St Wulfsige and Sherborne
Essays to Celebrate the Millennium
of the Benedictine Abbey
998–1998

St Wulfsige and Sherborne

Essays to Celebrate the Millennium of the Benedictine Abbey 998–1998

Edited by
Katherine Barker, David A Hinton and Alan Hunt

*based on papers given at the 1998 conference held in Sherborne
and with a new translation by Rosalind Love of the
Life of St Wulfsige by Goscelin of Saint-Bertin*

With contributions by
Katherine Barker, Aidan Bellenger, Joseph Bettey, Nicholas Campion,
David Farmer, J H P Gibb, Teresa Hall, Simon Keynes, Rosalind Love,
Timothy Reuter, Rebecca Rushforth, Rachel Stockdale,
Esther de Waal, Eric Woods and Barbara Yorke

Bournemouth University
School of Conservation Sciences
Occasional Paper 8

Published by
Oxbow Books

Published by
Oxbow Books, Park End Place, Oxford OX1 1HN

Bournemouth School of Conservation Sciences
Occasional Paper 8

Series Editor: Timothy Darvill

© Oxbow Books, Bournemouth University and the
Individual Authors 2005

ISBN 1-84217-175-5

A CIP record for this book is available from the British Library

This book is available direct from

Oxbow Books, Park End Place, Oxford OX1 1HN
(Phone: 01865-241249; Fax: 01865-794449)

and

The David Brown Book Co.
PO Box 511, Oakville, CT 06779
Tel: (860) 945–9329; Fax: (860) 945–9468
Email: david.brown.bk.co@snet.net

and via our website
www.oxbowbooks.com

*Cover image: A detail of the Feast Day of St Wulfsin from the
Sherborne Missal, BL Add MS. 74236, p 397, and is reproduced by
permission of the British Library. Colour reproduction has been made
possible by the generosity of Sherborne Historical Society.*

Printed in Great Britain by
Antony Rowe, Chippenham

'Et quonian ... nos sumus in quos fines seculorum devenerunt ...'

'And since ... we are those upon whom the ends of the ages
have come...'

*1 Corinthians 10:11, quoted in the King Æthelred charter authorising Bishop Wulfsige to
institute a Benedictine community at Sherborne, AD 998.*

GIRALDUS SCIREBURNENSIS

In Memoriam

Gerald Harold David Pitman of Sherborne
MBE, FRSA, Civic Honour of Sherborne

Contents

Contents

Contents

List of Figures

List of Tables

List of Contributors

Katherine Barker has lived in Sherborne for many years. Formerly part-time tutor with the University of Bristol Department of Continuing Education, it was as Senior Lecturer at Bournemouth University that she convened and organised the Sherborne Benedictine Millennium Conference. She has published a number of papers on West Country landscape archaeology and history. She contributed to, and edited, *The Cerne Abbey Millennium Lectures* (1988). She has recently taken on Editorship of the *Proceedings* of the Dorset Natural History and Archaeological Society.

Dom Aidan Bellenger is Prior of the Benedictine Downside Abbey. He has published numerous books and articles on monastic history and teaches at four universities. He is a Fellow of the Society of Antiquaries and of the Royal Historical Society.

Dr Joseph Bettey was formerly Reader in Local History at the University of Bristol. He is the author of numerous books and articles on West Country history, including many publications on the economic and social history of Dorset, and on the suppression of the religious houses.

Nicholas Campion is Principal Lecturer in History at Bath Spa University. He also teaches in the University's Study of Relgions department and lectures on the history of astrology at Kepler College, Seattle. He is author of *The Great Year, Astrology, Millenarianism and History in the Western Tradition* (Penguin 1994) and *Cosmos: A Cultural History of Astrology* (London Books 2006).

David Hugh Farmer was formerly Reader in History at the University of Reading. His books include *Magna Vita Sancti Hugonis; the Life of St Hugh of Lincoln* by Adam of Eynsham which he co-edited for the Oxford Medieval Texts Series. He is no stranger to West Country millennia having contributed to both the Amesbury millennium of 1979 and the Cerne Abbey millennium of 1987. He is editor of two volumes of Penguin Classics on *Bede and his Age*. He is perhaps best known to the wider world as author of the *Oxford Dictionary of Saints* now into a fifth edition – confirming its 'reputation as the standard one-volume work available in English'.

Jim Gibb was born in Canada and educated at King's School Canterbury and King's College Cambridge. Assistant master and then housemaster at Sherborne School from 1948 until his retirement from full-time teaching in 1980, he has made a special study of the architectural history of the Abbey at Sherborne. A Fellow of the Society of Antiquaries, he has published a number of papers on the medieval archaeology and history of Sherborne.

Teresa Hall, whilst resident in Dorset (1978–93), was involved in the archaeology and local history of the county representing Dorset on CBA Wessex and acting as secretary of the Dorset Archaeological Committee for several years. Moving to Somerset she became involved with the University of Bristol Shapwick Project and the local museum in Wells. She has recently completed an MPhil in English Local History at the University of Leicester entitled 'The Minster Church in the Dorset Landscape'.

David A Hinton is Reader in the Department of Archaeology at the University of Southampton. He teaches and researches the period from AD 400–1500 summarised in his book *Archaeology, Economy and Society*. Since 1991 he has been co-ordinating a research programme on Purbeck. Editor of the leaflet series 'The Making of Dorset', in 1998 he contributed a small volume on *Saxons and Vikings* to the 'Discover Dorset' series published by the Dovecote Press.

Alan Hunt is Head of Academic Development and Quality at Bournemouth University. Previously he was, in various capacities, a member of the University's School of Conservation Sciences, where he taught medieval and post-medieval archaeology. Until recently he was Chairman of the Dorset Archaeological Committee. His fieldwork, research, publications and backlog include extensive work in Dorset, particularly in the archaeology and history of rural settlements and churches.

Simon Keynes is Elrington and Bosworth Professor of Anglo-Saxon at the University of Cambridge and Fellow of Trinity College, Cambridge. He is author of many books and articles on Anglo-Saxon England, including *The Diplomas of Æthelred 'the Unready'* (1980) and *The 'Liber Vitae' of the New Minster and Hyde Abbey, Winchester* (1996). He is also co-editor of and contributor to *The Blackwell Encyclopaedia of Anglo-Saxon England* (1999).

Dr Rosalind Love has been Assistant Lecturer in the Department of Anglo-Saxon, Norse and Celtic, at the University of Cambridge, since January 2000, with especial responsibility for Insular Latin. Before that she was a British Academy Institutional Fellow based in Cambridge and working, as part of the Fontes Anglo-Saxonici research team, on the sources of Anglo-Latin literature, a project with which she continues to be actively involved. Her own particular field of research has been Anglo-Latin saints' lives, of which she has already published one set of editions and translations.

Timothy Reuter was Professor of Medieval History in the University of Southampton, Director of the Wessex Medieval Centre and a General Editor of Oxford Medieval Texts. His publications included *The Medieval Nobility* (1978), *Germany in the Early Middle Ages, c. 800–1056 (1991)*, *The Annals of Fulda* (1992) and *The New Cambridge Medieval History, III: c. 900–c. 1024,* (1999). Professor Reuter died while this volume was in preparation.

Rebecca Rushforth recently completed a PhD on the eleventh- and early twelfth-century manuscripts at Bury St Edmunds Abbey. She has been working at the Wren Library, Trinity College, Cambridge, on a project to make M R James's manuscript collection available on-line.

Rachel Stockdale was brought up in Dorset and has a special interest in the history of the county. She obtained a BA in Latin and German and an MA in Medieval Studies from the University of Reading, followed by a Diploma in Archive Studies from University College, London. Since 1973 she has worked for the British Library where she is now Head of Manuscripts Cataloguing, and she managed the recent project to mount the department's major catalogues on the Internet. In 1980, the British Library celebrated the fifteen-hundredth anniversary of the birth of St Benedict with an exhibition and a publication entitled *The Benedictines in Britain*, of which she was joint author.

Esther de Waal read history at Cambridge and then went to Leicester to do research in the Department of English Local History before returning to Newnham College as Research Fellow. There she wrote her first book, under her maiden name, Esther Moir, *The Discovery of Britain, English Travellers 1540–1840* (1964). After her marriage she taught in the Economic History department at Nottingham, for the Open University, and for Lincoln Theological College. Living for ten years in Canterbury in a house that had been the prior's lodging in the Benedictine monastery, led to the writing of *Seeking God, the Way of St Benedict* (1984), which has been widely translated. She has written numerous books and articles since then on monastic themes, Benedictine, Celtic and Cistercian and has travelled widely, most recently to the Philippines, leading retreats and organising conferences. Her latest book, *The Way of Simplicity, The Cistercian Tradition* (1998), was timed to coincide with the commemoration of the founding of the order in 1098.

Eric Woods has been Vicar of Sherborne since 1993. He read History at Magdalen College, Oxford, and Theology at Trinity College, Cambridge. He is a former Chaplain at the University of Bristol, where he was also a part-time Lecturer and Tutor in Theology for many years. He is a non-residentiary Canon of Salisbury Cathedral.

Barbara Yorke is Professor of Early Medieval History at King Alfred's University College, Winchester. She is author of *Kings and Kingdoms of Early Anglo-Saxon England* (1990), as well as author of numerous papers on the Anglo-Saxon period. Her book *Nunneries and the Anglo-Saxon Royal Houses* was published in 2002. She is currently working on the saints of Anglo-Saxon Wessex.

Preface

Katherine Barker

The conference and Sherborne

In April 1998 a one-day conference was held in Sherborne to mark the one-thousandth anniversary of the founding of the Benedictine Abbey by St Wulfsige through the granting of a charter by King Æthelred II. The conference formed part of a wider Sherborne Benedictine Millennium celebration programme of musical, literary and arts events mounted between 18 April and the Feast Day of St Benedict, 11 July. The conference convenor would like to thank both the Sherborne Millennium committee and Sherborne School for their wholehearted interest and support.

The conference was attended by Gerald Pitman, local resident extraordinary, whose infectious love for the history of his home town touched almost everyone in Sherborne over a period of nearly half a century. A capacity congregation packed Sherborne Abbey for his funeral requiem in February 2002. The editors have no hesitation in dedicating this small volume to his memory.

As it so happened, Gerald Pitman's death occurred within a month of the one-thousandth anniversary of the death of Bishop Wulfsige whose name we read in the opening lines of the foundation charter of 998.

> I, Æthelred, by the guiding control of God, king of the whole of Albion, persuaded by Archbishop Ælfric, with the advice of my bishops and leading men, and the of the nobility and faithful men in attendance on me, have given permission to Bishop Wulfsige to institute a rule of monastic life ... according to the practice of the holy father Benedict in the monastery church of Sherborne. (BL Add ms 46487, fo 3r)

Violence was never far away in Anglo-Saxon England; this is a time of 'warlord' history. And Viking warlords came by boat. In the very year of the Sherborne charter, they sailed into what is now Poole Harbour, and raided up the River Frome through Wareham to Dorchester, burning, pillaging and looting. The words of the Sherborne charter are those which attempt to bring

Figure 1. Sherborne Benedictine Millennium Celebration logo.

order and security, temporal no less than spiritual, to a troubled world. The close of the first millennium was imminent, and with it came a sense of purpose. Across western Europe, Christendom was reorganising and reforming in a powerful restatement of the hope brought by the Christian message. It was a time of looking forward in anticipation of a New Order inaugurated by an Event, the timing and character of which could not be known. And so it was the Benedictine House was to shape the next five and a half centuries of Sherborne's history, and then the next four and half, and so onwards. For the Dissolution itself was predicated on the Benedictine house, its removal left a 'footprint' of very distinctive form which continues to shape the character of the present town and the area round about. The memorial to the Benedictine millennium remains with us in the ground plan and pattern of everyday lives.

The conference papers

Nine speakers presented papers on various aspects of the Benedictine foundation which are published here. David Farmer explored the wider context of Benedictine reform, and Nicholas Campion, the wider significance of millennial movements. Simon Keynes explored the life and times of Wulfsige against the background of the charter itself, and Teresa Hall looked at the places recorded in the charter. After lunch the proceedings moved on to the 'hey day' of the Benedictines with Rachel Stockdale on book production and libraries; the Benedictines in education. Joe Bettey gave a powerful evocation of the 'pulling out' of the monastic house under the terms of the Dissolution of the Monasteries by Henry VIII's commissioners, the collapse of over five centuries of pastoral, social, and spiritual care for the Sherborne community and the 'revolution' in landholding effected across much of west Dorset as the abbot was obliged to relinquish his role as landowner. The conference was much enhanced by the presence of Dom Aidan Bellenger, with a timely and eloquent reminder that the Benedictines are alive and well. Former Abbot of Downside, his Benedictine habit brought an immediacy and sense of timelessness to the proceedings that no words could. Esther de Waal concluded the day by taking the words and teaching of St Benedict on into the future. They remain with us and for us, as they did for Wulfsige.

Post-conference contributions

Since the conference there have been two important developments. The first, through the good offices of Simon Keynes, is the inclusion of a new translation – indeed the first complete translation in English – of the *Life* of St Wulfsige written by Goscelin of Saint-Bertin not long after Wulfsige's death. Dr Rosalind Love was invited to speak about her work to Sherborne Historical Society in January of 2001; a Society of which Gerald Pitman was a founder-member. The editors are grateful to her for offering us a paper which is a valuable complement to those given at the conference.

And second, the editors are also pleased to include here several papers kindly submitted since the end of the conference. We would like to thank Timothy Reuter for his Introduction, Barbara Yorke, Simon Keynes, Eric Woods, and Rebecca Rushforth. One of the editors, Katherine Barker, has also made a number of contributions. Sadly, Timothy Reuter died while this volume was in preparation.

Each of those who witnessed the foundation charter appended a personal statement. Bishop Wulfsige wrote the following:

> Ego Wlsinus episcopus hoc meum desiderium ad perfectum usque perduxi.

> I, bishop Wulfsige, have brought this my wish all the way to completion.

A thousand years on, the next millennium now safely underway Katherine Barker, on behalf of the editors, would like to express her gratitude to everyone who has assisted in whatever way in the making of a volume which, it is hoped, may stand as a worthy contribution to the history of Sherborne. She has finally brought this her wish, *suum desiderium*, to completion in the year that celebrates the thirteen hundredth anniversary of the setting up of the Sherborne bishopric in 705.

Katherine Barker, Alan Hunt and David Hinton
Sherborne 2005

Acknowledgements

The editors would like to acknowledge permission to reproduce manuscript material from the Bibliothèque Nationale in Paris (Figs 5–6), the Bibliothèque Municipale in Orléans (Fig 22), the Domkapitel at Aachen Minster (Fig 23), and the British Library in London (Frontispiece and Figs. 4, 7–8, 17–20). They would like to thank Rachel Stockdale for very effective liaison on our behalf. They are grateful to Sherborne Town Council for permission to reproduce the Sherborne coat-of-arms (Fig 27e). The cover image has been reproduced in colour through the generosity of Sherborne Historical Society.

The editors also acknowledge their debt to both Professor Timothy Darvill, series editor, and to David Brown of Oxbow Books. This volume has been a long time in gestation. Katherine Barker would like to record her particular thanks to Simon Keynes for seeing the work through a number of vicissitudes and finally into print. She would also like to record her sincere thanks to Sherborne School for lecture theatre and photocopying facilities, to Wendy Sherlock for skilful copy-editing, to Susan Vaughan for the index and last – but not least – to H L Trump for financial assistance.

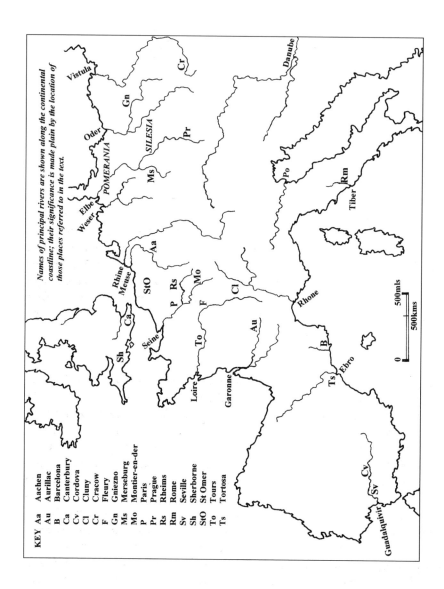

Names of principal rivers are shown along the continental
coastline; their significance is made plain by the location of
those places referred to in the text.

Figure 2. Map of Europe towards the end of the tenth century, showing some of the places mentioned in the text.

Introduction: Sherborne and the millennium[1]

Timothy Reuter[†]

Æthelred's charter of 998 for Wulfsige, which initiated (or marked the initiation of) the establishing of a monastery at Sherborne, quotes 1 Corinthians 10:11 'we, as the apostle says, upon whom the ends of the world are come'. It is tempting to see this as a reference to the millennium, something which loomed large in the thinking of Anglo-Saxon contemporaries (Byrhtferth of Ramsey, for example, or Wulfstan of York). Since the more recent millennium has brought about a substantial re-examination of contemporary attitudes to the first millennium, it may be helpful to draw on this to set the thoughts and actions of the founders of 998 in context.

Measurement of time

To understand attitudes to the first millennium it is important to understand attitudes to time, its passing and its measurement. We are not more surrounded by time than our predecessors, but we are surrounded by available measurements of time in a way which has only been true for the last one-hundred and fifty years or so. A thousand years ago, and indeed right across the period from late antiquity to the early modern era, time moved quite differently. Day and night were each divided into twelve hours – but that meant that hours varied in length according to the time of year. More important than hours were the liturgical divisions of the day, which was often considered to run, like the Jewish Sabbath, from sundown to sundown. Weeks, months and years also had their rhythms, determined by liturgy and agriculture. The agricultural year we know about – the main difference from today is that the hungriest time of the year was in July and August; the new harvest had not yet been gathered in, the fruits of last year were running short. Winter, provided that the harvest had not failed, was a time of plenty; livestock which was not kept over the winter had been slaughtered, the granaries were full of grain.

 The church year had different rhythms; concentrations of activity leading up to Christmas and Easter and in the week of Whitsun; a six-week period of fasting and sexual abstinence in Lent; a long 'fallow' period between Whitsun and Advent. Because Easter is celebrated on the Sunday after the first full moon following the spring equinox unless that full moon itself falls on a Sunday, the crucial part of the Christian year between the beginning of Lent and Whitsun shifted across the calendar from year to year. The moon's cycle does not mesh with the earth's cycle around the sun, and the Julian calendar, which inserts an extra day into the year every fourth year, complicates matters still further. Precise recurrences of weekdays, dates, and Christian feasts recur only once every 532 years. Within a human lifetime, no two church years would be exactly the same. Lying across these subtly varying rhythms determined by weather and the moon were cross-rhythms, the major feast days on which the deaths of the saints were celebrated and commemorated (and which saints these were varied from place to place). Theoretically, the week was the same as now, except that Saturday was a workday and many weeks would have had the equivalent of one or more bank holidays in the form of a saint's day.

If the rhythms of each year varied, so, for a long period, did the counting of years. Those who live in a Christian or post-Christian society today count from the year of Christ's birth (more strictly, from the year of the Incarnation, the Word made Flesh). But AD (or AI) is not a matter of contemporary record; it is simply the year in which a sixth-century monk, Denis the Short, calculated Christ's birth to have fallen. It's Denis who introduced this form of reckoning to give a permanent reminder of the distance from Christ's birth – before that, working out where you were on such a scale was a matter of learned calculation. And Denis' method was not widely adopted in Europe until the eighth century; we are basically talking about the cultural influence of Bede as disseminated across the continent by Anglo-Saxon missionaries. Even then, the use of AD/AI dating was by no means universal. In Spain, a version was used which started counting from the crucifixion. Much dating was done by years in office rather than referring to a single fixed point.

There was no universal agreement on when the year began. Our use of 1 January is a very recent convention. The Roman year had begun on 1 March (that is why September – *septem* – is the seventh month and October, November and December, *octo, novem* and *decem* are respectively, the eighth, ninth and tenth months). The Christian year could begin on 25 December (a date set in the third century – pretty arbitrarily – for Christ's birth), or on 25 March (nine months before 25 December, with the additional complication that counting could begin both logically, from 25 March preceding AD 1 and, illogically, from 25 March which fell within it). It could also begin on Easter Sunday, giving the years a variable length. The regnal years of kings and bishops began from the point their officials reckoned they had begun to rule; the Indiction could begin on 1 September or 24 September, to mention only the most common dates used (don't ask).

In short, the world a thousand years ago – and indeed the pre-industrial world generally – did not measure time as we do. There were at least four points at which the year could be said to have begun, and no way in which anyone could have calculated the precise point in the day or night at which the change took place. There was no equivalent to our decimalised sense of waiting for the odometer to tick over from 999999 to 000000; Roman numerals, with their mixture of counting down and counting up, allow at least half-a-dozen ways of expressing 999, from DCCCCLXXXXVIIII through DCDCCIX to IM. The year 1000 was simply one of many points to which a special significance could be attached.

Prediction and prophecy

What sort of significance was this? Essentially, we are talking about the prophetic element in both early Christianity and in many of the canonical books of the Old Testament. I'm going to be talking specifically about the Christian interpretation of these, but, though I do not claim to be more than vaguely informed on these matters, let alone an expert, many of these implications are probably shared with the Jewish and Islamic traditions. For the Christian tradition, the central point is that Christ will at some point return again to Earth to judge the righteous and the wicked and mark the ultimate triumph of good over evil and the merging of time with eternity. This is found at several points in the New Testament; but the idea that the time when this would happen could be calculated was explicitly rejected. The key text is 'Be vigilant, for you do not know the day nor the hour when the Son of Man shall come' (Matthew 25:13), which is warning both against trying to anticipate the second coming (perhaps by calculation or looking for signs) *and* against a too ready assumption that it would not happen in the near future. It could happen at any point – and the orthodox tradition made great use of this text; since you don't know when, you must live every day as if it might, but you should not look for signs: it will happen when it will happen. It's a classical example of the way in which revolutionary movements (whether they are consciously or unconsciously revolutionary), once they become established move to reinterpret their own doctrines in terms of stability, as witness the Gregorian papacy, Francis of Assisi or the early Protestant reformers.

A further key text in the Christian tradition is Paul's important warning in 2 Thessalonians 2:1–3: 'We beseech you, brethren, by the coming of our Lord Jesus Christ, that ye be not soon shaken in mind ... as that the day of Christ is at hand. Let no man deceive you, for that day shall not come, except there come a falling away first, and that man of sin be revealed, the son of perdition.' Note the implications of this text: Paul is already, at a very early point in the development of Christianity, concerned about apocalyptic beliefs (I am using Paul as a cipher at this point – for my argument it's irrelevant whether the historical Paul is indeed the author, since it's clearly a very early text whatever its authorship). Once again, this is essentially a stabilising text, but it stabilises in a rather different way, and one which would turn out to be a dangerous one in later centuries. Paul's argument was similar to that of Matthew 25:13. The end of the world *would* come, and it would be prefigured by the appearance of an opposite figure to Christ, later to be known as the Antichrist. But whereas Matthew 25:13 implied that the second coming could happen at *any* point, Paul's argument was that you could tell that it was not going to be soon, because there would be signs and these signs weren't present. The dangerous implication of the text, for those who chose to read it in a non-stabilising way, was that if you looked hard you might be able to find signs, and that would turn out to be a key point for the future.

Note that neither of these texts says anything at all about a thousand years. There is only one point at which that period occurs in this kind of context in the whole of the canonical bible, and that is in Revelations 20, where an angel appears and binds Satan for a thousand years, 'and set a seal upon him, that he should deceive the nations no more, till the thousand years should be fulfilled; and after that he must be loosed a little season'. During this time the righteous were to reign with Christ. This is a key point about almost all apocalyptic/eschatological thinking within the Christian tradition. What was anticipated was not so much the end of the world but its profound transformation in the period immediately preceding its end. Millennialism meant hope, as much as fear.

Predicting the new era
What ways were there of calculating when the new era would dawn? Well, there are two other key biblical passages which can be interpreted in terms of the end of the world as we know it. The first of these, surprisingly enough, is the story of the creation. God created the world in six days, and rested on the seventh. The methods of biblical interpretation developed in late antiquity assumed the existence of a fourfold truth in all biblical texts. The creation story was literally and historically true; but it was also prophecy: the Old Testament prefigured the New Testament (including the history anticipated in the New Testament); the New Testament fulfilled the prophecies of the Old. Since the Old Testament could be read as prefiguring all history from the coming of Christ, the six days of creation therefore could be and were read as prefiguring the six ages of the world. Once these were completed, the seventh day/age (the so-called 'world Sabbath') would be ushered in as a world-day (ie an age) of rest and peace. An 'age' *could* be (though need not be) interpreted as a period of a thousand years; on this reading we again have a point after which there would be a period of peace and rest.

But when did the world begin? It was possible to begin from the creation and then add up the history which follows down to the present, in a form of chronological calculation which as a long tradition extending into the nineteenth century if not beyond. But it was and is very difficult to arrive at a definitive result in doing so. Paradoxically, chronologists were generally more certain of the date than the year: the creation story gives us (or can be read as giving us) an equal division into day and night, followed by a period of growth – in other words, creation happened at the spring equinox. To get the year, however, one had to add up lives and reigns and make assumptions about simultaneities (especially in later and post-biblical histories), and within quite a wide range of time a whole number of results could be and were justified. One of the strange and fascinating stories of the first few centuries AD, uncovered in a brilliant article by Richard Landes, is the way in which clerics during the first millennium constantly recalculated the age of the world in order to move 6000 AM (*anno mundi*, the year of the world) into either the past or the more distant future. It's worth noting, incidentally, that by the time of the founding of Sherborne Abbey this game was over: whenever 6000 AM might have fallen, it was by 998 definitely in the past. The idea of six ages followed by a seventh age of peace remained to inspire people, but a literal calculation equating ages with periods of a thousand years was no longer possible.

The other crucial biblical text is the Book of Daniel. Daniel saw in a vision four beasts, of which the rule of the last would be the longest and most terrible; as in Revelations 20, and in the prophetic interpretation of the creation story, its end would be followed by the rule of the righteous. Very early on, a tradition set in of equating these four beasts (as the author probably intended) with historical empires: Babylonians, Medes, Persians. The fourth beast was the Roman Empire; when that ceased to exist, the last struggle and the final era of peace would begin. This early tradition was given definitive and mainstream validity by Jerome in his commentary on the Book of Daniel; it's important also to realise that Daniel's language and images (including the notion of the 'son of man' and the idea of the resurrection of the dead) are echoed at a number of points in the books of the New Testament. There is, however, a curious twist to all this. Daniel and his early interpreters saw the four empires as tyrannies; only when they were overcome would and could the thousand-year rule of the righteous begin. But the mainstream interpretation tended increasingly towards the view that the continued existence of the Roman Empire was a bulwark against the coming of the Antichrist.

What has just been said sets out the ways in which the passing of time was experienced a thousand years ago and the various strands of thought which could have allowed belief in the idea that the world as people knew it would end. It's important to realise that these strands did not necessarily produce a coherent or precise view of the end of the world, and also that most of them implied that the world would not end absolutely, but merely end 'as we know it', after which it would continue for a time, though in a different state. There might be a brief phase of terrible destruction and devastation, but in most views of the matter these were to be followed, for a time at least, by the rule of the righteous in a period of peace, plenty and prosperity. Whatever people expected at the end of the tenth century it was not the end of time and the Last Judgement; at most, it was the coming and defeat of the Devil or Antichrist. Such an End was to be hoped for as well as feared, and it was to be feared especially by the strong and powerful; the poor and meek might well have cause to rejoice.

The last decades of the tenth century

Was the end or transformation of the world anticipated more in the 990s than at other times? On the face of it, the answer is no. As we have seen, the period of a thousand years is one which had significance for what would come after the transformation of the world: it was the length of the rule of the saints. As we have already seen, an interpretation of the ages of the world which relied on precise periods of a thousand years yielded nothing particular for 1000: whenever the world had begun, it was already six thousand years old by then on any basis of calculation. An interpretation based on the four world empires, though it had perhaps slightly more substance, probably did not yield a great deal. There was little reason to suppose that the Roman Empire had ended. It may or may not be of significance that in Easter of the year 1000, Otto III, the ruling emperor in the west, who had recently fixed his title as being that of 'Roman emperor' (unlike his grandfather Otto I, who had tended to avoid such implications of his imperial coronation in 962), journeyed to Aachen, where Charlemagne was buried, and had the grave opened – perhaps with a view to having Charlemagne canonised as a saint, perhaps as a demonstration that the Roman Empire still lived in his own person.

So, did people immediately before the last millennium anticipate the transformation of the world? Historians' views on this have fluctuated considerably in the last two hundred years. Historians writing under the influence of the French Revolution saw millenialism as a liberating force; but, as so often in historical writing, their thesis came to be vulgarised and coarsened through repetition; increasingly it was presented as one of a world paralysed by fear of its own ending. In that form it was not difficult to counter, and by the time of the First World War the pendulum had swung the other way. The consensus was rather that for the mass of the population, few would even have known what year it was; this kind of calendrical consciousness is a back-projection from a much later era. The few references which we have to the millennium in the context of the end of the world, can be safely dismissed as the unrepresentative views of individuals rather than the tip of an iceberg of belief and fear, while occasional references to the end of the world in the dates of legal documents are offset by tens of thousands of documents which make no such invocation, and should in any case be seen as conventional rather than specific to a short period. Above all, there is no real evidence that people behaved differently as the millennium approached.

This consensus has continued for much of the twentieth century. There were some works written against the grain, such as Ter Braak's study of Otto III or Focillon's work on *L'An Mil*, but they made little impression. Recently, however, the issue has been reopened. Daniel Verhelst began the revival of interest with his impressive edition of Adso of Montier-en-Der's *On the Arising and Time of Antichrist* in 1976. Johannes Fried published a long piece on 'Expectations of the end of around the turn of the millennium' in 1989. And Richard Landes has made a series of contributions to our knowledge and understanding of the topic. Landes has argued in particular that implicit and possibly widespread expectations of the End existed throughout the west during the first millennium, keyed to the calculated age of the world and that because of the taboo in discussing the precise timing of the End, arguments from silence may be misleading. Occasional references to the End survived against heavy odds; they are therefore the tip of the iceberg, and are not outweighed by the vast number of non-references.

Now, the interesting things about the swings of this historiographical pendulum is that the evidential basis for discussion has hardly changed since the mid-nineteenth century; only a couple of minor passages are known to us which were not known to Michelet and Lot. So why has the discussion shifted? Mainly because of what seems plausible or implausible to historians at any given time. There are clear indications that there were indeed some people who were anticipating a radical change in the world around the year 1000, and we can perhaps even say there were rather more than there had been a century earlier or would be a century later. But there is no real objective basis for moving from that either to the claim that these views were those of a radical minority or to the assumption that they represented much more widespread hopes and fears; and we have no real means of assessing whether the reference to the end of the world in Wulfsige's foundation charter was merely conventional or deeply felt.

Growth of religious activity

What we can point to by way of context is both evidence for an intensification of religious experience in this period, and evidence for other changes at this time which were felt to be far-reaching. Late tenth- and early eleventh-century religious practice did indeed include a number of elements, not all new, but apparently on the increase, which may seem significant here. These include:

– an increase in pilgrimages by people from all classes of society, especially in really long-distance pilgrimages, for example to Rome or Jerusalem;

– a rise in the importance of saints' relics as focuses of more intense religious practice (as seen, for example, in the rebuilding of churches in the eleventh century to allow for the veneration of shrines by pilgrims, and in the function of displayed relics at public meetings such as church councils);

– the widespread building and rebuilding of churches, on a scale so large as to attract comment by contemporaries;

– the religiously sanctioned movements known as the peace and truce of God at which 'public' figures such as kings, bishops, dukes and counts, but also aristocrats and their fellow warrior followers, and the 'common people', met in large assemblies and swore oaths on relics to keep the peace;

– the appearance, for the first time for some centuries, of significant pockets of heretical belief across western Europe. We don't know much about these heretics, but what we do know is told to us by their enemies; but some groups at least seem to have been not so much rejecting the church's teaching as taking it too seriously – if you like, they were 'left-wing deviationists';

– more generally, the emergence of the crowd, the 'people', as participating actively in religious practice and as a force for religious reform. This is perhaps first visible at the assemblies at which the peace of God was proclaimed, but it can also be seen in the mass pilgrimages to Jerusalem of 1033 and 1065 in the early church councils at which measures of reform were proclaimed, and in the struggles to clean up the corrupt urban church élites found across western Europe in the eleventh century.

What we have, in other words, is more people taking a more active part in religious life. Some of this intensification may well have been linked with the belief in the coming end. But it may also be linked with the widespread social changes experienced around the year 1000. A whole series of regional studies published over the last fifty years have pointed to a number of features of post-Carolingian Europe which have made the decades around the millennium rather than the twelfth century the crucial era for most historians looking at the large-scale transformation of Europe from its Roman and post-Roman guise into the dynastic, courtly and feudal Europe of the long *ancien régime* from the fourteenth to the eighteenth centuries:

– a restructuring of settlement patterns, in many cases with those established later taking shape for the first time around the millennium;

– the extension of lordly authority over *all* the inhabitants of those settlements, with a levelling effect on those who had previously been free smallholders and those who had previously been slaves;

– the breakdown of Carolingian public authority as exercised by counts holding regular courts with application to all free men and landowners within a defined territory;

– the spread of locally controlled fortifications across western Europe, starting in Spain and Italy in the late tenth century and reaching the Channel by the mid-eleventh century;

– the transformation of two previously separate social groups, the landed aristocracy and their warrior followers into a group with common values and code of conduct, and the consequent transformation of the followers into a landed lesser aristocracy;

– last but not least, the accomplishing of all these transformations by the exercise of violence with little accompanying legitimation.

Inconclusive conclusion

The difficulty about applying all of this is that the model has been developed largely on the basis of evidence from France, northern Italy and eastern Spain. It does not obviously fit Ottonian Germany, nor the Kingdom of Wessex. The fact that it does not obviously fit does not mean that it does not fit at all, rather that we do not (yet) know. There are two main reasons for this. The first is that the nature and extent of available evidence varies greatly across Europe in the tenth and eleventh centuries. As a result, it is much easier to measure and discern social change in Burgundy or Catalonia than in Saxony or Wessex. The second is that the history of the regions of medieval Europe has been done on a national basis, each nation with its own historiographical traditions; French historians simply work with a different set of concepts and questions from those familiar to English or German historians (and *vice versa*).

The process of transnational understanding, of learning which differences between our various national pasts are and were real, and which are merely the product of a different perspective, has only just begun. Until it is much nearer to completion than it is now, we cannot fully contextualise the foundation of Sherborne. We can put it in a specifically ecclesiastical context, as a combination of pre-Gregorian piety and of the attempts to tidy up and define the relations between bishops and bishoprics on the one hand, and the clerical and monastic communities which served the cathedrals on the other, which is found not only in England following the reforms of Edgar and Dunstan but also across the continent. But we cannot so easily locate it in the context of fears of and hopes for the end of the world, or indeed of large-scale social transformation. It may turn out to have had such a context, but at present we simply do not know.

Note

1 Kindly agreeing, late in the day, to write an Introduction to the published papers, Professor Reuter has not included footnotes.

1. King Æthelred's charter for Sherborne Abbey, 998

Simon Keynes

In 998 King Æthelred the Unready issued a charter authorising Bishop Wulfsige to institute at Sherborne a community of monks living in accordance with the Rule of St Benedict. Wulfsige had been appointed bishop of Sherborne in 993, and had presided since then over a body of secular clergy. From 998 until his death in 1002 he was bishop, as before, but also abbot of the new monastic community. The original charter (presumably inscribed on a single sheet of parchment) is now lost, leaving us dependent for our knowledge of its text on a copy entered in the mid-twelfth century at the beginning of the Sherborne Cartulary (London, British Library, Add MS 46487, fos 3r–4r) (Frontispiece).

The charter begins with a dating clause (1). The text itself runs in the name of the king, stating the main business in hand (2) and then laying down the constitution of the new monastic community, including provision that Wulfsige's successors should rule the monks well, that any dispute should be referred to the archbishop and the king, and that the bishop himself would be abbot and father to the monks (3). The inwardness of the next section (4) is opaque, but it seems to reflect the settlement of an outbreak of disputes over land, and thereby to provide a context or pretext for listing of landed property belonging to the monastery (5). The grant of perpetual 'liberty' is extended to cover future gifts to the monastic community, with the usual reservation of military burdens, but with specific exemption from work on beacons (6). Dire punishment awaits anyone audacious enough to challenge the terms of the grant (7). The charter is attested by the king (8), whose attestation is followed by those of two archbishops, four bishops, two ealdormen, four abbots, and seven thegns (9).

For further discussion of the charter, see pp 69–72.

Latin text

English translation

(1)/fo 3r/Anno ab incarnatione
dominice . dcccc nonagesimo octauo .

In the year from the Incarnation of the Lord
998.

(2) Ego Æthelredus totius Albionis
Dei gubernante moderamine basileus
suadente archiepiscopo Ælfrico cum
consilio meorum episcoporum ac
principum seu nobilium michique
fidelium assistentium annui episcopo
Wlsino ordinare monachice
conuersationis normam . castamque
uitam et Deo amabilem secundum
institutionem sancti patris Bendedicti
in cenobio Scireburnensis ecclesie .

I, Æthelred, by the guiding control of God
king of the whole of Albion, persuaded by
Archbishop Ælfric, with the advice of my
bishops and leading men, and of the
nobility and faithful men in attendance on
me, have given permission to Bishop
Wulfsige to institute a rule of monastic life,
a life holy and pleasing to God, according
to the practice of the holy father Benedict,
in the monastery church of
Sherborne

(3) Ea ratione uidelicet ut quisquis
successor ei aduenerit siue pius siue
crudelis non habeat facultatem male
tractare res monachorum . sit pastor
non tirannus gubernet ad fratrum
utilitatem secundum pastoralem
auctoritatem non ad lupinam
rapacitem . pascat suos et se
sequentes . Habeat ipse solus uictum
inter fratres sicut scriptum est .
Principem populorum te constitui .
esto in illis quasi unus ex illis . Regat
ipse iuxta animarum et corporum
utilitatem substantiam monasterii ita
dumtaxat ut fratrum consilio non sit
ignotum quicquid agatur . Et si forte
quod absit euenerit ut pastor et grex
discordantur . semper ad examen
archiepiscopi reseruetur . et ipse regi
intimet ut iusta correctio sequatur . Et
quia mos minime apud nos consentit
ut in episcopali sede abbas constituatur
. fiat ipse episcopus eis abbas et pater .
et ipsi fratres obedientes ei sint sicuti
filii et monachi cum castitate et
humilitate et subiectione secundum
/fo 3v/disciplinam almi patris nostri
Benedicti . ut una brauium eterne
corone accipere mereantur .

On this condition, namely, that whomsoever
shall be his successor, whether a pious or a
cruel man, may not have the ability
(*facultas*) to deal wrongly with the affairs
of the monks: may he be a pastor, not a
tyrant, and rule in the interest of the
brothers in accordance with pastoral
authority and not with the greediness of a
wolf; may he nourish his men and those
who follow him. He is to take sustenance
only among the brothers, as it is written: 'I
have made you a prince of peoples [...]; be
among them as if one of them' [Eccl.
32:1]. May he rule the business
(*substantia*) of the monastery in
accordance with the interest of souls and
bodies, in such a way at least that whatever
may be set in motion may not be unknown
to the body of brothers. And if by chance it
should happen – and may it not be
so – that the pastor and the flock are in
disagreement, the matter should always be
reserved for the judgement of the
archbishop, and he himself should inform
the king so that lawful correction may
follow. And because the custom among us
in no way decrees that an abbot is to be
constituted in the episcopal see, may the
bishop himself be abbot and father to them,
and for their part may the brothers be
obedient to him as if sons and monks, with
chastity, humility and subjection according
to the discipline of our dear father Benedict,
so that together they may deserve to receive
the reward of the eternal garland [*cf.* I Cor. 9:24].

(4) Et quoniam sicut ait apostolos .
nos sumus in quos fines seculorum
deuenerunt . et multiplicato iam genere
humano . adeo ut perplures gratia
inopie ruris non habentes ubi uel
arando uel fodiendo agriculturam
exercentes uictum adipiscantur .
insuper et crescente philargiria non
nullorum ut quisque rapiat sibi quod
potuerit . optimum duxerunt priores
nostri ut omnis lis terminibus certis
adnulletur . ideoque territoria causa
concordie assuescere nuper inter
mundanos cepere ut portionem
quisque proprie telluris libere excolet .

And since, as the apostle said, we are those
'upon whom the ends of the ages have
come' [I Cor. 10:11], and with the human
race now multiplied so that very many, on
account of the lack of land, do not have
a place where they might get a living
through the exercise of agriculture – whether
by ploughing or by digging – and
especially with the greed of many
increasing in such a way that everyone
grabs for himself whatever he can, our
forebears thought it best that every lawsuit
be settled within clear limits, and therefore,
in the interest of harmony, they have
recently begun to grow accustomed [? to distribute]
lands among lay persons in such a way that everyone
could freely cultivate a portion of land for himself.

(5) Quorum ego exempla imitatus rus
predicti cenobii hac cartula annotari
censeo . Hoc est in ipsa Scireburna
centum agelli in loco qui dicitur
Stocland et predium monasterii sicut
Wlsinus episcopus fossis sepibusque
girare curauit . Deinde nouem cassatos
in loco qui ab incolis Holancumb
nuncupatur . Item in Halganstoke . xv .
in Thornford . vii . in Bradanford . x .
in Wonburna . v . in Westun . vii . in
Stapulbreicge . xx . in
Wulfheardigstoke . x . in Cumbtun .
viii . in Osanstoke . ii . et mansam
unam iuxta ripam maris qui dicitur aet
Lim .

Following the example of whom, I affirm
that the estate (*rus*) of the aforesaid
monastery be set down in this charter. That
is, in Sherborne itself one hundred plots
(*agelli*) in the place which is called Stockland,
and the estate (*predium*) of the
monastery just as Bishop Wulfsige took
care to enclose it with ditches and hedges.
Next, 9 hides in the place which is called
Holcombe [Rogus] by the inhabitants.
And 15 in Halstock, 7 in Thornford, 10 in
Bradford [Abbas], 5 in Oborne, 8 at
[Stalbridge] Weston, 20 in Stalbridge, 10 in
Wulfheardigstoke, 8 in [Nether and Over]
Compton, 2 in *Osanstoke*, and 1 hide
beside the shore of the sea which is called
Lyme.

(6) Et quicquid Deus his auxerit ex
donis fidelium continua securitate et
iugi libertate possideant fratres inibi
degentes . tribus exceptis que omnibus
communia sunt scilicet expeditione .
pontis arcisue restauratione . Tamen
nulli debitores sint/fo 4r/in rogi
constructione eo quod monasterium
hoc opus indigere nouimus .

And whatsoever God may increase for
them from the gifts of faithful men may the
brothers living therein possess in continual
security and perpetual liberty, three things
excepted which are common to all men,
namely military service, and maintenance of
bridge and fortress. However, they are to
owe no-one any service in the construction
of a beacon (*rogus*), because we recognise that the
monastery needs this work.

(7) Si forte quod absit hanc nostram donationem quispiam annullare temptauerit . et ad libitus proprios deflectere . sciat se equissimo iudici rationem redditurum . clangente tuba archangeli extremo examine . ubi omnis equitas et iustitia Christo iudicante cunctis manifestabitur.

If by chance, anyone – and may it not be so – should be tempted to annul this our donation, and to deflect it to his own purposes, let him know that he will render account to the most just judge, at the last judgement when the trumpet of the archangel is sounding, where every equity and justice shall be made known to all with Christ as judge.

(8) Ego Æthelredus rex Anglorum hanc libertatem concedo sepedicto monasterio sub episcopo quemcumque elegerit semper regendo et signaculo sancte crucis ✠ hanc munificentiam consigno coram his testibus.

I, Æthelred, king of the English, grant this privilege to the aforesaid monastery to be ruled always under the bishop, whomsoever he [the king] may have chosen, and I have marked this donation with the sign of the holy cross +, in the presence of these witnesses.

(9) Ego Ælfricus archiepiscopus hoc donum data michi benedictione firmaui. Ego Eadwulf archiepiscopus libens faui atque consensi. Ego Wlstanus episcopus hoc idem affirmaui.

I, Ælfric, archbishop [of Canterbury], having given my blessing have strengthened this grant. I, Eadwulf, archbishop [of York], acting willingly, have supported and consented. I, Wulfstan, bishop [of London], have affirmed this same thing.

Ego Ælpheagus episcopus consensum prebui
Ego Wlsinus episcopus hoc meum desiderium ad perfectum usque perduxi.
Ego Ælfwinus episcopus hilari mente concessi.

I, Ælfheah, bishop [of Winchester], have offered consent.
I, Wulfsige, bishop [of Sherborne], have brought this my wish all the way to completion
I Ælfwine, bishop [of Wells], with willing spirit, have granted.

Ego Æthelweard dux gratanter corroboraui.
Ego Ælfric dux consentaneus fui.

I, Æthelweard, ealdorman [of the western provinces], have confirmed gratefully.
I, Ælfric, ealdorman [of the districts of Winchester], have been in agreement.

Ego Ælfsige abbas.
Ego Wlfgar abbas.
Ego Leofric abbas.
Ego Godwine abbas.

I, Ælfsige, abbot [of the New Minster, Winchester]
I, Wulfgar, abbot [of Abingdon]
I, Leofric, abbot [of Muchelney]
I, Godwine abbot [unidentified]

Ego Æthelmær . minister.	I, Æthelmær, thegn
Ordulf . minister.	Ordwulf, thegn
Wulfget . minister.	Wulfgeat, thegn
Brihtmær . minister.	Brihtmær, thegn
Leowine . minister.	Leofwine thegn
Brihtric . minister.	Brihtric, thegn
Wulfnoth . minister.	Wulfnoth, thegn

Bibliography

Sherborne Cartulary. London. British Library, Add MS 46487.

2. Bishop Wulfsige's name: the writing and the spelling

Rebecca Rushforth and Katherine Barker

Pulfrige

This is how Wulfsige's name appears in a list of Sherborne bishops recorded in a book known as 'The Pontifical of St Dunstan', written in the second half of the tenth century almost certainly at Canterbury, and probably given to Wulfsige sometime after Archbishop Dunstan's death in 988 (Keynes, 'Wulfsige, monk of Glastonbury', Fig 5, this volume; Fig 3). The list of bishops was added to the 'Pontifical' early in the eleventh century, probably during the episcopacy of Wulfsige's successor Æthelric (1001–11/12), the last Sherborne bishop to be included in the original part of the list. This reproduction of Wulfsige's name has been much enlarged. The scribe has written the names of these bishops in a hand known as Insular Script (see below).

In the second half of the tenth century English scribes began to use Caroline minuscule for writing Latin texts, instead of the Insular minuscule which had previously been used (Brown 1990). Caroline minuscule had developed on the continent and is the ancestor of modern type: for example, the forms of **a** and **g** in type, which differ from our usual handwritten forms, come from Caroline script. However, the English scribes continued to use Insular minuscule for writing texts in English, and since Wulfsige is an English name, *wulf sige* 'wolf - victory',[1] it is written in Insular script. Here the name Wulfsige starts with an upper-case letter followed by seven lower-case letters, just as in modern English. However, some of the letters are not immediately recognisable to us.

The initial letter looks a little like a '**p**' but is in fact pronounced **w** and called *wynn*; the Anglo-Saxons adopted this rune because there is no **W** in the Latin alphabet. Every rune was named after a word containing the sound they represented: *wynn* means 'joy'.

The lower-case **u** and **l** are familiar today; note the wedge-shaped serifs which are typical of Insular script.

The **s** is quite different from that of today. It is one of the forms typical of Insular minuscule, and looks a little like a modern lower-case **r** with a descender. Wulfsige was the third bishop of this name at Sherborne; the other two bishops have their names written with the other typical Insular-minuscule **s**, a tall **s** looking much like an uncrossed modern **f**.

This **f** has the form found in Insular script. The little turn to the left on the bottom of the descender is typical of Insular minuscule in the eleventh century.

The **i** has no dot and will not have for at least another century; the dot was adopted to distinguish between **m**, **n**, **u**, and **i** all of which were formed from short vertical strokes and which could make words like '*minimum*' very hard to read.

The **e** has a 'hook' to the right; this is very characteristic of tenth-century Insular minuscule in England, and it survives into the eleventh century. The hook was a convenient way of joining the previous letter to the **e** as can be seen here with the **g** and the **e**. It was not a silent letter as in Modern English but would have been pronounced. Wulfsige is thus a three-syllable name pronounced 'wolf-see-er'.

The '**g**' is not like the modern typeface **g** which derives from Caroline minuscule; it is a typical Insular **g** with a flat top. In Old English, **g** could either be pronounced soft like a **y**, or hard, as in '*good*'; in Wulfsige's name it was pronounced like a **y**. In the twelfth century scribes started to distinguish between these two sounds when writing, using Insular **g** for a soft **g** and Caroline **g** for a hard **g**, and from this the Insular **g** developed into the Middle English letter *yogh*.

Figure 3. The name Wulfsige as it appears in a list of Sherborne bishops recorded in The Pontifical of St Dunstan but much enlarged (see Fig 5). Written in the second half of the tenth century, the list of bishops from Aldhelm to Æthelric was added a little later, sometime in the early eleventh century. (MS lat 943, fo 1v Pontifical of St Dunstan, Reproduced with permission from the Bibliothèque Nationale, Paris)

Some formal styles of writing known to Wulfsige's generation

Uncial – a style used in Latin manuscripts from the fourth to eighth centuries consisting of large, rounded letters. Uncial means 'inch-high' and we get this name from a letter in which Jerome complained about books being written in a script which was so uneconomical with expensive parchment. By Wulfsige's time this script was no longer used for whole books but only for chapter titles or the first letters of important words. Such titles were often written in a mixture of Uncial script and another Roman majuscule script called 'Rustic Capitals'; see the first line of Figure 6 (Keynes, 'Wulfsige, monk of Glastonbury', this volume).

Insular script – a system of writing which developed in Ireland in the sixth century and was used throughout the British Isles. It was characterised by some particular letter-forms and by the use of wedge-shaped serifs on the tops of letters like **I** and **l**. It could originally be written as a majuscule script, Insular half-uncial (found in the Lindisfarne Gospels and the Book of Kells), but by Wulfsige's time only the minuscule form was still in use for whole texts. After the adoption of Caroline minuscule in England, Insular minuscule was only used for English, not Latin, texts.

Caroline (Carolingian) minuscule – a style developed on the continent following the reforms of the Emperor Charlemagne. It spread through most of Europe, and was eventually adopted in England in the second half of the tenth century, but for more than a century was only used for writing Latin, not English, texts.

Runes – a Germanic system of writing, in use from the third century, designed for carving on hard surfaces (rather than writing with a pen on parchment). The symbols **ƿ**, wynn, and **þ**, thorn (pronounced **th**) were both adopted from the runic system into the Latin alphabet by the Anglo-Saxons for use in writing their own language. By Wulfsige's time runes were still known in England but (apart from **ƿ** and **þ** which had been thoroughly absorbed into the writing of Old English) they seem mostly to have been a literary curiosity, used in puzzles or recorded in manuscripts with other non-Latin alphabets.

Majuscule script – upper-case letters like modern Capitals, bounded between two lines (although straying above or below these lines was permissable), as opposed to minuscule script.

Minuscule script – small or lower-case letters; the bodies of the letters bounded between two lines, but may have ascenders (like **b, d, l**) which go above the line, or descenders (like **p, g, q**) which go below.

Figure 3. Extended caption.

Before the Germanic peoples converted to Christianity and started using Latin script they had a writing system known as runes, mainly used for inscriptions carved on to hard surfaces like stone, metal, wood or bone. When the Anglo-Saxons tried to use Latin letters to write Old English names and texts they found they needed some extra symbols for their specific linguistic requirements (Crystal 1995). Latin has no **w**; at first the Anglo-Saxons wrote **u** or **uu**, but sometime in the eighth century they began using the runic symbol p called *wynn* and pronounced 'w'. The first letter of Wulfsige's name as written above is an upper-case *wynn*. The symbol itself had meaning, 'joy' or 'glory'. *Wynn* began to go out of use in the twelfth century, perhaps because it was not familiar to the Normans; it was not a Latin Christian symbol, and our modern **w** developed in place of two overlapping **u**s. In the Middle Ages **u** and **v** were two different ways of writing the same letter; it was only later that these shapes began to have distinct meanings. This is why the French today call **w** 'double-v' while we call it 'double-u'.

In the other example of Wulfsige's name written in the same manuscript it has been Latinised as **Uulfsinus** (it looks like *Vvlsinus* to us) to fit in with the rest of the text, a Latin letter of which Wulfsige was the recipient. His name occurs on the first line of the letter; this line was written in majuscule or upper-case letters, while the rest of the test is in 'excellent Anglo-Caroline script' (Keynes, 'Wulfsige, monk of Glastonbury', Fig 6, this volume). The upper-case letters which the scribe uses are familiar to us today; the two **U**s (written like modern **V**s) are side by side, as **VV**, but are not yet the single letter **W**. By the time the mid-twelfth-century copy of the charter of 998 was made, the initial letter of Wulfsige was formed from two interlocking **U**s thus giving us something much closer to the modern **W**. However, the name is still **Wlsinus**; there is as yet no **u** to follow the **W** (see Frontispiece; Keynes, 'A note on Anglo-Saxon personal names', this volume).

The varying use of **W** and **V** in western Europe today remains to remind us both of the divide between those languages of Germanic/Norse origin and those descended from Latin, and of the alphabetic contribution made by the more recently Christianised north to the old Christianised south whence Christianity had originally come.

Note
1   The word 'wolf' itself also had a poetic significance for the Norse/Germanic world; the animal was associated with battle, with violence and places of danger, and with gallows sites; a remarkable story is told by Ælfric of Cerne of how the head of the martyred King Edmund had been protected by a Wolf from other beasts. For Christians, the Wolf was often a metaphor for the Devil (Magennis 1999, 66–74). The second element of the bishop's name, *-sige,* happily, means 'victory'.

Bibliography

Brown, M P, 1990, *A Guide to Western Historical Scripts from Antiquity to 1600*. London. British Library, pls 16–24, especially pl 22.

Crystal, D, 1995, *The Cambridge Encyclopaedia of the English Language*. Cambridge, see 16–18, 258–64.

Magennis, H, 1999, *Anglo-Saxon Appetites*. Dublin, 66–74.

3. A note on Anglo-Saxon personal names

Simon Keynes

Although a few of the personal names widely used in Anglo-Saxon England remain in common use to the present day (eg Alfred, Audrey, Edith and Edward, from Ælfraed, Æthelthryth, Eadgyth and Eadweard), the great majority of such names would strike a modern ear as outlandish. Even in the twelfth century, the Anglo-Norman chronicler William of Malmesbury was fearful that 'the uncouth barbarous names' of the English would offend the sensibilities of those not familiar with them; and it is difficult now to write of King Ecgfrith, King Ecgberht, and their like, without thinking of the 'wave of Egg-kings' pilloried by the authors of *1066 and All That* (1930). Perhaps the names are best consigned to oblivion; but it would be as well before doing so to understand them on their own terms, and to judge what they might have meant to contemporaries.

The stock of names from which parents could draw when naming their children was considerable, though it can be seen to have varied from one kingdom or region to another, from one end of the period to the other, and from the lower to the higher levels of the social hierarchy. In the earlier part of the period, monothematic or uncompounded names (such as Hild or Brorda) were almost as common as dithematic or compounded names (such as Æthelred or Wulfsige); but latterly, in the upper echelons of society, the monothematic names became less popular and dithematic names became the norm. The majority of names in common use were of west Germanic origin, though there was always a place for biblical and other names; the increasing use of names of north Germanic (Scandinavian) origin in the tenth and eleventh centuries reflects the pervasive influence of the Scandinavian settlements of the late ninth century, just as Norman names became more widespread following the events of 1066.

The majority of the names used by persons of rank in the tenth and eleventh centuries were dithematic, or compounded of two elements, known respectively as the 'prototheme' (or first element) and the 'deuterotheme' (or second element). There was of course a basic distinction between masculine names and feminine names; but whereas the first element was usually a word which could be used for either sex, the second was generally gender-specific. The relatively limited stock of protothemes by this stage in common use included the following words, of which some are adjectives and others are nouns (whether masculine, feminine or neuter): *ælf* (masc/fem 'supernatural being, elf'), *æthel* (adj 'noble, famous'), *beorht* (adj 'bright'), *ead* (neut 'riches, good fortune'), *eald* (adj 'old'), *ealh* (masc 'temple'), *ecg* (fem 'edge, sword'), *god* (masc 'god'), *guth* (fem 'battle'), *leof* (adj 'dear'), *ord* (masc 'spear'), *os* (masc 'god'), *sige* (masc 'victory'), *swith* (adj 'strong'), *wig* (neut 'battle'), *wulf* (masc 'wolf'). The more varied stock of deuterothemes in common use for masculine names included the following nouns: *gar* ('spear'), *lac* ('gift, present'), *mund* ('protection'), *noth* ('boldness'), *ræd* ('advice, counsel'), *ric[e]* ('power'), *stan* ('stone'), *weald* or *wold* ('power, dominion'), *weard* ('guardian, protector'), *wine* ('friend, protector'); some words used as protothemes for both sexes were also used as deuterothemes for masculine names, such as -*beald* (adj 'bold'), -*beorht*, -*sige*, and -*wulf*. The stock of deuterothemes in common use for feminine names included the following nouns: *burh* ('protection'), *flæd* ('beauty'), *gyfu* or *gifu* ('gift'), *gyth* ('battle'), *hild* ('battle'), *thryth* ('power, glory'), *wynn* ('delight, pleasure'). Some confusion arises from the fact that an element in one dialect (eg West Saxon *beorht*; later *byrht*, *briht*, 'bright') will seem to differ from the same element in another dialect (eg Anglian *berht*).

The stock of personal names formed in these ways was supplemented by the increasingly widespread use of pet-names (eg Ælle for Ælfwine), by-names – including nicknames (Wulfric Spot), occupational names, patronymics (Harold *Godwines sunu*), and locatives (Wulfstan of Dalham) – and double names (Lyfing Ælfstan), which must have been helpful when attempting to distinguish between namesakes. It is generally supposed that hereditary family names, which passed from father to son, were not generally used (if indeed used at all) before the Norman Conquest, and that their increasingly widespread use thereafter reflects the greater emphasis placed by the Normans on the inheritance of property from father to eldest son.

There were no fixed principles of name-giving, though it is apparent that certain conventions were observed from time to time within certain families. The use of names alliterating on a particular letter, or the repeated use of a particular element (which has much the same effect), was practised within certain royal dynasties, and may have been practised here and there at other levels of society. Perhaps more common, if not always (in our ignorance) so easy to detect, is the use of elements derived from the names of parents, grandparents, or more distant forebears, on one or on both sides of a family, in much the same way as forenames are used today. It was said of a boy born of good English stock in the early eleventh century that he was called Wulfstan, 'a name taken in the former part from his mother's [Wulfgifu], in the latter from his father's [Æthelstan]',[1] apparently in the hope that he would draw qualities from both of his parents. Somewhat more surprising are the recorded instances of the same name being used for two or more siblings. For example, we read in a Northumbrian context of an Earl Ealdred, in the eleventh century, who had five daughters: one called Æthelthryth, one called Ealdgyth, and three called Ælfflæd. But just as there were no rules, so too should we have no expectations; and it is accordingly dangerous to posit a family relationship between two people simply on the basis of the use of alliterating or shared name-elements.

The history of the English as a Christian people is said to have begun with Pope Gregory's ingenious if somewhat forced interpretation put upon names furnished to him when he encountered some slave-boys in the market place at Rome: not Angles, but angels; from the kingdom of Deira, so snatched from the wrath of God (*de ira Dei*); under their king Ælle, whence the exclamation Alleluia![2] This was the learned tradition, applied in the first instance to biblical names and by natural extension to names of Germanic origin. Some names doubtless carried associations invested in them by former or current holders of that name; but since each element in an Anglo-Saxon dithematic name was itself a meaningful word, many names had a resonance which would have been readily understood by contemporaries. Names such as Wigfrith ('war-peace'), and Wulfstan ('wolf-stone') cannot have left anyone much the wiser; but in those cases where a name was compounded of elements with more consistent or natural connotations, it might invite comparison (in the minds of those with heightened sensibilities) with the person's perceived status, demeanour, or behaviour. A girl born of lowly parents might not have been called Æthelthryth ('noble-glory'); while a prince called Æthelred ('noble-counsel') might on becoming king have been expected to follow sound advice or to make good policy, and would be judged all the more harshly by posterity if he had not.

There are many examples of passages in Old English and Anglo-Latin literature from the eighth century onwards which reflect awareness of the literal meaning of a personal name. In the late tenth century Ealdorman Æthelweard ('noble-protector'), the chronicler, identified himself in Latin as *patricius consul* ('noble-public servant'). At about the same time, the draftsman of a royal charter issued in 995 remarked on the fact that a Bishop Godwine ('god-friend') was so-called as much for the probity of his deeds as by the virtue of his given name; while the draftsman of another charter, issued in the same year, remarked how a certain Æthelsige ('noble-victory') had dishonoured his name by his manifold crimes. Unsurprisingly, there is little evidence for the use of intrinsically 'bad' names; but perhaps one should sense in Archbishop Wulfstan's use of Latin *Lupus* ('wolf'), as his pen-name, a warning to his flock that he was out on the prowl.

The difficulties now presented by Anglo-Saxon names arise in large measure from the vagaries which befell them with the passage of time, and from the indignities to which they were subjected by uncomprehending copyists. For example, the notionally 'proper' and quite distinct forms Æthelweard and Ælfweard converge latterly as 'Alward'; Ælfsige might be Latinised as Ælsinus;

Eadwig might be Latinised as Eaduuius and re-anglicised at Edwy; and so on. The wag who gave King Æthelred ('noble-counsel') the by-name *unræd* ('no counsel') had spotted a mismatch between name and recorded action, though it was simply the passage of time which corrupted the by-name from *unræd* to 'unready', and thereby dealt the king a further blow from which he never recovered. The name itself became Ailred, or Alred, and was (mis)interpreted already in the twelfth century as a fitting name for a counsellor, 'for the English Alred is in Latin *totum consilius* or *omne consilium* ["all counsel"]'.[3] The very common Anglo-Saxon name Wulfsige ('wolf-victory') was Latinised as Wlsinus; and in this way Wulfsige, bishop of Sherborne, came to be known as St Wlsinus, re-anglicised as St Wulsin, Wulfsin, or Wulfsy.

Notes
1   J H F Peile, 1934, *William of Malmesbury's Life of St Wulfstan*, 5–6.
2   Bede, *Eccl. Hist.*, ii.2.
3   *The Life of Ailred of Rievaulx by Walter Daniel,* M Powicke (ed) (Edinburgh, 1950), 8.

Bibliography
Bede, *Historia ecclesiastica gentis Anglorum* (*Ecclesiastical History of the English People*), B Colgrave and R A G Mynors (eds), 1969. Oxford.
Peile, J H F, 1934, *William of Malmesbury's Life of St Wulfstan*.
Powicke, M, (ed), 1950, *The Life of Ailred of Rievaulx by Walter Daniel*. Edinburgh.

4. The monastic reform of the tenth century and Sherborne

David Farmer

The Sherborne Millennium (998–1998) commemorates the return of monks to Sherborne and the appointment of one of their number as bishop of Sherborne. This paper links these events with the monastic reforms of the tenth century, with the history of the town of Sherborne and its later importance as an artistic centre.

The monastic revival of tenth-century England began with St Dunstan's installation as abbot of Glastonbury in 940. From the start the Rule of St Benedict was the chosen and predominant guide. News of similar continental movements had reached the court of King Athelstan (925–39), where Dunstan and his companion St Æthelwold served the king before they were ordained priests on the same day. Like their continental counterparts at Cluny and Gorze, they opted for a life of liturgical worship, chastity and renunciation of all individual ownership. Their standard book of Customs, the *Regularis Concordia* was closely based on Cluny's equivalent *Customary,* which came to England through the influence of Fleury, which claimed and still claims to possess the relics of St Benedict. Although there is no record of Dunstan having visited Fleury, his two principal followers, Æthelwold of Winchester and Oswald of Worcester, certainly did so, and helped their disciples to do the same. The form and text of the Rule they used came from the same source, as presumably did much of their music and liturgy. But the English revival soon revealed its own characteristics also. It developed English vernacular prose writings and collected extant Old English poems, it fostered the dramatic Easter Sepulchre, and more important than these, it provided many bishops for the Church in England for over more than fifty years. This was largely due to the movement's close connection with the kings of England. This was most notable in the reign of Edgar (959–75), who, although younger than either, was closely associated with both Dunstan and Æthelwold.

The foundation of Sherborne as a monastic cathedral came comparatively

Figure 4. Portrayal of King Edgar; the frontispiece preceding the charter by which he refounded New Minster, Winchester as a Benedictine house. Dated 966, it may in fact be slightly later. Edgar is flanked by the foundation's two patron saints, the Virgin and St Peter, and is offering up the charter to Christ seated in a mandorla supported by four angels.

The iconography is very similar to that for King Cnut and Queen Emma [Ælfgifu] shown presenting an altar cross to New Minster some fifty years later. Christ sits high in his mandorla and it is He who is this time flanked by the Virgin and St Peter. The two women, the Virgin and the Queen are shown on the left-hand side of the picture, the men on the right (see Barker, 'Picturing the beginning of the Age of Saints', Fig 20e, this volume). (BL Cotton MS Vespasian A VIII, fo 2v Portrayal of King Edgar. Reproduced by permission of the British Library) late in the revival. It took place during the troubled reign of Æthelred the Unready when hostile Viking forces were active in Dorset as well as central Wessex. The monastic Order strongly supported the king through its principal writers, Ælfric of Cerne and Wulfstan of York, who both stressed the duty of loyalty. In many parts of the country the abbeys were prominent in local government. Political as well as religious considerations may well have led to the re-establishment of Sherborne. It was essential that this diocese should be held by one utterly loyal to the king, and its monastic character made it likely that this security would be a permanent feature. In point of fact, for the century 978–1078, the see of Sherborne was held continuously by monks with only two exceptions. Usually its bishops came from either Glastonbury or Winchester. Moreover there were already monks of the revival at Cerne and Milton, while the monastic see of Winchester, the then capital of England, was extremely important as a wealthy landowner, as a centre of vernacular art, music and literature and the founder of several dependent monasteries. All this had been the achievement of St Æthelwold, its bishop from 963 to 984, while the new bishop of Sherborne in 998, St Wulfsige, had been a disciple of St Dunstan at Glastonbury and had ruled his abbey of Westminster before his promotion. Thus Sherborne was closely connected with the two most important figures of the tenth-century monastic revival.

Sherborne had in fact long been a bishopric and its first bishop, Aldhelm of Malmesbury (died 709), was a monk. Related to the royal family of Wessex by blood, he became a monk and abbot at a comparatively early age and was the first notable Anglo-Saxon writer of Latin. Bede knew and admired his works but did not imitate their often verbose style; they were widely read and diffused until the eleventh century. As abbot he wrote several letters which have survived; one to Geraint, king of Dumnonia (in the Devon-Cornwall area) in favour of keeping the synod of Whitby's sound decision in favour of keeping the feast of Easter on the same day as the rest of the Western Church, while another was written to the clerics of St Wilfrid (Whitby's principal spokesman) exhorting them to fidelity during his exile. His most famous Latin work, *De Virginitate* (in poetry and prose) is a collection of examples of virginal consecration to God's service, drawn from the Bible and early Church history. His vernacular works, unknown to Bede but known to King Alfred, included Old English poems sung to his own harp accompaniment at Malmesbury to entice pagans into the Church.

It may well be that Bede did not know the full importance of Aldhelm. He was not very well informed about Wessex, for which his only acknowledged source was Daniel, bishop of Winchester. He said little about King Ine (688–726), for example, whose law code reveals a confident Christian society in which civil law enforced church law and in which native British men of high status could flourish; however, Bede did record his abdication and death soon afterwards in Rome. Similarly the *Life and Letters* of St Boniface (died 754) reveal a flourishing monasticism in Wessex of which Bede said little, for the excellent reason that his sources were limited. Aldhelm was certainly a builder of note; Malmesbury, Bradford-on-Avon and Frome were his monastic churches, and when he was bishop he apparently built churches at Sherborne, Wareham and possibly other churches in the Isle of Purbeck. His important connection with this area is preserved in the authentic place-name St Aldhelm's Head, later corrupted to St Alban's Head.

The choice of Sherborne as the western see is difficult to understand. It was less notable than the Roman towns of Dorchester and Ilchester; the presence of a Celtic monastery there but on a different site from the cathedral may or may not be a pointer. Another reason for choosing Sherborne may have been simply that Aldhelm owned all or part of it through his close connection with the Wessex kings. Centuries later, William of Malmesbury (writing in 1125) described Sherborne as 'a small village, attractive neither for the density of population nor eminence of its site. It is a source of wonder and almost shame that an episcopal see lasted here for so many centuries' (Preest 2002, 116). It should be noted, however, that there was a certain rivalry between Aldhelm's monastery (the very word Malmesbury arguably means *Aldhelm's burg*) and Aldhelm's see [bishopric]. When the saint died at Doulting, his body was taken not to Sherborne but to Malmesbury, where it was enshrined. It should also be noted that when the Sherborne see had a vast territory covering Devon, Somerset, Dorset, Wiltshire and possibly Berkshire, whereas by the tenth century bishoprics had been set up for Devon, Somerset and Wiltshire, so Sherborne was a diocese for Dorset only. Owing to its poverty it was sometimes united with Ramsbury, and this union was eventually made permanent when the see of Salisbury was established in 1078.

One aspect of the monastic revival in England and at Sherborne, was its close association with saints. Monasteries needed living exemplars as well as the text of the Rule, however venerable that may have been. They also needed monastic heroes of the past, sometimes vividly recalled through their relics, whether these were bones or books like Dunstan's famous class-book of Glastonbury. They also needed *Lives* of saints of varying length, both for private and public reading. Sherborne had both memory of Benedict in life and of his lively cult at Fleury and Orléans, and also of Aldhelm, its first bishop. More will be said below about Wulfsige, Sherborne's bishop of the monastic revival who was venerated as a saint after his death in 1002. Here, however, we may recall other saints connected with Sherborne; the British Juthwara, of whom we know virtually nothing for certain except the connection of her relics with Sherborne, which were translated *c* 1050 with Wulfsige's to a new shrine, and two unusual dedications from the twelfth century may well point back further to local interest in two different saints; Probus of Cornwall and Emerenciana of Rome. Knowledge of the second may have come from Canterbury or from Aldhelm, who had visited Rome and was specially interested in saintly virgins; the cult of Emerenciana is closely linked with that of the much more famous Agnes, of whom she was the nurse. Probus' dedication could be linked to continuing Celtic interests, as does the cult of Juthwara. Possibly her enshrinement with Wulfsige indicates a recognition and appreciation of Christianity in western Britain before the Anglo-Saxons penetrated it.

It is interesting to note that the monastic element at Sherborne proved to be more permanent and, it seems, more relevant to the town's wealth than the diocesan one. When Salisbury became the diocese of Wiltshire, Dorset and Berkshire in 1078, Sherborne was a priory. But in 1122 it became an abbey of fifty monks, had foundations at Horton (Dorset) and Kidwelly (Carmarthenshire). Although electoral registers show that there were fewer monks there in the later Middle Ages, at the time of the Dissolution it had an income of over £682, more than Cerne, Milton, Pershore or Selby, but considerably less than the thirty wealthiest abbeys in England. The rebuilding of the nave of the abbey church, the fan-vaulting of the nave and aisles and the completion of the eastern chapel before 1500, took place when the community of monks seems to have numbered less than twenty. By this time they had the two hospitals in the town, and a Sherborne monk, copying William of Malmesbury's passage cited above, inserted negatives to his condescending description of the town. In fact, for a medium-sized monastery, they contributed notably to the country's artistic heritage not only by rebuilding the church, but also by commissioning the justly famous Sherborne Missal. This is one of the richest liturgical manuscripts to survive from medieval England and is a worthy successor to the two Sherborne Pontificals of the eleventh century.

It is also interesting to note that St Stephen Harding, abbot of Citeaux from 1109 to 1134, who received St Bernard as a novice there and appointed him abbot of Clairvaux, had been a monk at Sherborne and commissioned or wrote at Citeaux a large number of manuscript biblical and patristic works which survive to this day at Dijon. It is by no means impossible that Stephen, who was a monk at Sherborne had, as a young monk, acquired his artistic and literary skills here at Sherborne. A large statue of him on the place where he received Bernard's monastic profession, survives to this day at Citeaux. Thus his and Sherborne's contribution to Cistercian as well as Benedictine history is appropriately recorded.

The refounding of Sherborne as a Benedictine monastery just a thousand years ago is indeed worthy of commemoration both in the history of the town and in that of the monastic Order.

Bibliography

Campbell, James, 1982, *The Anglo-Saxons*. London.

Farmer, David, 1997, *The Oxford Dictionary of Saints* (4th Edition). Oxford.

Head, Thomas, 1990, *Hagiography and the Cult of Saints: the Diocese of Orléans 800–1200*. Cambridge.

Ker, N R, 1964, *Medieval Libraries of Great Britain* (2nd Edition). Royal Historical Society.

Knowles, David, 1959, *The Religious Orders in England, Volume 3*. Cambridge.

Knowles, David, 1966, *The Monastic Order in England* (2nd Edition). Cambridge.

Knowles, D, and Neville Hancock, R, 1953, *Medieval Religious Houses: England and Wales*. London.

Parsons, David (ed), 1975, *Tenth-Century Studies*. Chichester.

Preest, D (trans), 2002, *William of Malmesbury: the Deeds of the Bishops of England*. Woodbridge. Gesta Pontificum Anglorum.

5. The Revelation of St John: the last book of the Bible

Eric Woods

The literal translation of the last book of the Bible is 'The Revelation of John', but in both Greek and English this is ambiguous. However, the opening lines of the book make the meaning clear:

> This is the account of a revelation which God gave to Jesus Christ. He gave it to show his servants what must soon take place. Christ sent his angel to inform his servant John of it, and told John everything that he saw.
> (Rev. 1:1–2)

Debate about authorship, date and historical context of the Apocalypse (as the book is often known) continues unabated at the start of the third Christian millennium. St Wulfsige, at the end of the first, would probably have been content with the book's own testimony, that it was written by 'John', in exile on the island of Patmos. Perhaps Wulfsige would have known of the evidence of Irenaeus, bishop of Lyon, writing *c* AD 180, that the Apocalpyse and the Fourth Gospel were written by one and the same person, none other than the Apostle St John. Irenaeus also asserts that the book was 'seen' at the end of the reign of the Emperor Domitian. Domitian died in AD 96, and most scholars date Revelation to the last decade of the first Christian century – which almost (but not quite) rules out authorship by John the Apostle. However, I prefer the view that places Revelation shortly before the fall of Jerusalem, in AD 70, during the Jewish War which began in AD 66.[1]

Whatever the truth of the matter, the Apocalypse (a difficult book to understand at the best of times) is only intelligible if the author himself had indeed shared with his readers, as he claimed, 'the persecution, the royal status and courage that are ours as Christians' (Rev. 1:9).[2] In other words, whichever Roman Emperor was responsible for the particular persecutions endured by John and his fellow Christians, it was out of that suffering (and aware that more was to come) that the Apocalypse was born.

This brings us to the heart of the meaning of 'apocalyptic', which is a literary genre which emerged in Judaism during the reign of the Seleucid King, Antiochus Epiphanes (175–163 BC). The world 'apocalyptic' comes from the Greek *apokalypsis*, meaning 'revelation'. And all apocalyptic writings (Daniel in the Old Testament, Revelation in the New, a number of intertestamental Jewish works such as 1, 2 and 3 Enoch, 4 Ezra and Jubilees, as well as a few passages in the New Testament such as Mark 13 and parallels) have this in common: they grow out of times of oppression and persecution, and employ cryptic language, colourful imagery and confident pronouncement about the fulfilment of God's promises, in order to encourage, strengthen and inspire their readers. The principal difference between Jewish and Christian apocalyptic is that the latter centres, as we might expect, on the person of Jesus Christ in whom hopes of God's people have been and will continue to be fulfilled. But all use metaphor, allegory and symbolism to help the reader to understand the significance within God's plan of the troubled times through which they are living.

So apocalyptic is usually more concerned with 'forth-telling' than 'fore-telling'. It contains not so much detailed prediction about what will happen this year or next as a sketch of the background – past, present and future – against which current events are being worked out. This is the function of that famous passage in Revelation (20:1–11):

> Then I saw an angel coming down from heaven ... He seized ... Satan, and chained him up for a thousand years ... that he might no longer lead the nations astray until the thousand years were over. After that he must be released for a little while ... And I saw the souls of those who had been beheaded because they had witnessed to Jesus and proclaimed God's message ... They came to life and reigned with Christ for a thousand years ... Then when the thousand years have been completed, Satan will be released from his prison, and he will go out and lead astray Gog and Magog, the nations which are in the four corners of the earth, to bring them together for war ... and fire came down out of heaven and consumed them ... Then I saw a great white throne and him who sat on it. Earth and heaven fled from his presence, and vanished away.

John reassures those enduring present tribulation that at some point in the future all will be resolved by God himself, who will establish that Holy City where God 'will wipe every tear from their eyes; and there will be no more death, no more mourning, crying and pain; for the old order has gone' (Rev. 21:4).

Almost certainly, John did not intend his readers to understand his reference to a 'thousand years' as a precise prediction of time. They would have recognised instead the broad brush-stroke of biblical prophecy. Later generations have sometimes been more literal in their approach, which is when apocalyptic gives way to apocalypticism, 'a way of looking at the world, and a way of constructing or maintaining communities, which stir up and keep at boiling point, certain types of end-of-the-world speculations'.[3] It is that sort of biblical literalism which causes some sects to perpetrate all sorts of bizarre acts, some of which – such as the events near Waco, USA, in 1993 which culminated in seventy-nine members of the Branch Davidian cult dying in a spectacular fire – end in tragedy. As Stephen Jay Gould puts it, 'Apocalypticism is the province of the wretched, the downtrodden, the dispossessed, the political radical, the theological revolutionary, and the self-proclaimed saviour – not the belief of people happily at the helm'.[4]

So was Wulfsige – 'happily at the helm' of his diocese – affected by some kind of apocalypticism when in 998 he engineered the dismissal of the secular canons from Sherborne, and their replacement by Benedictines? Somehow I doubt it. I suspect he stood more in the mainstream of Christian understanding, concerned – like John himself – to reach backward and into the present and the future, to interpret God's word to his own community. The invitation to the Benedictines would not have been to help the diocese prepare for the end of the world, but rather to bring a clearer glimpse of heaven and eternity to the company of believers, struggling as so many have done before and since to maintain and commend their faith in dark and difficult times.[5]

Notes
1   J A T Robinson, 1976, *Redating the New Testament*, and S S Smalley, 1994, *Thunder and Love*. *cf* J Knight, 1999, *Revelation*, arguing for the 'traditional' date just prior to AD 96.
2   All biblical quotations are from *The Translator's New Testament*, 1975, Bible Society.
3   T Wright, 1999, *The Myth of the Millennium*, 31.
4   S J Gould, 1997, *Questioning the Millennium*, 45.
5   The best introduction to apocalyptic remains D S Russell, 1978, *Apocalyptic Ancient and Modern*.

Bibliography
Boxall, I, 2002, *Revelation: Vision and Insight*. SPCK.
Gould, S J, 1997, *Questioning the Millennium*. Jonathan Cape.
Knight, J, 1999, *Revelation*. Sheffield Academic Press.
Robinson, J A T, 1976, *Redating the New Testament*. SCM Press.
Russell, D S, 1978, *Apocalyptic Ancient and Modern*. SCM Press.
Smalley, S S, 1994, *Thunder and Love*. Nelson Word.
Wright, T, 1999, *The Myth of the Millennium*. Azure.

6. 'Thousand is a perfect number ...' quoth Ælfric of Cerne

Nicholas Campion

The guide to Sherborne Abbey on sale in the visitors' bookstall records the events of the abbey's early years from its consecration over twelve hundred years ago, including such celebrated happenings as the future King Alfred's visit on Good Friday 865 on the occasion of the granting of a charter by his elder brother, Æthelberht. St Wulfsige's installation of Benedictine monks as a replacement for the secular canons, from which the abbey's millennium is dated, is credited as part of the wider reformation of the English church by St Dunstan, archbishop of Canterbury from 960 (Gibb 2000, 2). The charter by which this event is recorded is dated to the year 998, ten years after Dunstan's death. The question we should pose though, is whether it took place precisely because the year was 998, and the end of the first Christian millennium was but two years in the future. Did Dunstan, Wulfsige and the reformers believe that they were living in the 'last days', and were their actions prompted by the urgent need to prepare the church for Christ's longed-for return, one thousand years after his birth? Ælfric, abbot of Cerne, had been in Dorset for five years by the time of Wulfsige's arrival in 993–4. Already a 'scholar of fame and distinction', it may be presumed that it was Ælfric who must have exercised the most direct influence on Wulfsige (Keynes, 'Wulfsige, monk of Glastonbury', this volume). And it is Ælfric's words which form the title of this paper. They are taken from his *Homilies* (Thorpe 1844–6, I, 189), the second edition of which was in production at the time.

Was one thousand a significant number?

The belief that thousand year periods are historically significant is not well-attested in Scripture. There is but one mention in the Old Testament, a famous quote from Psalm 90:4, in which the psalmist's praise of God includes the lines 'for a thousand years in thy sight are but as yesterday when it is past'. 2 Peter, 3:8, paraphrased the Psalm in similar words: 'with the Lord one day is as a thousand years, and a thousand years is one day'. However, it was St John who established the thousand year period as a unit within Christian historiography. In Revelation, Chapter 20, he set out the basic chronology in which Christ's return would be followed by the defeat of Satan and the judgement of the righteous, who would then sit in splendour with Christ while he ruled for a thousand years. At the end of this period Satan, who had been bound and cast into a pit, would be set free and engage in a last cosmic battle with Christ. Satan's defeat would precipitate the Last Judgement, that of the unrighteous, to be followed by the establishment of the New Jerusalem, the eternal Kingdom of God.

St John's chronology appears to have been imported from contemporary Persian religion, in which it was believed that *Zurvan* (fate, destiny) ruled for a thousand years prior to the creation, and that history then passed through thousand year phases culminating in the triumph of *Ahura Mazda*, the god of light, and the consignment of *Ahriman*, the god of darkness, to his pit (Campion 1994, 288, 322). Whether the theory was Persian in origin or not, Church Fathers such as Irenaeus, Lactantius and Clement of Alexandria believed it was significant. In the fifth century St Augustine gave it his blessing, converting the six days of Creation and seventh day of rest into a chronology of six great historical periods, of which the last was the reign of Christ and the saints, followed by the seventh phase, that of the Kingdom of God (Campion 1994, 33–5; Augustine 1972, XI 30–1, XV 12, XX 6–9, 16–19, XXII).

These, then, would have been the millenarian sources from the Gospels and the Church Fathers with which Dunstan, Ælfric and Wulfsige would have been familiar. There are thus three obvious flaws in the argument that a devout Christian would have necessarily viewed the approach of the year 1000 as significant. Firstly, the countdown to the millennium could not begin until after Christ's Second Coming, which was still awaited. Secondly, Augustine, impressed by the Christianisation of the Roman Empire had argued that the rule of Christ had in effect commenced with his first appearance, and that there was therefore no pressing need to look forward to the Second Coming. Thirdly, he abandoned the literalism of thousand year periods, preferring to talk of past ages in terms of numbers of generations and refusing to place a time limit on the current age. Thus, to a conservative, scholarly Christian with a belief based exclusively on Scripture, it might be positively an anathema to see the year 1000 as being significant in any way.

Millenarian forecasts

However, religious devotion is based as much on emotion as intellect and, regardless of the strict interpretation of Scripture, millenarian themes have always been present in Christianity. For many Christians, the hope that Christ's return is imminent has sustained their belief through times of trouble. Indeed, for evangelists, the threat that Christ might return to punish the ungodly tomorrow is a major tool of conversion. Forecasts of when he will return are less important than the belief that he could arrive at any moment, and in that context almost any year can be shown to have suitable Scriptural authority. For millenarians any numerology or chronology based on Scripture will suffice as a timing measure, and any celestial omen, natural disaster or political upheaval can be seen as evidence that the Second Coming is nigh.

The first revolutionary Christian millenarian movement can be dated to AD 156 when a certain Phrygian named Montanus declared himself to be the incarnation of the Holy Ghost and proclaimed the Third Testament (Cohn 1970, 25). From then on the expectation that Christ was about to return and inaugurate the Rule of the Saints was to become one of the most powerful motivating ideologies in European history.

While the belief in Christ's return, whether tomorrow or in the distant future, is central to Christian theology, it comes in different forms. We may define millenarianism as a more revolutionary version, appealing to revolutionary armies and religious enthusiasts, culminating in the Reformation. Eschatology may be defined as a more scholarly appreciation of the approaching End, which appealed to influential scholars such as Alcuin and Dante, and which climaxed in the Renaissance and found secular echoes in the Enlightenment (Campion 1994, 31–3). If Dunstan was motivated by pressure of the approach of the judgmental year, 1000, then he would have belonged to the more revolutionary, millenarian camp. The suffering inflicted by a wrathful God on southern England through the agency of Viking raiders during the final two decades of the century would have served only to increase a sense of urgency (Keynes, 'Wulfsige, monk of Glastonbury', this volume).

Millenarians and eschatologists may have differed according to whether they were scholarly monks or revolutionary peasants, on whether they thought that history was primarily composed of four phases or seven. But what united them all from the fifth century to the sixteenth was a vigilance for signs of the End. As Pope Gregory I wrote to Æthelbert, king of Kent in June 601:

> Further we also wish Your Majesty to know, as we have learned from the words of Almighty God in Holy Scripture, that the End of the present world is already near and that the unending kingdom of the Saints is approaching. As this same End of the world is drawing nigh, many unusual things will happen – climate changes, terrors from heaven, unseasonable tempests, wars, famines, pestilences, earthquakes. All these things are not to come in our own days, but they will all follow upon our times. (McGinn 1979, 64)

Five hundred years later Hildegard of Bingen (1098–1179), one of the great Catholic reformers, warned that 'countless signs will appear in the sun, moon and stars, in the waters and in the other elements as well as in all creation, so that people will be able to predict the disaster that is to come through these signs as through a painting' (Fox 1987, 1.28). Otto of Friesing (c 1110–58), another reformer, himself discussed the effects of the 1066 appearance of Halley's comet, considering its consequences in the Norman Conquest of

England and the excommunication of the Emperor Henry IV in 1076, the latter a traumatic event for those who believed that the Papacy and Empire were to jointly fulfil a divinely authorised joint destiny in bringing about the Kingdom of God on Earth. Otto compared this event to the shattering of the statue in the Book of Daniel, signifying the approach of the last times (McGinn 1979, 98–9). Thus, prophecies of the End are perpetual, appealing to every generation, particularly to church reformers.

Was the year 1000 seen as an apocalyptic year?
There is considerable argument as to whether or not the year 1000 was awaited as the year of the Apocalypse. The evidence that it was is scattered and anecdotal, and some of it dates from after the event. For example, Thietmar of Merseburg described 1000 as the 'best year since the immaculate Virgin brought forth our salvation, when a radiant dawn was seen to shine upon the world'. In the late 1030s the author of the *Annales Hildesheimenses* recalled that 'With Otto III ruling, the thousandth year passing the number of established reckoning according to that which is written: the thousandth surpasses and transcends all years' (Thompson 1996, 48).

We also have occasional accounts of the signs and wonders seen during the course of the year. In Lotharingia the celebrations of Easter were interrupted by an earthquake, while shortly afterwards a comet appeared and stayed in the sky for three months. That in turn was followed by the destruction by fire of the church of St Michael the Archangel (France 1989, Glaber III, ch 3; Thompson 1996, 35).

However, the evidence is slight and there is considerable scepticism that anyone in the year 1000 believed that anything of supernatural significance was about to take place. The prevailing belief that Europe was shaken by a millenarian outburst can be attributed largely to the fictionalising instincts of a number of nineteenth-century historians, whose legacy is found in modern works such as Stephen Skinner's *Millennium Prophecies* (1994). In 1994 Skinner described vividly the scene in the year 999 as pre-millennial tension drove bands of flagellants through the countryside causing disturbances. In a flight of fancy he reports that 'mobs called for the execution of supposed sorcerers or unpopular burghers, and even some farm animals were freed to roam through the towns, giving a slightly surrealistic air to the proceedings' (Skinner 1994, 69; Thompson 1996, 35–55).

As we have seen, the argument that the 990s were years of apocalyptic fever is difficult to sustain. The lack of literary evidence is compounded by the clear exaggeration amongst those who report the alleged instances of millennial hysteria. Then there is the problem that the historiography of church conservatives, following St Augustine, was positively antithetical to any notion that the prevailing order was about to be overthrown. We can add to this list the following objections: the poor and illiterate did not know what year it was, the educated would have used material from the Islamic world, such as planetary tables, which were set for the *Hejira*, and the calendar was often based on regnal years, so that for Wulfsige 1000 was the 22nd year of Æthelred the Unready's reign. Meanwhile, as we have seen, such was the flexibility of scriptural numerology that then as now, any year can be shown to have millenarian properties. Thus Abbo of Fleury, writing in 995, described a prediction he heard that the Antichrist would come in 960 (Thompson 1996, 38). One of the most influential prophecies of the Middle Ages, that of Joachim of Fleury, had the 'Age of the Holy Spirit' commencing in 1260 (Campion 1994, 372–9). In this sense, the year 1000 could provide a useful hook for millenarian prophecies, but not necessarily any more so than many other years.

The final argument which is consistently used to demonstrate the absence of millenarian feeling in the Middle Ages rests on the evidence for ecclesiastical endowments. Why, it is asked, would anyone endow a chapel or church at great expense for a great number of years if it was believed that the end of the world was due imminently? Thus, in 998 the Council of Rome imposed a seven year penance on King Robert II of France while in 999 Pope Sylvester II granted to the archbishop of Rheims the privilege of crowning all future kings of France. To apply this argument to Sherborne, why would Wulfsige have bothered to reform the abbey if Christ was coming in a couple of years, and could have done the job for him?

There are a number of flaws in this argument, which is based on sweeping assumptions rather than textual evidence. Firstly, those in positions of ecclesiastical authority were generally more concerned with maintaining their power and unimpressed by religious prophecies which had, in any case, proved repeatedly to be false. Thus, even if the popes did not believe that Christ was about to return, this does not mean that Wulfsige didn't. Secondly, any true believer in Christ's return would be likely to go to great lengths to prove his or her devotion, and this could be proved both by spending a large amount of money and making an endowment for as long as possible. Thirdly, nowhere in the Scriptures is it forecast that places of worship or pilgrimage will become redundant after the Second Coming. It is only after the end of the millennium, when Christ's thousand year rule comes to an end, that all earthly existence will be replaced by the new heaven and new earth. Fourthly, the argument assumes that there is some rationale in millenarianism, and that nobody who believed that the world was about to end would spend their money in such an illogical manner.

Yet it is foolish to look for logic in areas of activity driven by fear, faith and blind hope. As an example, in May 1998 I was watching an evangelical television station in Louisiana. An item in which a teenage boy's dreams had been interpreted as revealing that the last days were due in November was followed by an appeal for $5,000 to purchase news items of an apocalyptic nature over the next three years. These two segments were juxtaposed without even the merest trace of irony and with no attempt to justify the obvious contradiction between them. Lastly, the argument misunderstands the paradoxical nature of prophecy which, as Karl Popper showed, should be understood as a call to action rather than an injunction to wait passively while fate unfolds (Campion 1994, 11–14; Popper 1986). Thus, if Wulfsige did believe that the Second Coming was due in two years time, his reform of Sherborne in 998 can be seen as a direct preparation for the greatest supernatural event since the Resurrection, or perhaps since the Creation itself. While the evidence suggests that the general population was entirely uninfluenced by millenarian fever, it is fair to assume that a church reformer such as Wulfsige would have been, partly because those who set out to clean the church's augean stables so often saw themselves as preparing Christ's path. It might, therefore, be surprising if Wulfsige did not believe that Christ was about to return.

There is now, as happens in academic debates, a revisionist movement, pioneered by Richard Landes and Henri Focillon, promoting the evidence that, while there might not have been the sort of millenarian outbreaks described by Skinner, there were significant events which can only be explained by the belief in the imminence of the Second Coming (Thompson 1996, 42–52). It is alleged, for example, that those historians who denied the reality of millenarian feeling were Marxists who were uncomfortable with the notion that revolutionary movements could be driven by ideology rather than economic pressure.

The revisionist argument relies heavily on the existence of the 'Peace of God', a devotional and evangelical movement which flourished from the 990s to 1030s, partly in protest against the prevailing abuses perpetrated by the political and military powers. The fact that it lasted until the 1030s is significant, for 1033 was the thousandth anniversary of the Resurrection, hence a possible date for the Second Coming if 1000 proved disappointing. As it happened, 1033 was also to bring disillusionment. At the movement's height there were enormous gatherings, such as that at Limoges in 994, and even though such events were orchestrated by clergy who were concerned to bolster their position and protect their estates against predatory nobles, they seem to have tapped a deep vein of religious feeling (Thompson 1996, 49). The question we must ask if we are to gain an insight into Wulfsige's motives, but which I cannot answer here, is whether the English reformers were influenced by the Peace of God, or by parallel developments, such as the apparent extraordinary growth in the cult of relics.

The main item of evidence from the political world, but one which is significant on account of its leading players, finds the Emperor Otto III occupying Rome in 996. He installed his cousin Bruno on the papal throne as Gregory V with the aim of restoring the Christian Roman Empire under his sway. In 998 he had to return to depose John XVI and install, in 999, his protégé, Sylvester II. From there he journeyed to Aachen where, with great ceremony, he reinterred the bones of Charlemagne, the empire's founder. The evidence suggests that Otto saw himself as the Last Emperor, the secular ruler whose task was to prepare the way for Christ's arrival (Campion 1994, 337–9, 341–2, 435–40). If Otto could be moved to such lengths by the ticking of the calendar, then why not Wulfsige?

Seen in this light Sherborne Abbey is less the charming old building at the centre of one of England's most picturesque market towns, or one of the jewels in the crown of the burgeoning heritage industry. Instead it is the living testimony of an extraordinary moment when a small band of religious revolutionaries set out to prepare the way for the most extraordinary event any of them could imagine, an occurrence so rich in supernatural splendour that it is beyond our limited modern comprehension: the dead were to be raised, the righteous were to be judged, celestial trumpets were to be sounded, kings were to be overthrown, the sky was to be filled by angels battling with Satan and the entire world as we know it was to come to an end.

Wulfsige was not just one figure in a wave of popular millenarian fever. He was in all likelihood the leader of a minority who alone had seen the future. If we can translate Wulfsige's probable millenarianism into twentieth-century terms then we might compare it to a combination of the single-minded determination of the Bolsheviks seizing the Winter Palace in 1917 with the wide-eyed spiritual optimism of San Francisco's summer of love. The church reform did not take place in isolation from the political events of the time. Dunstan's term as archbishop had seen the formalisation of Wessex's domination of the Anglo-Saxon kingdoms and, in 973, Edgar's coronation as first king of England. Yet, in the endless competition between the spiritual and secular powers, Wulfsige was essentially a dissenter and Sherborne Abbey embodies the alternatives to all existing earthly political orders. It is an image of the future heaven on earth.

Bibliography

Augustine, *City of God*, 1972, H Bettenson (trans). London. Penguin Books.

Campion, N, 1994, *The Great Year, Astrology, Millenarianism and History in the Western Tradition*. London. Penguin Arkana.

Cohn, N, 1970, *The Pursuit of the Millennium* (Revised Edition). London. Paladin.

Fox, M (ed), 1987, *Hildegard of Bingen, Book of Divine Works*. Santa Fe, New Mexico.

France, J (ed and trans), 1989, Rodulfi Glabri, *Historiarum Libri Quinque* [Rudolfus Glaber *The Five Books of the Histories*]. Oxford. Clarendon Press.

Gibb, J H P, 2000, *Sherborne Abbey* (3rd Edition). Friends of Sherborne Abbey.

McGinn, B, 1979, *Apocalyptic Traditions in the Middle Ages*. New York.

Popper, K, 1986, *The Poverty of Historicism*. London, New York.

Skinner, S, 1994, *Millennium Prophecies*. London. Virgin.

Thompson, D, 1996, *The End of Time: Faith and Fear in the Shadow of the Millennium*. London. Sinclair Stephenson.

Thorpe, B (ed), 1844–6. *Ælfric's Homilies of the Anglo-Saxon Church* (Two volumes). London. The Ælfric Society.

7. *Anni Domini Computati*
or counting the years of the Lord 998–1998: the Sherborne Benedictine millennium

Katherine Barker

ð cccc nonageſimo octauo

The significance of the seven figures written above – 998 and 1998 – is so obvious to us it is a conscious effort-of-mind to see the sequence of symbols for what it actually is. We read just seven digits divided by a dash. The nines appear no less than four times, the eights appear twice, and the one – only once. The meaning we attach to these seven digits would not have been obvious to Wulfsige, nor to his contemporaries.

Digits they may be, but just like writing, we know they read from left to right, and further, that they read according to the place-value system. That is, also reading in the reverse direction from right to left, each digit represents a sum ten times larger than its immediate neighbour. The digits include no commas (that is, 1998 and not 1,998) and therefore we understand them to represent years, and – more than that – linked by a short horizontal dash they will denote a passage of time which will be from an earlier (lower) figure to a higher (later) figure. The simple addition of the digit 1 at the beginning of the second set makes it ten times larger than the first set, that is, of course, nineteen ninety eight as against nine ninety eight. We have thus conveyed on paper in just three systematically arranged 'coded' symbols – one thousand years – a millennium.

This abbreviated, easily understood coded shorthand, derives from the simple brilliance of the place-value system.[1] These are the thousands, hundreds, tens and units we all learned in primary school which enable us to write down the very smallest number to the very largest we can ever conceive of by the use of just ten symbols, 1, 2, 3, 4, 5, 6, 7, 8, 9, and 0, the zero. Ultimately of Indian origin, Hindic-Arabic place-value notation has been described as 'perhaps one of the most successful intellectual innovations ever devised by human beings' (Barrow 2001, 46).

This is now so successful – indeed so fundamental – to our world-view that it is almost impossible to reconstruct the 'mind-set' of a time when it did not exist. Through its use the most complex of mathematical thinking can be shown in writing, on paper – or screen. Such a system is not unlike that of the alphabet which, adopted many centuries earlier, established the use of twenty-six symbols (more or less) by which the most sophisticated of verbal ideas could be expressed in writing. Unlike verbal literacy, however, mathematical literacy (numeracy?) is relatively recent; its adoption by what we now call the western world post-dates the birth of Christianity by many centuries. It is a lot younger than the Church.

The year which to us is AD 998 was to Wulfsige and his clerk, rendered in Latin as *anno ab incarnationis dominice . dcccc nonagesimo octavo* (see Frontispiece and above). That is, 'in the year of the incarnation [birth] of our Lord' (we still use AD, *Anno Domini*, in the year of the Lord), and then follow five Roman numerals, **dcccc**, that is 500 + 100 + 100 + 100 + 100 (making nine hundred) and then, in words, **nonagesimo octavo**, or ninety eight, written in the ablative case, responding to ***anno ab***, 'the year from'. The system here is additive, there is no significance whatever in the position of the symbols which are in part abbreviated words; **d** for 500 was adopted early in the first century, a modification of another non-alphabetic symbol, and similarly with **c**, although here the coincidence with **centum**, 'hundred', was a useful one (Ifrah 1998, 188). The rest is spelled out in full. If we treated 998 in this way (9 + 9 + 8), the answer would be 26; 1998 would add up to 27, and 2005 to precisely seven.

Only a little thought will show that it is all but impossible to show working in Roman numerals, **I** (1), **V** (5), **X** (10), **L** (50), **C** (100), **D** (500) and **M** (1000). Everyday computation for Wulfsige (as it had been for generations) required the use of an abacus or other counting device. Such a task was, and continued to be, the profession of the skilled *computator* or *calculator* who did the calculation – as for us, based on tens – but who only *then* wrote down the result; the answer. Numbers, like the dates of years, were essentially static items; they were symbols. They were not tools which could be manipulated through the business of writing them down. The Romans ran a successful trading empire and were surveyors, builders and engineers second to none. And so it was *computation* – the use of the abacus or similar device – which became the corner-stone of the practical, everyday world inherited almost in entirety by the early medieval church and its builders. We now take both literacy and numeracy as the two fundamental communication skills of life but tend to forget that both are dependent on written systems. The manipulation of rational sequences of computational and mathematical ideas by way of written symbols was, to Wulfsige's world, simply not possible. The arithmetic *literacy* so commonplace to every primary school child today thus was not in approved use in the Christian tenth century.[2] The role of the zero had yet to be accepted.

The meaning of numbers and St Augustine

Numbers had for centuries before Wulfsige been more than a means of recording the results of computation. To those knowledgeable, numbers and number patterns gave access to a wider cosmos, to a rich philosophical and spiritual world which formed an important symbolical and allegorical element in literary and scriptural writing. For many centuries, *Millennium* had connoted apocalyptic prophecy – the End of Things (Cohn 1970). But we mislead ourselves today if we treat **M**[ille], **ten** times **ten** times **ten**, and **1,000** as precisely one and the same thing. Each has different properties and behaves in a different way. The first is a perfect number which betokens the Divine,[3] the second constitutes a tangible, three-dimensional form on the lines of a *Rubik's Cube*, and the third is licensed to perform in the place-value system. This is a conceptual separation we make with some difficulty.

St Augustine, late Roman scholar and Early Christian father writing at the turn of the early fifth century, was deeply concerned with 'squaring' (as we might say), the practical meaning of numbers with their spiritual significance. His *Civitas Die* [City of God] is regarded as one of the milestones in the history of western thought (see Reuter, 'Introduction', this volume). For God's real purpose in creating the world was the creation of the Heavenly City. As a highly trained legal man, Platonist and Rhetor, concerned with precision in thinking, Augustine was confronted with the revelatory or *apocalyptic* aspects of the new faith as expressed in the Bible, and how best to understand their implications in the unfolding of human history. His extensive writings remained among the most influential in the early medieval church (Knowles 1972).

Augustine pondered the significance of the Six plus One days of the Creation told in *Genesis* at the beginning of the Bible in relation to the thousand year period described in *Revelation* at its very end (Woods, 'The Revelation of St John', this volume). 'People ... have been particularly excited' he wrote,

> by the actual number of a thousand years ... taking it as appropriate that there should be a kind of Sabbath for the saints ... after the labours of six thousand years since man's creation ... 'one day is like a thousand years' – a kind of seventh day of rest for a thousand years. Now the thousand years, it seems to me, can be interpreted in two ways ... it may indicate that this event happens in the last thousand years ... the sixth millennium [anticipating the seventh millennium as the rule of the Saints after the appearance and final defeat of the Devil (or *Antichrist*)] ... [or] the thousand years [stands] for the whole period of the world's history signifying the entirety of time by a perfect number ... of course the number thousand is the cube of ten ... it seems that sometimes a hundred is used to stand for a totality ... how much more does one thousand! (Knowles 1972, 907–8)

Thousand stood as an 'incalculable number; a round number denoting a great multitude' (Boxall 2002, 9, 62).

Augustine reckoned the temporal scheme of the Scriptures to indeed be based on Six Ages – echoing the writings of Lactantius a century earlier (today we reckon things in three – Stone, Bronze and Iron Ages). But these Six Ages betokened something profoundly incomplete; the Seventh Age, was ultimately one of fulfilment.[4] Thus the whole history of the world spanned exactly seven thousand years, 'but we know that the six thousandth year is not yet completed, and when this number is completed the consummation must take place' (Jay Gould 1997, 75–6). Augustine knew he was living in the Sixth, the last old Age of the World (Brown 2000, 294) and the sack of Rome by the Goths in AD 410 served to strengthen his conviction. 'History [for Augustine] ... was ... an essentially divinatory pursuit as it was to remain for Christian theologians throughout medieval Europe (Campion 1994, 327).

So given an allegorical matching of God's days with experienced human millennia, when would the actual End begin? That is, the appearance of the Devil to inaugurate the thousand-year run-up to the Last Judgement and Rule of the Saints? Early Christianity sought a closure of the Ages and the turning of centuries was – each time – a time of significance.[5] And this was surely of no less significance to Wulfsige and his contemporaries at the turn of the tenth century – it was probably the greater. '*Et quoniam sicut ait apostolos nos sumus in quos fines seculorum devenerunt* (and as the Apostle said, we are those "upon whom the ends of the ages have come")' are words from Corinthians quoted in the charter of 998 (Keynes, 'King Æthelred's charter', this volume).

The passing of centuries

Pope Gregory the Great despatched Augustine (of Canterbury) to England in 597 – in time for 600. 'The end of the present age is already drawing near' wrote Gregory, 'the kingdom of the saints is approaching ... by our good actions may we be found ready for the Judge' (McGinn 1995, 66). Archbishop Theodore of Canterbury (668–90), Aldhelm's teacher and patron, who effected a major reorganisation of the church in England, is credited with the writing of a work the *Laterculus Malalianus* in which he expounds on the seven ages of the world. This text is the source for the statement that the Crucifixion took place in *anno mundi* 6000, thus making *anno mundi* fall not in AD 1000 but in AD 1033 (Stevenson 1995, 212–13). Aldhelm, first bishop of Sherborne, wrote a lengthy treatise on the meaning and significance of Seven (based on an earlier work by Isidore of Seville) 'perennial felicity of the blessed life ... shall be paid to each and every one according to ... his merits ... granted to the innocent ... only through a sevenfold increment of times, one thousand in number, after the throng of the impious has been separated' (Lapidge and Herren 1979, 35). We might pause to reflect on how he may have seen the dawn of the year 700.

Aldhelm did not become bishop of the new see based at Sherborne until 705/6 (*ibid*, 10).

Charlemagne was crowned Holy Roman Emperor in what is now Aachen on Christmas Day 800, a time scheme for the beginning of the End favoured by Eusebius four centuries earlier (McGinn 1995, 62). It was Charlemagne who first appointed *compotistae*, experts in ecclesiastical time-reckoning; calendar dates of Easter, of Saint's days of Feast and Fast.[6] And the chronicling of events by calendar year (not, for example, by regnal year) and which is now normal to us, is a characteristically Carolingian development. One which was to be taken up by Alfred in the compiling of the Anglo-Saxon Chronicle. Whilst Reuter ('Introduction', this volume) draws attention to the paucity of material on the reaction to the approach of the year ten hundred – 1000 – we surely note some of the increased activity of which he spoke in the career of Otto III who, in 998, set out his programme on a seal based on that of Charlemagne, surrounded by the words *renovatio imperii Romanorum*, 'his imperial role ... being to possess the summit of power in both temporal and spiritual matters ... establishing an unambiguously Rome-based concept of Christian emperorship' (see Barker, 'Picturing the beginning of the Age of Saints', Fig 14, this volume). What precisely this *renovatio* was about is not clear and met with mixed reactions at the time (Warner 2001, 12).[7] The preferred titles of the rulers of both Frankish and Anglo-Saxon worlds reflect the aspirations of their illustrious Ottonian contemporary further east (Canning 1996, 75–6, 78–81).

Otto III sent a crown to King Stephen of Hungary in 1000 (a replica was recently on display at Greenwich, the first of a thousand years of European crowns), and in the same year Otto pilgrimaged to Gniezo to the shrine of St Adalbert setting up the bishoprics of Cracow, Silesia and Pomerania. He then went on to open the tomb of Charlemagne in Aachen; 'as he had doubts regarding the location of the bones of Emperor Charles [Charlemagne] he secretly had the pavement over their supposed remains ripped up ... after taking a gold cross which hung around the emperor's neck ... he replaced everything with great veneration' (Warner 2001, 184–5).

With everything well-disposed north of the Alps, Otto 'betook himself off to the Roman Empire and, arriving at the Romulan citadel [Rome], was received with great honour by the pope' on 14 August 1000 (Warner 2001, 186). This was a time when the supernatural – the Christian supernatural – could, quite legitimately, be invoked in the furtherance of the personal agenda (*ibid*, 4, 185). There is a powerful spiritual element here serving to endow dynastic ambition with a justification that Scriptural interpretation could readily provide, creating a momentum which was to take Christian rule and its institutions deep into eastern Europe. It may be that our current ideas on the relative insignificance of the year ten hundred are at least in part a reflection of our own twentieth-century history. The Iron Curtain also severed scholarship (see Leong 1990). Otto's career is surely a striking complement to that *crescendo* of activity that finds its consummation in the subject of this volume; that spiritual fuel that drove the leaders of the Benedictine re-formation from Carolingia, to Franconia and thence north into Anglo-Saxon England.

Computation and 'Saracen magic'

There is another element to explore here which relates to *computation* and the signification of number. Among the first travellers who left a record of Prague was Ibrahim ibn Yacoub, an erudite Jew from Tortosa in Spain who wrote in Arabic. Probably sent on a diplomatic and trading mission to Otto I in the 960s, it was scholars at Cordova who preserved his extensive observational and scientific writings for later generations (Demetz 1997, 14). It was during the tenth century that Arab texts in mathematics and astronomy were translated into Latin for the first time (Bakar 1999, 141). The source of these texts was Spain. 'I am convinced that the schools of Lorraine in the last half of the tenth century were the seedplot in which the seeds of Arabic science first germinated in Latin Europe … to Germany, France, and especially to England' (Thompson in Bakar 1999, 141). The use of the zero came to the west certainly by 970, but remained something of a mystery and it acquired the reputation for being dangerous Saracen magic. Said to have been invented by one 'King Algor' (Abu Jafar Muhammed ibn Musa al-Khwarizmi) it became a matter of abacist versus algorist or *gerbertistas* after Gerbert of Aurillac who was consecrated pope on Easter Day, 999 (Swetz 1987, 27; Kaplan 1999, 98, 103; Warner 2001, 182).

   Gerbert (born 940), began as a monk in the French abbey of Aurillac, then studied in Muslim Spain obtaining the best scientific education of his day. Appointed bishop of Rheims, he was then appointed pope by Otto III taking the name of Sylvester II – a symbolic move indeed, for the first Sylvester had crowned Constantine first Christian emperor. Gerbert was one of the first Latin authors to use Arabic numerals (Colish 1997, 165). 'One of the greatest writers of the Age [Gerbert] was also one of the most aware of the period's historical context … an intellectual who [held] the reins of power … Gerbert plunged [historiography] into politics' (Leonardi 1999, 209). Not surprisingly, Gerbert was believed to have made a pact with the Devil so successful was his career. It was one of Gerbert's older friends Adso, abbot of Montier-en-Der (born 910) who 're-introduced the eschatalogical reading of the Apocalypse' (*ibid*, 210). In a work dedicated to Gerberga, sister of Otto I and wife of Louis IV of West Francia he gave a full account of the Antichrist. Circulating from about 950 it proved very popular, 'the critical edition uses 171 manuscripts … 9 different versions of the text survive' (McGinn 1995, 101). Through Augustine, Adso saw human history as the story of the playing out of the relations between God and the Devil, and when the latter was finally overcome history would end. 'He saw the one thousand of the Apocalypse to mean the historical millennium' (Leonardi 1999, 210). The last battle would take place in Jerusalem. Adso set sail for the east in 992 and died on the way. Gerberga, the dedicatee of his apocalyptic thesis, was great-aunt to Otto III who succeeded Otto II at the age of five.

Gerbert was clearly resented by Thietmar of Merseburg writing *c* 1014:

> [Gerbert was] illegally promoted to the rulership over the city of Rheims ... skilled in discerning the movements of the stars and surpassed his contemporaries in his knowledge of various arts ... driven from his diocese he sought out Emperor Otto ... resided with him at Magdeburg ... and there built an *oralogium*, positioning it correctly after he had observed through a tube the star that sailors use for guidance. (Warner 2001, 303)

Gerbert was, in short, highly skilled in the use of the Arab astrolabe 'the earliest "analogue" reckoning device in European history of science' (Borst 1993, 59) – and an instrument associated with pagan Saracen astrology and magic. He also used the *clepsidra* or water clock, not the sun dial (Borst 1993, 57–9). To Gerbert, correct time-keeping was indispensable to worship; things should be done at the right time. His vision of God has much in common with Boethius, perhaps his most influential model (Leonardi 1999, 210, note). Boethius (480–524), author of the *Consolation of Philosophy* was later credited with the invention of Arabic numerals, a woodcut of 1503 shows him pointing at the zero, smiling, whilst Pythagoras looks disconsolately at his abacus (Guedj 1997, 52–3; Ifrah 1998, 578–9; Kaplan 1999, 113).

Evidence suggests that while Gerbert was teaching at Rheims, he had begun to study the Boethian canon. He passed this legacy on to his pupils, which included Abbo of Fleury (born *c* 945), who later taught in France (Colish 1997, 167). It was Abbo who witnessed a Viking assault on Paris and then wrote it up, creating 'an epic of the historic present' (Wallace-Hadrill 1983, 354). It was also Abbo who reported that in his youth in Paris he had heard a preacher announcing the end of the world for the year one thousand, to be followed shortly by the Last Judgement. He related a rumour current in Lorraine (see above) that the world would end in the year in which the Feast of the Annunciation fell on a Good Friday. Such occurred in 992; Abbo's *Apologia* in fact dates from 998 (Focillon 1969, 54–5). Certainly as important, was the fact that Abbo, like Gerbert, was highly skilled in the use of the *clepsidra* – and calculating the passing of time by observing the heavens. He criticised Bede (died 735), whose tables were demonstrably wrong by twenty years.[8] The monastery at Fleury in the Loire Valley was marked for special consideration as housing the bones of St Benedict and surviving Viking raids in 855, 865 and again in 878. It went on to become 'a centre of intellectual distinction in the tenth century' (Wallace-Hadrill 1983, 358). Traube considered that Fleury possessed the 'completest collection of classical texts in ninth-century Franconia ... there was almost no intellectual field in which Fleury showed no interest' (Wallace-Hadrill 1983, 355–8).

Benedictine reform of Cluny and Fleury – and Sherborne

It was Abbot Odo of Cluny who effected the Benedictine reform of Fleury – having finally overcome the resistance of the monks who feared for the legal status of their monastery (Wollasch 1999, 176). Cluny grew to be head of a whole group of monasteries; the power of Odo's reforming initiatives (927–42) were also felt at Aurillac – as they were to be at Sherborne.[9] It was Rodulfus Glaber (born 980) who dedicated his *History* to St Odilo of Cluny (994–1049). As a chronicler, his writing is framed by an intense awareness of the possible significance of what he was living through. He records 'the many events which occurred with unusual frequency about the millennium of the Incarnation of our Lord ... when that year approached ... almost the whole world suffered the loss of great men', and shortly after that year 'the whole world was ... clothed in a white mantle of new churches ... a little later ... the relics of many saints were revealed' (France 1989, 94, 115). White was the colour associated with Heaven, with Victory and with God/the Son of Man (Boxall 2002, 60). '*Et quoniam sicut ait apostolos nos sumus in quos fines seculorum devenerunt* (and as the Apostle said, we are those "upon whom the ends of the ages have come")' are words from Corinthians included in the text of the legal document which set in motion the refounding – and rebuilding – of the church at Sherborne. As has already been noted. We have an interconnectedness of things here, a single inspirational theme which mobilised able and scholarly men who carried kings with them. The imperial style of Edgar's coronation in Bath in 973 hints of an awareness of Otto II's coronation as Holy Roman Emperor in 962 (Lawson 1982, 170); Carolingian precedent conferred both spiritual *kudos* and political authority.

Oswald, bishop of York had received much of his training at Fleury, and it was Abbo who was sent to teach at the Abbey of Ramsey in the Fens for two years where he produced a major *Vita*, the *Life* of St Edmund King and Martyr, the *Passio sancti Edmundi Regis et Martyris*, between 985 and 987. Edmund died a horrible death at the hand of the Vikings in the winter of 869–70. Abbo's version of events, although not in that of Asser or the Anglo-Saxon Chronicle, may in fact be a more reliable source (Ridyard 1988, 67) – he did, after all, know something of Viking practices. Abbo was murdered at St Benoit-sur-Loire [Fleury] in 1004 – recorded by Glaber; Gerbert of Aurillac, Pope Sylvester II, died of malaria south of Rome in the summer of 1003 and Wulfsige of Sherborne died in Beaminster, Dorset, in 1002, earlier in the same year that witnessed the death of Otto III. And so it came to pass that 'almost the whole world suffered the loss of great men' and shortly after that year 'the whole world was ... clothed in a white mantle of new churches ... a little later ... the relics of many saints were revealed'. The new church at Sherborne was by then under construction and suitably interred there, in due course, were the relics of Saints Wulfsige and Juthwara.

1000: committing one thousand, mille, to writing

Thietmar of Merseburg (975–1018) in his *Chronicon* was clearly aware of the millennium that had elapsed since the birth of Christ and made reference to it with particular reference to the career of Henry II, described by Glaber as 'a most Christian king'. But the words the former chooses are interesting – the way he expresses numbers. 'After the unstained maiden had given birth ... *in the numerical series of the millennium in the fourth place according to the series of ordinal numbers* [1004], the year in which King Henry wished to secure his salvation', and again, 'since that Incarnation of the Lord *a full millennium and thirteen years had passed* [1013]' in which Henry was received in Rome by the pope (Warner 2001, 237, 307 – author's italics). He succeeded Otto III in 1002 and died in 1024.

We note the way – even in translation – Thietmar needs somehow to explain the reckoning of the years given the tenor of the events he describes; the style in which he writes it down: '*in the fourth place according to the series of ordinal numbers*'. This is not the writing of a Latin date; he is using an alternative system. Much has been written on the significance of the growth of literacy in the Frankish and Carolingian world of the eighth and ninth centuries – the huge increase in the production and distribution of books – both in terms of learning and as gift exchange – explored most notably by McKitterick (1989, 1990). Rather less explored, it seems, is the matter of 'numerical literacy' – the arrival and adoption of a system by which numbers could be manipulated on paper (see above) and how numbers thus joined the world of the written word. Truth was The Word comprising a finite number of what we might now call 'set' texts and commentaries, edited and approved and published (to which more approved commentaries could be added) from which the unacceptable and/or non-Christian were excluded and thus, soon enough, lost. A carefully selected canon of works of inspirational writing, a *corpus* of received wisdom was in circulation, expressed in the Latin alphabet, and available to those trained to be able to read it.

So what about numbers? During the same period these were items which, having hitherto belonged either to Market place or to Metaphor, were finding a literate life of their own. With the use of the zero, numbers could behave through writing like writing itself – an alternative form of language. And this was an integral part of a school of learning promoted from the south, by those Moslem scholars who had already come into conflict with the Christian world and who (with armed support) occupied Spain and southern Italy. Arab attacks on Italy started again in earnest in the 990s (Kennedy 1999, 644); Barcelona had fallen the previous decade. In parallel, as it were, with the thought-world of the *computator* and his abacus on the Christian side of the Mediterranean was another coming from the other side, the pagan *computator* with a numerical 'alphabet' validated through the use of the zero – a very effective system indeed of committing calculation processes to writing. This was a technique which could only serve to increase philosophical and spiritual *angst* in the Latin and

Christianised world; that is, through the introduction – if not invasion – of a communications system in mathematical literacy which was non-Latin, and non-Christian and therefore deeply suspect, and which was to remain so for a considerable period of time.[10]

A thousand years ago tenth-century Christian thinkers were thus faced by an intellectual dilemma perhaps as great as that faced by Augustine. Here was a philosophical conundrum for which there was – almost by definition – no answer. What *was* the scriptural significance of *thousand* – what *did* it betoken in terms of history and the future? 'For a thousand years in thy sight are but as yesterday when it is past, and as a watch in the night'[11] cannot be conveyed on an abacus. Neither can the Seven days of the Creation. But these things are written in Words in the Scriptures and must therefore demand very careful thought. 'Thousand' may be represented by the perfect form of the ten-sided cube. It may betoken human perfection; the Ultimate. It may even signify the ten hundredth year since the Incarnation. But it is very certainly not the four digits comprising 1,000 which read in the direction of the Devil; a One displaced to the Left no less than three times and – furthermore – by a sign representing Nothing.[12] And that was surely an affront – if not deeply sinister – to informed Christian Latin thinking.

And there was more. The adoption of referencing events by chronological year – the 'chronicle' – had heightened awareness of the 'open-endedness' of time when Christians knew it was closed. And further to that, irrespective of the numbering system used, things simply did not add up. People expert in *computus* had made mistakes about years and dates. Abbo, following Gerbert, had had to make a division between nature, *ordo natura*, and tradition, *historiae fides*. The authority of God was no longer directly manifest in time and numbers as it had been for Isidore of Seville (died 636). It had come to lie somewhere else; somewhere between observed natural order on the one hand and received Christian order on the other. They had to be reconciled. As the skills of astrolabe computation could now eloquently demonstrate, in the closing years of the tenth century, the time of God and his Saints simply did not tally with the time of human experience. 'Did, in fact, the Church and the World live in the same Time?' (Borst 1993, 64). Was there in fact 'a parallel universe'? Christ could not be subject to the uncertainties of human history which he would, at the appropriate time, bring to an End.[13]

With the pagan (semi-literate) Viking threat from the north and the pagan (counter-literate) Arab threat from the south, were these things really not the harbingers of the beginning of the End – just as predicted? Were these not the signs? Could there be any better century for perplexed Christian rulers to get things into good order? Could there be any time which offered such entitlement for action – for the Benedictine-led reform of Christ's church and the making of a new beginning – to await consummation of the Christian promise?

The wonderful extra-natural world of the late tenth/early eleventh century is foreign country to those of us who inhabit the materialistic, secular world of the turn of the twentieth/twenty-first century. Numbers no longer promise Revelation. Those symbols of divine order and purpose have been reinterpreted through the mundane principles of place-value mathematics. Time itself may be explained by the laws of physics, whilst its passing is measure only of our own mortality. Those of us who have now lived through the turn of the second millennium may perhaps pause a moment to ponder the spiritual resolution that watched so carefully – and so advisedly – over the end of the first.

Notes

1   A row of figures can, of course, present another 'code' and have another significance. No one would attempt to read (say) 0199 819980 in terms of the place-value system.

2   Numbers included in a written text can still give problems and there remain standard conventions for the appropriate use of figures or words. Rees, *Rules of Printed English* (1970) includes four pages of instructions as to correct usage. The Bettenson translation of *Augustine City of God* (Knowles 1972, 908) uses both thousand and 1,000 on the same page; the former as an adjective and the latter as a noun.

3   'Thousand is a perfect number and no number extends beyond it. With that number is betokened the perfection of those men who nourish their souls with God's precepts' (Thorpe 1844–6, I, 189). See Campion ('Thousand is a perfect number', this volume). Ælfric also observed that 'immoderate curiosity is a sin'.

4   The number Six has recently been cited by the world of science. There is Richard Leakey's *The Sixth Extinction, Biodiversity and its Survival* (1996), Richard Fenyman's *Six Not-So-Easy Pieces* (1997) and Martin Rees' *Just Six Numbers, the Deep Forces that Shape the Universe* (1999).

      To Augustine the Six Ages were (1) from Adam to the Flood, (2) from the Flood to Abraham, (3) from Abraham to David, (4) from David to the Exile in Egypt, (5) from the Exile to Christ, (6) from Christ to his Second Coming, culminating in the seventh and final age, the Eternal Sabbath and Rule of Saints. Other 'histories' were fitted into this framework.

5   Dionysius Exiguus (literally Denis the Short) was commissioned by Pope John I (AD 523–6) to prepare a Christian chronology. Fixing the year of Christ's birth as Year 1 (he was in fact about four years out) he calculated on from there. And everything since has been built on this. Not recognising the zero of course, subsequent generations have never really resolved the vexed question as to whether centuries change on the 00 or on the 01.

6   Work published at the time included an update of Bede's tables, tables of the lunar and Easter cycles, and a chronicle of world-years to the present [AD 809]; that is, the 4,761 years since the Creation (Borst 1993, 44). That would make 239 years to the year 5000, thus the year 1048; the year 6000 will begin (on this reckoning) in 2048.

7   In 996, the year of his coronation, Gerbert wrote elegantly to Otto III: '*Extremus numerorum abbaci vestrum definiat*' – the highest number that could be represented on an abacus – 'let it/may it define you[rs]'; that is, 27 counters, and each greater by the power of ten than the one before. Borst (1993, 58) suggests this was an

allusion to the length of the emperor's life. Playing with numbers we note that the year 999 (9 + 9 + 9) adds up to 27. Could this not rather be a reference by Gerbert to the 'defining' year of Otto's career? And with *definiat* in the subjunctive, Gerbert is expressing a wish.

8   Abbo carried out the most important computation, that of the 'Easter cycle'. The first ended in 533, the second would end in 1065 (Borst 1993, 54). The first year of the Third Cycle thus fell in 1066.

9   The administrative and tenurial relationship of the Benedictine Abbey of Cluny with its dependent community at Lournand and the area around it is the subject of Bois (1992) which offers a number of insights relating to the (re)structuring of the Sherborne estate of 998 (see Barker, 'Sherborne in AD 998', this volume).

10   The advantages of the system eventually became compelling, but not for several centuries. In 1299 an ordinance was passed in Florence forbidding its use – for fear of fraud. The zero could easily be turned into a 6 or a 9, or worse still, a single digit slipped in could increase a sum by the power of ten, sums in account books had to be written in words. In Venice too, 'old figures' (ie Roman numerals) were alone to be used because they could not be falsified. As late as 1494 the mayor of Frankfurt instructed his master calculators to refrain from using digits. Even today we still write both words and figures on High Street bank cheques (Barrow 2001, 48).

11   Psalm 90:4.

12   To Christians, following Jewish tradition, the state of Nothing represented a turning away from God, an ultimate state of sin. God had created the world out of Nothing. Nothing represented the greatest evil; to Augustine it was equated with the Devil (Barrow 2001, 42, 72–4).

13   Something of this is surely echoed in the writing of Francis Fukuyama, a political scientist from Cornell University. *The End of History and the Last Man* (1992) is the development of a thesis that sees history as a process. With the end of the Cold War and the universal adoption of western-style liberal democracy, mankind has reached some kind of collective Fulfilment.

Bibliography

Bakar, O, 1999, *The History and Philosophy of Islamic Science*. Cambridge. Islamic Texts Society.

Barrow, J D, 2001, *The Book of Nothing*. Vintage UK.

Bois, G, 1992, *The Transformation of the Year 1000. The Village of Lournand from Antiquity to Feudalism*, J Birrell (trans). Manchester.

Borst, A, 1993, *The Ordering of Time, from the Ancient Computus to the Modern Computer*. Polity Press with Blackwell.

Boxall, I, 2002, *Revelation: Vision and Insight, an Introduction to the Apocalypse*. SPCK.

Brown, P, 2000, *Augustine of Hippo, a Biography* (Revised Edition). Faber.

Campion, N, 1994, *The Great Year, Astrology, Millenarianism and History in the Western Tradition*. Penguin Arkana.

Canning, J, 1996, *A History of Medieval Political Thought*. Routledge.

Cohn, N, 1970, *The Pursuit of the Millennium* (3rd Edition). Oxford.

Colish, M L, 1997, *Medieval Foundations of the Western Intellectual Tradition, 400–1400*. Yale University Press.

Demetz, P, 1997, *Prague in Black and Gold, the History of a City*. Allen Lane, Penguin.

Focillon, H, 1969, *The Year 1000*. London. Harper Torchbooks.

France, J (ed and trans), 1989, *Rodulfi Glabri, Historiarum Libri Quinque, Rodulfus Glaber*. The Books of the Histories. Oxford. Clarendon Press.

Guedj, D, 1997, *Numbers, The Universal Language*. Thames and Hudson.

Ifrah, G, 1998, *The Universal History of Numbers*. London. Harvill Press.

Jay Gould, S, 1997, *Questioning the Millennium*. Jonathan Cape.

Kaplan, R, 1999, *The Nothing That Is; a Natural History of Zero*. Penguin.

Kennedy, 1999, Sicily and al-Andalus under Muslim Rul'. In T Reuter (ed), *The New Cambridge Medieval History, Volume 3*. Cambridge, 646–69.

Knowles, D (ed), 1972, *Augustine, Concerning the City of God against the Pagans*, H Bettenson (trans). Penguin.

Lapidge, M, and Herren, M, 1979, *Aldhelm, The Prose Works*. Brewer, Roman and Littlefield.

Lawson, M K, 1982, Late Anglo-Saxon England and the Continent. In J Campbell (ed), *The Anglo-Saxons*. Phaidon Press, 170–1.

Leonardi, C, 1999, Intellectual Life. In T Reuter (ed), *The New Cambridge Medieval History, Volume 3*. Cambridge, 186–211.

Leong, A (ed), 1990, *The Millennium, Christianity and Russia 988–1988*. Crestwood, NY. St Vladimir's Seminary Press.

McGinn, B, 1995, The End of the World and the Beginning of Christendom. In M Bull (ed), *Apocalypse Theory and the Ends of the World*. Oxford. Blackwell, 58–89.

McKitterick, R, 1989, *The Carolingians and the Written Word*. Cambridge.

McKitterick, R (ed), 1990, *The Uses of Literacy in Early Medieval Europe*. Cambridge.

Ridyard, S, 1988, *The Royal Saints of Anglo-Saxon England, a Study of West Saxon and East East Anglian Cults*. Cambridge.

Stevenson, J B, 1995, Theodore and the *Laterculus Malalianus*. In M Lapidge (ed), *Archbishop Theodore, Commemorative Studies on his Life and Influence*. Cambridge Studies in Anglo-Saxon England, 11. Cambridge.

Swetz, F J, 1987, *Capitalism and Arithmetic, the New Math of the 15th Century*. La Salle, Illinois. Open Court.

Thorpe, B (ed), 1844–6. *Ælfric's Homilies of the Anglo-Saxon Church* (Two volumes). London. The Ælfric Society.

Wallace-Hadrill, J M, 1983, *The Frankish Church*. Oxford History of the Christian Church. Oxford. Clarendon Press.

Warner, D A (trans), 2001, *Ottonian Germany, the* Chronicon *of Thietmar of Merseberg*. Manchester.

Wollasch, J, 1999, Monasticism, the First Wave of Reform. In T Reuter (ed), *The New Cambridge Medieval History, Volume 3*. Cambridge, 186–211.

8. Wulfsige, monk of Glastonbury, abbot of Westminster (*c* 990–3), and bishop of Sherborne (*c* 993–1002)

Simon Keynes

This volume commemorates the passage of a thousand years from the occasion, in 998, when King Æthelred the Unready authorised Wulfsige, bishop of Sherborne, to effect a significant change in the organisation of his church. The church of Sherborne had been served up to that point by a bishop with a community of secular clergy; but it was served thereafter by a bishop with a community of monks, living according to the Rule of Benedict. The question arises as to whether this was a truly significant event in a long and complex story extending from the earliest days of Christianity in the kingdom of the West Saxons, in the second half of the seventh century,[1] to the dissolution of Sherborne Abbey in 1539. After all, Wulfsige himself has not made much of an impression on the historical consciousness of the English nation. He qualified *ex officio* for a place in the *Oxford Dictionary of Saints*.[2] Yet he was not included in the old *Dictionary of National Biography*, or even in the *DNB*'s supplementary volume of *Missing Persons* (published in 1993); so one can but hope that he will be discovered again, at Oxford, in good time for inclusion in the *New DNB*. One has also to admit that 998 is not exactly a date that rings across the centuries, like 1066, and that charters of King Æthelred the Unready are not normally the stuff of millenary celebrations. It is the case, however, that Wulfsige is one of the relatively small number of bishops in Anglo-Saxon England who have left rather more than the barest trace of their existence; and as we piece together the fragments of evidence, and try to bring them into sharper focus, a picture emerges of a bishop who can be seen to have played a significant and certainly a most honourable part in the affairs of his day.

The early bishops of Sherborne
The twelfth-century historian, William of Malmesbury, described Sherborne

rather contemptuously as a 'small place, distinguished neither for the number of its inhabitants nor for the beauty of its location, so that it is remarkable and almost shameful that it lasted as an episcopal see for such a long time'.[3] William had reasons of his own for being scornful of Sherborne and at least some of its bishops, but there is no reason why we should share his prejudices. According to the venerable Bede, the West Saxons were converted to Christianity during the reign of King Cynegisl (611–42), 'through the preaching of Bishop Birinus'.[4] An episcopal see for the West Saxons was established initially at Dorchester (on Thames), and was then re-established at Winchester. In these matters as in other respects the pattern was set, however, during the reign of King Ine (688–726). Following the death of Hædde, bishop of Winchester, in 705, the episcopal see for the West Saxons was divided in two: Daniel became the new bishop of Winchester, and Aldhelm, formerly abbot of Malmesbury, became the first bishop of Sherborne.[5]

Aldhelm, bishop of Sherborne (705–9), is renowned as a distinguished scholar with a large vocabulary and a fine turn of phrase; his treatise on virginity, in verse and prose, written for the nuns of Barking Abbey, ranks with Bede's *Ecclesiastical History* as one of the major works of Anglo-Latin literature to survive from the early part of the Anglo-Saxon period, and is studied as intensively in the twentieth century as ever it was in the seventh, or in the tenth.[6] Yet Aldhelm was only the first in the procession of interesting figures who have lent their distinction to the history of the church of Sherborne.[7] **Ealhstan**, bishop of Sherborne from *c* 824 to 867,[8] would appear to have played a significant role in the emergence of the kingdom of the West Saxons from the shadow of Mercian supremacy, and its transformation under King Æthelwulf (839–58) into a kingdom which extended across the whole of England, south of the Thames, from Cornwall to Kent. Æthelwulf seems to have had particular plans for the division of his extended kingdom after his death; and Bishop Ealhstan is alleged to have been involved in a plot hatched while the king was absent in Rome, in 855–6, aimed at preventing his resumption of power on his return.[9] Æthelwulf came back, albeit under reduced circumstances, but only lasted another two years, to 858; whereupon he was succeeded by his son Æthelbald in the west and by his son Æthelberht in the east. The fact that Bishop Ealhstan presided over the burials of King Æthelbald at Sherborne in 860, and of King Æthelberht at Sherborne in 865,[10] is arguably an indication that he had approved of Æthelbald's actions after Æthelwulf's death in 858, and that he had endorsed the unification of the eastern and western parts of the extended kingdom, under Æthelberht, in 860.[11] Ealhstan's own death is reported in the Anglo-Saxon Chronicle for 867: 'and he had held the bishopric of Sherborne for 50 years, and his body is buried in the cemetery there.'[12]

There is reason to believe that Ealhstan's successor, **Heahmund**, had served as a priest in the royal household in the early 860s,[13] in which case his appointment as bishop of Sherborne in 867, during the reign of King Æthelred

(865–71), represents an early example of what would become a standard path of promotion. Heahmund was among those killed at *Meretun* in 871, in battle against the Danes, and was buried at Keynsham in Somerset. **Æthelheah**, bishop of Sherborne in the 870s, is effectively a nonentity; but, for all we know, he might well have played a significant role in maintaining support for Alfred the Great during his darkest hours in 878, and might then have officiated in the baptism of the Danish leader, Guthrum, at Aller and Wedmore. **Wulfsige I**, bishop of Sherborne in the 880s, is known to have moved in King Alfred's literary circles. Like his episcopal colleagues, he received a copy of Alfred's translation of Pope Gregory the Great's *Pastoral Care*,[14] and he wrote a preface to accompany a copy of Bishop Wærferth's translation of Gregory's *Dialogues*.[15]

Asser was a priest from St David's, in Wales, who had entered Alfred's service in the mid-880s, and wrote a *Life* of the king in 893, generally accepted as one of the most important historical and literary works of the period; he became bishop of Sherborne during the course of the 890s, and is said to have died in 909.[16]

The opportunity was taken at about the time of Asser's death to effect a major reorganisation of the West Saxon dioceses, reducing their size and increasing their number by bringing them more into line with the ancient shires of Wessex: where previously there were two sees, at Winchester and Sherborne, now there would be five, at Winchester (Hampshire) and Ramsbury (Wiltshire and Berkshire), and at Sherborne (Dorset), Crediton (Devon), and Wells (Somerset). The tenth-century bishops of Sherborne were thus not quite as influential in Wessex as their predecessors had been in the eighth and ninth centuries; and the political changes in the tenth century which gave the kingdom a new identity, and different centres of activity, contributed further to a process which took Sherborne out of the busy mainstream and into a quieter backwater. So, while it is possible to reconstruct the succession of bishops of Sherborne in the tenth century, it proves to be the case that the bishops themselves are scarcely more than names.

It is only when we reach **Wulfsige III**, in the last decade of the tenth century, that the evidence begins to flow. The basic information is supplied by charters, some interesting letters, and a manuscript, now in Paris, which has the distinction of being Wulfsige's own pontifical, all of which are discussed further below. We also have a *Life* of St Wulfsige written in the late eleventh century (*c* 1078) by Goscelin, a monk from the monastery of Saint-Bertin, in Flanders, who was at Sherborne under Bishop Herman, and who pursued his career as a wandering hagiographer for some time thereafter.[17] Further information on Wulfsige is supplied by William of Malmesbury.[18] And of course Wulfsige continued to make an impression on later Sherborne tradition.[19] In a period for which evidence of any kind is scarce, a superfluity of evidence is all too easily regarded as an accident of survival; but it is sometimes the case that such superfluity is better regarded as a product of particular distinction.

Wulfsige, abbot of Westminster

It is generally assumed that Wulfsige was constituted the first abbot of
Westminster from its refoundation in the early years of the reign of King Edgar,
and that he continued to hold this office for some time after his appointment as
bishop of Sherborne, *c* 993, during the reign of King Æthelred.[20] It is important
to note, however, that the 'traditional' view of Wulfsige's career took some
while to assume any consistent form. We have it on Goscelin's authority that
Wulfsige was born in London, and that he was entrusted by his parents into the
care of the church at Westminster, where he soon displayed his great promise.[21]
There is reason to believe, on the other hand, that Wulfsige had been trained at
Glastonbury, under Abbot Dunstan, in the early 950s.[22] Goscelin states further
that Wulfsige became a monk at Westminster under Archbishop Dunstan (959–
88); that King Edgar appointed him abbot of the community (presumably in the
960s); that he continued to hold office as abbot of Westminster after King
Æthelred appointed him bishop of Sherborne; and that he was bishop for '25'
years.[23] Sulcard of Westminster, writing in the late eleventh century, focused his
attention on Dunstan's role in the foundation of the abbey, and appeared to
know nothing of Wulfsige.[24] In his account of Sherborne, William of
Malmesbury presumed that it was Dunstan, as bishop of London (957–9), who
had made Wulfsige abbot of Westminster, placing him in charge of a community
of twelve monks, and that Wulfsige later became bishop of Sherborne,[25] yet in
his main account of Westminster, Wulfsige is not mentioned.[26] According to a
later form of the 'Westminster' tradition, represented by John Flete's 'History'
(written in the mid-fourteenth century), Wulfsige became a monk at Westminster
under Dunstan, who was at that time bishop of Worcester and London; he was
appointed Dunstan's deputy at Westminster, with King Edgar's approval, in
958; he was made abbot of Westminster, by King Æthelred, in 980; and a few
years later he was made bishop of Sherborne.[27]

   The early history of Westminster Abbey, in the second half of the tenth
century, is shrouded in the fog generated by those who formed the abbey's view
of itself in the late eleventh and early twelfth centuries,[28] and the respective roles
played by King Edgar, Archbishop Dunstan and Abbot Wulfsige remain
somewhat unclear.[29] The whole story has yet to be taken apart and put back
together from first principles; but special interest must be attached to three
documents, extant in the form of single sheets of parchment written in the late
tenth century, which in combination represent what might be dignified as the
earliest form of a local 'Westminster' tradition. The first document is a charter,
dated 951, by which King Edgar granted land at Westminster to the church of
Westminster, so that Archbishop Dunstan could re-establish monastic life
there.[30] The date is obviously impossible, and since it was probably determined
by the particular charter which seems to have been used as a model,[31] there is
little point in trying to emend it to something historically more acceptable. The
charter itself is good evidence, none the less, of Dunstan's direct involvement in

the refoundation of the abbey. The second document is a composite record, concerning an estate near Hendon (Middlesex).[32] Archbishop Dunstan bought the estate from the king, after the death of its former owner (Wulfmær), and King Edgar granted it to the abbey in 972; there were complications in the disturbed times after Edgar's death, but in the event Archbishop Dunstan was able to purchase more land in the same place from King Edward, in 978.

The third document is ostensibly a charter of King Æthelred, dated 986, by which he granted land at Hampstead (Middlesex) to Westminster Abbey; again, it is clear that Archbishop Dunstan was the interested party.[33] The document was not drawn up in the manner of a normal royal diploma; but there seems no reason to doubt that it is a genuine record, produced at Westminster, of a transaction which took place in the given year. All three of these documents were produced at Westminster in the late tenth century,[34] and all three display traces of a very distinctive type of formulation which is associated principally with Dunstan's Glastonbury but which might well have spread from there to Dunstan's Westminster,[35] in which connection we should bear in mind that Wulfsige was apparently among those trained at Glastonbury, under Abbot Dunstan, in the early 950s.[36] It is striking, however, that the three earliest documents which deal explicitly with the first stages in the endowment of Westminster Abbey focus on Archbishop Dunstan as the moving force, and do not mention Wulfsige; and if we leave aside two patently spurious charters from Crowland, dated 966,[37] it is the case that Wulfsige does not attest any surviving charters as abbot in the 960s, 970s, or 980s.[38] In fact, the first appearance of Wulfsige as abbot is in a list of those present at a 'great synod' at London convened under the auspices of Archbishop Æthelgar in 989–90;[39] he occurs thereafter in 990, and again in 993.[40]

There is one other charter which bears rather more helpfully on the position of Wulfsige at Westminster. It is the so-called 'Telligraphus' of King Æthelred, concerning the privileges and estates of Westminster Abbey, dated 998.[41] The 'Telligraphus' is closely related to Æthelred's charter of the same year for Wulfsige and the church of Sherborne, to the extent that they have to be considered in relation to each other; but the Westminster charter is generally dismissed as spurious, and the connection between them explained by assuming that a copy of the Sherborne charter was taken to Westminster and was used, at some later date, as a model for yet another of the Westminster forgeries.[42] The 'Telligraphus' is certainly not, as it stands, a royal diploma of normal type; but it is conceivable that it was produced at Westminster at the end of the tenth or in the early eleventh century, to take its place alongside other documents recording essential information on the abbey's endowment (noting which estates the abbey already owned, and in what other estates it had a reversionary interest). The grants represented by the three charters mentioned above were grouped together at the head of the document, suggesting that, as a group, they represented what was seen to be the basic story.[43] More to the immediate point, the draftsman of the 'Telligraphus' states what may have been the simple truth about Wulfsige: that Dunstan had loved him as if he were his son, and had entrusted the abbey to him *ad regendum regulariter* ('for ruling in accordance with the Rule'); that King Æthelred had subsequently made him abbot there (apparently after Dunstan's death); and that a few years later King Æthelred had appointed him bishop of Sherborne, on the understanding that Sherborne would be ruled *secundum suum regimen* ('according to his own form of discipline'), and that after his days it would be as 'free' as other monasteries. It is said of one estate (Cowley, in Middlesex) that after the days of a certain Ælfric it would revert to the control of Bishop Wulfsige, presumably in accordance with an earlier arrangement, and perhaps supporting Goscelin's notion that, as bishop, Wulfsige retained an interest in Westminster; since the estate belonged to Westminster in 1066, it would appear that in the event Wulfsige did the honourable thing. A point in favour of a relatively early date for the 'Telligraphus' is the contrast between it and two gloriously spurious charters, known to have been fabricated by a single hand in the mid-twelfth century: one, in the name of Bishop Dunstan, dated 959, proclaims the refoundation and endowment of Westminster, and mentions Wulfsige as the monk to whom Dunstan had entrusted the care of his abbey;[44] the other, in the name of King Edgar, dated 969, rehearses the legend from the king's point of view, and does not mention Wulfsige at all.[45]

So much for the evidence, such as it is; but at least it leaves plenty of room for manoeuvre (and speculation). It would appear that Dunstan himself was directly responsible for the foundation of Westminster Abbey, and that he retained control of its affairs for the duration of his lifetime (setting an example that a number of his episcopal colleagues are known to have followed).[46] He would doubtless have brought in some monks who had been trained under his regime at Glastonbury, in the early 950s, and seems to have entrusted responsibility for the ordinary administration of the abbey to one of their number, Wulfsige, from some point in the early or mid-960s onwards. Wulfsige may not, however, have held office as abbot during Dunstan's lifetime, and it seems likely that he only attained that office after Dunstan's death on 19 May 988. It is interesting that the monks of Westminster were by that time producing charters on behalf of themselves (perhaps under Wulfsige's direction), and that the charters in question bear traces of the distinctive formulation which seems to have originated at Glastonbury in the 940s, and which was employed there in the early 950s; for we can sense in this way that Westminster remained conscious of its origins and associations. It is also interesting that relations between Dunstan and Wulfsige would appear to have been especially close, for this establishes the context in which (as we shall see) one of Dunstan's service-books was passed on to Wulfsige.

More generally, we should bear in mind that Wulfsige would have been well placed, in the 960s and 970s, to observe the monastic reformers in action. After a period in the 950s when progress was impeded by political complications, the reform movement gathered momentum as well as pace, and began to penetrate more deeply during the 960s into the fabric of English society. At Winchester, in 964, King Edgar and Bishop Æthelwold collaborated in what seems to have been a carefully staged display of royal and monastic power: the supposedly disreputable secular clergy were forcibly ejected from the Old and New Minsters, and replaced with monks; whereupon Bishop Æthelwold became the head of the monastic community in the Old Minster, and Æthelgar was appointed abbot of the New Minster. Not all the secular clergy would have been as wicked as the reformers were concerned to make out, and not all the monks would have been so determined to have it exclusively their own way; but we may suppose that Wulfsige was among those who would have derived much satisfaction from the dramatic turn of events. He would have beamed with pleasure as the reformed monasteries (including his own) accumulated lands and privileges, and steadily increased their influence, stature, and power; and he would have shared in the excitement as religious houses vied with each other to get the newest buildings, the best relics, and the most impressive array of church plate, vestments and books. Many factors combined to create a need for new buildings, and the increased resources of a church would provide new opportunities to satisfy those needs. Relics were treasured as part of the cults which lent their distinctive identity to a church, and drew in the pilgrims; and if there were not any in the bottom drawers, they could be brought in from outside. The increased demand for the equipment of the monastic life would revitalise craftsmanship and scholarship, with a multiplier effect operating down all the lines of production. Services for the dedication of a new church, or for the translation of a saint's relics, would raise the profile of a church in the public eye, and generate yet more support. The monks, in short, were on a roll; and some among their number would be looking to spread their influence more widely and deeply within the church.

Wulfsige, bishop of Sherborne

In 993 (or 994) King Æthelred the Unready appointed Wulfsige bishop of Sherborne. After many years in Dunstan's shadow, and after five years (perhaps) as abbot of Westminster, Wulfsige might have regarded the appointment as a golden opportunity to make his own mark, by developing what he had seen and done at Westminster in a different setting. Yet in order to understand Wulfsige's activities at Sherborne, it is necessary to bear in mind that his career did not unfold only against the background of the extension of monastic reform. These were troublous times in England, and the English were in disarray. After many years of peace, Viking raiders had resumed their activities in the 980s; but a more substantial force had arrived in 991, and seemed reluctant to leave the kingdom. The intensification of Viking activity in the early 990s seems to have concentrated the collective mind. Vikings had long been regarded as instruments of divine punishment for the sins of the English people, and their activities made the king and his councillors more acutely aware than ever of the need to do what was pleasing in the sight of God.[47] It is also clear that churchmen, and pious laymen, might have regarded the Viking invasions as one of the signs of the 'last days', leading up to the Day of Judgement (with or without any presumption that it would happen in or about the year 1000), putting even more of a premium on the need to set their respective houses in order.[48] Nor is it likely to be a coincidence that these were momentous times in the internal politics of King Æthelred's reign: the king felt that he had wandered off the correct path, after the death of Bishop Æthelwold in 984, and seems in the early 990s (by 993) to have resolved to mend the errors of his ways.[49]

For all that is said or imagined about King Æthelred's wicked councillors, they were now, and would continue to be for some years, men whom we might judge to be of the highest calibre. On the episcopal bench, pride of place would seem to have belonged to those who had risen to prominence in the context of the monastic reform movement. For example: **Æthelgar**, monk of Abingdon, abbot of the New Minster (964–88), bishop of Selsey (980–8), and archbishop of Canterbury (988–90); **Sigeric**, monk of Glastonbury, abbot of St Augustine's, Canterbury (980–90), bishop of Ramsbury (985–90), and archbishop of Canterbury (990–4);[50] **Ælfric**, monk of ?Abingdon and abbot of St Albans (*c* 970–*c* 995), who succeeded Sigeric as bishop of Ramsbury in the early 990s and who retained that see when he succeeded Sigeric as archbishop of Canterbury (995–1005); and **Ælfheah**, monk of Deerhurst or Glastonbury, abbot of Bath (?963–84), bishop of Winchester (984–1006), and archbishop of Canterbury (1006–1012).[51] Among the abbots, those who seem to have been most prominent in the deliberations of the king and his councillors were again from the front line of monastic reform. For example: **Ælfweard**, abbot of Glastonbury (*c* 975–1009); **Ælfsige**, abbot of the New Minster, Winchester (988–1007); and **Wulfgar**, abbot of Abingdon (990–1016).[52] The leading ealdorman of the day was **Æthelweard** of the western provinces, a kinsman of the king, renowned in his own right as author of a Latin translation of the *Anglo-Saxon Chronicle*, and also renowned as the patron of Ælfric of Cerne (the homilist). In the king's immediate household, we need only mention Æthelweard's son **Æthelmær**, who had founded or endowed the church at Cerne, in Dorset, and who is also renowned as a patron of Ælfric, initially at Cerne (Dorset) and later at Eynsham (Oxfordshire).[53]

We see these men attesting the king's charters; we may suppose that they drew strength from each other; and we can imagine the networking, the gossip, and the intrigue. Dunstan, Æthelwold and Oswald were all dead, buried, and awaiting translation; yet one can be sure at the same time that the Glastonbury mafia, the Winchester mafia, and the Worcester mafia were active behind the scenes, and infiltrating each other's camps. It would be helpful to know more about the relationship between Ealdorman Æthelweard, his son Æthelmær, and Bishop Wulfsige, in Dorset as well as at court. It is with **Ælfric** of Cerne, however, that we come to the person who must be presumed to have exercised the most direct influence on Wulfsige hereafter. Ælfric had been a pupil of Bishop Æthelwold, at Winchester, and had there been exposed to the monastic reform movement at full power. He was established by Æthelmær at Cerne in 987, and remained there until 1005, when he became abbot of Eynsham.[54] Ælfric had thus been in Dorset for about five years when Wulfsige arrived at Sherborne, and was already the scholar of fame and distinction to whom a bishop might turn for advice and support. He had produced his 'First Series' of Catholic Homilies, dedicated to Archbishop Sigeric, in 990–1,[55] and in 993–4, when Wulfsige became bishop of Sherborne, he was in the process of producing his 'Second Series' of homilies, also dedicated to the archbishop.[56] Wulfsige may have been the diocesan bishop, but Ælfric had style, and the archbishop's ear.

It so happens that the process of Wulfsige's appointment as bishop of Sherborne has left a trace of a kind which takes us deep into the rarefied worlds of Anglo-Saxon diplomatic, palaeography, and prosopography. The scribe of a charter by which King Æthelred granted privileges to Abingdon Abbey, in 993, incorporated in his text a detailed list of those who had been present on the occasion at Winchester, on 4 June, when the grant was made, though for various reasons the charter itself was drawn up a few weeks later, on 17 July, at Gillingham (probably the place of that name in Dorset).[57] Curiously, the scribe left a gap where he had intended to put the name of the bishop of Sherborne, as if at the time there was a vacancy at Sherborne (following the death of Bishop Æthelsige I). Wulfsige himself appears in the witness-list as abbot of Westminster, which must have been his position in June; yet it is clear from the charter that sooner or later his name was inserted by a different scribe, in darker ink, in the space originally left blank for Sherborne, and is there accompanied by what would appear to be an autograph cross.[58]

Unfortunately we have no means of knowing precisely when the witness-list was 'updated' in this remarkable way. Wulfsige was certainly a bishop before the death of Archbishop Sigeric, on 28 October 994,[59] so we may infer that he took office some time after 4 June in 993 (when the see was vacant), and before 28 October in 994 (when Sigeric died). It is possible that Wulfsige retained a direct interest in Westminster; but, if so, the arrangement cannot have lasted long. The name of Ælfwig, abbot of Westminster, was added at the end of the list of abbots in the charter of 993, apparently by the scribe who had inserted Wulfsige's name in the space for Sherborne, and presumably at the same time. The presumption might be that the witness-list was updated at the earliest convenient opportunity, in 993 or 994, and that Wulfsige relinquished Westminster when he moved to Sherborne. It is conceivable, however, that the list was updated a few years later, and that for a while Wulfsige retained control of his abbey. It would be possible on this basis to accommodate Goscelin's remarks to the effect that, as bishop of Sherborne, Wulfsige continued to act as abbot of Westminster. The remarks seem to have been based on testimony bearing on the monastic proclivities which Wulfsige displayed at both places, and, more particularly, on the fact that both houses had 'their own charters carefully written out under his name and authority' (*singula priuilegia sua ipsius nomine et auctoritate uigilanter conscripta*).[60] The fact remains, however, that Ælfwig attested a charter, as abbot of Westminster, in 997,[61] so we must presume that Wulfsige had relinquished his former office by then.

It would be difficult to characterise Wulfsige's activities as bishop of Sherborne in the 990s, except in the general sense that he presumably participated in the routine business of his diocese, and from time to time attended meetings of the king and his councillors wherever they were held. One special event which took place not long after his appointment as bishop was the dedication of the new tower at the Old Minster, Winchester, in the latter half of 993 or in the first ten months of 994. The event is described in a verse letter prefixed to Wulfstan Cantor's 'Metrical Account of St Swithun', addressed to Ælfheah, bishop of Winchester (984–1006); the point being that Wulfsige, bishop of Sherborne, is registered among those present.[62] It is a pleasant thought that Wulfsige might have been impressed by the occasion, and resolved not to be outdone by the bishop of the neighbouring West Saxon diocese; but while we may presume that Wulfsige's activities at Sherborne involved some new building, it is difficult to attribute any part of the surviving Anglo-Saxon fabric to him, as distinct from his successors in the eleventh century.[63]

We come now to what is certainly the most outwardly attractive object associated with Bishop Wulfsige. In order to perform his appointed tasks, a bishop needed a pontifical, that is to say a book which contained the orders of service for the kinds of religious ceremony in which a bishop might expect to be involved (the consecration of a church, the ordination of a priest, the coronation of a king, and so on).[64] One such pontifical, now known as the Pontifical of St Dunstan, was written in the second half of the tenth century, almost certainly at Christ Church, Canterbury.[65] In its original form, the book began with a famous set of three prefatory images, depicting Christ in different guises as King (5v), God (6r), and Man (6v),[66] followed on fos 7r–8v by the text of a letter from Pope John XXII (955–64) to Dunstan, dated 21 September 960, which accompanied the grant of the pallium.[67] It is difficult indeed to resist the natural inference that the book was written for Archbishop Dunstan himself, at any stage during his pontificate (959–88), but probably during the 960s or 970s.[68]

Dunstan died in 988, and one imagines that his pontifical stayed for the time being at Canterbury. In view of the close relationship formed between Dunstan and Wulfsige, at Glastonbury (perhaps) and at Westminster, it is entirely appropriate that the pontifical would appear to have been given to Wulfsige, presumably on his becoming bishop of Sherborne five years later, in 993/4, or some time thereafter. It was probably at this stage that a preliminary quire (fos 1–4) was added at beginning of the book, in order to provide space for additional items. The first leaf was originally left blank; but a list of the bishops of

Sherborne from Aldhelm to Æthelric was added on fo 1v (Fig 5),[69] showing that the book was at Sherborne in the early eleventh century. Most interestingly, a letter of exhortation from an archbishop to a bishop, specified as Bishop Wulfsige, was added in excellent Anglo-Caroline script on fos 2r–3r (Fig 6),[70] and a drawing of the Crucifixion was added on fo 4v.[71] It is conceivable that the additions were made when the book was still at Canterbury, once it had been decided (whether by Archbishop Sigeric or, later, by Archbishop Ælfric) that Dunstan's book should be given to Wulfsige; but it is also possible that they were made on Wulfsige's instructions once the book had arrived at Sherborne, as the first and most important of several 'local' additions.[72] The archbishop who wrote the letter of exhortation to Wulfsige might therefore have been Archbishop Sigeric (990–4), or Archbishop Ælfric (995–1005). After the salutation, the letter begins as follows: 'We give thanks to God who set us up – unworthy and least of his servants – to the governance of his holy church *in such dangerous and difficult times*. And now we pray together for the mercy of Almighty God that he may help us in every good work.' The bulk of the letter is lifted verbatim from a much earlier letter of Alcuin to an archbishop of York, and comprises general advice on how it behoves a bishop to behave. The letter continues as follows: 'Give guidance to the ealdorman, and all secular *principes*, that they keep piety and mercy in judgements'; and so on. The archbishop was aware that these were dangerous times; and it is interesting that he should have urged the bishop to ensure that the ealdorman (Æthelweard) and the *principes* (no doubt including the king's reeves and thegns) conducted their business and discharged their duties in accordance with good Christian custom, presumably in their deliberations and judgements at meetings of the shire-court.

To have a letter sent to Bishop Wulfsige by Archbishop Sigeric, or Archbishop Ælfric, is good enough; so the fact that we also have a letter sent to him by another hand constitutes a veritable *embarras de richesses*. It seems that Wulfsige had asked Ælfric of Cerne to give him some advice for the guidance of secular clergy, and also some advice on the episcopal office. Ælfric responded to the effect that Wulfsige ought to know how to conduct himself,[73] but produced a 'Pastoral Letter' cast in Wulfsige's name for the guidance of the clerics subject to him.[74] Three copies of this letter have been preserved, in variant forms: one, added to a manuscript at Exeter in the late eleventh century, provides what appears to be an 'early' and complete version of the text, incorporating a section which may have been added by Wulfsige (chs 150–8), and ending with what may have been Ælfric's own peroration (chs 159–61), but not including a passage derived from Ælfric's *De oratione Moysi* (chs 105–10);[75] a second version, written *c* 1000 and corrected by Ælfric himself, breaks off incomplete in chapter 108, soon after the beginning of the passage from Ælfric's *De oratione Moysi*, leaving the ending unknown;[76] a third version, written at Worcester in the late eleventh century, includes the passage derived from *Ælfric's De oratione Moysi* (chs 105–10) but ends at chapter 149 (omitting Ælfric's peroration).[77]

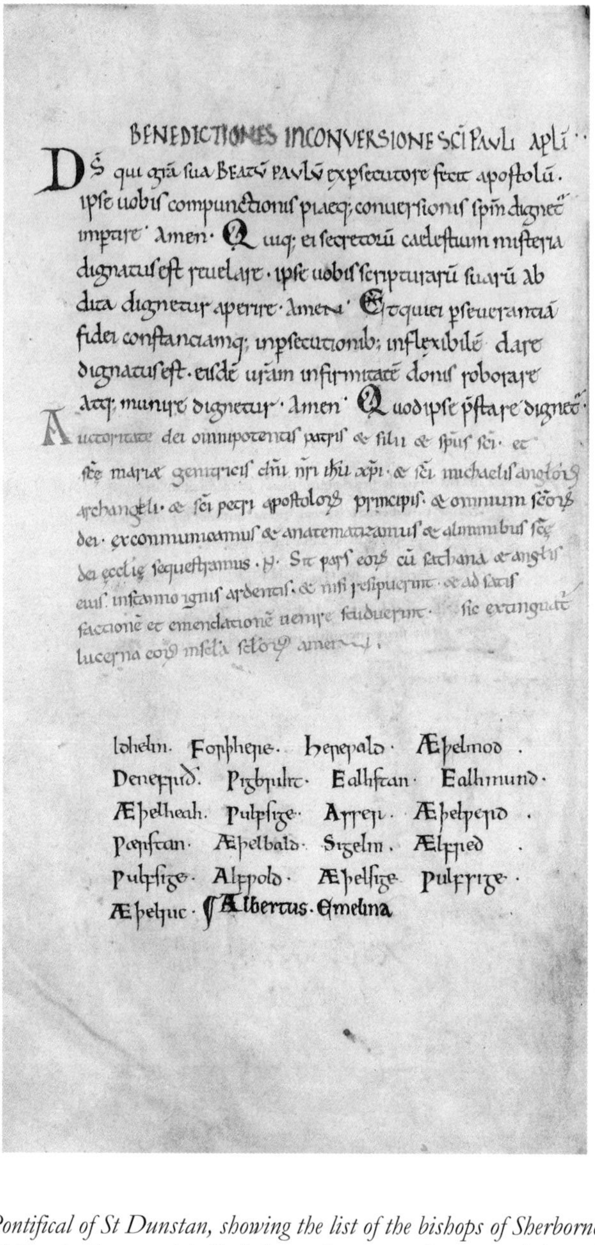

Figure 5. The Pontifical of St Dunstan, showing the list of the bishops of Sherborne from Aldhelm to Æthelric. Written in the second half of the tenth century almost certainly at Canterbury, the Pontifical was probably given to Bishop Wulfsige sometime after Archbishop Dunstan's death. The first leaf was originally left blank. The list of bishops was added – in Sherborne – sometime in the early eleventh century. Note the rendering of the name Wulfsige towards the bottom right-hand corner (see Rushforth and Barker, 'Bishop Wulfsige's name', this volume). (Pontifical of St Dunstan, Paris, BN Lat. 943, fo 1v)

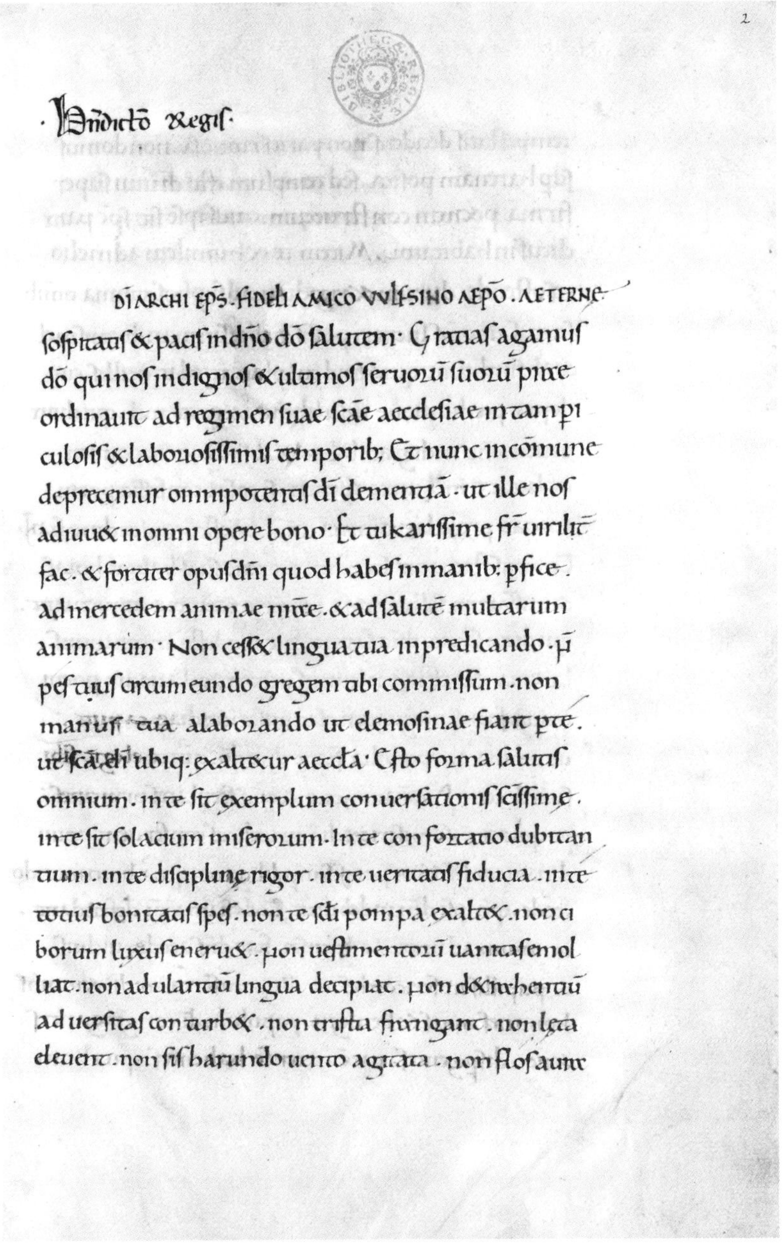
2

·Bndicto Regis·

DI ARCHI EPS. FIDELI AMICO VVLFSINO AEPO. AETERNE

sospitatis & pacis in dño dō salutem· Gratias agamus
dō qui nos indignos & ultimos seruorū suorū p te
ordinauit ad regimen suae scāe aecclesiae in tam pi
culosis & laboriosissimis temporib; Et nunc in cōmune
deprecemur omnipotentis dī clementiā. ut ille nos
adiuuet in omni opere bono· Et tu karissime fr̄ uirilit̄
fac. & fortiter opus dñi quod habes in manib; pfice.
Ad mercedem animae tuae. & ad salutē multarum
animarum· Non cesset lingua tua in predicando. pi
pes tuus circumeundo gregem tibi commissum. non
manus tua a laborando ut elemosinae fiant p te.
ut scā dī ubiq; exaltetur aecclā· Esto forma salutis
omnium. in te sit exemplum conuersationis scissime.
in te sit solacium miserorum. In te con fortatio dubitan
tium. in te disciplinę rigor. in te ueritatis fiducia. in te
totius bonitatis spes. non te scli pompa exaltet. non ci
borum luxus eneruet. non uestimentorū uanitas emol
liat. non adulantiū lingua decipiat. non detrahentiū
ad uersitas conturbet. non tristia frangant. non leta
eleuent. non sis harundo uento agitata. non flos autur

Figure 6. The Pontifical of St Dunstan, showing the beginning of a Pastoral Letter from Archbishop Sigeric or Ælfric to Bishop Wulfsige probably written in the mid-990s. Wulfsige's name can be seen in the first line, Latinised as VVLFSINO, Wlsino that is, Wulsin. (Pontifical of St Dunstan, Paris, BN Lat. 943, fo 2r)

The letter, which was probably written in the mid-990s,[78] contains useful guidance for secular clergy, presumably directed at the parish priests throughout the diocese of Sherborne, yet also applicable to the canons in Bishop Wulfsige's episcopal household. It represents a fine expression of the monastic point of view, displaying deep disapproval of the lax standards which prevailed among the secular clergy (eg chs 1, 14–15), who ignored their own Rule (ch 102), and a strong conviction in the superiority of the monastic orders (chs 46–7, 101); priests are urged to pray for the king (ch 51), and are told what things they needed (chs 52–60), what their duties might be (chs 61–2), and what they should not do or be (chs 73–82).

No less interesting is the fact that the letter also reflects Ælfric's response to the Viking invasions. In his 'First Series' of homilies, despatched to Archbishop Sigeric before the arrival of a Viking army in eastern England in the late summer of 991, Ælfric did not seem unduly concerned.[79] In his 'Second Series' of homilies, despatched to Archbishop Sigeric in 992 or 993, he mentioned the activities of hostile pirates as if they had been not very much more than a passing inconvenience.[80] It was in the mid-990s that Ælfric undertook the compilation of the collection known to modern scholarship as his Lives of Saints.[81] The collection incorporates a homily for Mid-Lent, on the 'Prayer of Moses' (De oratione Moysi), which seems to have originated separately, and which represents a sustained exposition of the necessary response to contemporary troubles.[82] Taking his cue from an episode in Israel's struggle against the Amalekites (Exod 17:9–13), Ælfric enlarges on the need for Christians to call on God in times of distress, especially in the last age before the end of the world. His analysis was conventional, and his response predictable. Men had rejected monastic life, and held God's services in contempt; so God sent his punishment in the form of a heathen army, as had been seen 'nu on niwum dagum and undigollice' ('now in recent times, so clearly', line 177). The solution was to stop bickering, live wisely, and order one's deeds in accordance with the Lord's will.[83]

Ælfric's homily De oratione Moysi is a clear expression of the received view that Viking invasions were a manifestation of divine displeasure; and his letter to Wulfsige is an equally clear exposition of the standard monastic view of secular clergy. It is easy to see how the two could merge; and the fact that a passage from De oratione Moysi, stressing the need for a virtuous life, was inserted by Ælfric into one of his own copies of the letter to Wulfsige suggests how, in his mind, the two texts may have complemented each other. One should add that the earliest and only 'complete' version of the letter to Wulfsige contains a seemingly intrusive section on the duty of priests in enforcing good Christian practices (chs 150–8), apparently derived from a set of pronouncements originating at a council of bishops (and thus not improbably inserted on the authority of Wulfsige himself), which stipulates (among other things) that the mass 'Contra Paganos' should be sung 'every Wednesday in every minster'.[84] The impression made by Ælfric's letter to Bishop Wulfsige, when read in relation to its historical context, is that separate threads were beginning to become entangled with each other: Viking invasions were a manifestation of God's displeasure with the English people; the monastic life was superior to the life of secular clergy; and it was essential that all men should mend the errors of their ways, in order to gain God's favour. The question remains: what would Bishop Wulfsige do about it, at Sherborne?

The reform of the community at Sherborne (998)

Several different factors may have combined to induce Bishop Wulfsige, in 998, to effect a change in the organisation of his church at Sherborne. It is not inconceivable, in the first place, that he was conscious of the impending millennium, and felt a need to take action before it was too late.[85] Nor could anyone forget, in the second place, that Viking activity in the 990s put great pressure on all those in positions of authority. Raids of the kind experienced in the 980s were sources of local irritation; but in the early 990s the nature of Viking activity in England took such a dramatic turn for the worse that many more people, even in those areas not yet directly affected, must have begun to fear for the future. We may imagine that the news spread like wildfire: the loss of Ealdorman Byrhtnoth at the Battle of Maldon in 991; the introduction of the desperate policy of buying off the invaders with payments of *gafol*, or tribute, also in 991; the attack on the very heart of the kingdom, at London, in 994; the employment of the Danes as mercenaries, to protect the country against other Viking forces, also in 994; and the wretched fact that the mercenaries turned against those whom they had been hired to protect, in 997.

It is significant, in the third place, that the direction of the kingdom's domestic affairs had itself taken a turn in the 990s which would favour a bold initiative of precisely this kind. As we have seen, a striking feature of domestic affairs at this time was the king's concern, in general terms, to make amends for earlier mistakes, and in so doing to promote all causes conducive to the welfare of the Church and by extension to the welfare of the kingdom. The direction of royal policy finds its most obvious expression in a series of charters which extend throughout the closing decade of the tenth century, and into the opening years of the new millennium. In 993, King Æthelred reaffirmed the privileges of Abingdon Abbey (S 876). In 994, he granted privileges to Ealdred, bishop of Cornwall (S 880). In the same year, the king granted land to Wilton Abbey, where lay his half-sister St Edith (S 881). Also in the same year, he granted land to Æscwig, bishop of Dorchester (S 882). In 995, the king granted land and privileges to Muchelney Abbey (S 884). In the same year, he granted land to the bishopric of Rochester (S 885). In 996, he granted land to St Albans Abbey (S 888). In 996 and 997, he restored land to the Old Minster, Winchester (S 889, 891). In 998 he restored land to the see of Rochester (S 893). And so on. It is the combination and more particularly the *concentration* of such charters, in the 990s, that lend special significance to them as a group, and give substance (in the simplest terms) to the notion that they were manifestations of a desire in high places to do what was pleasing in the sight of God. One should add, in the same connection, that there was an increased incidence, in the 990s, of formal ceremonial for the promotion of the cults of saints, including those saints who stood in close relationship to the king.[86] Æthelred the Unready seems to have been anxious, indeed, to wrap himself in the vicarious sanctity of his half-siblings. A new abbey was founded in the early 990s at Cholsey, in Berkshire, in honour of St Edward the Martyr;[87] a few years later, apparently on 3 November 997, the cult of St Edith was endorsed by the ecclesiastical establishment in a ceremony at Wilton Abbey;[88] and on 20 June 1001 the relics of Edward were translated from one site to another in their resting-place at Shaftesbury Abbey.[89]

We come, in the fourth place, to the more particular ecclesiastical context for Bishop Wulfsige's reform at Sherborne. It is axiomatic, of course, that one of the most distinctive aspects of the monastic reform movement, in England, is the extent to which monasticism penetrated the episcopacy in the late tenth and first half of the eleventh centuries. During this period, a high proportion of those who attained preferment as bishops had risen to prominence as monks or abbots of the reformed monasteries.[90] To judge from the *Regularis Concordia*, it may have been the intention or expectation of the reformers, in the early 970s, that bishops' sees would, as a matter of course, come to be served by monastic as opposed to secular communities.[91] Yet on their appointment to bishoprics, the monastic bishops generally felt free to adopt practices of their own, determined by whatever circumstances they found, and by whatever changes they were moved or able to introduce.[92] One strategy was sooner or later to impose the monastic Rule on the community, whether by force of royal authority or by strength of episcopal personality. At the Old Minster, Winchester, under Bishop Æthelwold (963–84), the clerks were famously ejected, in 964, and replaced by monks drawn from Abingdon and elsewhere; but, whether adopted at a monastery or at an episcopal see, the uncompromising ejection of incumbent secular clergy was a tactic which risked alienation of an important sector of the local society, on which any religious house depended for support, and may not have been to the taste or indeed to the advantage of all.

An alternative strategy was for a monastic bishop to set an example of personal discipline, by living his life in accordance with the Rule (perhaps in association with a few other monks), in what would become a mixed community of monks and clerks, and in this way the more gently to encourage the secular clergy of an episcopal see to adopt monastic discipline. At Worcester, under Bishop [later Archbishop] Oswald (961–92), there seems to be a choice between a sudden change in the composition of the community in the mid-960s (as suggested by the notorious 'Altitonantis' charter),[93] and a more gradual transformation from a secular to a monastic community (as suggested by attestations of clergy in the Worcester leases).[94] There is reason to believe, however, that some of the 'clerks', 'deacons' and 'priests' who attest the

Worcester leases from the 960s onwards may (on the analogy of terminology
employed at Winchester) have been monks who had taken higher orders, in
which case it is possible that the conversion to a monastic community began
earlier than is apparent from the leases, and that Worcester was more 'monastic',
by the time of Oswald's death, than might have been supposed.[95] The process
may have been similar at Canterbury. Dunstan (959–88), Æthelgar (988–90) and
Sigeric (990–4) were committed reformers, and would have continued to
maintain their own monastic way of life; yet according to Canterbury tradition,
it was Archbishop Ælfric (995–1005), on his return from Rome in 997, who
drove out the clerks and replaced them with monks.[96] The truth is more likely to
be that the process began in the 960s, and was brought in the 990s to a state
which in monastic retrospect could be represented as completion,[97] for nothing
would be more appropriate, from a monastic point of view, than to turn a
period of transition into a dramatic moment of change.

It follows that when Wulfsige arrived at Sherborne, *c* 993, a preference for
the monastic life, which had been imposed by force at Winchester in 964 (with
consequences felt after Edgar's death in 975), could be seen to have been
implemented on a more gradual and relaxed basis at Worcester and at Canterbury
in the 970s and 980s; and the circumstances may have seemed right, therefore,
for a return to affirmative action. The archbishop had despatched a letter of
general encouragement, but Ælfric (of Cerne) left Wulfsige in no doubt where
his duty lay. Matters were complicated, in 997, when the Viking mercenary force
turned against its employers, and when it was the south-west that bore the brunt
of their unwanted attention. The Vikings ransacked Ordulf's monastery at
Tavistock, Devon, in 997, and in the following year struck deep into Dorset:

> In this year the [Danish] army turned back east into the mouth of the Frome,
> and there they went inland everywhere into Dorset as widely as they pleased;
> and the English army was often assembled against them, but as soon as they
> were to have joined battle, a flight was always instigated by some means, and
> always the enemy had the victory in the end.[98]
>
> (see Barker, 'Bishop Wulfsige's lifetime', this volume)

Unfortunately, we cannot say precisely when, in 998, the ravaging of Dorset
took place, or whether it affected Sherborne, or, indeed, whether it has any
bearing whatsoever on the matter in hand. Equally, we cannot be prevented
from wondering whether the ravaging of Dorset prompted Bishop Wulfsige to
take measures of a kind which might help to prevent a repetition of such a
pointed manifestation of divine displeasure.

And so we come to the charter, drawn up in the name of King Æthelred,
which is the main focus of our attention[99] (see Keynes, 'King Æthelred's charter',
this volume). In 998, at the instigation of Ælfric, archbishop of Canterbury,
Æthelred gave permission to Bishop Wulfsige 'to institute a rule of monastic
life, a life holy and pleasing to God, according to the practice of the holy father
Benedict, in the monastery of the church of Sherborne'. Wulfsige's successor,

whomsoever it might be, was to act as shepherd of the monks, and to live as one of the community; any dispute between bishop and monks was to be referred to the archbishop, who would report to the king; and because custom hardly allowed an abbot to be set up over an episcopal see, the bishop himself would be abbot and father to them, and they would be obedient to him, according to the Rule of St Benedict. The charter does not lay down provisions affecting Wulfsige himself, as if the point in his case was essentially to consolidate or regularise a position which had already been reached, and the draftsman seems to have been more concerned to ensure that Wulfsige's successors would not abuse their position. The implication seems to be that the successor might well come from outside the community, presumably in accordance with the circumstances envisaged in the *Regularis Concordia*.[100]

It is always difficult to judge the authenticity of a charter preserved not in what might purport to be its original form (written on a single sheet of parchment, in handwriting contemporary with the given date), but only in a later copy or transcript. Moreover, judgements on the authenticity of Anglo-Saxon charters are rarely capable of anything approximating to proof, and tend to depend on the cumulative force of a combination of separate considerations: awareness of the particular circumstances in which a charter was produced, preserved and transmitted; close examination of the form, integrity and substance of the received text, whether in Latin or in the vernacular; and understanding of the place of that text in whatever historical, diplomatic and literary contexts seem to be appropriate. It has to be admitted that King Æthelred's charter for Bishop Wulfsige displays certain features which render it at first sight vulnerable to doubt, but closer analysis reveals nothing that constitutes a decisive objection to its authenticity, and much that stands in its support.[101]

The charter was accorded pride of place in the twelfth-century cartulary of Sherborne Abbey, presumably copied from a single-sheet exemplar now lost[102] (Frontispiece). In terms of its formulation, or diplomatic, the charter contains no words or formulas which might be regarded as out of place in a document of this period, and some forms of wording which are particularly appropriate to its immediate context. The structure of the text is unusual in comparison with other charters of the late tenth century, for it begins with a dating clause, suggestive of the influence of the 'Dunstan B' formulation known to have been employed at Glastonbury in the 950s; but, as we have seen, the 'Dunstan B' formulation would appear to have spread from Glastonbury to Westminster, and is arguably not out of place, therefore, at Wulfsige's Sherborne. The charter otherwise stands apart from 'normal' royal diplomas of the period for the excellent reason that it deals with matters which of their nature are peculiar to itself. Its most remarkable feature is the statement that any disagreement between the bishop (*pastor*) and the community (*grex*) should be referred to the archbishop (*ad examen archiepiscopi reseruetur*), who would in turn advise the king of the action to be taken (*et ipse regi intimet ut iusta correctio sequatur*). The arrangement accords well in spirit with the advisory role envisaged for the king in the *Regularis Concordia*, and would be out of place in any other context. The see was transferred from Sherborne to Salisbury (Old Sarum) in 1078, and for a while Sherborne was a subordinate priory; but in 1122 it gained its independence as an abbey, and soon came into conflict with the bishop. The monks of Sherborne took a close interest, therefore, in documents which concerned their own rights; and in fact it has been shown that the Sherborne cartulary was compiled in the late 1140s, soon after the community had (with help from the pope) defended its right to elect its own abbot without interference from the bishop of Salisbury.[103] It is remarkable that the monks of Sherborne should have given pride of place, under these circumstances, to a document which might have been as useful to the bishop of Salisbury as they evidently hoped it would be to themselves; and the fact that they did so can perhaps be construed as a sign of their own confidence in its authenticity.

No less interesting is the reference to the social and economic factors which had prompted the bishop to demarcate his property, and which had prompted the king to confirm the abbey in the possession of its estates. The list of estates provided in this connection begins with 'one hundred plots (*agelli*) in Sherborne itself, in what is called Stockland, and the estate (*predium*) of the monastery, just as Bishop Wulfsige enclosed it with ditches and hedges', reflecting the care he was taking to protect the interests of his community in times of great stress.[104] The rest of the list is acceptable as a record of the abbey's endowment in the late tenth century, and is notable for its omission of Corscombe, Dorset, a Sherborne property known to have been out on lease since the 970s.[104a] Another point in favour of the charter's authenticity is the statement added to the standard reservation of the military burdens: 'however they are to owe no-one any service in the construction of a beacon, because we recognise that the monastery needs this work'.[105] Nothing could be more appropriate, in 998, than a special provision intended to ensure that the monastery would be able to give priority to its own defence, when the Viking army threatened to come its way.

There are no discernible anachronisms in any other part of the text. The list of witnesses, although short, is impeccable in its selection of names; and Wulfsige himself attests with a sentence to the effect that he has brought his plan to fruition, suggesting the possibility that he played some part in the drafting of the text. One should bear in mind, finally, that a text of the charter for Wulfsige at Sherborne seems to have found its way to Westminster, where it was used as a model for the 'Telligraphus' of King Æthelred, also dated 998. Of course it is possible to imagine circumstances in which the monks of Westminster might have gained access to a copy of the charter for Bishop Wulfsige; but it must be said that the connection is easier to understand if both texts originated in the late tenth century, and if we may suppose that it reflects the real links which existed at that time between Sherborne and Westminster.

Little is known of Wulfsige's activities as bishop of Sherborne in the few years that remained of his life. He was present, styled 'bishop of Dorset', at a meeting of the king and his councillors held at Cookham, Berkshire, in the late 990s,[106] and, more significantly, is known to have been involved in the translation of the relics of Edward the Martyr, at Shaftesbury, in June 1001,[107] he also attested the charter by which King Æthelred granted Bradford-on-Avon, in Wiltshire, to the nuns of Shaftesbury, in the closing months of the same year.[108] Other routine aspects of his episcopal business are suggested by some of the texts added to the Pontifical of St Dunstan. It may have been Wulfsige himself who arranged for a copy of Ælfric's homily on the dedication of a church to be added on spare leaves at the end of the original manuscript.[109] Another homily on the dedication of a church was added on an extra quire, apparently in the early eleventh century, and on the recto of a leaf left blank at the end of this quire we find two forms of words for two penitential letters issued in Bishop Wulfsige's name, for homicides.[110] Bishop Wulfsige died on his estate at Beaminster, Dorset, on 8 January 1002.[111] His body was borne with great honour to Sherborne, where it was placed in a sarcophagus and buried in a porch or side-chapel (*porticus*) of the church.[112] His crozier (*baculus*) and other insignia of his office were still preserved at Sherborne in the twelfth century.[113]

The church of Sherborne in the eleventh century

Wulfsige was succeeded as bishop of Sherborne by a certain Æthelric, who had been a monk at Glastonbury Abbey,[114] and who held the bishopric from 1002 to 1011 x 1012.[115] It was evidently during his episcopacy that a list of the bishops of Sherborne was entered quite carefully in the lower part of a blank page at the beginning of the Pontifical of St Dunstan (Fig 5),[116] and it is as if by placing the list on the first opening of the book that Æthelric intended to establish his own position in the line of succession reaching back to Aldhelm, and to put the equivalent of a Sherborne stamp on what may have become one of the church's principal treasures.

According to Goscelin, it was twelve years after Wulfsige's death that miracles began to occur at his tomb.[117] Bishop Æthelric drew this to the attention of Archbishop Ælfheah, and King Æthelred; whereupon the archbishop authorised him to translate Wulfsige's remains, and to establish an annual festival for him in his province.[118] Accordingly, Æthelric presided over the translation of his predecessor's body from the *porticus* to a better place on the right-hand side of the high altar.[119] Goscelin's 'twelve' years would take us from *c* 1002 to *c* 1014; but if we choose to be guided (as well we might) by the reference to the involvement of Archbishop Ælfheah, the translation would seem to have taken place before his capture by the Danes in 1011, and so perhaps *c* 1010. The suggested date for the first translation of St Wulfsige thus falls within the period when Thorkell's army was active in England (1009–12), and it may be no coincidence that it was a period when Danish activity had its most devastating effect throughout the kingdom.

The impact is clearly visible at Sherborne. Bishop Æthelric used his pontifical as a convenient place for recording the text of a letter he wrote to Æthelmær (evidently the principal secular official in Dorset, in the absence of an ealdorman), complaining about a short-fall in his receipts of ship-scot in respect of thirty-three out of the three hundred hides for the diocese (and a potential further short-fall in respect of nine hides at Holcombe), and suggesting that Æthelmær might be able to set matters straight.[120] The complaint can be understood in the light of a statement in the Chronicle, for 1008, to the effect that the king 'ordered that ships should be built unremittingly over all England, namely a warship from 310 hides, and a helmet and corselet from eight hides'. It would appear, in other words, that the bishop had been made responsible in some way for the provision of one ship, but that he was not receiving due payments from some of the estates which in combination made up the three hundred (or three hundred and ten) hides required by him to discharge the obligation. This may have been in (or before) 1008, but is more likely to have been two or three years later, when the community is known to have been coming under pressure to grant the use of its estate at Holcombe Rogus, in Devon, to the king's son Edmund the Ætheling.[121]

The burdens imposed on land-owners by the need to provide for the defence of the country against Viking attack are made vividly apparent in another way. The church of Sherborne's estate at Corscombe, in Dorset, which had been leased out by Bishop Ælfwold for two lives, during the reign of King Edgar, was duly returned to the church during the episcopacy of Bishop Æthelric; but it emerges from a charter that Æthelric was then obliged to give the estate to Ealdorman Eadric, 'on account of the ravages of wicked men and the attacks of the Danes' (*ob malorum infestationes direptionesque Danorum*), which appears to mean that the bishop had been compelled to give up the estate in order to discharge an obligation forced upon him by the authorities when raising the funds required for defensive purposes.[122] The specific involvement of Eadric in this connection suggests the period 1009–12, when he can be shown to have gained a position of great power in the land.[123] Bishop Æthelric was succeeded by Æthelsige II, who held office at Sherborne from *c* 1012 to an indeterminate point between 1014 and 1018. It was during his time that Wulfgar, described as a servant (*famulus*) of the monastery, bought the estate at Corscombe from Ealdorman Eadric, for a large sum of gold and silver, and gave it back to the abbey for the good of his soul; the happy event was duly confirmed by charter of King Æthelred, issued after Æthelred's return from Normandy in the spring of 1014.[124]

In 1016 the English finally succumbed to the Danes. For reasons or under circumstances that may not yet be fully understood, Cnut and his closest followers appear to have taken a special interest in Dorset, as if they had decided to make the base of their operations in the south-west. Several of Cnut's Scandinavian followers settled in the county, notably Orc at Abbotsbury, Bovi at Horton, and Agmund at Cheselbourne; there were housecarls at Dorchester, Bridport, Wareham, and Shaftesbury; and of course it was at Shaftesbury that King Cnut died, in 1035.[125] The Danish interest in Dorset was also felt at Sherborne. A certain Brihtwine had succeeded Æthelsige II as bishop of Sherborne, probably in 1015 or 1016, and continued to hold that office in the opening years of Cnut's reign; but it emerges from Goscelin's *Life* of St Wulfsige that Brihtwine was presently 'ejected' from the bishopric, and replaced by Ælfmær, abbot of St Augustine's, Canterbury.[126] It was this Ælfmær who seems to have been implicated (with an archdeacon of the same name) in the treachery by virtue of which the Danes had been able to capture Canterbury in 1011,[127] so it looks as if he was being rewarded for his assistance, and placed in a position where he could continue most effectively to represent the Scandinavian interest. It is not exactly clear when Ælfmær was appointed, but it was probably in the mid-1020s.

Interestingly, we learn (in yet another charter preserved at Sherborne) of a Dane called Toki, who seems to have managed to obtain an interest, at about this time, in the abbey's property at Holcombe (which would have reverted to the abbey after the death of Edmund Ironside in 1016), and who passed that interest on to his sons, among them Care and Ulf. After some dispute, Ulf was allowed to remain in possession of the estate, with reversion to Sherborne after his death.[128] No less interestingly, Goscelin states opaquely that Ælfmær 'harassed the Lord's flock (*grex*) which had been established by the true shepherd (*pastor*), Wulfsige, and made efforts to appropriate one of the monks' estates'; for which Ælfmær went blind, and returned whence he came (where he recovered his sight), whereupon Brihtwine was restored, and passed the see on to his brother Ælfwold.[129] If the charter and Goscelin's story are put together, we see what may have been an instance of Bishop Ælfmær favouring his Danish friends in leasing a prime monastic estate to one of Cnut's followers, and an ensuing dispute over its ownership in the next generation; and since Holcombe was evidently such a coveted property, we understand, perhaps, why the community of Sherborne was seemingly not sorry to see Ælfmær go back to Kent.

From the English viewpoint, all this looks like the unacceptable face of Scandinavian conquest; yet it is clear that Sherborne also worked its charm on the Danish conqueror. Goscelin describes how King Cnut and Queen Emma visited the church in an unspecified year (perhaps while Ælfmær was bishop), and were shocked to see that the roof was leaking, and the saint's tomb exposed to the elements; whereupon Queen Emma, always keen to gain some credit, gave £20 of silver towards its repair.[130] If the king himself stood back on this occasion, he eventually saw the need to get some credit of his own. In 1035, presumably not long before his death at Shaftesbury, he gave a large estate at Corscombe, Dorset, to Sherborne Abbey, 'for the redemption of my soul and the absolution of my sins', stipulating in the charter that the community were to pray hard for him, 'so that after my death, through God's mercy and by virtue of their holy prayers, I might be able to reach the kingdom of heaven'.[131] The irony is, in this instance, that the king may have been party to the appropriation of the same estate from Sherborne, at an earlier stage[132] but, from his point of view, it was never too late to ingratiate himself with the monks.

The bishop who would appear to have done most for the church of Sherborne in the eleventh century, and perhaps also for promoting the cult of St Wulfsige, was Ælfwold II (1045–(1062 x ?)), brother of Bishop Brihtwine. It is not obvious why or under what circumstances Wulfsige came to be revered as a saint: perhaps because he was renowned for his prophetic powers,[133] but more probably because Sherborne needed a saint of its own who could compete with the saints of other churches in the competitive religious market of the eleventh century. As we have seen, in *c* 1010 Bishop Æthelric had moved Wulfsige's body from its grave in the porticus to a better place near the high altar. Goscelin describes at some length how Ælfwold brought the sarcophagus in which Wulfsige had been buried into the main church, how the bishop commissioned numerous shrines and crosses in gold and silver, and how he undertook further building work at the abbey,[134] and it is a pleasant thought that the church depicted on the 'Seal of the church of St Mary of Sherborne', probably made in the eleventh century and used as a conventual seal for some time thereafter, may represent the church as it appeared after Ælfwold's building works in the 1050s.[135] Yet Bishop Ælfwold wanted nothing more than to put Sherborne firmly on the map of the resting-places of saints. According to Goscelin, it was he who brought the relics of St Juthwara from Halstock to Sherborne, which soon proved most efficacious.[136] But it is William of Malmesbury who supplies the information which helps us to understand where Ælfwold was coming from, and what he was up to. Ælfwold had been trained as a monk at the Old Minster, Winchester,[137] and it is this link which explains his activities at Sherborne in the mid-eleventh century.[138] As one might have expected of an Old Minster man, Ælfwold brought with him to Sherborne a statue of St Swithun,[139] and since a manuscript containing Wulfstan of Winchester's *Narratio metrica de S. Swithuno*, copied directly from a late tenth-century manuscript at Winchester, was seen by Leland at Sherborne in the 1540s, it may be that he brought the poem of the statue as well.[140]

There is one other dimension to this story. It is often supposed that Bishop Ælfwold died in 1058, and was succeeded at that point by Herman, bishop of Ramsbury, who brought Goscelin with him to Sherborne.[141] In fact there is good reason to believe that Ælfwold was still alive and active, as bishop of Sherborne, in 1062, and was only then or thereabouts succeeded by Herman.[142] The most helpful consequence of extending Ælfwold's life into the early 1060s is that he can be credited with commissioning a sacramentary (known as the 'Red Book of Darley') which in itself is symbolic of the Winchester-Sherborne axis.[143] The manuscript contains Easter Tables for the years 1061–98, starting near the end of one Dionysiac cycle (1045–63) and continuing towards the end of another (1083–1101); so the implication is that it was produced in 1060–1. It is generally supposed that it was written at Winchester, at the Old or the New Minster; yet it seems clear that it must have been intended from the outset for use at Sherborne, since the calendar for January contains a prominent commemoration of Bishop Wulfsige (*Sancti Wulfsini Scirburnensis episcopi*), who is not known to have been honoured outside that church.[144] Bishop Ælfwold was also keen on St Cuthbert,[145] but the cult was too widespread for it to be easy to judge whether its treatment in the sacramentary is also indicative of Ælfwold's special devotion to the Northumbrian saint.

Ælfwold's successor, Bishop Herman (*c* 1062–78), was footloose if not fancy-free. He had been appointed bishop of Ramsbury (for Wiltshire and Berkshire) in 1045, but left the country in 1055 having failed in an attempt to move his see to Malmesbury. After three years of self-imposed exile at the monastery of Saint-Bertin, in Flanders, Herman came back to England in 1058, probably accompanied by the monk Goscelin, and returned initially to Ramsbury.[146] A few years later, in or soon after 1062, he sought and gained permission to move his see to Sherborne, and from there presided over a large diocese which now included Dorset as well; but in 1075 he was authorised to move from Dorset back into Wiltshire, and soon afterwards established his see at Salisbury (Old Sarum), where in 1078 he died.[147] Herman was quick to take advantage of Wulfsige's thaumaturgical powers, for Goscelin relates how on one occasion the bishop brought forth the relics of St Wulfsige in a lawsuit, and how effective they were in silencing the opposition.[148] It is otherwise in connection with Herman that we might understand how a manuscript of the Romano-German Pontifical, written in Germany in the eleventh century, came to be at Sherborne in the second half of the eleventh century, where it received numerous additions in Latin and in the vernacular.[149] It can easily be imagined, on the other hand, under what circumstances the Pontifical of St Dunstan had found its way by the end of the eleventh century to the Cathedral of Notre Dame in Paris.[150]

Goscelin's *Life* of Wulfsige, written in 1078–9, represents only the first stage in the development of traditions about Sherborne's past.[151] A collection of material put together at Sherborne in the fourteenth century includes an extended tract on the kings of England (from Ecgberht to Edward I) followed by a regnal list from Cerdic to Ecgberht.[152] These items of general historical interest are themselves followed by two of more parochial concern: a narrative account of successive bishops of Sherborne, from Aldhelm to Herman, of uncertain authority[153] and an important list of the royal benefactors of Sherborne Abbey.[154]

The most famous of all manuscripts associated with Sherborne is, however, the great Missal produced *c* 1400, known to posterity as the 'Sherborne Missal'.[155] Included in the spectacular scheme of decoration, we find symbolic or imaginary portraits of the successive bishops of Sherborne[156] and of many of the church's royal benefactors.[157] Our attention turns, however, to the section covering saints' days.[158] The page containing the mass for St Wulfsin's Day (p.397) contains, in the lower margin, a scene which appears to relate directly to the events of 998 (Fig 7).[159] One commentator has taken the view that it shows Wulfsige 'first as Abbot of Westminster presiding over his monks, then journeying on foot to Sherborne as bishop of Sherborne leading monks thither to serve the cathedral (afterwards abbey) church, and finally enthroned in the church'.[160] Another commentator interprets the scene rather differently. Wulfsige, on the left, receives the monks in their black habits at Sherborne, while a group of the expelled canons stand disconsolate behind him; the expelled canons, in the middle, are led out and away from Sherborne past a different church, until they arrive at Old Sarum, on the right, where they are welcomed by Bishop Osmund.[161]

Figure 7. The Sherborne Missal c 1400; the Mass for St Wulfsin's Day, the scene from the lower part of the page. Reading from left to right the picture probably tells the whole of the Wulfsige story from his welcome into the church at Sherborne, the leading away of the secular canons and the welcoming of the Benedictine monks, and then moving on to the activities of his successors, Bishops Herman, Richard Poor, and Richard Mitford. (BL Add MS 74236 p 397, The Sherborne Missal. Mass for St Wulfsin's Day. Reproduced by permission of the British Library)

The most natural interpretation is, however, that the scene represents the whole of the story: a group of monks, on the left, comes from Westminster, and is welcomed into the church at Sherborne by a bishop [Wulfsige in the 990s], while the incumbent secular clergy take shelter behind him; some secular clergy are led away from Sherborne by another bishop [Herman, in the 1070s], and are taken up the hill towards the rather modest church at Old Sarum (Salisbury), in the middle, where the cathedral stood beneath a great castle; and, to complete the story, a third bishop [Richard Poor, in the 1220s], leads his clergy down the hill from Old Sarum towards a far more magnificent church, on the right, with a great spire, evidently the thirteenth-century cathedral at New Sarum (Salisbury), wherein sits (perhaps) the present incumbent [Richard Mitford, *c* 1400].[162] Evidently they knew at Sherborne, even four hundred years after the event, that Wulfsige's introduction of monks into his church was the principal act for which the bishop deserved to be remembered.

* * * * * * * *

The millennium in 1998 of King Æthelred's charter authorising Bishop Wulfsige to institute monastic life in his church, according to the Rule of St Benedict, is by no means the only event worthy of commemoration at Sherborne. The millennium of the death of St Wulfsige himself fell on 8 January 2002; the 1300th anniversary of the foundation of the bishopric of Sherborne might reasonably be celebrated in 2005; and the 1100th anniversary of the death of Alfred's biographer, Bishop Asser, should not pass without notice in 2009. Yet the events at Sherborne in 998 signify far more than just Wulfsige's approach to monastic reform, to be compared with the activities of others at Winchester, Canterbury, Worcester, and elsewhere. These were perilous times in England, and it is almost painfully apparent that the English were forced to ask what they had done, or not done, to deserve such terrible punishment at the hands of a wrathful God. The events at Sherborne cannot be understood except in relation to the conditions which prevailed among the English in the 990s, in the midst of the Viking raids which loomed so large during the reign of King Æthelred the Unready. So in commemorating Wulfsige, we should also remember the anguish and the anxiety endured throughout this period by his long-suffering flock.

Notes

1   Cenwealh, king of the West Saxons (642–72), is said to have given one hundred hides at *Lanprobi* (in or near Sherborne) to the church. For the suggestion that *Lanprobi* was the site of an earlier British monastery, see K Barker, 'The Early History of Sherborne', *The Early Church in Western Britain and Ireland*, (ed) S M Pearce, British Archaeological Reports, British ser 102 (Oxford, 1982), 77–116;

see also *Charters of Sherborne*, (ed) M A O'Donovan (Oxford, 1988), xliii–xliv and 83–8.

2   D H Farmer, *The Oxford Dictionary of Saints* (2nd edition) (Oxford, 1987), 448–9.

3   William of Malmesbury, *Gesta Pontificum Anglorum* [hereafter *GP*], ii. 79: 'Scireburnia est viculus, nec habitantium frequentia nec positionis gratia suavis, in quo mirandum et pene pudendum sedem episcopalem per tot durasse sæcula' (*Willelmi Malmesbiriensis Monachi De Gestis Pontificum Anglorum Libri Quinque*, (ed) N E S A Hamilton, Rolls ser (London, 1870), 175); trans D Preest, *William of Malmesbury: the Deeds of the Bishops of England* (Gesta Pontificum Anglorum), (Woodbridge, 2002), 116. A new edition of the *Gesta pontificum Anglorum*, (ed) M Winterbottom and R M Thomson, with accompanying translation and commentary, is forthcoming.

4   Bede, *Historia ecclesiastica gentis Anglorum* [hereafter *HE*], iii. 7 (Bede's *Ecclesiastical History of the English People*, (eds) B Colgrave and R A B Mynors (Oxford, 1969), 232–6).

5   Bede, *HE* v.18 (ed Colgrave and Mynors, 514).

6   For an authoritative account of Aldhelm, with further references, see M Lapidge, 'Aldhelm', *The Blackwell Encyclopaedia of Anglo-Saxon England*, (eds) M Lapidge *et al* (Oxford, 1999), 25–7.

7   On the bishops of Sherborne, see J Fowler, *Mediaeval Sherborne* (Dorchester, 1951), 35–67; see also J H P Gibb, *The Book of Sherborne* (2nd edition), (Buckingham, 1984), 19–26. There is much of value in D P Kirby, 'Notes on the Saxon Bishops of Sherborne', *Proceedings of the Dorset Natural History and Archæological Society* 87 (1965), 213–22.

8   The Anglo-Saxon Chronicle [ASC], s.a. 867, gives him a career of '50' years as bishop of Sherborne; but it seems likely that he became bishop in 824, and that '50 years' was essentially the chronicler's way of expressing 'a long time'. See S Keynes, 'The West Saxon Charters of King Æthelwulf and his Sons', *English Historical Review* 109 (1994a), 1109–49, at 1111 n 2.

9   Asser, *Vita Ælfredi regis Angul-Saxonum*, ch 12 (S Keynes and M Lapidge, *Alfred the Great: Asser's 'Life of King Alfred' and Other Contemporary Sources* (Harmondsworth, 1983), 70). Asser remarks elsewhere (ch 28) that Ealhstan held his bishopric 'honourably', perhaps suggesting that he was concerned to clear him of the charge; see S Keynes, 'On the Authenticity of Asser's *Life of King Alfred*', *Journal of Ecclesiastical History* 47 (1996a), 529–51, at 545. For Ealhstan's avaricious streak, which extended to the seizure of Malmesbury Abbey, see WM, *GP* ii. 79 (ed Hamilton, 176–7; trans Preest, 116–17).

10   ASC, s.a. 860. According to a vernacular record originally entered in a gospel-book (S 813), King Edgar granted land to the church of Sherborne specifically for the sake of Kings Æthelbald and Æthelberht; see *Anglo-Saxon Charters*, (ed) A J Robertson, 2nd edition (Cambridge, 1956), 104–6 (no 50), and *Charters of Sherborne*, (ed) O'Donovan (1988), 36–9 (no 10). In references to Anglo-Saxon charters, 'S' signifies P H Sawyer, *Anglo-Saxon Charters: an Annotated List and Bibliography* (London, 1968), with number of charter. A revised and updated version of the main part of this list, compiled by S E Kelly, is available on the web site of the British Academy/Royal Historical Society Joint Committee on Anglo-Saxon Charters (www.trin.cam.ac.uk/chartwww).

11   S 333 is a charter of King Æthelberht granting privileges to the church of Sherborne, issued at Dorchester on 26 December 863 and confirmed at Sherborne

on 31 March 864; see Keynes, 'West Saxon Charters of King Æthelwulf and his Sons', 1125.

12 A ninth-century ring inscribed with the name 'Alhstan' (Ealhstan), found in Wales, has no necessary connection with Bishop Ealhstan: see E Okasha, *Hand-List of Anglo-Saxon Non-Runic Inscriptions* (Cambridge 1971), 98–9 (no 86).

13 Keynes, 'West Saxon Charters of King Æthelwulf and his Sons', 1132–4.

14 See N R Ker, *Catalogue of Manuscripts Containing Anglo-Saxon* (Oxford, 1957), 27–8 (no 19) and 132–3 (no 87); for the latter, see also S Keynes, *Anglo-Saxon Manuscripts and Other Items of Related Interest in the Library of Trinity College, Cambridge*, Old English Newsletter, Subsidia 18 (Binghamton, NY, 1992), 29 (no 17). It has been suggested (Ker, *Catalogue*, 28) that Wulfsige, bishop of Sherborne, may be the Wulfsige who succeeded Heahstan as bishop of London in the late 890s. There is no obvious reason for making this identification, unless the idea had been to release a position in the west for Asser.

15 Keynes and Lapidge, *Alfred the Great*, 187–8.

16 ASC, MSS ABCD, s.a. 909. See S Keynes, 'Asser', *Blackwell Encyclopaedia of ASE*, (ed) Lapidge *et al*, 48–50. Asser was succeeded as bishop by a certain Æthelweard, who is sometimes identified as King Alfred's younger son of the same name; *cf* Keynes and Lapidge, *Alfred the Great*, 256. To judge from episcopal lists, the division of the diocese of Sherborne was effected after Æthelweard's demise.

17 For the Latin text of Goscelin's *Vita S. Wlsini,* see C H Talbot, 'The Life of Saint Wulfsin of Sherborne by Goscelin', *Revue Bénédictine* 69: 1–2 (1959), 68–85, with P Grosjean, in *Analecta Bollandiana* 78 (1960), 197–206; and for a translation, see R Love, 'The Life of St Wulfsige of Sherborne by Goscelin of Saint-Bertin', this volume. For Goscelin himself, see *The Life of King Edward Who Rests at Westminster*, (ed) F Barlow, 2nd edition (Oxford, 1992), 133–49, at 135. For some discussion of the historical value of his *Life* of Wulfsige, see F Barlow, *The English Church 1000– 1066* (2nd edition) (London, 1979), 222–4, and M A O'Donovan, 'Studies in the History of the Diocese of Sherborne', PhD dissertation, Univ of Cambridge (1972), 333–45.

18 William of Malmesbury, *GP*, ii. 79–82 (ed Hamilton, 175–81; trans Preest, 116– 20).

19 For later traditions at Sherborne, see further below, this paper.

20 F E Harmer, *Anglo-Saxon Writs* (Manchester, 1952), 579; *The Heads of Religious Houses England and Wales 940–1216,* (eds) D Knowles, C N L Brooke, and V C M London, 2nd edition (Cambridge, 2001), 76; Barlow, *English Church, 1000–1066*, 222, n 6; C R Hart, *The Early Charters of Northern England and the North Midlands* (Leicester, 1975), 374–5.

21 Goscelin, *Vita S. Wlsini*, chs 1–2 (ed) Talbot, 75; trans Love, this volume.

22 A lost Glastonbury calendar contained the obit of 'Bishop Wulfsige, monk of Glastonbury' on 13 January ('Idus Ianuarii', presumably for 'VI Idus Ianuarii'): see J Scott, *The Early History of Glastonbury: an Edition, Translation and Study of William of Malmesbury's 'De Antiquitate Glastonie Ecclesie'* (Woodbridge, 1981), 138.

23 Goscelin, *Vita S. Wlsini*, chs 3 (ed) Talbot, 75–6, clarified in the chapter-heading, 73; trans Love, this volume), 4 (ed) Talbot, 76; trans Love, this volume, and 5 (ed) Talbot, 76–7; trans Love, this volume). The '25' years may represent no more than a rough calculation from Æthelred's accession in 978 to Wulfsige's death in 1002. For a different view of the chronology implicit in Goscelin's work, see Barlow, *English Church 1000–1066*, 222[–3], n 6.

24 B W Scholz, 'Sulcard of Westminster: "Prologus de Construccione Westmonasterii"', *Traditio* 20 (1964), 59–91, at 67 and 86–7.

25 WM, *GP* ii. 81 (ed Hamilton, 178–9; trans Preest, 118–19).

26 WM, *GP* ii. 73 (ed Hamilton, 141; trans Preest, 92–3).

27 *The History of Westminster Abbey by John Flete,* (ed) J A Robinson (Cambridge, 1909), 79–80. Flete cites the 'Telligraphus' of King Æthelred (S 894), on which see further below. He also cites verbatim a passage from Goscelin, *Vita S. Wlsini,* ch 4 (*haec ex vita sancti Wulsini capitulo iv*); so he was, in effect, providing details to compensate for Goscelin's basic ignorance of Wulfsige's career at Westminster.

28 For some of the Westminster forgeries, see *Facsimiles of Anglo-Saxon Charters,* (ed) S Keynes (London, 1991a), 10–11, with further references; see also P M Korhammer, 'The Origin of the Bosworth Psalter', *Anglo-Saxon England* 2 (1973), 173–87, at 182–6.

29 For the early history of Westminster Abbey, see B Harvey, *Westminster Abbey and its Estates in the Middle Ages* (Oxford, 1977); R Gem, 'The Origins of the Abbey', in C Wilson *et al, Westminster Abbey,* New Bell's Cathedral Guides (London, 1986), 6–21; *Westminster Abbey Charters 1066 – c. 1214,* (ed) E Mason (London, 1988), 1–3; D Sullivan, *The Westminster Corridor: an Exploration of the Anglo-Saxon History of Westminster Abbey and its Nearby Lands and People* (London, 1994); and J Field, *Kingdom, Power and Glory: a Historical Guide to Westminster Abbey* (London, 1996), 8–15. See also D Whitelock, 'Some Anglo-Saxon Bishops of London', reptd in her *History, Law and Literature in 10th–11th Centuries* (London, 1981), no II, 22.

30 S 670 (BCS 1048), from Westminster Abbey Muniments V (*OSFacs.* ii, Westminster 4; Sullivan, *Westminster Corridor,* plate 7). For valuable explication of the topography, with map, see Sullivan, *Westminster Corridor,* 79–80, 166, and map M.

31 S Keynes, 'The "Dunstan B" Charters', *Anglo-Saxon England* 23 (1994b), 165–93, at 177.

32 S 1451 (BCS 1290), from BL Stowe Charter 32 (*OSFacs.* iii. 33), written apparently by three hands in different stages (main text, boundary clause, and dating clause). For valuable explication of the topography, with map, see Sullivan, *Westminster Corridor,* 87–9, 168, and map N.

33 S 1450, MS. 1 (*cf* BCS 1351), from BL Stowe Charter 33 (*OSFacs.* iii. 34; Sullivan, *Westminster Corridor,* plate 11). For valuable explication of the topography, with map, see Sullivan, *Westminster Corridor,* 99–108, 169, and map O.

34 There can be little doubt that Stowe Charter 32 and Stowe Charter 33 were produced in close association with each other. The parchment used is very similar for both charters, and it is possible they were cut from the same sheet. The main hand in Stowe charter 32 is hybrid, and seems curiously affected, but the dating clause (with which it ends) is in the same more consistently Square Minuscule hand as Stowe charter 33.

35 S 670 is fundamentally a 'Dunstan B' charter (above, n 29); S 1451 is cast in a narrative form, but has elements of 'Dunstan B' formulation (eg the sentence introducing the boundary clause); S 1450, MS 1 also has elements of 'Dunstan B' formulation. A charter recording Dunstan's grant of land at Hendon to Westminster Abbey (S 1295 (BCS 1263)) might deserve reconsideration as part of the same group. S 753 (BCS 1198), from Westminster Abbey Muniments VII (*OSFacs.* ii. Westminster 8), is probably to be regarded as another late-tenth-century forgery, produced at Westminster in the 'Dunstan B' mode, and naming Dunstan as the beneficiary of a grant in fact intended for Westminster; see Keynes, 'The

"Dunstan B" Charters', 178 n 55.

36 Above, n 22.

37 S 741 (BCS 1178) and 1294 (BCS 1179).

38 S Keynes, *An Atlas of Attestations in Anglo-Saxon Charters c. 670–1066*, I: *Tables*, ASNC Guides, Texts and Studies 5 (Cambridge, 2002), table LXI. While it is always dangerous to rely on negative evidence, the non-appearance of Wulfsige, as abbot, in the charters of the later 960s, 970s and 980s has cumulative significance.

39 S 877, *Anglo-Saxon Charters*, (ed) Robertson, 130 (no 63); *Charters of the New Minster, Winchester*, (ed) S M Miller (Oxford 2001), no 31.

40 Keynes, *Atlas of Attestations*, table LXI.

41 S 894 (B Thorpe, *Diplomatarium Anglicum Ævi Saxonici* (London, 1865), 296–8), preserved only as a copy entered in a fourteenth-century Westminster cartulary. For discussion, see Sullivan, *Westminster Corridor*, 63 and 164–5.

42 *cf* Goscelin's remarks on the existence, at Westminster as well as at Sherborne, of charters drawn up in Wulfsige's name (below, n 60).

43 The three grants were still associated with each other in the twelfth century, when they were combined to produce a composite record of the early stages in the endowment of Westminster Abbey: S 1450, MS 2 (BCS 1351), from Westminster Abbey Muniments VI (*Facsimiles of Anglo-Saxon Charters*, (ed) Keynes, no 36).

44 S 1293 (BCS 1050), from Westminster Abbey Muniments IX (*OSFacs.* ii. Westminster 5), incorporating a simplified version of the information about Westminster estates in the 'Telligraphus' of King Æthelred (most of which is wholly out of place in a charter dated 959, albeit 1 April 959). See also T A Heslop, 'Twelfth-Century Forgeries as Evidence for Earlier Seals: the Case of St Dunstan', *St Dunstan: His Life, Times and Cult*, (ed) N Ramsay *et al* (Woodbridge, 1992), 299–310, with plates 53 and 54 (a).

45 S 774 (BCS 1264; *The Crawford Collection of Early Charters and Documents*, (eds) A S Napier and W H Stevenson (Oxford, 1895), 12–18 (no 6), from Oxford, Bodleian Library, MS Eng. hist. a. 2, no IV (*Facsimiles of Anglo-Saxon Charters*, (ed) Keynes, no 37).

46 It was not considered inappropriate in the late tenth century for a bishop (or, in certain cases, an archbishop) to retain control of the abbey from which he had come: Dunstan, archbishop of Canterbury (959–88), retained an interest at Westminster; Oswald, archbishop of York (971–92), at Ramsey; Æthelgar, as bishop of Selsey (980–8), at the New Minster, Winchester; Sigeric, as bishop of Ramsbury (*c* 985–90), at St Augustine's, Canterbury; Ælfric, as bishop of Ramsbury (*c* 991–5), at St Albans; and Wulfsige, bishop of Sherborne, at Westminster. In some cases it may be that the bishopric conferred the status, and the abbey conferred the distinction and the wealth.

47 S Keynes, 'The Vikings in England, c. 790–1016', *The Oxford Illustrated History of the Vikings*, (ed) P Sawyer (Oxford, 1997), 48–82.

48 M Godden, 'Apocalypse and Invasion in Late Anglo-Saxon England', *From Anglo-Saxon to Early Middle English: Studies presented to E. G. Stanley*, (eds) M Godden *et al* (Oxford, 1994), 130–62; S Keynes, 'Apocalypse Then: England AD 1000', *Europe Around the Year 1000*, (ed) P Urbanczyk (Warsaw 2001), 247–70.

49 S Keynes, *The Diplomas of King Æthelred 'the Unready' 978–1016: a Study in their Use as Historical Evidence* (Cambridge, 1980), 186–93.

50 For Sigeric, see Keynes, *Diplomas*, 189–90, and N P Brooks, *The Early History of the Church of Canterbury: Christ Church from 597 to 1066* (Leicester, 1984), 279 and 281–

3. On the date of his death (28 October 994), see Keynes, *Diplomas*, 251–3; S Keynes, 'The Historical Context of the Battle of Maldon', *The Battle of Maldon AD 991*, (ed) D Scragg (Oxford, 1991b), 81–113, at 112, n 75; and below, n 79.

51 For Æthelgar, see *The Liber Vitae of the New Minster and Hyde Abbey, Winchester*, (ed) S Keynes, Early English Manuscripts in Facsimile 26 (Copenhagen, 1996b), 26–32. For the successive archbishops of Canterbury in Æthelred's reign (Æthelgar, Sigeric, Ælfric, Ælfheah, Lyfing), see N P Brooks, *The Early History of the Church of Canterbury: Christ Church from 597 to 1066* (Leicester, 1984), 278–87.

52 For Ælfsige, see *Liber Vitae*, (ed) Keynes, 32–3.

53 S Keynes, 'Cnut's Earls', *The Reign of Cnut: King of England, Denmark and Norway*, (ed) A R Rumble (London, 1994c), 43–88, at 67–8.

54 C A Jones, *Ælfric's Letter to the Monks of Eynsham*, Cambridge Studies in Anglo-Saxon England 24 (Cambridge, 1999), 4–15.

55 *Ælfric's Catholic Homilies: the First Series/Text*, (ed) P Clemoes, Early English Text Society s.s. 17 (Oxford, 1997); B Thorpe, *The Homilies of the Anglo-Saxon Church*, 2 vols. (London, 1844–6), I (with translation). For a translation of the Latin preface (ed Clemoes, 173–4; ed Thorpe, 1–2), see *Ælfric's Prefaces*, (ed) J Wilcox, Durham Medieval Texts 9 (Durham, 1995), 127–8.

56 *Ælfric's Catholic Homilies: the Second Series /Text*, (ed) M Godden, Early English Text Society s.s. 5 (Oxford, 1979); Thorpe, *Homilies of the Anglo-Saxon Church*, II (with translation). For a translation of the Latin preface (ed Godden, 1; ed Thorpe, 1–2), see *Ælfric's Prefaces*, (ed) Wilcox, 128–9. For the dating of Ælfric's 'First' and 'Second' series of homilies, see further below with n 79.

57 S 876: *Charters of Abingdon Abbey*, (ed) S E Kelly, 2 vols. (Oxford, 2000–1), no 124. For the view that S 876 is an authentic and original charter, which spawned a number of spurious imitations, see Keynes, *Diplomas of King Æthelred*, 98–102. Kelly (*Charters of Abingdon*, I, cxi–cxv) takes the view that the 'older' charters of the same group, in the names of Kings Eadwig and Edgar, are authentic, and that S 876 was drawn up, or fabricated, at Abingdon in imitation of them. For further discussion, see S Keynes, 'Wulfgar, abbot of Abingdon (990–1016), and King Æthelred's charter for Abingdon abbey (993)', *Anglo-Saxon England* (forthcoming).

58 Keynes, *Diplomas*, 101 nn 54 and 251. A digital facsimile of the charter, in colour, is available on the web site of the BA/RHS Joint Committee on Anglo-Saxon Charters (above, n 10).

59 Wulfsige attests S 880 and 881, both of which were issued in 994, before the death of Sigeric; see Keynes, *Atlas of Attestations*, table LXa.

60 Goscelin, *Vita S. Wlsini*, ch 4 (ed) Talbot, 76; trans Love, this volume.

61 S 891, and Keynes, *Atlas of Attestations*, table LXI.

62 *Wulfstan Cantor, Narratio metrica de Sancto Swithuno*, Epist. line 225: edited, with translation and commentary, in M Lapidge, *The Cult of St Swithun*, Winchester Studies 4.2 (Oxford, 2002), 390–1; *Frithegodi Monachi Breuiloquium Vitæ Beati Wilfredi et Wulfstani Cantoris Narratio Metrica de Sancto Swithuno*, (ed) A Campbell (Zürich, 1950), 65–177, at 65–75. See also R N Quirk, 'Winchester Cathedral in the Tenth Century', *Archaeological Journal* 114 (1959), 28–68, at 33 and 62.

63 For the (mid-eleventh-century) date of the surviving Anglo-Saxon fabric, see J H P Gibb, 'The Anglo-Saxon Cathedral at Sherborne' [with an appendix on Documentary evidence by R D H Gem], *Archaeological Journal* 132 (1975), 71–110, at 90–1 and 101.

64 H Gneuss, 'Liturgical Books in Anglo-Saxon England and their Old English

Terminology', *Learning and Literature in Anglo-Saxon England: Studies presented to Peter Clemoes*, (eds) M Lapidge and H Gneuss (Cambridge, 1985), 91–141, at 131–3; *The Liturgical Books of Anglo-Saxon England*, (ed) R W Pfaff, Old English Newsletter Subsidia 23 (Kalamazoo, MI, 1985), 87–98.

65 Paris, BN, MS lat. 943. For accounts of the manuscript, see: E Temple, *Anglo-Saxon Manuscripts 900–1066* (London, 1976), no 35; Ker, *Catalogue of Manuscripts containing Anglo-Saxon,* no 364; Brooks, *Church of Canterbury,* 244; *The Golden Age of Anglo-Saxon Art 966–1066,* (eds) J Backhouse, D H Turner and L Webster (London, 1984); *Anglo-Saxon Litanies of the Saints,* (ed) M Lapidge, Henry Bradshaw Society 106 (London, 1991), 79–80; D N Dumville, 'Liturgical Books for the Anglo-Saxon Episcopate: a Reconsideration', in his *Liturgy and the Ecclesiastical History of Late Anglo-Saxon England: Four Studies* (Woodbridge, 1992), 66–95, at 82–4; J Rosenthal, 'The Pontifical of St Dunstan', *St Dunstan,* (ed) Ramsay, 143–63; *Liturgical Books,* (ed) Pfaff, 89–90; and B Ebersperger, *Die angelsächsischen Handschriften in den Pariser Bibliotheken*, Anglistische Forschungen 261 (Heidelberg, 1999), 32–44 (no 5). I am grateful to Dr Richard Gameson for a sight of his notes on the manuscript, incorporating details of its collation.

66 For an explication of the iconography, see Rosenthal, 'The Pontifical of St Dunstan', 154–9.

67 *Councils & Synods with Other Documents Relating to the English Church I: A.D. 871–1204,* (eds) D Whitelock, M Brett and C N L Brooke, 2 pts (Oxford, 1981), i [871–1066], 88–92 (no 25).

68 Rosenthal ('The Pontifical of St Dunstan', 151) dates the manuscript post 973, because of its inclusion of a text of the 'Second Anglo-Saxon Coronation Ordo', in a particular form. There is, however, no reason to believe that this version of the ordo was devised specifically for the purposes of Edgar's coronation at Bath, in 973. The driving force behind successive versions of the coronation ordo was the need periodically to produce a new pontifical for a new bishop or archbishop, and it is hazardous, therefore, to associate a version of the text in a particular manuscript with the coronation of a particular king. It is apparent on other grounds that the 'Second' ordo itself originated in the late ninth or early tenth century.

69 Later additions on 1rv show that the book was at Notre Dame, Paris, before the end of the eleventh century; see below, n 150.

70 *Councils & Synods,* (eds) Whitelock *et al,* 226–9 (no 41).

71 For a reproduction in colour, see Rosenthal, 'The Pontifical of St Dunstan', plate IV.

72 For further discussion, see Rosenthal, 'The Pontifical of St Dunstan', 159–62.

73 See *Ælfric's Prefaces,* (ed) Wilcox, 123 (text) and 133 (translation), *cf* n 55.

74 *Councils & Synods,* (eds) Whitelock *et al,* 191–226 (no 40).

75 Cambridge, Corpus Christi College, MS 190, 295–308 (Ker, *Catalogue,* no 45, art 17).

76 Cambridge, University Library, MS Gg. 3. 28, fos 264r–266v (Ker, *Catalogue,* no 15, art 97).

77 Oxford, Bodleian Library, MS Junius 121, fos 101v–110r (Ker, *Catalogue,* no 338, art 26).

78 P Clemoes ('The Chronology of Ælfric's Works', *The Anglo-Saxons,* (ed) P Clemoes (Cambridge, 1959), 244) placed the letter in the period 992 x 1002 (where '1002' should be corrected to '*c* 998', as above); Whitelock (*Councils & Synods,* 191 and 193) placed it in the period 993 x *c* 995, soon after Wulfsige's translation to

Sherborne, *cf* n 81.

79 The dating of Ælfric's 'First' and 'Second' series of homilies (above, nn 55–6), turns in part on our assessment of the impact on Ælfric of the Viking raids in the early 990s, and in part on the date of the death of Archbishop Sigeric. It is clear from charter and other evidence that Sigeric died on 28 October 994 (above, n. 50); but the alternative view, that he died on that day in 995, has proved difficult to dislodge. In 1979 Godden (*Ælfric's Catholic Homilies; the second series*, xci–xciv) placed the First Series *c* 993–4, and the Second Series in 995; see also Godden, 'Apocalypse and Invasion', 133. For a reassessment of the evidence, see M Godden, *Ælfric's Catholic Homilies: Introduction, Commentary and Glossary,* Early English Text Society, Supplementary Series 18 (Oxford, 2000), xxix–xxxvi, placing both series more loosely in the period 990–5, within a year or two of each other.

80 Keynes, 'Historical Context of the Battle of Maldon', 99; Godden, 'Apocalypse and Invasion', 132–3.

81 *Ælfric's Lives of Saints*, (ed) W W Skeat, 4 pts, Early English Text Society, original series 76, 82, 94 and 114 (Oxford, 1881–1900), reptd 2 vols (London, 1966), based on BL Cotton Julius E vii (Ker, *Catalogue*, no 162). It is generally assumed that Ælfric published his 'Lives of the Saints' some time after the publication of his 'Second Series' of homilies (Clemoes, 'The Chronology of Ælfric's Works', 219–22), in the mid- or later 990s, and certainly before the death of Ealdorman Æthelweard (*c* 998). Godden's statement, to the effect that 'the collection in which it appears was begun after 995 and completed by 1002' ('Apocalypse and Invasion', 133), should be emended on historical grounds to read 'after 994' (death of Archbishop Sigeric) and 'by *c* 998' (death of Ealdorman Æthelweard).

82 *Lives of Saints*, (ed) Skeat, I, 282–306 (no XIII); see also EHD, (ed) Whitelock, no 239 (f)), and Clemoes, 'Chronology of Ælfric's Works', 220–1. The text in Julius E vii (Ker, *Catalogue*, no 162, art 17) is collated by Skeat with an 'earlier' version of the homily in Cambridge, Corpus Christi College, MS 162 (Ker, *Catalogue*, no 38, art 6), and with versions in two other manuscripts (Ker, *Catalogue*, nos 21, art 15, and 57, art 68).

83 For a most instructive discussion of the homily, in the context of other works by Ælfric, see Godden, 'Apocalypse and Invasion in Late Anglo-Saxon England', 133–7.

84 See *Councils & Synods*, (eds) Whitelock *et al*, 194–5. Provision for the mass 'Contra paganos' was subsequently incorporated in VII Æthelred, a programme of public prayer drawn up by Archbishop Wulfstan in response to the Viking invasion of 1009.

85 For indications that some churchmen in tenth-century England might have attached particular significance to the year 1000, see Keynes, 'Apocalypse Then: England AD 1000', 264–6.

86 Keynes, 'Apocalypse Then: England AD 1000', 264.

87 Goscelin, *Vita S. Yvonis,* ch 3, cited in S Keynes, 'King Alfred the Great and Shaftesbury Abbey', *Studies in the Early History of Shaftesbury Abbey*, (ed) L Keen (Dorchester, 1999b), 17–72, at 50.

88 Goscelin, *Translatio S. Edithae*, ch 1 (ed A Wilmart, 'La légende de Ste Édith en prose et vers par le moine Goscelin', *Analecta Bollandiana* 56 (1938), 5–101 [*Vita*] and 265–307 [*Translatio*], at 265–8; *Writing the Wilton Women,* ed S Hollis (Turnhout, 2004), 69–71.

89 *Passio S. Eadwardi*, cited in Keynes, 'King Alfred the Great and Shaftesbury

Abbey', 52–3.

90   The presentation of the evidence by D Knowles, *The Monastic Order in England*
     (2nd edition), (Cambridge, 1963), Appendix IV, 697–701, is most instructive (but
     remains in need of revision in points of detail). See also *Heads of Religious House*,
     (eds) Knowles *et al*; and Keynes, *Atlas of Attestations*.

91   *Regularis Concordia*, Proemium, ch 9 (*Regularis Concordia/The Monastic Agreement of
     the Monks and Nuns of the English Nation*, (ed) T Symons (London, 1953), 6.

92   For the distinctively English cathedral-monastery, see P Wormald, 'Æthelwold
     and his Continental Counterparts: Contact, Comparison, Contrast', *Bishop
     Æthelwold: His Career and Influence*, (ed) B Yorke (Woodbridge, 1988), 13–42, at 37–
     8. For a lucid exposition of the wider context, see J Barrow, 'English Cathedral
     Communities and Reform in the Late Tenth and the Eleventh Centuries', *Anglo-
     Norman Durham*, (eds) D Rollason, M Harvey and M Prestwich (Woodbridge,
     1994), 25–39.

93   S 731: Keynes, *Facsimiles of Anglo-Saxon Charters*, no 40.

94   For further discussion, see P H Sawyer, 'Charters of the Reform Movement: the
     Worcester Archive', *Tenth-Century Studies*, (ed) D Parsons (Chichester, 1975), 84–
     93 and 228, and J Barrow, 'The Community of Worcester Cathedral, 961 – c.
     1100', *St Oswald of Worcester*, (eds) N Brooks and C R E Cubitt (London, 1996),
     84–99.

95   For more detailed discussion, see *Liber Vitae*, (ed) Keynes, 64–5, and *Atlas of
     Attestations*, table LXXVI.

96   ASC, MS F, s.a. 995, and S 914, dated '1006'.

97   Knowles, *Monastic Order*, 696–7. See also Korhammer, 'Origin of the Bosworth
     Psalter', 181–2; Brooks, *Early History of the Church of Canterbury*, 255–60; and M
     Lapidge, 'B. and the Vita S. Dunstani', *St Dunstan*, (eds) Ramsay *et al*, 247–59, at
     258; Barlow, *English Church 1000–1066*, 222–3.

98   ASC, MSS CDE, s.a. 998.

99   S 895: *Charters of Sherborne*, (ed) O'Donovan, no 11.

100 *Regularis Concordia*, Proemium, ch 9 (*Regularis Concordia*, (ed) Symons, 6).

101 There is a full and effective discussion of the charter in *Charters of Sherborne*, (ed)
     O'Donovan, 41–4; see also Keynes, *The Diplomas of King Æthelred*, 256, and *Councils
     and Synods*, I.i, (ed) Whitelock, 193 n 7.

102 There was another copy of the charter in a twelfth-century manuscript of
     uncertain origin (? Worcester), badly damaged by fire in 1731: BL Cotton Otho A.
     xviii, fo 132r, printed in *Anglia Sacra*, (ed) H Wharton, 2 vols. (London, 1691) I,
     170–1. The same manuscript contained a copy of King William I's diploma for
     Bury St Edmunds, concerning the abbey's freedom from episcopal interference
     (*Regesta Regum Anglo-Normannorum/The Acta of William I (1066–1087)*, (ed) D Bates
     (Oxford, 1998), 201–9 (no 39)). See also *Charters of Sherborne*, (ed) O'Donovan,
     xviii–xix.

103 F Wormald, 'The Sherborne "Chartulary"', *Fritz Saxl: a Volume of Memorial Essays*,
     (ed) D J Gordon (London, 1957), 101–19, at 108–9; see also *Charters of Sherborne*,
     (ed) O'Donovan, xiv–xviii.

104 For an important discussion of the Sherborne estate, see K Barker, 'Sherborne in
     Dorset: an Early Ecclesiastical Settlement and its Estate', *Anglo-Saxon Studies in
     Archaeology and History* 3 (1984), 1–33, esp. 10–11; see also R Faith, *The English
     Peasantry and the Growth of Lordship* (London, 1997), 18–22. A remark in Goscelin's
     Vita S. Wulsini, ch 18 (ed) Talbot, 83; trans Love, this volume) suggests that

Wulfsige had been concerned to apportion estates between the monks and the bishop; see also S 1382, in *Charters of Sherborne*, (ed) O'Donovan, 45–6 (no 12).

104a For the suggestion that Corscombe is represented in the charter by the reference to twenty hides at Wulfheardigstoke, see Barker ('Sherborne in AD 998', this volume); but *cf* below (The church of Sherborne in the eleventh century) which might indicate that Corscombe was not in the abbey's hands at the time.

105 *Charters of Sherborne*, (ed) O'Donovan, 42. See also D Hill, 'An Anglo-Saxon Beacon System', *Names, Places and People: an Onomastic Miscellany in Memory of John McNeal Dodgson*, (eds) A R Rumble and A D Mills (Stamford, 1997), 157–65, at 164.

106 S 939: *Anglo-Saxon Wills*, (ed) D Whitelock (Cambridge, 1930), 44–6 (no XVI.2).

107 Keynes, 'King Alfred the Great and Shaftesbury Abbey', 52–3.

108 S 899: *Charters of Shaftesbury Abbey*, (ed) S E Kelly, Anglo-Saxon Charters 5 (Oxford, 1996), 114–22 (no 29).

109 Paris, BN Lat. 943 (Ker, *Catalogue*, no 364), fos 156r–160r, characterised by Ker as written in 'a fine square Anglo-Saxon minuscule of s. x/xi'. Edited by Ebersperger, *Die angelsächsischen Handschriften in den Pariser Bibliotheken*, 236–62. There are other texts in Ker, *Catalogue*, nos 283, art 8, and 331, art 77. Clemoes assigns the composition of the homily to Ælfric's 'middle period' ('Chronology of Ælfric's Works', 238).

110 Paris, BN Lat. 943 (Ker, *Catalogue*, no 364), fo 170r: *Councils and Synods* I.i, (ed) Whitelock, 230–1 (no 42) and 237 (no 43.IX). See also *Memorials of St Dunstan*, (ed) W Stubbs, Rolls Series (London, 1874), 406–9. For the bishop's role in such matters, *cf* II Edmund, ch 4.

111 For the place of his death, see Goscelin, *Vita S. Wlsini*, ch 6 (ed) Talbot, 77; trans Love, this volume. The day is given in the 'Red Book of Darley' (see below); *cf* Goscelin, *Vita S. Wlsini*, ch 9 (ed Talbot, 79; trans Love, this volume). The year is established by analysis of charters, in relation to obits (Keynes, *Diplomas*, 257–8).

112 Goscelin, *Vita S. Wlsini*, chs 6–9 (ed) Talbot, 77–9; trans Love, this volume.

113 WM, *GP* ii. 81 (ed Hamilton, 178–9).

114 The obit of 'Bishop Æthelric, monk of Glastonbury' was commemorated in Glastonbury (8 May); see Scott, *Early History of Glastonbury*, 138.

115 For the terminal date, see Keynes, *Diplomas*, 264 n 64, and *Charters of Sherborne*, (ed) O'Donovan, 50–1.

116 Paris, BN Lat. 943 (Ker, *Catalogue*, no 364), fo 1v. Heahmund is wrongly called 'Ealhmund', presumably because the scribe was infected by Ealhstan.

117 Goscelin, *Vita S. Wlsini*, chs 9–11 (ed) Talbot, 78–80; trans Love, this volume.

118 Goscelin, *Vita S. Wlsini*, ch 12 (ed) Talbot, 80; trans Love, this volume.

119 Goscelin, *Vita S. Wlsini*, chs 12–13 (ed) Talbot, 80–1; trans Love, this volume; Gibb, 'The Anglo-Saxon Cathedral at Sherborne', 106.

120 Paris, BN Lat. 943 (Ker, *Catalogue*, no 364), fo 170v: *Anglo-Saxon Writs*, (ed) Harmer, 266–70 (no 63); *Charters of Sherborne*, (ed) O'Donovan, 46–8 (no 13).

121 S 1422: *Anglo-Saxon Charters*, (ed) Robertson, 146–8 (no 74), and *Charters of Sherborne*, (ed) O'Donovan, 49–51 (no 14). The document was probably drawn up *c* 1012; and note that in it Æthelmær is styled 'ealdorman'.

122 S 933: *Charters of Sherborne*, (ed) O'Donovan, 51–4 (no 15). *Cf* M K Lawson, *Cnut: the Danes in England in the Early Eleventh Century* (London, 1993), 39 ('the attacks and plunderings of the evil Danes').

123 Keynes, *Diplomas of King Æthelred*, 213–14.

124 S 933: *Charters of Sherborne*, (ed) O'Donovan, 51–4 (no 15). For the possibility that Bishop Æthelsige II died in 1016, see Goscelin, *Vita S. Wlsini,* ch 16 (ed) Talbot, 82; trans Love, this volume, and Barlow, *English Church 1000–1066*, 222 n 1.

125 For further details, see S Keynes, 'The Lost Cartulary of Abbotsbury Abbey', *Anglo-Saxon England* 18 (1989), 207–43, at 230–1, and 'King Alfred the Great and Shaftesbury Abbey', 55.

126 Goscelin, *Vita S. Wlsini,* ch 16 (ed) Talbot, 82; trans Love, this volume; see also Barlow, *English Church 1000–1066*, 223 n. 5. *Cf Charters of St Augustine's, Canterbury*, (ed) S E Kelly (Oxford, 1995), xix.

127 ASC, MSS CDE, s.a. 1011; see Lawson, *Cnut*, 150 n 141.

128 S 1474: *Anglo-Saxon Charters*, (ed) Robertson, 200–2 (no 105), and *Charters of Sherborne*, (ed) O'Donovan, 59–61 (no 17).

129 Goscelin, *Vita S. Wlsini,* ch 16 (ed) Talbot, 82; trans Love, this volume.

130 Goscelin, *Vita S. Wlsini,* ch 14 (ed) Talbot, 81; trans Love, this volume; Gibb, 'The Anglo-Saxon Cathedral at Sherborne', 106–7. For the contemporary perception of Cnut and Emma *as a pair*, see Keynes, 'Queen Emma and the *Encomium Emmae Reginae*', *Encomium Emmae Reginae*, (ed) A Campbell, Camden Classic Reprints 4 (Cambridge, 1998), xiii–lxxxvii, at xxiv–xxvi.

131 S 975: *Charters of Sherborne*, (ed) O'Donovan, no 16. Lawson, *Cnut*, 66 and 113.

132 The estate had been restored to Sherborne by King Æthelred in 1014 (above, n 124); so it looks as if Cnut had taken it into his own hands.

133 Goscelin, *Vita S. Wlsini,* ch 6 (ed) Talbot, 77–8; trans Love, this volume; see also WM, *GP*, ii. 81 (ed Hamilton, 178–9; trans Preest, 118–19).

134 Goscelin, *Vita S. Wlsini,* chs 17–18 (ed) Talbot, 82–3; trans Love, this volume.

135 See Gibb, 'The Anglo-Saxon Cathedral at Sherborne', 107–9. Remarkably (although not exceptionally), the seal-matrix still existed at Sherborne in the sixteenth century, and was used for sealing the abbey's Deed of Surrender in 1539: London, PRO, E322/212, now a fragment.

136 Goscelin, *Vita S. Wlsini,* chs 21–5 (ed) Talbot, 84–5; trans Love, this volume; Gibb, 'The Anglo-Saxon Cathedral at Sherborne', 109.

137 WM, *GP* ii. 82 (ed Hamilton, 179; trans Preest, 119–20.

138 Gibb, 'The Anglo-Saxon Cathedral at Sherborne', 101–2. For Ælfwold, see also Barlow, *English Church 1000–1066*, 223–4, and Lapidge, *Cult of St Swithun*, 185.

139 *Miracula S. Swithuni*, ch 44 (Lapidge, *Cult of St Swithun*, 680–1); WM, *GP* ii. 82 (ed Hamilton, 179; trans Preest, 119–20). See also Gibb, 'The Anglo-Saxon Cathedral at Sherborne', 102 and 109. On the fate of the statue, see Fowler, *Mediaeval Sherborne*, 66.

140 Oxford, Bodleian Library, MS. Auct. F. 2. 14 (S.C. 2657): Ker, *Catalogue*, 353–4 (no 295); M Lapidge, in *Manuscripts at Oxford*, (eds) A C de la Mare and B C Barker-Benfield (Oxford, 1980), 21; and Lapidge, *Cult of St Swithun*, 364 and 366–7.

141 The assumption derives ultimately from WM, *GP* ii 83 (ed) Hamilton, 183; trans Preest, 121–2). For Herman and Goscelin, see Barlow, *Life of Edward*, xlix and 133–4.

142 See further below, n 147.

143 Cambridge, Corpus Christi College, MS 422. See *English Kalendars before A.D. 1100*, (ed) F Wormald, Henry Bradshaw Society 72 (London, 1934), no 14; *Anglo-Saxon Litanies*, (ed) Lapidge, 66; Dumville, 'Liturgical Books for the Anglo-Saxon Episcopate: a Reconsideration', 74–5; *The Liturgical Books of Anglo-Saxon England*,

(ed) R W Pfaff, Old English Newsletter Subsidia 23 (Binghamton, NY, 1995), 21–4; M Budny, *Insular, Anglo-Saxon, and Early Anglo-Norman Manuscript Art at Corpus Christi College, Cambridge: an Illustrated Catalogue* (Two volumes) (Kalamazoo, MI, 1997) I, 645–66 (no 44), and II, plates 604–8; and R Rushforth, *An Atlas of Saints in Anglo-Saxon Calendars*, ASNC Guides, Texts and Studies 6 (Cambridge, 2002), no 19.

144 Budny, *Insular, Anglo-Saxon, and Early Anglo-Norman Manuscript Art*, II, plate 604 (showing the calendar for January). The book was also provided with a distinctive daily mass for St Swithun; see Lapidge, *Cult of St Swithun*, 80–2. For full details of saints entered in calendars in tenth- and eleventh-century manuscripts, laid out in tabular form, see Rushforth, *Atlas of Saints*.

145 WM, *GP*, ii.82 (ed Hamilton, 180; trans Preest, 19–20); see also Kirby, 'Notes on the Saxon Bishops of Sherborne', 219–22.

146 For Herman's exile and return, see JW, s.a. 1055 and 1058 (*The Chronicle of John of Worcester*, II: *The Annals from 450 to 1066*, (eds) R R Darlington and P McGurk (Oxford, 1995), 578 and 584).

147 S Keynes, 'Giso, Bishop of Wells', *Anglo-Norman Studies* 19 (1996c), 203–71, at 208–9, with further references.

148 Goscelin, *Vita S. Wlsini*, ch 20 (ed) Talbot, 83–4; trans Love, this volume.

149 BL Cotton Tiberius C. i: Ker, *Catalogue*, 260–1 (no 197). The manuscript was later moved from Sherborne to Salisbury. See N R Ker, 'Three Old English Texts in a Salisbury Pontifical, Cotton Tiberius C I', *The Anglo-Saxons*, (ed) Clemoes, 262–79, and T Webber, *Scribes and Scholars at Salisbury Cathedral c. 1075–c. 1125* (Oxford, 1992), 10 and 143–4.

150 It has been said that Wulfsige 'created a library at Sherborne' (Barlow, *English Church 1000–1066*, 223). The evidence is a late eleventh-century booklist in the Pontifical of St Dunstan, which in fact relates to the library of the cathedral church of Notre-Dame, Paris (Ker, *Catalogue*, 438).

151 For Goscelin's *Life*, see Talbot, 'The Life of Saint Wulsin of Sherborne by Goscelin', 68–73; Barlow, *Life of Edward*, 135; and esp. Love, 'The Life of St Wulfsige of Sherborne by Goscelin of Saint-Bertin', this volume.

152 BL Cotton Faustina A. ii fos 14–23 and 23v.

153 BL Cotton Faustina A. ii, fos 24r–25r. It should be noted that the list includes a certain 'Brichtelm' between Ælfwold I and Ælthelsige I. Ælfwold I died in 978, and was buried at Sherborne (ASC); Æthelsige I attests for the first time in 979 (S 834). One might suppose, therefore, that Brihthelm was chosen as bishop, but died before he could formally take up his office. *Cf* Keynes, 'King Alfred the Great and Shaftesbury Abbey', 58 and n 148.

154 BL Cotton Faustina A. ii, fo 25rv. See *Charters of Sherborne*, (ed) O'Donovan, xx, xxxvii–liii and 81–2.

155 The manuscript, long in the possession of the dukes of Northumberland, was secured for the British Library in 1998 and is now BL Add. MS 74236. For an excellent (and well illustrated) account of the manuscript, in all its glory, see J Backhouse, *The Sherborne Missal* (London, 1999) which has now been joined by an educational CD-ROM. For an earlier account, see J A Herbert, *The Sherborne Missal: Reproductions of Full Pages and Details of Ornament from the Missal Executed between the Years 1396 and 1407 for Sherborne Abbey Church and now preserved in the Library of the Duke of Northumberland at Alnwick Castle* (Oxford, for the Roxburghe Club, 1920).

156 Backhouse, *Sherborne Missal*, 34–5, with illustration on 42 (Aldhelm *et al*); for Bishop 'Brithelin', ie Brihthelm, see above, n 126.

157 Backhouse, *Sherborne Missal*, 35 and 37, with illustrations on 47 (King Cenwalh, King Cynewulf) and 48 (King Eadwig, King Edgar). The texts are printed by Herbert, *Sherborne Missal*, 24–5; see also *Charters of Sherborne*, (ed) O'Donovan, xxi and xxxvii–liii.

158 Backhouse, *Sherborne Missal*, 41 and 44–54.

159 Reproduced in Backhouse, *Sherborne Missal*, 56. A colour postcard showing the main part of the scene was published by the Friends of Sherborne Abbey in 1998.

160 Herbert, *Sherborne Missal*, 26.

161 Fowler, *Mediaeval Sherborne*, 61. The composition as a whole is then interpreted as a subtle way of assuring Richard Mitford, bishop of Salisbury (1396–1407), and patron of the book, that the canons expelled by Wulfsige from Sherborne had not been left out in the cold.

162 Backhouse, *Sherborne Missal*, 44–5.

Bibliography

Ælfric's Lives of the Saints, W W Skeat (ed), 1881–1900 (4 parts, reprinted in two volumes, 1996). Early English Text Society. London.

Ælfric's Prefaces, J Wilcox (ed), 1995, Durham Medieval Texts 9. Durham.

Ælfric's Catholic Homilies: the First Series/Text, P Clemoes (ed), 1997, Early English Text Society s.s. 17. Oxford.

Ælfric's Catholic Homilies: the Second Series /Text, M Godden (ed), 1979, Early English Text Society s.s. 5. Oxford.

Backhouse, J, 1999, *The Sherborne Missal*. London.

Backhouse, J, Turner, D H, and Webster, L (eds), *The Golden Age of Anglo-Saxon Art 966–1066*. London.

Barker, K, 1982, The early history of Sherborne. In S M Pearce (ed), *The Early Church in Western Britain and Ireland*, British Archaeological Reports, British Series, 102. Oxford, 77–116.

Barker, K, 1984, Sherborne in Dorset: an early ecclesiastical settlement and its estate. *Anglo-Saxon Studies in Archaeology and History* 3, 1–33.

Barlow, F, 1979, *The English Church, 1000–1066* (2nd edition). London.

Barlow, F (ed), 1992, *The Life of King Edward Who Rests at Westminster* (2nd edition). Oxford.

Barrow, J, 1994, English Cathedral Communities and Reform in the Late Tenth and Eleventh Centuries. In D Rollason, M Harvey and M Prestwich (eds), *Anglo-Norman Durham*. Woodbridge, 25–39.

Barrow, J, 1996, The Community of Worcester Cathedral, 961–c. 1100. In N Brooks and C R E Cubitt (eds), *St Oswald of Worcester*. London, 84–99.

Bates, D (ed), 1998, *Regesta Regum Anglo-Normannorum/The Acta of William I (1066–1087)*. Oxford.

Bede, *Historia ecclesiastica gentis Anglorum (Ecclesiastical History of the English People)*, B Colgrave and R A G Mynors (eds), 1969. Oxford.

Brooks, N P, 1984, *The Early History of the Church of Canterbury: Christ Church from 597 to 1066*. Leicester.

Budny, M, 1997, *Insular, Anglo-Saxon, and Early Anglo-Norman Manuscript Art at Corpus Christi College, Cambridge: an Illustrated Catalogue* (Two volumes). Kalamazoo, MI.

Campbell, A (ed), 1950, *Frithegodi Monachi Breuiloquium Vitae Beati Wilfredi et Wulstani Cantoris Narratio Metrica de Sancto Swithuno.* Zurich.

Clemoes, P, 1959, The Chronology of Ælfric's Works. In P Clemoes (ed), *The Anglo-Saxons.* Cambridge, 212–47.

Darlington, R R, and McGurk, P (eds), 1995, *The Chronicle of John of Worcester, II: the Annals from 450 to 1066.* Oxford.

Dumville, D N, 1992, Liturgical Books for the Anglo-Saxon Episcopate: a reconsideration. In his *Liturgy and the Ecclesiastical History of Late Anglo-Saxon England: Four Studies.* Woodbridge, 66–95.

Ebersperger, B, 1999, *Die angelsächsischen Handschriften in den Pariser Bibliotheken,* Anglistische Forschungen 261. Heidelberg.

Faith, R, 1997, *The English Peasantry and the Growth of Lordship.* London.

Farmer, D H, 1987, *The Oxford Dictionary of Saints* (2nd Edition). Oxford.

Field, J, 1996, *Kingdom, Power and Glory: a Historical Guide to Westminster Abbey.* London.

Fowler, J, 1951, *Mediaeval Sherborne.* Dorchester.

Gem, R, 1986, The Origins of the Abbey. In C Wilson *et al* (eds), *Westminster Abbey.* New Bell Cathedral Guides. London, 6–21.

Gibb, J H P, 1975, The Anglo-Saxon Cathedral at Sherborne [with an appendix on the documentary evidence by R D H Gem]. *Archaeological Journal* 132, 71–110.

Gibb, J H P, 1984, *The Book of Sherborne* (2nd edition). Buckingham.

Gneuss, H, 1985, Liturgical Books in Anglo-Saxon England and their Old English Terminology. In M Lapidge and H Gneuss (eds), *Learning and Literature in Anglo-Saxon England, Studies presented to Peter Clemoes.* Cambridge, 91–141.

Godden, M, 1994, Apocalyse and Invasion in Late Anglo-Saxon England. In M Godden *et al* (eds), *From Anglo-Saxon to Early Middle English: Studies presented to E G Stanley.* Oxford, 130–62.

Godden, M, 2000, *Ælfric's Catholic Homilies: Introduction, Commentary and Glossary.* Early English Text Society, Supplementary Series 18. Oxford.

Goscelin, *Translatio S. Edithae.* In A Wilmart (ed), 1938, La légende de Ste Édith en prose at vers par le moine Goscelin, *Analecta Bollandiana* 56, 5–101, and 265–307.

Harmer, F E, 1952, *Anglo-Saxon Writs.* Manchester.

Hart, C R, 1975, *The Early Charters of Northern England and the North Midlands.* Leicester.

Harvey, B, 1977, *Westminster Abbey and its Estates in the Middle Ages.* Oxford.

Herbert, J A, 1920, *The Sherborne Missal: Reproductions of Full Pages and Details of Ornament from the Missal executed between the Years 1396 and 1407 for Sherborne Abbey Church and now preserved in the Library of the Duke of Northumberland at Alnwick Castle.* Oxford, for the Roxburghe Club.

Heslop, T A, 1992, Twelfth-Century Forgeries as Evidence for Earlier Seals: the case of St Dunstan. In N Ramsay *et al* (eds), *St Dunstan: His Life, Times and Cult.* Woodbridge, 299–310.

Hill, D, 1997, An Anglo-Saxon Beacon System. In A R Rumble and A D Mills (eds), *Names, Places and People: an Onomastic Miscellany in Memory of John McNeal Dodgson.* Stamford, 157–65.

Jones, C A, 1999, *Ælfric's Letter to the Monks of Eynsham.* Cambridge Studies in Anglo-Saxon England, 24. Cambridge.

Kelly, S E (ed), 1995, *Charters of St Augustine's Canterbury.* Anglo-Saxon Charters 4. Oxford.

Kelly, S E (ed), 1996, *Charters of Shaftesbury Abbey.* Anglo-Saxon Charters 5. Oxford.

Kelly, S E, 2000–1, *Charters of Abingdon Abbey* (Two volumes). Anglo-Saxon Charters

7–8. Oxford.

Ker, N R, 1957, *Catalogue of Manuscripts containing Anglo-Saxon.* Oxford.

Ker, N R, 1959, Three Old English Texts in a Salisbury Pontifical, Cotton Tiberius C I. In P Clemoes (ed), *The Anglo-Saxons.* Cambridge, 262–79.

Keynes, S, 1980, *The Diplomas of King Æthelred 'the Unready' 978–1016: a Study in their Use as Historical Evidence.* Cambridge.

Keynes, S, 1989, The Lost Cartulary of Abbotsbury Abbey. *Anglo-Saxon England* 18, 207–43.

Keynes, S (ed), 1991a, *Facsimiles of Anglo-Saxon Charters.* Oxford.

Keynes, S, 1991b, The Historical Context of the Battle of Maldon. In D Scragg (ed), *The Battle of Maldon AD 991.* Oxford, 81–113.

Keynes, S, 1992, *Anglo-Saxon Manuscripts and Other Items of Related Interest in the Library Trinity College Cambridge.* Old English Newsletter, Subsidia 18. Binghamton New York.

Keynes, S, 1994a, The West Saxon Charters of King Æthelwulf and his Sons. *English Historical Review* 109, 1109–49.

Keynes, S, 1994b, The 'Dunstan B' Charters. *Anglo-Saxon England* 23, 165–93.

Keynes, S, 1994c, Cnut's Earls. In A R Rumble (ed), *The Reign of Cnut: King of England, Denmark and Norway.* London, 43–88.

Keynes, S, 1996a, On the Authenticity of Asser's *Life of King Alfred. Journal of Ecclesiastical History* 47, 529–51.

Keynes, S (ed), 1996b, *The Liber Vitae of the New Minster and Hyde Abbey, Winchester.* In Early English Manuscripts in Facsimile 26. Copenhagen.

Keynes, S, 1996c, Giso, Bishop of Wells. *Anglo-Norman Studies* 19, 203–71.

Keynes, S, 1997, The Vikings in England c. 790–1016. In P Sawyer (ed), *The Oxford Illustrated History of the Vikings.* Oxford, 48–82.

Keynes, S, 1998, Queen Emma and the *Encomium Emmae Reginae, Encomium Emmae Reginae,* A Campbell (ed). Camden Classic Reprints 4. Cambridge.

Keynes, S, 1999a, Asser. In M Lapidge *et al* (eds), *The Blackwell Encyclopaedia of Anglo-Saxon England.* Oxford, 48–50.

Keynes, S, 1999b, King Alfred the Great and Shaftesbury Abbey. In L Keen (ed), *Studies in the Early History of Shaftesbury Abbey.* Dorchester, 17–72.

Keynes, S, 2001, Apocalypse Then: England AD 1000. In P Urbanczyk (ed), *Europe Around the Year 1000.* Warsaw.

Keynes, S, 2002, *An Atlas of Attestations in Anglo-Saxon Charters c. 670–1066.* ASNC Guides, Texts and Studies 5. Cambridge.

Keynes, S, forthcoming, Wulfgar, Abbot of Abingdon (990–1016). King Aethelred's charter for Abingdon Abbey (993). *Anglo-Saxon England.*

Keynes, S, and Lapidge, M, 1983, *Alfred the Great: Asser's 'Life of King Alfred' and Other Contemporary Sources.* Harmondsworth.

Kirby, D P, 1965, Notes on the Saxon Bishops of Sherborne. *Proceedings of the Dorset Natural History and Archaeological Society* 87, 213–22.

Knowles, D, 1963, *The Monastic Order in England* (2nd Edition). Cambridge.

Knowles, D, Brooke, C N L, and London, V C M (eds), 2001, *The Heads of Religious Houses in England and Wales 940–1216* (2nd Edition). Cambridge.

Korhammer, P M, 1973, The Origin of the Bosworth Psalter. *Anglo-Saxon England* 2, 173–87.

Lapidge, M, 1991, *Anglo-Saxon Litanies of the Saints.* Henry Bradshaw Society 106. London.

Lapidge, M, 1992, B and the Vita S. Dunstani. In N Ramsay *et al* (eds), *St Dunstan: His Life, Times and Cult.* Woodbridge, 247–59.

Lapidge, M, 1999, Aldhelm. In M Lapidge *et al* (eds), *The Blackwell Encyclopaedia of Anglo-Saxon England.* Oxford, 25–7.

Lapidge, M, 2002, *The Cult of St Swithun.* Winchester Studies 4.2. Oxford.

Lawson, M K, 1993, *Cnut: the Danes in England in the Early Eleventh Century.* London

de la Mare, A C, and Barker-Benfield, B C (eds), 1980, *Manuscripts at Oxford.* Oxford.

Mason, E, 1988, *Westminster Abbey Charters 1066–c 1214.* London.

Miller, S M (ed), 2001, *Charters of the New Minster, Winchester.* Oxford.

Napier, A S, and Stevenson, W H (eds), 1895, *The Crawford Collection of Early Charters and Documents.* Oxford.

O'Donovan, M A, 1972, Studies in the History of the Diocese of Sherborne. Unpublished PhD dissertation, University of Cambridge.

O'Donovan, M A, 1988, *Charters of Sherborne.* Oxford.

Okasha, E, 1971, *Hand-list of Anglo-Saxon Non-Runic Inscriptions.* Cambridge.

Pfaff, R W (ed), 1985, *The Liturgical Books of Anglo-Saxon England.* Old English Newsletter Subsidia 23. Kalamazoo, MI.

Preest, D (trans), 2002, *William of Malmesbury: the Deeds of the Bishops of England (Gesta Pontificum Anglorum).* Woodbridge.

Quirk, R N, 1959, Winchester Cathedral in the Tenth Century. *Archaeological Journal* 114, 28–68.

Robertson, A J, 1956, *Anglo-Saxon Charters* (2nd edition). Cambridge.

Robinson, J A, 1909, *The History of Westminster Abbey by John Flete.* Cambridge.

Rosenthal, J, 1992, The Pontifical of St Dunstan. In N Ramsay *et al* (eds), *St Dunstan: His Life, Times and Cult.* Woodbridge, 143–63.

Rushforth, R, 2002, *An Atlas of Saints in Anglo-Saxon Calendars.* ASNC Guides, Texts and Studies 6. Cambridge.

Sawyer, P H, 1968, *Anglo-Saxon Charters: An Annotated List and Bibliography.* London.

Sawyer, P H, 1975, Charters of the Reform Movement: the Worcester Archive. In D Parsons (ed), *Tenth Century Studies.* Chichester, 84–93.

Scholz, B W, 1964, Sulcard of Westminster: 'Prologus de Construccione Westmonasterii'. *Traditio* 20, 59–91.

Scott, J, 1981, *The Early History of Glastonbury: an Edition, Translation and Study of William of Malmesbury's 'De Antiquitate Glastonie Ecclesie'.* Woodbridge.

Stubbs, W, 1874, *Memorials of St Dunstan.* Rolls Series, London.

Sullivan, D, 1994, *The Westminster Corridor: an Exploration of the Anglo-Saxon History of Westminster Abbey and its Nearby Lands and People.* London.

Symons, T (ed), 1953, *Regularis Concordia/The Monastic Agreement of the Monks and Nuns of the English Nation.* London.

Talbot, C H, 1959, The Life of Saint Wulfsin of Sherborne by Goscelin. *Revue Bénédictine* 69, 1–2, and 68–85.

Temple, E, 1976, *Anglo-Saxon Manuscripts 900–1066.* London.

Thorpe, B, 1844–6, *The Homilies of the Anglo-Saxon Church* (Two volumes). London.

Thorpe, B, 1865, *Diplomatarium Anglicum Ævi Saxonici.* London.

Webber, T, 1992, *Scribes and Scholars at Salisbury Cathedral c. 1975–1125.* Oxford.

Wharton, H, 1691, *Anglia Sacra* (Two volumes). London.

Whitelock, D (ed), 1930, *Anglo-Saxon Wills.* Cambridge.

Whitelock, D, 1981, Some Anglo-Saxon Bishops of London. In *History, Law and Literature in the 10th and 11th Centuries* (Volume 2). London.

Whitelock, D, Brett, M, and Brooke, C N L (eds), 1981, *Councils and Synods with Other Documents Relating to the English Church I: AD 871–1204* (2 Parts; Part 1, *871–1066*). Oxford.

William of Malmesbury, *Gesta Pontificum Anglorum*, N E S A Hamilton (ed), 1870, Rolls Series. London.

Wormald, F (ed), 1934, *English Kalendars before AD 1100*. Henry Bradshaw Society, 72. London.

Wormald, F, 1957, The Sherborne 'Chartulary'. In D J Gordon (ed), *Fritz Saxl: a Volume of Memorial Essays*. London, 101–19.

Wormald, P, 1988, Æthelwold and his Continental Counterparts: Contact, Comparison, Contrast. In B Yorke (ed), *Bishop Æthelwold: his Career and Influence*. Woodbridge, 13–42.

9. Saints' Lives in Anglo-Saxon Wessex

Barbara Yorke

By the time the West Saxons were introduced to Christianity in the seventh century the writing of saints' *Lives* (or 'hagiographies' or Latin *vitae* as they are often known) was a well-established literary genre. The convention of the Latin *vita* was to begin with portents at the birth of a future saint, followed by coverage of their early education and renunciation of secular life for the religious; details of their ecclesiastical career would then be given, including the performance of miracles and further portents as death approached as foreseen by the saint; after a holy death and burial, there would be further miracles at the tomb and often instructions from the dead saint for furthering his or her cult by reopening the grave where the body could be found uncorrupted. The final stage in the launching of the cult was the translation of the body from burial ground to church, where miracles might then be expected on a regular basis for those who visited the saint's tomb.

There was no official papal recognition of cults at this date and affirmation by the local community was all that was required to launch a cult. The written saint's *Life* therefore potentially had an important role in publicising the cult of the saint, and perhaps in defending their reputation if it was at all controversial (like that of Bishop Æthelwold of Winchester who died in 984). The aim was not to write a strikingly original piece of work, but to prove that the saint in question conformed to an established prototype, so extensive use might be made of 'model' *Lives* such as those of St Anthony by Athanasius or St Martin by Sulpicius Severus. It was assumed that all saints could perform miracles of the type recorded in the Bible, and in the earliest *Lives* many saints are recorded as performing remarkably similar miracles in healing the sick or the raising of the dead. *Lives* were also designed to instruct members of religious communities and secular society in the ideals of Christian behaviour.

Because of the established conventions it was possible to produce a written *Life* with very few basic facts, as can be illustrated, for example, by the eleventh-century *Life* of Birinus, the first bishop of Dorchester on Thames (the first West Saxon see). The value of hagiographies for reconstructing the real lives of their subjects depends upon whether the author knew the subject or not, was in a position to talk to others who had, or had access to reliable written sources of information. However, even the most speculative *Lives* have valuable information about contemporary beliefs and the practice of religion. For Wessex, as for other areas of Anglo-Saxon England, three main phases in the writing of *Lives* can be identified. Although a number of West Saxon saints such as Bishop Aldhelm of Sherborne and Malmesbury (Wiltshire) are known from the conversion period of the seventh and eighth centuries, and may be referred to in Bede's *Ecclesiastical History*, the only extant *Lives* for saints from this period are for those West Saxons who went to work in Germany either converting pagans or reinforcing the faith in nominally Christian areas. The *Lives* of Boniface from Nursling (Hampshire) and his kinswoman Leoba from Wimborne (Dorset) were written respectively by Willibald of Mainz and Rudolf of Fulda, while the Anglo-Saxon nun Hygeburg of Heidenheim produced a *Life* of her kinsmen, the brothers Willibald and Wynnebald from Bishop's Waltham (Hampshire).

A more significant period of hagiographical writing in Wessex was that of the monastic reform of the later tenth century. Winchester was a major centre for the writing of Latin *Lives*, including those of its leading saints and former bishops, Swithun and Æthelwold. However, Old English was probably more widely understood and utilised in the church at this time and Ælfric of Winchester produced Old English versions of the *Lives* of most of the significant saints, though St Swithun was the only West Saxon included. It may be suspected that the vernacular *Lives* were produced for other West Saxon saints, but that they were superseded by subsequent Latin versions, for when foreign bishops came to hold positions in the West Saxon church – a practice which begun under King Cnut and continued apace after the Norman Conquest – they expected reputable saints to have Latin *Lives*. Goscelin, the author of the *Life* of St Wulfsige, was among those of foreign birth employed in England to produce Latin versions for the saints whose *Lives* were written in Old English, or whose reputations rested mainly on oral tradition. Goscelin was also the author of a *Life* of St Edith of Wilton (Wiltshire) who died at a date between 984 and 987 and was the daughter of King Edgar. Goscelin records that he used both written sources concerning her and her mother, Wulfthryth, who was also revered at Wilton as a saint, as well as oral traditions about their lives and miracles which were still current in the nunnery and often associated with specific items that they had owned. Goscelin may also have been the author of a different type of saint's *Life*, the *passio* of King Edward the Martyr which presented his murder in 978 as a martyrdom. The author reports that he made use of an earlier *Life*, and possibly this was a vernacular version produced for the Shaftesbury nunnery where the king was buried. Slightly later *Lives* survive for Eadburga of Nunnaminster, Winchester and Ælfflaed of Romsey (Hampshire).

The West Saxon saints culted in Wessex for whom written *Lives* survive fall into two main categories, bishops of West Saxon sees and members of the West Saxon royal house who were all, with the exception of Edward the Martyr, princesses or former queens. Wessex is not as well served as are some other parts of the country by local saints, usually from the conversion period, whose cults are often only cursorily recorded in later medieval sources, but may have been passed down through oral tradition. These saints are often associated with more fantastical stories and elements of popular religious practice such as the use of holy wells. The cults of some British saints that fall into this category are recorded from the western shires of Wessex, such as St Sidwell of Exeter and St Decuman of Watchet (Somerset), who were believed to have been martyred for their faith with springs appearing miraculously where their blood had been shed. For Dorset there is St Juthwara of Halstock (that is *halganstoke* or 'holy place') who, beheaded by her own brother, placed her severed head on the altar and whose feast day was celebrated at Sherborne on 13 July. Sherborne also marked the feast day of St Emerenciana on 18 January, stoned to death in third-century Rome. Her association with the *scir burn*, the 'clear stream' of the place-name may suggest a Latinised version of a name related to a water cult of pre-Saxon, British origin.

10. The Life of St Wulfsige of Sherborne by Goscelin of Saint-Bertin

a new translation with introduction, appendix and notes

Rosalind Love

Introduction

The *Life* of St Wulfsige is generally counted among the earliest works of the Flemish hagiographer Goscelin who did so much to commemorate the Anglo-Saxon saints in the later eleventh century. His career has been described in detail elsewhere; it is sufficient background for our consideration of this text to recall that Goscelin, a monk of Saint-Bertin at Saint-Omer, had come to England under the patronage of Bishop Herman, probably in the early 1060s.[1] We have it on Goscelin's own authority that he joined the monks at Sherborne, as well as functioning as chaplain to the nuns at Wilton, but also on occasion accompanied Herman as he went about his business within and beyond the diocese. Not long after Herman died, in 1078, the hagiographer was obliged for some undisclosed reason to leave the area, embarking upon the peripatetic life of an exile, until he settled at St Augustine's, Canterbury in the early 1090s.

The prologue of Goscelin's *Life* of Wulfsige, as transmitted, is addressed to an unnamed bishop, and includes fairly explicit information about the circumstances of composition. Goscelin says that he had learnt about Wulfsige from his fellow-monks at Sherborne, at least one of whom, Ælfmær, was old enough to have nursed Wulfsige on his death-bed. He was spurred on to begin writing up an account of Wulfsige's life, with the intention of dedicating it to Herman, but before he could finish the task, Herman died, 'and the eagle's youth has replaced him with you, to whom I am now writing'. This confession is very similar to Goscelin's prefatory remarks to his *Life* of Edith of Wilton, composed in about 1080. Addressing himself to his dedicatee, Lanfranc, he there admits that Herman had first asked him to write about Edith, 'but I, hindered until now by modesty or carelessness, have dedicated the first-fruits of my efforts to your excellency' (Wilmart 1938). Goscelin's words surely imply that the anonymous dedicatee of the *Life* of Wulfsige is Herman's immediate successor, Osmund. Given the fact that he had left Sherborne perhaps by about 1080, the likely date of the composition of the *Life* would therefore be between 1078 and 1080. C H Talbot (1955), the editor of the text had, however, conjectured that the dedicatee might be Roger of Caen (consecrated in 1107) rather than Osmund, his reasoning being that Osmund is referred to in chapter XXI '*sub pontifice Osmundo* (as if he had already passed into history)'. This would mean assigning the text to a date after 1099. Reviewing Talbot's edition, Grosjean (1960), likewise expressed the view that the text must, as it stands, be regarded as a late work of Goscelin. Yet there is nothing about the reference to Osmund in chapter XXI which does actually suggest that he was already dead at the time of writing, and no events or persons datable to after 1078/9 are referred to in the text, so that there seems to me to be little warrant for rejecting Osmund as the recipient.

The only surviving complete copy of Goscelin's *Life* of Wulfsige is preserved in the compilation of British saints' Lives in Gotha, Forschungsbibliothek MS I.81, of unknown (English) origin and provenance, which was written by a single scribe in the second half of the fourteenth century. The manuscript is of some interest insofar as a good number of the texts are not preserved elsewhere. It is often thought to have connections with the West Country, on account of the presence of several saints with Cornish/Devon connections: Nectan of Hartland, Petroc, Pyran, Rumon (whose relics were translated to Tavistock in the tenth century), Sativola/Sidwell of Exeter; but a detailed study of the collection, which might shed more light, has yet to be made. A heavily abridged version of the *Life* of Wulfsige occurs in the fourteenth-century collection of saints' Lives in London, British Library, Lansdowne 436, probably made at Romsey Abbey (Fig 8). The version of the *Life* preserved there is much curtailed and contributes no new material, but is nevertheless on occasion a useful guide to what might have been in Goscelin's original text in the places where the Gotha version has only a muddle or an apparent omission. A yet more brusquely abridged version of the *Life* is to be found in John of Tynemouth's *Sanctilogium Angliae, Walliae, Scotiae et Hiberniae*, compiled probably during the first half of the fourteenth century (Horstman 1901).

The *Life* of Wulfsige was edited, regrettably with very little annotation, for the first time by C H Talbot,[2] who had already published a substantial later work by Goscelin, his highly personal *Liber Confortatorius*. Talbot's transcription of the Gotha text is, alas, faulty, as Grosjean pointed out in his review, and this highlights the fact that it is only in attempting to translate a text that one discovers the problems with it. Inspection of the manuscript shows that there are still further emendations which need to be made to Talbot's text, in addition to those noted by Grosjean. The latter also suggested some textual emendations, taking into account the sense of the Latin and the orthographical oddities which are characteristic of the scribe of the Gotha manuscript. I have included as an

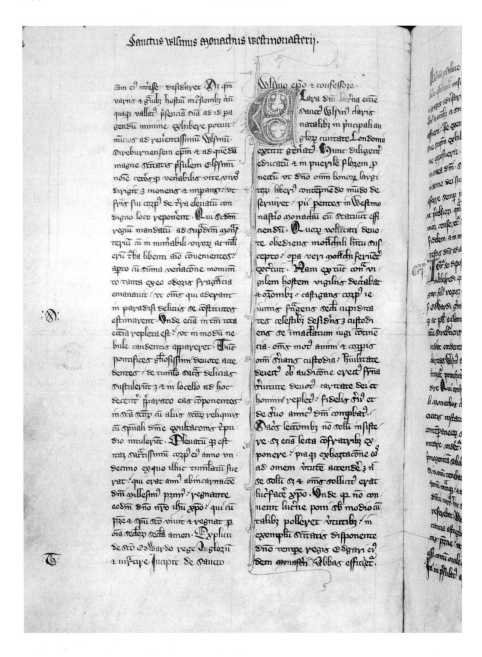

Figure 8. Goscelin's Life of Wulfsige is likely to have been written between 1078 and 1080, this is the first page of a fourteenth-century, heavily abridged edition probably made at Romsey Abbey. (BL Lansdowne MS 436, fo 48v The Life of St Wulfsige. Reproduced by permission of the British Library)

appendix a list of all the corrections and emendations to Talbot's Latin text which I have incorporated into my translation.

Goscelin apparently had little documentary evidence on which to base his composition, and certainly no pre-existing *Life* of Wulfsige; as he says himself (a standard claim which he makes in all his attested hagiographies), his sources are house tradition, hearsay and, just to establish the most direct line of authority possible, some first-hand eye-witness evidence. He refers to the '*privilegia*' of Westminster and Sherborne, but it is hard to find any sign that he actually used them as a source for what he wrote about his subject. Although Goscelin would have been the first to admit that miracles are worth nothing without a virtuous life,[3] his description of Wulfsige's life, which only occupies eight out of the twenty-five chapters of the text, appears very much like mere background for his account of the various translations and attendant miracles, the hard-core material of all relic-cults. Certainly a large part of his portrayal of Wulfsige's character and career is the commonplace stuff of hagiography, some of it going back to the paradigm established by Sulpicius Severus' depiction of St Martin of Tours in the late fourth century: noble birth, handsome looks coupled with intelligence and evident holiness, swift progress up the careers ladder having come to the attention of the monarch and the prominent churchmen of the day, chastity, humility and diligent exercise of authority, the inclination to withdraw from the affairs of the world, foreknowledge of death, and a death-bed speech of valediction and prophecy. It is interesting, however, to see Goscelin along the way taking pains to gloss over, even beautify, the matter of Wulfsige's simultaneous involvement with both Sherborne and Westminster, held in plurality. But he is at his best and most lively as a narrator of the miraculous in the lives of ordinary mortals, of little vignettes full of circumstantial detail.

The other document Goscelin refers to, in chapter 21 and again in chapter 24, is a '*Passionale*' or '*Libellus*' concerning St Juthwara, presumably a short account of her supposed martyrdom attached to some record of her miracles, which may perhaps have been supplied at the time when Ælfwold introduced her relics, in order to certify their authenticity. Quite possibly the last traces of that document can be seen in the only other known account of Juthwara's martyrdom, which John of Tynemouth incorporated into the *Sanctilogium* mentioned above, presumably again an abbreviated version of a Passion of St Juthwara which John had come across during his researches.[4] Whilst corresponding to the essence of Goscelin's brief notice of her murder, John's account makes no mention of Halstock, nor of the translation of Juthwara's relics to Sherborne, and certainly not of the particular miracle associated with her relics which forms the penultimate chapter of the *Life* of Wulfsige, where Goscelin makes an explicit cross-reference to the book of Juthwara's miracles. Possibly the text John saw had come from Halstock, or reflected only the interests of Halstock, but it may also simply be the case that the ruthless paring knife of his anthologising style did away with the portion of her '*Libellus*' which related to her cult at Sherborne. At any rate, this particular martyr remains a relatively mysterious little figure.

If the testimony of the Gotha manuscript is at all trustworthy – and it is very possible that some errors can be attributed to successive copyists, since after all the fourteenth-century manuscript stands at quite some remove from eleventh-century Sherborne – Goscelin appears to have committed one or two errors, for example in mistakenly referring to Edmund Ironside as Eadwine, and in writing of a non-existent Bishop Wulfsige of Worcester, and his time-scale for Wulfsige's career has also caused some puzzlement, as will be noted in due course. Perhaps historical inaccuracies, if they are Goscelin's, are less excusable when we recall that he was writing within less than a century of Wulfsige's death, and had talked to at least one person who had witnessed it. Certainly Goscelin is generally regarded as a fairly accurate reporter of the information he was given and a respectful interpreter of historical record.[5] Yet the hagiographer's brief was principally to emphasise and advertise sanctity rather than to write history, and to ensure that the holy portrait shone out clearly from a background landscape which only really needed to be sketched in lightly.

Even though among Goscelin's works the *Life* of Wulfsige is by no means the most flowery and expansive, nevertheless, in many places, the strongly poetic flavour of his prose renders the task of translation into idiomatic, flowing English quite difficult. He was a great lover of the grandiose – not to say obfuscating – circumlocution, a touch of abstruse vocabulary, a sprinkling of home-made adjectives, and carefully balanced phrases linked by rhyme, sometimes expanding a single idea into a lengthy peroration, sometimes veering towards a more terse, allusive narrative voice. The list of chapter-headings, for example, is composed almost as if it were poetry, in compact newspaper-headline style. I have tried very hard to provide a translation which might serve as a guide to the Latin text, rather than take on a life of its own, but at the same time it has proved impossible sometimes not to stray further away from Goscelin towards slightly more readable English.

HERE BEGINS THE PROLOGUE TO THE LIFE OF SAINT WULFSIGE, BISHOP AND CONFESSOR, WHICH THE VENERABLE PRIEST AND MONK GOSCELIN HAS COMPOSED

Long ago I learnt of the celebrated merits of the holy Bishop Wulfsige, whom you have in the care of your episcopal zeal, not only from the present brothers, who like thirsty sucklings eagerly drank in these stories from their predecessors who had known the great father, but also from the very one who nursed him, a monk named Ælfmær, whom I myself have known, seen and heard as fellow-monk. He was with the saint himself not only during his life but also as he lay dying, and stated that at his death among other prophetic utterances he said that he saw the secrets of heaven, which he was about to enter, laid open to him. And his many miracles demonstrate that he lives on after death. As I say, I learnt these things from the brothers' most truthful testimony, and at their request, with the good will of the venerable prior Wulfric, I had undertaken to write them down with the intention of presenting them to your remarkable predecessor, Bishop Herman. But lo! while I was day-dreaming death snatched him prematurely from me on swift wings and the eagle's youth[6] has replaced him with you, to whom I am now writing. I therefore commend to your watchful[7] eminence not so much the skill of the writer as the trustworthiness of the account, not so much the clumsiness of the workman as the evidence of the truth, so that under your bright gaze the night and gloom of bombastic incredulity might not mar the bright radiance of sanctity.

Here ends the preface.

Here begin the chapter-headings:

I	Born of noble stock in the city of London, dedicated to God and educated in the district of Westminster, dear Wulfsige showed by his progress that divine grace was not inactive in him.
II	Reaching the priesthood by passing through the degrees of office and of virtue, and shining out as a perfect man he was also a notable benefit in the management of Christ's household.
III	Raised to the rank of abbot he so watched over the Lord's flock that he showed himself worthy of a loftier station than the one he was occupying.
IV	At the consent of King Æthelred he was made bishop of the province of Dorset and had oversight of both monasteries as bishop and abbot, by the Lord's example and encouragement doubling his talent in hymn-singing and works of mercy.
V	Secluded from the whirlwind of the world for the discipline of Lent he strove to be completely the Lord's, making his life a rich burnt-offering with tithes,[8] and running in the race for the crown for twenty-five years of episcopacy.[9]
VI	In his final illness he foretells to a servant who is also ill that he will go with him the next day to the court of the high King, and indicates in a prophecy the place and the sarcophagus where he will be buried when he has died.
VII	And he announces to a weeping priest that twelve years after his burial the mourning of his companions will be turned into joy at the manifestation of his miracles.
VIII	As he is being anointed with holy oil on the point of death, he cries out that he can see the heavens opened wide and the Saviour standing at the right hand of God awaiting his arrival; and thus expiring he is buried at Sherborne with his companion.
IX	The remains of the holy body, being longer than the sarcophagus from the shoulders upwards, make it longer through divine power by stretching themselves out inside it; the mourning people rejoice at the miracle.

X	The Bishop of the Hwicce, bearing both the name and the status of St Wulfsige, is instructed in a vision and brought to his tomb, and there received relief from protracted illness.
XI	Among many miracles, on the Lord's Epiphany five infirm persons pushed over on to his tomb are suddenly restored to health.
XII	A hunch-backed woman, having received in a vision the saint's message about asking for the return of his staff, brought it to Sherborne and went away with her health.
XIII	On the authority of Archbishop Ælfheah a festal translation of St Wulfsige takes place, after which widespread news of his power draws a great multitude of people.
XIV	Amongst others drawn to the father's great miracles come the King and Queen.
XV	A woman who flouts his feast day is stuck to her seat and distaff and spindles by divine power, is brought with these, in the act of spinning, and is released at his shrine.
XVI	St Wulfsige's successors are listed, among whom is included a bishop who was made blind until he vacated the see and left the position free for the pastor who had been expelled.
XVII	The Bishop and prior while they were discussing the translation of his sarcophagus into the church, were, at one and the same hour, both encouraged by a marvellous revelation, so that they hastened the matter forward.
XVIII	When the tomb is opened it gives out lovely fragrances; once it is positioned in the heart of the church it bears the remains of the holy father placed within.
XIX	Concerning the theft from the church, while the brothers are in turmoil, a voice, issuing from Wulfsige's grave with the words: 'Revenge is mine, I will repay saith the Lord'[10] is heard by everybody, and on the same day not only are the lost holy things restored but also the thieves perish.
\<XX\>	At a time when the judgement of the wicked was prevailing against the rights of the church, St Wulfsige is brought into the midst, and soon, struck by divine power, they condemn their own fiction and adjudge to the saint his rightful possession.
XXI	As the relics of SS Wulfsige the confessor and St Juthwara the virgin are being put into silver reliquaries, the water used to wash them becomes holy, and is made health-giving for many sick persons.
XXII	At the drinking of this water it is related that a few of the many were delivered from the verge of death.
XXIII	A woman dead in both feeling and body, yet still breathing her last breaths, having drunk this water immediately rose up whole.
XXIV	A dying priest was swiftly aided by the healing of water in which only the holy limbs of St Juthwara had been dipped.
\<XXV\>	Praise and salvation where these saints dwell together.

Here end the chapter headings.

HERE BEGINS THE LIFE OF WULFSIGE, BISHOP AND CONFESSOR

I   The illustrious light of the Lord's church, St Wulfsige, was born of illustrious lineage in the principal city of the English, London, which, watered by the famous River Thames, with her great size and wealth welcomes the traffic of visitors from overseas. Here he was carefully brought up and when he reached blossoming boyhood his devout parents decided that he should be offered to the Lord, the Giver of all good things. Within the walls of that very city there shines the church of the celestial keybearer [ie St Peter], now made splendid by royal involvement and wealth, which in the English tongue, because of its western position, is called Westminster. There they gave him to the Lord, consecrated in the sacrifice of holy Samuel,[11] a perpetual servant under the patronage of St Peter, and at the same time, in accordance with their status and their religious devotion, they also made a solemn offering of riches. When the school-master of the church examined him and saw that he was endowed with elegance of form and outstanding robustness, such as might commend him as an increase of good hope and a vessel of divine election,[12] he determined that he should be instructed extensively in the Holy Scriptures. Accordingly Wulfsige by God's inspiration advanced in age and wisdom,[13] and showed more and more clearly what he was destined to be in the future by the grace of God.

II   Having therefore innocently shaken off his sweet and loveable boyhood he passed upwards through the holy ranks of office to the summit of holy priesthood, now by virtue of his maturity and good character made a bright mirror of sanctity; and having long since put on the armour of God, equipped with the breastplate of faith and the helmet of salvation,[14] he battled against the watchful enemy in watchings and prayers, punishing his body[15] with fastings and breaking the appetites of this world with heavenly longings, guarding his holy celibacy with constant continence, keeping full guard over every stirring of both soul and body, submissive in humility, attentive in obedience, devoted in service to his brothers, filled with love of God and of men, a faithful servant, and once a servant, then a proven friend of the Lord.[16] He gave himself over not only to reading the Holy scriptures, but also to expounding to his brothers the things he had read and inciting them to all virtue by affectionate encouragement, eager to gain not only himself, but others, for Christ.[17] Thus from his boyhood upwards growing in holiness towards perfection and ascending from strength to strength the great lover of God strove to produce, like the kingdom of God, first the blade, then the ear, afterwards the full corn in the ear.[18] Living such a way of life he was a brilliant hope for building up and increasing Christ's household.

III   At that time the excellent King Edgar was directing the affairs of the English with all divine peace and justice, in accordance with the heavenly promise which he was fortunate to have received at the very moment of his birth, in the hearing of Archbishop Dunstan who now dwells in heaven, namely that he would be the Peace of the English church, deservedly preferred before not only his father Eadwine[19] and his uncles Æthelstan and Eadred but also all kings of the English before him.[20] One of many signs of God's justice was that the King admitted none to ecclesiastical preferment except any whom the Metropolitan himself, the father of the English [ie Dunstan] by divine foreknowledge judged to be worthy. With his holy assent and commendation, therefore, the devout King put Wulfsige, the chosen one of God, now excelling in monastic orders under the charge of that same father [scil Dunstan], in charge of that very monastery of St Peter [ie Westminster]. How strenuously he kept watch for the salvation of many, how strongly he rose up against that most insidious of adversaries of the Lord's flock, with what fatherly care he attended to each and every one, how fine an example of all his teachings he displayed in himself, who can rightly express? He laboured so hard in the Lord's vineyard,[21] he so amply bore fruit in the house of his God,[22] that he was always regarded as being fit to bear still more fruit, indeed so that he was reckoned as being worthy of a more exalted position than the one he was occupying. The Lord, himself bearing testimony, raised to yet higher things the one who was faithful in a small matter and faithful in a greater matter.[23]

IV   At the time, therefore, when King Æthelred, the son of the glorious King Edgar, and brother of the precious martyr Edward and the most holy virgin Edith, followed his father and his brother to the lofty heights of kingship, the church of Sherborne, which fell in the west of England,[24] was bereft, and the eminence of the east, Wulfsige, prize-fighter for the Lord, was asked for. And so it was that by God's ordinance and by royal assent and at the general acclamation of the clergy and people, he was enthroned on the episcopal throne of that church. Yet he could not abandon his own child [ie Westminster], but held and cherished both houses in one, as the remarkable driver of the Lord's chariot.[25] Here he called himself bishop, there abbot. In this way he drew together under the wings of his fatherly love two places separated by some distance, so that both communities might be one single sheepfold under one shepherd. Certainly they testify that he first founded a community of monks in both places, and that at each house he shone out brilliantly, as the first abbot and also in the lofty position of bishop. And it is evident that he kept them safe from any harm with the sharp blade of the anathema, lest anyone ravage or destroy the Lord's sheepfold; as the divine prophetic voice warns: 'Awake, oh sword, against those who scatter my flock!';[26] on which subject also the apostle says 'he that troubleth you shall bear the judgement, whosoever he be'.[27] Both houses have their own charters carefully written out under his name and by his authority, which quite clearly demonstrate to the reader his prudence and providence most worthy of mention, and the esteem and reverence in which he was held among the princes of the realm. In taking up his episcopacy, therefore, reflecting not so much on the honour as on the burden, not so much that he was rising in rank as rising to the task, and recognising that the more he was given the more he owed, he applied himself to working more and more to double and increase the Lord's talent,[28] and forgetting what lies behind strained forward to what lies ahead,[29] running about, making haste, stirring up his friend,[30] doing the work of an evangelist, fulfilling his ministry,[31] preaching the Lord's commandment, heralding the kingdom of God; he was a refuge for the poor, eyes for the blind, feet for the feeble, a crutch for the infirm, food for the hungry, clothing for the naked and redemption for the guilty. Wherever he went, with his feet shod with the preparation of the gospel of peace[32] he scattered the fruitful seed of the word of the Lord, and strengthened faith in God by giving his blessing to the faithful populace, christening infants so as to make them the adopted sons of their Father on high.[33] Whenever he travelled on horseback the Church was nevertheless with him: a choir of psalm-singing monks and clerics surrounded him as he passed along every journey, ringing out psalmody and the praises of Christ, and he did not put meeting and talking to those who came to greet him before the singing of hymns, and once he had given his blessing to those who asked for it, he gave no place to idleness.

V   In his Lenten preparation he seemed more like a hermit than a church dignitary.[34] For having withdrawn into the confines of the cloister and having shrugged off the tumult of the world, he enclosed himself in a secret life of simplicity with the monks and relinquished the reins of worldly affairs. Yet meanwhile he did not use this leisure in leisurely fashion and his was no indolent repose, but he made his flight from the world a fleeing to God, and took upon himself hard-working peace and silence resounding with praise, and contemplative inactivity. He stood before his Lord a servant ready for action, as if to say to Him, with the full and direct gaze of his heart: 'To Thee have I lifted up my eyes; who dwellest in heaven, Behold as the eyes of servants are on the hands of their masters; as the eyes of the handmaid are on the hands of her mistress, so are our eyes unto the Lord our God, until He have mercy on us.[35] And I shall praise Thee with uprightness of heart,[36] and the meditation of my heart shall be always in Thy sight'.[37] On Maundy Thursday, emerging as if from the Lord's bedchamber to proclaim His commandments and to commemorate His act of service,[38] he enacted the holy mystery of the Eucharist and the chrism oil,[39] teaching and blessing the people, and having completed the Easter rite he visited the remainder of his diocese preaching the good news of the Lord. In this manner he fought the good fight for the Lord's strongholds through twenty-five years of episcopacy until he came within reach of the finishing-line, so that like a good competitor he might receive the prize for having run the race.[40] His extraordinary death testifies to the fact that his life was more extraordinary than can be conveyed.

VI   As the ministry of this good steward[41] drew to a close, the day of the Lord's birth approached. The Lord came to the door of his watchful servant, knocking that it might be opened to Him.[42] At his manor called Beaminster, blessed Wulfsige was seized by his last illness, in order that, released from mortality, he might enter into the joy of his Lord[43] as an immortal one. Now the day of Holy Epiphany had dawned brightly, and the dear bishop offered to his Lord instead of gold confession, instead of incense thanksgiving, instead of myrrh his imminent death. At the same time, one of his knights named Æthelwine, who had always been very faithful and of great service to him, also fell ill. He, hearing of Wulfsige's sickness and moved to yet deeper pain on his beloved lord's behalf, anxiously sent someone to find out what hope, if any, there might be of recovery. And the bishop having received his caring servant's messenger, said 'Quickly send word, brother, to your very dear lord from me, that he should put his affairs in order and prepare himself with all care, for tomorrow he will go with me to the court of our supreme King, where he will receive from our shared Lord the reward set aside for him for faithful service'. The messenger went away, and the bishop roused the brothers who are present with this petition: 'My dear ones, give heed to the request of my fatherly love that you make sure that this faithful servant of mine, well known to all of you, who is going to pass over with me to the Lord's mercy, but will die a little before I do, is borne with me to Sherborne, and properly buried in that same monastery with me, so that he who has always been devotedly by my side in this present life may also in death be by my side in perpetual peace.' O blessed faithfulness of the righteous! O how true the Lord's words: 'whoever hears you, hears me, and whoever receives a righteous man in the name of a righteous man, will receive the reward of the righteous'.[44] If it may be permitted to apply great examples to a small matter, in just this same way also the Forerunner in the Gospels [scil John the Baptist] from his prison-cell sent a messenger to ask his Lord whether they should look for another.[45] By this means he was able to learn that the Lord Himself would follow his herald to death. And it seems that St Wulfsige was filled with the spirit of prophecy, in that he foretold both his own certain death and that of the other man. They all marvelled at this prediction, and they marvelled still more when it came to pass. But their hearts fell at the extinguishing of such a bright light. Yet just as long ago the disciples did not understand what was said to them about the Lord's passion and it was hidden from their dulled senses, so now likewise they failed to take in what they were clearly hearing. Indeed we are usually slow to believe in that which we do not wish to occur. At length they asked him with a deep sigh – for they already believed what he had said – where he wanted to be buried after his death, and he intimated that the place was very definitely in Sherborne and also that there was a sarcophagus already prepared in which he would be laid without any difficulty.

VII   Foremost among the mourners was a certain priest who had been a particularly close acquaintance of the holy bishop by virtue of his honesty, and especially party to his innermost secrets in God; his name was Wulfric. With fatherly compassion the man of mercies consoled him in the Holy Spirit, speaking confidently as if already released from the bondage of the flesh and already established in heaven: 'Do not weep', he said, 'my dearest brother, because I am going to enter the joy of my Lord who is summoning me. Take heart, rather, and have faith because from the twelfth year after my death and thereafter the Lord, remembering His generosity, will show forth His wonderful mercies[46] towards me by the testimony of miracles, and He will visit His people through me by the revelation of His grace, so that just as you now grieve over me, so then you will all rejoice at heaven's regard for me.' His prophesy brought forth the promised fruit in due season.[47]

VIII   Accordingly when his last hour pressed upon him, as is customary the sick man was put in his episcopal throne and the prize-fighter, ready to triumph against the powers of the air,[48] was anointed with the powerful mystery of holy unction, and when the priest's hand touched with holy oil his breast, that secret store of divine gifts, then lifting his eyes to the Lord his protector[49] he broke forth into the remarkable exclamation uttered by the blessed observer Stephen: 'Behold', he said, 'I see the heavens opened and Jesus standing on the right hand of God',[50] and with these prophetic words he breathed his spirit into the Lord's hands. O what blest and pure and clear-sighted eyes of faith you were granted, blessed father Wulfsige, with which you were made worthy to see the glory of such great majesty! Indeed blest are the pure in heart for they shall see God.[51] O truly must the blest bishop, enabled to pierce the heavens with such sharpness of vision, be worthy of special grace that the Lord Jesus Christ should have deigned to reveal Himself on the right hand of God the Father, as He did to the great protomartyr [Stephen]! Blessed is he who has seen the joy he is about to enter! Blessed is the man to whom the heavens lie open![52] When, therefore, the bier had been made for the venerable body it was borne to the diocese of Sherborne by his orphaned flock, singing hymns mingled with sighs. The above-mentioned knight Æthelwine had preceded his lord in death by about an hour, and having waited for him on the way, as had been instructed, accompanied him as far as the appointed burial-place, the extraordinary faithfulness of the prophetic bishop creating an extraordinary spectacle for the people who flocked together. When the funeral rites had accordingly been carried out by the bishops, abbots, clergy and the crowds of people who were present, he was buried with his companion, according to his instructions, in the porticus (?transept) – that is that one he had chosen for himself in advance – waiting to be revealed by God's providence in his due time.[53]

IX   When, however, he was placed in the very sarcophagus that he had given instructions about, the bishop's body was found to be too long so that his neck and shoulders were hanging out, and there was no way that he could be squeezed into the confines of the hollow, which was too short. They were all agitated and were in a bind about what they should do. For although they had known in advance that this sarcophagus would not fit his size they did not dare to put him anywhere other than where he had instructed, or make any change. But presently the grace of Heaven deigned publicly to manifest in His beloved servant an immense and unheard-of miracle, which was witnessed at the time by the populace and by hitherto wholly trustworthy corroborators. For during the hiatus, two provincial or neighbouring bishops had come up close to the burial-place, so that the holy father's merits might the more clearly be evident to noble witnesses; suddenly there was a noise in the tomb, the living corpse moved on its own and drew inside the short hollow all the parts which had been sticking out, and as if just waking from sleep on a bed the dead man stretched out his whole body within the hard stone, which yielded like sand or snow. And what is more remarkable still, the tomb appeared to be longer than the body, and was now as much too large as it had previously been too small. What praises the surrounding crowd raised to heaven then! How their bereft hearts wept more freely, joy mingling with their sorrows! Then the lid was put on with tender care and the heavenly treasure was laid up, ready, that is, for the time of divine visitation which he had himself promised. But just in case anyone should be dubious about such great miraculous power, almost unheard of, a similar miracle is to be found in the English History of the venerable Bede, concerning King Sebbi,[54] but also we read that other saints' remains came to life in various different ways. Blessed Wulfsige died in the twenty-fifth year of his pontificate, as has already been noted, on the eighth of January,[55] on the third day of Epiphanytide, on the day which bears witness to the Lord's resurrection [scil Sunday],[56] ready to offer to Christ the gifts of his faith along with the Magi: gold for the son of a King, incense for the son of God, myrrh for the son of man; ready to celebrate with the angels the everlasting feast of Christ's nativity. This blest inhabitant of heaven rested in the tomb for twelve years, just as a grain of wheat lies dead under the earth while it gathers the strength with which to burst forth into the shoot and the fruit in due season.[57] And then in the twelfth year after his death, he began, as he had promised, to make known in the promised miracles his long-concealed merits; out of the very many which occurred, it seems good to describe just a few which will be sufficient for faith.[58]

X   St Wulfsige's fellow-bishop and namesake Wulfsige presided over the church
of the Hwicce,[59] elected for the salvation of many but by God's fatherly correction
tried in the fire of prolonged illness, so that when health was restored to him by the
father of mercies it would be all the more precious. He was told in a vision to visit St
Wulfsige's tomb for the sake of healing, and was brought to the saint's monastery in a
litter, like the paralytic's bed. The living yet sick man stayed there overnight and was
cured by the health-bringing yet dead man, so that he who had only just made it there
in a litter, returned home riding on a horse, whole and cleansed, and the exhortation
from the Gospel could fitly be applied to him: 'Take up your bed and walk!'[60] The day
before he rose up healed the other priests were in conference with the King about
appointing a successor to that same Wulfsige because of his illness. And when it was
decided to postpone the decision for his consent, behold suddenly to the amazement
of everyone he entered the royal court with his retinue. When he had told them
everything they marvelled praising God and speaking warmly of His most worthy
confessor, Wulfsige. This great man's reputation spread widely and drew crowds of
people here; no small number of persons with various illnesses received healing, and
the ceremonies of feast-days were regularly thronged by joyful participants. One of the
very many of these also was the occasion of that glorious and memorable event which
was seen on the holy feast of the Purification of the Blessed Mother of God, Mary,
when the yearly purification ceremonies of the Christian rite were being carried out
with the candles twinkling like stars:[61] as the procession for that festival was
approaching St Wulfsige's shrine five invalids were knocked over on to the very tomb
by the pushing and shoving of the large crowd, and were suddenly restored to health.
What a good fall it was from which they rose up again healed! By this the joy of the
festival was increased; praise and glory to God, glorious in His saint!

XI   A certain woman from St Wulfsige's birth-place, London, was bent double,
with her heels digging into her rear. She had wandered all over seeking the patronage
of many saints, and now had returned home despairing of her health. In a dream she is
said to have been advised by the kindly father in this way: 'Go to Sherborne', he said,
'to my resting-place and tell the brothers of the monastery this secret from me, that
they must ask for the episcopal staff which I entrusted to the Mother of the nuns at
Shaftesbury, that they must bring it back with them to my shrine and that they will
know by this sign and message that you are to be healed in memory of me.' What a
wonderful revelation! The brothers did not know about such a relic of their bishop
until the woman told them about it and they made enquiries with that abbess, and the
staff was found and brought home. She who had received it, had kept it for so many
years that she had almost forgotten about it. The woman, receiving at the saint's shrine
reward for her journeying, toiling and obedience, released and restored took her full
health home with her; as for the rest, if her faith merited it, she would in the future
enjoy that eternal light which will be granted to all of us through that great intercessor
and patron by the Lord who lives and reigns forever and ever.

XII   We are adding here the following miraculous events relating to his translation
which are well-established fact. At that time an outstanding man, Æthelric, had charge
of the see, elected bishop after the blessed Wulfsige. He had decided to translate the
saint's body from the portico where it lay buried like heavenly treasure, into the

church, and to accord it higher importance, because the occurrence of so many miracles demanded this. He delayed carrying it out, afraid that he might perhaps be condemned for his temerity by those who are slower to believe, but the hand of God as if to shake him from his slumber wrought still more frequent glistering miracles and more and more clearly demonstrated that the confessor was worthy of all ceremonial honour. At long last, therefore, he took news of God's very obvious favour, now well-known to everyone as word had spread throughout England, to the blessed archbishop of Canterbury, Ælfheah, and also to King Æthelred, whom we mentioned above as having accepted the noble Wulfsige as bishop. Now the divine and prophetic father Dunstan had elected the most holy Ælfheah as abbot of the monastery which is called Bath, and then made him bishop of Winchester, and lastly had him as his successor – after Ælfric – in the archbishopric; the church now has him as a martyr. At any rate, this captain of the church, worthy of God, together with the King and all the faithful who were of goodwill, rejoiced greatly at the very clear sign and trustworthy affirmation of the holy man's merits, and that out of an earthly citizen they had gained a patron in heaven; and he determined that Wulfsige should be translated with the utmost solemnity and that he should be suitably celebrated in his province with a yearly festival. And so the venerable Bishop Æthelric, summoning his fellow bishops, the abbots and clergy and a great multitude of people pouring in from every quarter, began the task of raising the health-bringing corpse from the tomb as if from the cavern of death.[62] When lid was turned over, the opened coffins suddenly gave vent to the force of their sweetness as if they were store-rooms full of aromatic spices, and filled those who were close by, and those who came running up, with a new fragrance never experienced before. Then that place seemed less a cemetery for the dead than the courts of paradise breathing forth the perfume of life. From this everyone understood more profoundly the merits of dear father Wulfsige, as their aroma poured over them all, and every tongue blessed him and all lungs rejoiced to be breathing in air full of such grace.

XIII   Then his holy relics were lifted out of the tomb and out of the portico and placed with due devotion in a new reliquary, and amidst the singing of praises, are transferred into the church as if into the heart of Jerusalem, and reburied on the right-hand side of the high altar, where suppliants' prayers are answered in accordance with their faith. And since that time such great miracles are taking place here all the time, and his reputation has attracted such great crowds of sick people of every kind here, that you might think that the sick people of the whole of England have poured into Sherborne. Neither the vestibules nor the porticoes nor the church itself seemed large enough to accommodate such great crowds; the greater part – those who were good honest folk – were cured. Although these miracles have passed from our common memory either because there were just too many or because of the frequent upheavals of war or because of the scarcity of writers available to record them, yet they are all stored up in heaven. May these few most notable ones which we record here bear sufficient testimony of how true the merits of this saint are, and of how truly those miracles also are to believed which have been passed over in silence.

XIV   With the passing of time King Eadwine succeeded to his father Æthelred,[63] and after he had seven times over forged a peace to put an end to war, he was murdered by the deceit of his companion, and the king of the Danes, Cnut, obtained complete control of the English realm. But the famed father Wulfsige still continued his accustomed miracles, and still great crowds of both the whole and the sick flocked to him as their spiritual physician. Such was the intensity of the devotion to him that even the King himself, with Queen Emma and all the solemn retinue of the realm, came as suppliant to seek his patronage, and prostrating himself there offered gifts with regal generosity and poured out prayers so as to commend himself to the saint's favour. After praying, while he was examining the state of the church with inquisitive eyes, he drew the queen's attention to the roof above, crumbling with age and full of gaping cracks. 'Do you see', he said, 'how the shrine of most holy Bishop Wulfsige is exposed to all the rain and every kind of harm from the sky above? It is for you to see to it that all this is restored.' The prince, turned from tyrant into religious man, seemed to be intimating something more with these instructions: 'The impoverished circumstances of this angelic citizen in our midst accuses and rebukes us, arrogantly got up in our gold and gem-studded finery. You have more leisure: see to this, and defend me and yourself by giving money.' Straightway the Queen offered twenty pounds of silver to repair the holy roof. Having paid this much out, she hinted that they should make recourse to her again as if to a public treasury. Such was the privilege of blessed Wulfsige that he could call forth royal obedience.

XV   Of his very many miracles, we here faithfully report in addition to the above those which have been wrought in modern times, just as we have heard them from truthful witnesses who saw them with their own eyes. The revered feast-day of the glorious father was approaching. The priest gave instructions for it to be celebrated, as was the custom, with due solemnity. Everyone obeyed him, and broke off from work. Just one woman of the parish of Sherborne, a person of no small reputation, impudently scorned this injunction, priding herself in being, as she thought, more prudent and bolder than all the others. That feast day dawned and she, neglecting church and its holy observances, hastened to her distaff, clasped it to her side, and got briskly on with the business of spinning. Neither her neighbours nor her relatives, not even her own husband, were able to restrain her. For there is indeed a certain type of perverse person, stiff-necked and of obstinate heart,[64] as incorrigible as unpersuadable, who is prepared to believe in nothing except their own opinion, and whom it will never be possible to turn back from the trouble that is coming straight at them. Even as she was still laughing at those who were chiding her, suddenly she was brought by a bitter blow to perceive the saint's power, which she had not believed in from hearing words alone.[65] All of a sudden she was stuck rigid to the stool she had been sitting on, her upper hand, where it was drawing out the twisted flax, was suspended on the distaff, her lower hand was stuck to the spindle, and in the middle the fine thread hung from her frozen arms. Trying to get up was like wanting to uproot an oak-tree or shift a rock, and it seemed easier to pull the fingers from their joints than to free them from the distaff and spindle with which they seemed to be fused. Thus in an extraordinary way she was now inextricably taken hold of by the very work which she had irreverently been holding just before, and that which she had of her own will presumed to embark upon she was not able of her own will to persist with, and the hated punishment prevented her from doing so. The wretched woman began to mourn, reproached both by her own body and by her own ill-advised actions. The whole house resounded with her weeping and groaning, and a crowd gathered to gape at the sight. Eventually they thought of a plan for her remedy. She was carried, with her stool and the tangle of threads she was in the act of spinning, into the church during the celebration of mass, through the midst of dense crowds of people, a new offering, a new spectacle, as extraordinary as it was pathetic, and she was placed, like some statuette, before the healing relics of St Wulfsige. There with mournful complaint she began begging earnestly for forgiveness of her sin, and promising to observe his feast-day with as much reverence as she could from then on and for as long as she lived, and at the same time the whole crowd was offering up a prayer, when suddenly before everyone's eyes she was granted absolution and fully restored to control over herself as before. She got up and threw down the distaff and spindles as if they had been her shackles, and they have been hung up by the saint's shrine in commemoration of such a great miracle. And so she who had been a monstrosity of disaster was turned into a miracle of health, and out of a spectacle of horror was made a spectacle of happiness. In place of distress she received composure, for infirmity vigour, for mourning exultation, for the confusion of correction she received the favour of grace, having thus experienced the holy father's sternness and fairness in binding and loosing,[66] his power to smite and to heal; furthermore she was made an example both for herself and for everyone else of the veneration which is his due. Hence by all exultant voices songs of praise were joyfully raised heavenward to the Lord of miracles.

XVI   These are known to be Wulfsige's successors up to the present day. The venerable Æthelric took his place, as has already been described. He died in the time of King Eadwine whom we mentioned above,[67] and in his place was elected Æthelsige, and Brihtwine succeeded him. When he was ejected, Ælfmær, a monk of Canterbury usurped his position.[68] He harassed the Lord's flock which had been established by the true shepherd, Wulfsige, and made efforts to appropriate one of the brothers' endowments and because of this lost the sight of his eyes which is more precious than any endowment, and the blindness of greed was turned into physical darkness, and he lost the ability to perceive the form and beauty of all things for the sake of one small thing which belonged to the servants of Christ. And he did not even get that. However, it is reported that back at his own monastery he did eventually regain his sight, so that he might know that he had been punished by the judgement of St Wulfsige for exercising tyranny over his flock, and having put off the episcopacy which was not his due he was reclothed with his sight by the saint's mercy. Brihtwine gained back the see which was now opened to him, and afterwards passed it on to his brother Ælfwold.[69]

XVII   To return to our elaboration of St Wulfsige's miracles: this same Ælfwold, with the prior of his monastery, Ælfweard, had decided to move the sarcophagus, from which we have already said the saint had been translated, into the church to where his glorious relics were. While they were lingering in uncertainty over this plan they were each individually warned or rather rebuked by the following vision on one and the same night, at the very same hour even. The prior was brought in his dream into the portico where the saint's tomb used to stand, and from it he saw himself gathering up golden honey-combs as if from an opened bee-hive, and their incredible fragrance wafted through the whole monastery. And waking up he still thought he could smell that wonderful sweetness, so that he cried out in joy: 'Truly, honey-sweet father, we have in this place experienced your nearness and you have granted these tokens of your presence.' He rushed straight to the bishop hoping to find in him a listener for his tale but found instead that he was more eager to describe his own vision. There was an amicable dispute as to which should speak first and which listen attentively. For the bishop himself had in a vision found himself in an orchard full of blossom and before him was the most holy and vigilant guardian of his flock, shining like the captain of the heavens. He was standing by an incredibly bright fountain and was washing his head in it: the observer was seized with fear and joy and made to approach and address such a lovely apparition. 'What', he said, 'are you doing, o fairest father?' The saint replied to him, 'That which it would have been proper for you to have done long ago'. Accordingly, when both the prior and the bishop had recounted their visions to one another, their awe was much increased, and where just one vision, appearing to just one person, would have been enough for amazement and belief, the double manifestation amplified the miracle and the message of the repeated mystery confirmed them both in their conviction. Brooking no further procrastination, and having got together a band of men and some of the brothers, that same day and hour they carried out the desired ceremony.

XVIII   When, therefore, the tomb was opened, every corner of the church was filled with wonderful sweetness so that what the prior had smelt in his dream was experienced in truth and physical reality. And the incense of these aromas did not die away at all until everything had been completed concerning the sacred tomb. This was carried into the church and fittingly placed on the north side of the high altar, and the bones of the blessed confessor, which as we described above had been translated to the north side, were reverently washed and put in a chest on top of that same north-side monument, once a reliquary-shrine had been prepared, and at its head an altar was set up, where the Morrow Mass was to be celebrated daily. In saying the bones were washed we prove the vision to have come true, in which Bishop Ælfwold saw the saint washing his head. When he joined the new monastery to the old one, he translated the holy patron again into the new one, since the old one was in a dilapidated state. The same bishop had very many adornments made for the church in the form of shrines and crosses covered in gold and silver. In fact, the blessed Wulfsige had granted to the brothers of his monastery the tithes and the half carucate of plough-land which were the possession of the bishop.[70] Certainly he has the reward of his fatherly care – may all who make offerings have it! – of the Judge who is Judge of all.

XIX   Under Herman, Ælfwold's successor, one of the church's golden shrines was stolen. Whereupon the brothers, exhausted with searching, succumbed to bitter grief. The sacristan was even more upset, since he had the charge of keeping watch over the church. Later on, as one night he came out of matins and went in the direction of the sanctuary, lo and behold suddenly from St Wulfsige's resting-place a loud voice rang out, clearly audible both to his ears and to those of all the brothers who were in the choir: 'Revenge is mine, I will repay saith the Lord.' They were all stunned and began tremulously to be comforted by the hope of consolation in the merits of the holy bishop. For nobody doubted that this saying had been sent there from heaven. And so they prayed all the more earnestly because they strongly believed that they had been comforted by this prophetic utterance from their father. What more is there to say? The same day not only was the stolen shrine restored completely but also the thieves were arrested and punished, and the prophetic and divine nature of the voice was proved by its obvious effectiveness.

XX Another time the king's judges attempted to appropriate into royal control no small parcel of land belonging to the bishop. Because of this there were many law-suits, and many objections and invented stories were hurled like darts. Depending upon reasoning and testimonies the defenders of the church put forward evidence of the truth in order to gain justice, but were not able to check the violence: at the last session of the law-suit they [the aggressors] had conspired to seize and cut off from the bishop the property at stake – assailing equity with force. But then by order of Bishop Herman, who succeeded Ælfwold, and under whom two episcopal sees became one, the holy relics of Wulfsige were brought in for a holy adjudication. In their presence the unruly chatter of the crowd was silenced as if at the arrival of some magnate, and as if the saint himself were the tribunal passing sentence there was suddenly such a great transformation that the opposition, who had been battling for a victory with all their effort, became favourably inclined towards the saint, and some of the more hostile ones swore on oath in the presence of everyone that the property about which the case was being fought had always from ancient times been the inheritance and property of the bishop and the church of God. And that it should forever remain the possession of the saint was decided by the unanimous agreement and acclamation of the whole assembly. The whole affair taught the lesson that the palm of victory is to be ascribed to the merits of St Wulfsige.

XXI From this point all that follows are the miracles common to the blessed confessor Wulfsige and the most holy virgin and martyr Juthwara. Now the blessed Juthwara was long ago made manifest by bright signs and visions, and Bishop Ælfwold had translated her from the chapel at the place called Halstock to Sherborne amidst great glory. Once upon a time she was beheaded there by her brother, as is related in the account of her Passion, and after her head had been cut off, her mutilated body is said to have run after it and with both hands to have put it back on to the neck from which it had fallen. So then, under Bishop Osmund, their precious relics were placed with solemn honour in individual reliquaries splendidly adorned with gold, by the venerable prior Ælfric, at the desire and with the consent of the brothers, having first come before the face of the Lord in fastings and prayers, and with the favourable intercession of the saints themselves. And the water in which the bones of both saints had been washed became consecrated by the double holiness, as it were, and thus endowed by the combined powers of two occupants of heaven for a yet greater number of remedies, it was made into a source of healing for many sick people. We shall recount just a few of the many, so that the many may be verified from the few.

XXII A brother of the monastery was bitterly afflicted for almost half a year first by fevers every two days and subsequently by daily fevers. He shuddered at food and hated to sit at table. He was dragged to meals as if to an inquisition. When on the feast day of the translation of dear Juthwara he was on his way to sing in choir after the procession, trembling and pallor abruptly took hold of him. He began to retreat further off as if taken captive. Then the brothers, calling to mind the favours bestowed by the saints, poured out for him to drink as an antidote some of the water used to wash them. And that very moment in which he tasted it, it was as if health entered in and fever was driven out, and he was so improved that he thought himself renewed by the sweetness and exulted in the complete restoration of his strength, and longed for the food he had hated, and from groaning became happy and cheerful as if a changed man. Now he looked like the same man who took the drink and was healed, yet at the same time a different, healthy, man had been made out of the sick man. Quite soon at his example sick persons began to be accustomed to come for that holy fluid as if to some healing well, and to carry away healing with the draught they took. It is said that both another brother and also someone from among the servants of the monastery were stricken by the same illness and were swiftly cured by the same medicine in the sight of all the other brothers. Another one, worn down by a similar fever for a whole year, was so near to death that the breath scarcely remained in him, but when he drank the water of the saints his former strength and health returned immediately. So even a sick man close to the end still quickly received the life he had despaired of and his health from this small draught.

XXIII   Who can worthily tell the story of the wife of a certain nobleman brought back from the very jaws of death? She lay for three whole days without voice, without hearing, without sensation, as if lifeless, her whole body immovable as stone. Her eyes were wide open not in direct gaze but with deathly glaze, her head thrown back, her pupils unmoving, her eye-lashes unflickering. She gave no sign of life to those around her who called to her or shook her, and if she was lifted up or carried, her neck drooped, and all her other limbs too, unless she was held up by the assistance of others. Only her breath trembled within the dead body, so that for the time being one might call her not dead but dying. Nothing except her death was expected, and all the talk was of her burial only. On the third day of this three-day agony, consecrated to the commemoration of the Resurrection [scil Sunday], her son, who had been brought up as a monk of our two saints' community, came with the natural affection of a son to visit both parents, desiring to care for her and to console him. As far as human agency was concerned he saw in her no remedy for the present life. But remembering the power of his own patron saints, when he returned to the monastery he sent some of the oft-mentioned water to help her. Scarcely had the messenger crossed the threshold of the house and the sick woman – such was the strength of the heavenly cure – moved her foot and restored the hope that had been despaired of, and when they put drops of the healing fluid on her lips, straightway, as if waking from heavy sleep, she came to life again, then looked at those standing over her with eyes, as it were, spinning, sat straight up and seizing hold of the cup full of healing she had just tasted, drank it down more intently. Without delay, as if the Lord were calling her, she rose up restored. At this all her friends and her husband rejoiced as heartily at having received her as if from the grave, as they had lamented despairingly over her before. And at the miraculous powers of the blessed Wulfsige and also the blessed Juthwara, the brothers and all the people raised loud praise to the Lord who is glorious in his saints, by the touch of whose relics such great power is given to the element of water.

XXIV   A miracle particular to saint Juthwara, since it is similar to these, will briefly be recounted here even though it is adequately described in her own book of miracles. Under Bishop Ælfwold there was a well-known priest called Wulfric, learned and orderly. Illness caused him to despair of his life, and he had received the unction of holy oil for the remission of his sins and in preparation for his spiritual journey, and then he remembered the recognised powers of the dear virgin, and sent an errand boy, saying, 'Hurry to Sherborne and take to the brothers my request that they dip the relics of blessed Juthwara, which Ælfwold translated thither, into some water and send it to me to drink. For by this I believe that I shall receive my life and my former health.' The messenger went and fetched it, and he drank and that same hour was restored by the virgin's grace.

XXV   And so while we have been escorting the holy Bishop Wulfsige with a helping hand, we have added to his noble train the martyred virgin Juthwara, and have woven roses among lilies, so that, while they each separately give pleasure on their own, by being blended they might give a more splendid display: having these heavenly flowers the church of Sherborne shines with twin brightness. It is beautiful the way that the starry virgin has migrated to be with this ethereal standard-bearer, so that with episcopal honour he might conduct her to her King, like the friend of the Bridegroom and the bridesman of the Bride, like the doorkeeper and the custodian of the King's bridal-chamber. May all who venerate them faithfully be blessedly assisted by their patronage, and be permitted to rejoice in their heavenly presence on high, through the Lord the giver of all good things, who reigns forever and ever, amen.

Appendix

Emendations to Talbot's text (G = emendations suggested by Grosjean):

A Talbot's errors of transcription from Gotha I.81

Pref. line 3 allactancius *hec apotarunt*; line 5 qui *ipsi* sancto (G); line 13 aquile *restituit* (G); Capitula ch i *in* suburbano (G); ch vii conuertendos *suorum* luctus; ch viii cum *suo* comite; ch x presul *Wycciorum* (G); ch xviii portat *ipsius* sancti patris; ch xxiiii de solis *sancte* Iudware; ch **I**, line 5 *omnium* bonorum largitori; line 10 perpetuum *famulum* (G); ch **III**, line 6 ad *ecclesiasticam* prelacionem (G); ch **III**, line 9 fauore et *preconio* (G); ch **III**, lines 17–18 alciora *promouit* (G); ch **IV**, line 36 data *tantum* benedictione (G); ch **VIII**, line 4 carismatum *reconditorium* (G); ch **VIII**, line 20 mirum spectaculum *faciens*; ch **IX**, line 4 *praescissent hanc* tumbam; ch **IX**, line 12 se *mouit* uitalis (G); ch **IX**, line 13 *attraxit* duroque lapide (G); ch **IX**, line 13 harena uel *niue* cedente; ch **IX**, line 19 in tempus *scilicet*; ch **XI**, line 15 nobis *tribuat* dominus (G); ch **XII**, line 18 clarum *indicium*; ch **XII**, line 18 et fidelem *assertionem* (G); ch **XIV**, line 17 .xx. *libras* argentorum; ch **XV**, lines 37–8 *recipit* gracie fauorem; ch **XVII**, lines 12–13 uisionem *referendam*; ch **XVII**, lines 17–18 fontem *perlustrissimum* (G); ch **XVIII**, line 4 *complerentur* omnia (G); ch **XIX**, line 3 amplius *tribulabatur*; ch **XX**, line 2 iuris *in dictionem* (G); ch **XX**, line 4 ueritatis *indicia* protendebant; ch **XX**, line 15 ad sancti *dicionem* (G); ch **XXII**, line 10 *escas* quas fastidierat (G); ch **XXII**, line 16 eodem morbo *correptos* (G); ch **XXIII**, line 15 baiulus *attigit*

B Errors made either by the scribe of Gotha I.81 or in his exemplar

Capitula ch viii Dum *ungitur* (G); ch xv *selle* et colo (G); ch xvii sub *una* hora (G); ch xxiiii *cito* subuenitur (G); ch xxiiii salus *cohabitacionis* ipsorum (G); ch **III**, line 4 *patruis*que Aethestano (G); ch **III**, line 11 *Quantum* tunc ... *quantum* contra (G); ch **V**, line 2 uidebatur quam *ierarcha* (G); ch **VIII**, line 1 *Vrgente* ergo extrema hora (G); ch **XII**, line 24 mortis *speleo assumere* aggressus est; ch **XVIII**, line 6 *que* in aquilonale latus (G); ch **XVIII**, line 12 ueteri *dilapso* (G); ch **XX**, line 9 uelut *si* principe (G); ch **XXI**, line 11 *domini* facie (G); ch XXII, lines 1–2 *prius* biduanis (G); ch **XXIII** *Sed* quis digne (G); ch **XXIII** cuiusdam *primarii* (G)

Notes

1   See F Barlow (ed and trans), *The Life of King Edward Who Rests at Westminster*, 2nd Edition (Oxford, 1992), 133–49. The dating of Goscelin's arrival at Sherborne depends heavily upon the date assigned to the start of Herman's involvement there, which should probably be somewhere in the early 1060s rather than 1058 as has often been proposed; see S Keynes, 'Giso, bishop of Wells (1061–88)', *Anglo-Norman Studies* 19 (1997), 203–71 at 208–9.
2   C H Talbot, 'The Life of Saint Wulfsin of Sherborne by Goscelin', *Revue Bénédictine* 69 (1959), 68–85; the edition needs to be read with Grosjean's review, referred to above, alongside it.

3   As he does explicitly in his *Life* of St Wærburh (*Patrologia Latina* 155, cols. 93–110), ch 9, where he apologises for keeping his readers waiting for what they really want, namely miracles, but reminds them that 'a virtuous life can be perfectly complete without miracles, but miracles are nothing without virtue'.

4   See Horstman (1901), *Nova Legenda Angliae*, I.98–99; Juthwara is beheaded by her brother Bana, who mistakenly believes her to be pregnant because her wicked stepmother has tricked her into using two cheeses as a poultice for chest-pains, and these drip milk and look like a pregnant woman's milk-laden breasts.

5   See the appraisal of Goscelin's methodology by Barlow, *The Life of King Edward*, 143–4.

6   *cf* Ps. 102(103):5 ('*renovabitur ut aquilae iuventus tua*').

7   Goscelin, in applying here the adjective *speculatiuus* to his episcopal dedicatee, may well have intended a pun which it is impossible to convey adequately in English, namely that the Latin noun *speculator* is equivalent to the Greek *episcopos*, one who keeps watch in a watch-tower, or, a bishop; the joke goes back at least as far as Columbanus who addressed the Pope as *reuerendissimo Speculatori* in his fifth letter, written in about 613.

8   *cf* Ps. 65(66):15 ('*holocausta medullata offeram tibi*'); see also Deut. 12:6.

9   A mistake seems to have been made somewhere along the line: by Goscelin, or by his informants, or during the transmission of the text, since the length of Wulfsige's episcopacy is nearer ten than twenty-five years. Grosjean, in his review (202–3) suggested that the error arose from here in the chapter-headings, advancing the ingenious hypothesis of a scribal confusion between **.II.** and **.V.**, ie between 'two quinquennia' [=10 years] and 'five quinquennia' [=25 years]. There seems to be no way of sorting it out now. A further problem arises later on with Goscelin's continued assertion that miracles only started to occur twelve years after Wulfsige's death, a figure which is again difficult to accommodate; see below.

10   Romans 12:19.

11   I Samuel 1:19–2:11 recounts the story of how the Samuel's parents promised their child to the Lord as his servant.

12   *cf* Acts 9:15, where God calls Paul his 'vessel of election'.

13   Luke 2:52 ('*et Iesus proficiebat sapientia et aetate*').

14   Ephes. 6:11 ('*induite vos armaturam Dei*') and 1 Thess. 5:8 ('*induto loricam fidei ... et galeam spem salutis*').

15   1 Cor. 9:27 ('*castigo corpus meum*').

16   *cf* James 2:23 ('*Abraham ... amicus Dei appellatus est*').

17   1 Cor. 9:21 ('*ut lucrifacerem eos*').

18   Mark 4:28 ('*primam herbam, deinde spicam, deinde plenum frumentum in spica*').

19   Edgar's father was Edmund (Ironside) not Eadwine; a mistake which Goscelin perpetrates again in ch XIV.

20   This is Goscelin's rather terse way of referring to an event described in most of the Lives of Dunstan – see W Stubbs, *Memorials of St Dunstan* (London, 1874), 56 (Adelard), 93 (Osbern), and 183 (Eadmer) – in which Dunstan, just elected abbot of Glastonbury, at the time of Edgar's birth (ie 943) received a revelation of heavenly voices singing '*Pax anglorum ecclesie exorti nunc pueri et Dunstani nostri tempore* (Peace for the church of the English in the time of the boy now born and of our Dunstan)'; the prophecy is reported in this form by Adelard and Eadmer. He also refers to the prophecy at greater length in Bk 1, ch 2 of his *Vita S. Edithe*, ed.

Wilmart, 'La légende de Sainte Édithe', (1938), 40.

21 *cf* Matt. 20:1–16, the parable of the labourers in the vineyard.

22 *cf* Ps. 51(52):10 ('*oliva fructifera in domo Dei*').

23 *cf* Luke 16:10 ('*qui fidelis in minimo, et in maiori fidelis est*').

24 Goscelin here makes a pun, impossible to convey in English, on the root '*occid-*', by saying that Sherborne falls ('*occiderat*') in the region of the setting ('*occidentalis*') sun.

25 *cf* Goscelin's comment in his *Life of Wulfhild*, ch 4, on Wulfhild's control of the convents at both Barking and Horton: '*binas itaque eclesias ut Christi bigas et unam domum unica caritate aurigabat* (with undivided affection she controlled the two churches, like two of Christ's chariots, as one single house)' (M L Colker, 'Texts of Jocelyn of Canterbury which Relate to the History of Barking Abbey', *Studia Monastica* 7 (1965), 383–460, at 424).

26 This is a conflation of two separate portions of scripture, Zach. 13:7 ('*framea suscitare super pastorem meum*') and Jer. 23:1 ('*vae pastoribus qui disperdunt et dilacerant gregem pascuae meae*'); in fact Goscelin appears to be quoting, absolutely verbatim, one of the standard antiphons for matins on the Tuesday after Palm Sunday: '*framea suscitare adversus eos qui dispergunt gregem meum*'; see R.-J. Hesbert, *Corpus Antiphonalium Officii*, Four volumes (Rome, 1963-70), III no 2893.

27 Gal. 5:10.

28 *cf* Matt. 25:14–30, the parable of the talents.

29 Phil. 3:13 ('*quae quidem retro sunt obliviscens, ad ea vero quae sunt priora, extendens meipsum*').

30 Prov. 6:3 ('*discurre festina suscita amicum tuum*').

31 2 Tim. 4:5 ('*opus fac evangelistae ministerium tuum imple*').

32 Eph. 6:15 ('*calceati pedes in praeparatione Evangelii pacis*').

33 *cf* Rom. 8:15 ('*spiritum adoptionis filiorum*'), and Gal. 4:5, Eph. 1:5 ('*adoptionem filiorum*').

34 The MS reads '*ierarchia*'; for better sense Grosjean suggested emendation to '*ierarcha*', a reading also supported by the version of the *Life* in Lansdowne 436. Here Goscelin subtly echoes a phrase from Sulpicius Severus' *Life* of St Martin of Tours which had long since become a commonplace of hagiography: 'at that time he was reckoned not so much a soldier as a monk' (bk II.7, '*illo tempore non miles sed monachus putaretur*', ed J Fontaine, *Sulpice Sévère, Vie de Saint Martin* (three volumes), Sources Chrétiennes 133–5, Paris, 1967, I.256).

35 Ps. 122(123):1–2 verbatim.

36 Ps. 118(119):7 ('*confitebor tibi in directione cordis*').

37 Ps. 18(19):15 ('*et meditatio cordis mei in conspectu tuo semper*').

38 By '*annunciacionem mandatorum eius et officium seruitutis ipsius*' presumably Goscelin here alludes to the *Mandatum* ceremony of Maundy Thursday which commemorates Christ's act of service in washing the disciples feet (as recounted in the John's Gospel, chapter 13); here 'commandments' is perhaps an allusion to first antiphon sung during the *Mandatum*, which gives the ceremony its name, that is '*Mandatum novum*', John 13:34, 'a new commandment I give unto you: That you love one another'.

39 Presumably the Chrism Mass, at which the bishop blessed the oils used for anointing the sick and dying, and for baptism.

40 *cf* 1 Cor. 9:24 ('*ii qui in stadio currunt, omnes quidem currunt, sed unus accipit bravium. Sic currite ut comprehendatis*'). See note 9 above on the matter of Wulfsige's supposed twenty-five-year episcopacy.

41 *cf* 1 Pet. 4:10 ('*sicut boni dispensatores*') and Luke 12:42 ('*quis est fidelis dispensator*').

42 *cf* Luke 12:36 ('*cum venerit et pulsaverit, confestim aperiant ei*') and *cf* also Revelation 3:20.

43 *cf* Matt. 25:21 and 23 ('*intra in gaudium domini tui*').

44 Matt. 10:41 (or Luke 10:16) verbatim.

45 Matt. 11:2–3 ('*an alium exspectamus?*').

46 Ps. 16(17):7 ('*mirifica misericordias tuas*').

47 Ps. 1:3 ('*fructum suum dabit in tempore suo*').

48 *cf* Eph. 2:2 ('*principem potestatis aeris huius*').

49 *cf* Ps. 3:4, 41(42):10, 90(91):2.

50 Acts 7:56.

51 Matt. 5:8.

52 This is the responsory for the second nocturn of the vigil of the Feast of Stephen, as prescribed in the *Antiphonale Missarum Sextuplex,* ed R-J Hesbert (Brussels, 1935).

53 *cf* 2 Thess. 2:6 ('*ut reveletur in suo tempore*').

54 Bede, *Historia Ecclesiastica* IV.11.

55 The text actually has '*viii idus ianuarii* (on the eighth ides of January)', which is the 6th, and must be a scribal error, contradicting, as it does, other evidence for the day of Wulfsige's death.

56 It is nowhere else mentioned that the day of Wulfsige's death fell on a Sunday – if indeed this is the correct interpretation of Goscelin's characteristically oblique phrase. It is generally accepted that Wulfsige died in 1002, yet 8 January fell on a Sunday in 999, so perhaps this is merely a piece of embroidery by Goscelin, or an erroneous story which had circulated at Sherborne.

57 *cf* John 12:24–5.

58 Since Archbishop Ælfheah, who was murdered in 1012, is said to have sanctioned the first translation of Wulfsige, the twelve years which Goscelin refers to more than once would have to be only an approximation, as Wulfsige's death occurred in 1002.

59 The bishop of Worcester at this date would have been Wulfstan; at no time was the position occupied by a namesake of Wulfsige. See F Barlow, *The English Church, 1000–1066* (London, 1979), 68 n 2 for the suggestion that this 'Wulfsige' is a conflation of Wulfstan and Leofsige, his successor, perhaps reflecting a joke about Leofsige's subordination to his superior.

60 Mark 2:9 or John 5:11.

61 This long sentence is hopelessly confused in its syntax and it is quite likely that the text is corrupt at this point; in an attempt to sort it out I have wondered tentatively whether the verb *lustrat* might be an error for *lustra* (= 'offerings' or 'purificatory sacrifices'; perhaps alluding to the fact that Candlemas marked the Purification of Mary). The solution is only partial, and not entirely satisfactory, but fortunately the general sense is clear enough, namely that the miracle occurred during the ceremonies of Candlemas (ie 2 February).

62 Talbot's text here reads *corpus de sepulcro uelud de mortis speculo aggressus est*; which makes little sense as it stands, not least because there seems to be a verb missing from the text as preserved by Gotha I.81; at this point the version in Lansdowne 436 reads *de sepulcro uelud de mortis speleo assumere aggressus est*, which I have accordingly adopted in my translation.

63 Goscelin here seems to have got into confusion over his kings of England (this

may just conceivably be a scribal error at some stage in the transmission of the text, though the mistake is consistent throughout), since he must mean here Edmund Ironside, rather that Eadwine, and it is not clear quite what he means by this reference to the death of 'Eadwine' Edmund, nor yet to what the '*septies* (seven times over)' might refer.

64   *cf* Ezech. 2:4 ('*dura facie et indomabili corde*').

65   Here again Goscelin indulges in word-play which it is hard to replicate in English: the woman who won't be convinced by words alone (*ex verbis*) is brought up short by a beating instead (*ex verbere*).

66   *cf* Matt. 16:19, where Peter is promised the power of binding and loosing.

67   Again Goscelin refers to Edmund as Eadwine. Moreover, he is mistaken to say that Æthelric died during the reign of Edmund: this must apply rather to his successor Æthelsige, whose date of death could therefore be assigned to before 1016.

68   Ælfmær was abbot of St Augustine's, Canterbury, 1006–23. In his later work, the *Historia translationis S. Augustini (Patrologia Latina* CLV.30), composed for that house, Goscelin, not surprisingly, gives a version of this story with a different slant, saying that Ælfmær, being struck blind 'by the judgement of the mercy of God, who smites those He loves', voluntarily left the see of Sherborne 'which he had unwillingly taken up'.

69   Ælfwold's succession is dated to 1045.

70   This and the following sentence make very poor sense as they stand, and the text seems in some way to be corrupt (Talbot just printed them and put [*sic*] at the end). Literally we have: 'but the blessed Wulfsige had granted to the brothers of his monastery the tithes and the half carucate of plough-land from the bishop. Certainly he has the reward of his fatherly care (patronage?), who (which?) offerers may have of the judge is of all'; my translation is merely an attempt to convey what appears to be the broad sense. It has been suggested that the reference to tithes may be an interpolation; see the discussion of a spurious Sherborne charter which records a similar grant to the monks by Wulfsige, in M A O'Donovan (ed), *Charters of Sherborne*, Anglo-Saxon Charters III (Oxford, 1988), no 12. There Wulfsige is purported to be granting '*unum cassatum in ipsa uilla* [Sherborne] *et omnem decimam episcopii* [sic] *eiusdem uille in omnibus rebus* (one hide in that same town, and all the tithes of the bishop in the same town in all things)'.

Bibliography

Barlow, F, 1979, *The English Church, 1000–1066*. London.

Barlow, F (ed and trans), 1992, *The Life of King Edward Who Rests at Westminster* (2nd Edition). Oxford.

Colker, M L, 1965, Texts of Jocelyn of Canterbury which Relate to the History of Barking Abbey. *Studia Monastica* 7, 383–460.

Fontaine, J (ed), 1967, *Sulpice Sévère, Vie de Saint Martin* (Three volumes). Paris. Sources Chrétiennes, 133–5.

Grosjean, P, 1960, review of C H Talbot, The Life of Saint Wulsin of Sherborne by Goscelin. *Analecta Bollandiana* 78, 197–206.

Hesbert, R-J (ed), 1935, *Antiphonale Missarum Sextuplex*. Brussels.

Hesbert, R-J, 1963–70, *Corpus Antiphonalium Officii* (Four volumes). Rome.

Horstman C (ed), 1901, *Nova Legenda Angliae* (Two volumes). Oxford.

Keynes, S, 1997, Giso, bishop of Wells (1061–88). *Anglo-Norman Studies* 19, 203–71.

O'Donovan, M A (ed), 1988, *Charters of Sherborne*. Anglo-Saxon Charters III. Oxford.

Stubbs, W, 1874, *Memorials of St Dunstan*. London.

Talbot, C H, 1955, The *Liber Confortatorius* of Goscelin of Saint Bertin. *Analecta Monastica, Studia Anselmiana*, 37, 1–117.

Talbot, C H, 1959, The Life of Saint Wulsin of Sherborne by Goscelin. *Revue Benedictine* 69, 68–85.

Wilmart, A, 1938, La légende de Sainte Édithe en prose et vers par le moine Goscelin. *Analecta Bollandiana* 56, 5–101, 265–307.

11. Bishop Wulfsige's lifetime: Viking campaigns recorded in the Anglo-Saxon Chronicle for southern England

Katherine Barker

Viking raids were a part of life during the ninth, tenth and eleventh centuries. For over two hundred years people in southern England lived with an ever-present threat which could turn into a nightmare. Sightings of Viking [Danish] ships evoked fear. Anyone living upstream of an estuary or harbour could be seriously at risk. The entries in the Anglo-Saxon Chronicle tell us, in bald terms, of English kingdoms highly organised on a war-footing – a state of alert – in an attempt to deal with an often desperate situation. The pages are full of references to sub-divisions of the kingdoms, the *shires*[1] – in the south, to Dorsetshire, Somersetshire and Devonshire; to the other *shires* of the kingdom of the West Saxons (Wessex), and to *shire* levies of men – or tribute; to *shire* leaders or *ealdormen* [aldermen]; to the military role of various other senior and/or high-born officials and, not least, to bishops with responsibilities for defence, including the provision of ships and their crews (see Barker, 'Sherborne in AD 998', this volume). In 848, a century and a half before Wulfsige, Bishop Ealhstan of Sherborne joined with others and 'fought against a Danish host at the mouth of the [River] Parrett'. A respite finally came with the famous victory by King Alfred in Somerset in 878.

Viking activity increased again in the course of the tenth century, and the decades of the 980s and 990s were 'dangerous and difficult times' as we hear in an episcopal letter to Wulfsige (Keynes, 'Wulfsige, monk of Glastonbury', this volume). As Keynes points out, the very year of Wulfsige's charter, 998, witnessed the 'host' land at the mouth of the River Frome – Poole harbour – and 'push up into Dorset in whatever direction they pleased' (Fig 9). 'Many a time levies were gathered to oppose them; but as soon as battle was about to begin, word was given to withdraw, and always in the end the host had the victory.' Figure 10 is an evocative view of the mouth of the Frome nine centuries

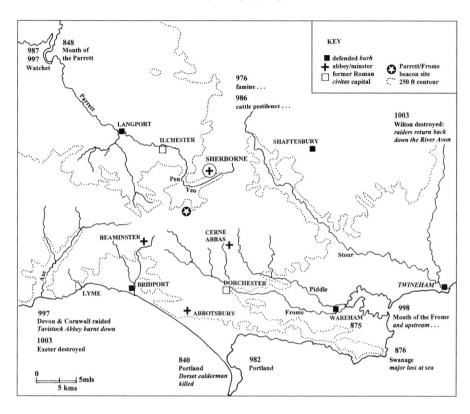

KEY

- ■ defended *burh*
- + abbey/minster
- ▢ former Roman *civitas* capital
- ✪ Parrett/Frome beacon site
- ⋰ 250 ft contour

848
Mouth of the Parrett

987
997
Watchet

976
famine . . .

986
cattle pestilence . . .

1003
Wilton destroyed:
*raiders return back
down the River Avon*

LANGPORT

ILCHESTER

SHAFTESBURY

SHERBORNE

Pen

Yeo

BEAMINSTER

CERNE ABBAS

Stour

BRIDPORT

DORCHESTER

Piddle

TWINEHAM

LYME

997
Devon & Cornwall raided
Tavistock Abbey burnt down

1003
Exeter destroyed

ABBOTSBURY

Frome

WAREHAM
875

998
Mouth of the Frome
and upstream . . .

876
Swanage
major loss at sea

840
Portland
*Dorset ealdorman
killed*

982
Portland

0 ⊢——————⊣ 5mls
5 kms

Figure 9. Map of the area around Sherborne; including the whole of Dorset and parts of Somerset, Devon and Wiltshire, to show Viking raiding activity as recorded in the Anglo-Saxon Chronicle in the years between 848 and 1003 in relation to the main river systems of the region.

later after a considerable rise in sea level. Ælfric, abbot of Cerne, scholar and writer, predictably concluded that God had sent punishment in the form of a heathen army because men had rejected the monastic life in favour of the lax standards of the secular clergy (Keynes, 'Wulfsige, monk of Glastonbury', this volume). Such a comment might reflect the state of things in Sherborne in the years before 998; Ælfric was sent to Cerne in 987. The Vikings, ('the pirate host') were heathen and pillaged their Christian neighbours with notorious savagery. There is, however, no reference to damage done to any Dorset abbey in 998.

Whilst it might be tempting to suggest this was because the levies of Dorsetshire were particularly well-organised, there is no evidence either one way or the other. Faced with a water-based enemy, Sherborne itself was geo-

Figure 10. Poole Harbour from Studland looking northwards towards the Borough of Poole. It is also the mouth of the River Frome which flows into the harbour on the left-hand side of the picture. 'In this year [998] the [Viking] host turned eastward into the mouth of the Frome, and pushed up into Dorset in whatever direction they pleased. Many a time the levies were gathered to oppose them; but as soon as battle was about to begin, word was given to withdraw, and always in the end had the victory' (Anglo-Saxon Chronicle). A thousand years ago sea level was lower and some of the marshy ground in the picture was probably dry land. (E Haslehurst, watercolour c 1910; published source not located)

graphically rather well placed. While not actually very far from the coast as the crow flies, Sherborne is sited a long way upstream and is impossible to access – or escape – by boat. Confronted by organised resistance, raiders coming up the Parrett could not have penetrated further than Pen at Yeovil – possibly not further than Ilchester – and those approaching from the south coming up the Frome could not navigate the narrow chalk valley tributary streams leading north and west into the heart of the county without leaving the safety of their boats.

It may be noted that the year before Edgar sanctioned the setting up of the Benedictine House at Winchester in 963–4, there had been a 'very great pestilence'. Edgar's legislation on church dues of the year 962 related the origins of the pestilence with the wages of sin and the non-payment of tithes (Chaney 1999, 239). There is no recorded outbreak of pestilence for the year 996–7, but the wording of the Sherborne charter of 998 could possibly reflect some of the longer-term changes effected by such a calamity of a generation earlier (Barker, 'Sherborne in AD 998', this volume). Whatever befell the human population, this was followed up in 976 by famine, and in 986 by the 'first [coming] to England' of 'the great pestilence among cattle'. In the event, King Æthelred's reign (979–1016), was to produce more law codes than of any other Anglo-Saxon monarch, including the royal protection of churches (Chaney 1999, 230).

By 1016 the Viking menace was, in effect, all over. King Cnut became king of the English and his wife, Queen Emma [Aelgifu], gave money to repair the roof of the cathedral church at Sherborne. In the fullness of time Cnut died at Shaftesbury. But the organisation of the kingdom into shires (*counties* to the Normans) for purposes of tax, justice and military service remained. The shire boundaries recorded in the Domesday Book of 1086 are to an overwhelming extent exactly what they were hundreds of years later (Campbell 1993). When the Normans conquered the kingdom they took over a structured and systematic administrative system which remained largely unaltered into the nineteenth century. The key official, that of county sheriff, the *shire reeve*, was already established by the year 1000.

The passages below are selected from entries in the Anglo-Saxon Chronicle (Garmonsway 1954; see also Swanton 1996) with special reference to south and south-west England, and are left to speak for themselves. Wulfsige's parents were surely alive by the 940s if not before; his grandparents would probably have remembered Alfred. The map (Fig 9) illustrates Chronicle entries relating to Dorset and Somerset which are referenced by their dates, together with brief notes as to their significance.

We cannot know exactly how news spread, and what news would have reached Wulfsige, or how quickly – nor as to its precise on-the-ground significance at the time (propaganda or 'spin' is evidenced in the Chronicle; it is not a new art) – nor have any idea as to what might be missing from the story in events that were not recorded. But we are left in no doubt whatever that the threat from the coast was very real; the manning and maintenance of cross-country early warning beacons, *rogi*, was clearly important (Keynes, 'Wulfsige, monk of Glastonbury' and Barker, the Sherborne Estate at Lyme', this volume). The first Viking raids reported in western Europe were in the final decades of the eighth century. Most notorious were the attacks on coastal monasteries on the north-east coast of England, Lindisfarne and probably Jarrow. One incident, however, is recorded along the south coast. The crews of three ships, described later as from Hordaland in Norway, landed on Portland during the reign of the West Saxon king Beorhtric (786–802). The Dorset reeve rode out to investigate, and was killed.

Selected entries from the Anglo-Saxon Chronicle from the years 838 to 1003 relating to southern England

References to the Sherborne region, Somerset, Dorset and the West Saxon kingdom are in bold type. Chronicle entries 992–1002, for the years Wulfsige was at Sherborne, are denoted by asterisks.

838   In this year came a great pirate host to Cornwall, and they [the Danes and the Britons of Cornwall] united, and continued against **Egbert, king of Wessex.** Then he heard this and proceeded with his levies and fought them at Hingston Down, and there put to flight both Britons and Danes.

840   In this year ealdorman Wulfheard fought at Southampton against thirty-three ships' companies, and made great slaughter there and won the victory ... And the same year ealdorman Æthelhelm fought against a Danish host at Portland **with the men of Dorset**, and for a considerable time they drove back the host, but the Danes had possession of the place of slaughter and **slew the ealdorman [of Dorset]** ...

848   In this year ealdorman Eanwulf with the **men of Somerset** and bishop Ealhstan **[of Sherborne]** and ealdorman Osric with the **men of Dorset** fought against a Danish host at the mouth of the Parrett, and made great slaughter there and won the victory.

850   In this year ealdorman Ceorl with the men of Devon fought against the heathen at Wiceganbeorg, and made great slaughter there and won the victory ... And the heathen for the first time remained over the winter. And the same year [851] came three hundred and fifty ships to the mouth of the Thames, and stormed Canterbury and London, and put to flight Beorhtwulf, king of Mercia, with his levies, and went south over Thames into Surrey; and king Æthelwulf and his Æthelbald, **with the West Saxon levies**, fought them at Acleah, and there made the greatest slaughter of a heathen host that we have heard tell of up to this present day, and there won the victory.

866   ... and in the same year died bishop Ealhstan, and he held the episcopal see at **Sherborne** fifty years; and his body lies there in the churchyard.

870   In this year came the host to Reading in Wessex ... four days afterwards ... king Æthelred and Alfred his brother, led great levies there to Reading ... great slaughter on either side ... Ashdown ... Basing ... and there the Danes had a great victory ... then **Alfred** succeeded to the **kingdom of Wessex** ... in the course of the year nine engagements were fought ... south of the Thames ... and the West Saxons made peace. At Easter, king Æthelred died and ... his body lies **at Wimborne**.

875   In this year the host eluded the **West Saxon levies** and got into **Wareham** ... and the king made peace ... that they would quickly leave the kingdom;

and then under cover of this agreement they evaded the English levies by nights and the mounted host got to Exeter.

876   In this year came the host into Exeter from **Wareham** ... and were caught in a great storm at sea, and there off **Swanage** one hundred and twenty ships were lost ... and Alfred rode to Exeter ... [the host] were in the fortress where they could not be got.

878   In this year the host went secretly to Chippenham and rode over Wessex and occupied it ... and drove a great part of the inhabitants oversea ... Alfred took refuge in inaccessible places ... then after Easter ... rode to Egbryhtesstan, to the east of Selwood, and came to meet him there all the **men of Somerset** and Wiltshire and that part of Hampshire ... on this side of the water. [This leads on to the well-known story of Alfred hiding in the Somerset marshes – and the burning of the cakes – the defeat of the Danes, the baptism of Guthrum their leader and the creation of the Danelaw. For the next few years raiding was concentrated along the rivers of northern France and the Low Countries].

889   In this year no journey was made to Rome, except by two couriers whom Alfred sent with letters.

897   Then on one occasion in the same year came six ships to the Isle of Wight and did much harm there, both in Devon and almost everywhere along the coast. The king ordered nine of the new ships to put out and they blockaded the entrance from the sea ... three of the ships were beached on dry land at the upper end of the harbour [**?Poole/Hamworthy**] and the crews had gone off inland ... they escaped because the ships of the others were aground.

899   In this year Alfred died ...

962   In this year there was a very great pestilence, and a destructive fire in London burnt down St Paul's: it was rebuilt the same year.

963   In this year St Æthelwold was chosen by King Edgar to be bishop of Winchester, and St Dunstan archbishop of Canterbury ... in the year after he was consecrated he established many monasteries, and drove out the secular clergy because they would not observe any monastic rule and replaced them with monks. Then he came to king Edgar and asked him to give him all the monasteries which the heathen had destroyed, because he wished to restore them and the king cheerfully granted it.

976   In this year there was great famine in England.

980   ... the same year Southampton was ravaged by a pirate host and most of the citizens were slain or taken hostage.

981   In this year Padstow was laid waste, and in the same year much destruction was done everywhere along the coast, both in Devon and Cornwall. In the same year passed away Ælfstan bishop of Wiltshire ...

982   In this year three pirate crews landed in **Dorset** and **ravaged Portland**. The same year there was a great fire in London ... two ealdormen passed away, Æthelmaer of Hampshire and Eadwine of Sussex ... and two abbesses of Dorset ... Herelufu **of Shaftesbury** and Wulfwynn **of Wimborne** ...

986   ... the great pestilence among cattle first came to England ...

987   In this year **Watchet** was ravaged ... and Goda the Devonshire thegn was slain.

991   In this year Ipswich was harried, and ... ealdorman Byrhtnoth was slain at [the battle of] Maldon. In this year it was decided for the first time to pay tribute to the Danes because of the great terror they inspired along the sea coast. This course was adopted on the advice of archbishop Sigeric.

992*   In this year ... the king ... decided that all ships ... should be collected at London and ... gave command of the levies to ealdorman Ælfric, earl Thored, bishop Ælfstan and bishop Æscwig ... the host was engaged [at sea] and [they] made great slaughter of them ...

994*   In this year Anlaf and Swein came to London with ninety four ships and kept up an unceasing attack on the city and they ... set it on fire ... went away doing as much harm as they could ... burning, harrying and slaughter both along the coast and in Essex, Kent and Hampshire ... took up winter quarters in Southampton ... Then the king ... decided to offer them tribute ... this was done and they accepted it, together with provisions which were given to them from the whole of the **West Saxon kingdom** ... sixteen thousand pounds ... conducted with great ceremony at Andover ...

997*   In this year the host went round Devonshire into the mouth of the Severn, and they harried, both in Cornwall, Wales and Devon, and landed at **Watchet**; they wrought great havoc by burning and killing people and then went back round Land's End ... and entered the estuary of the Tamar, and so up it until they came to Lydford. There they burned and slew everything they met and burnt to the ground Ordwulf's abbey church at Tavistock, carrying off an indescribable amount of plunder ...

998*   In this year the host turned eastward again into **the mouth of the Frome**, and pushed up into **Dorset** in whatever direction they pleased. Many a time levies were gathered to oppose them; but as soon as a battle was about to begin, word was given to withdraw, and always in the end the host had the victory. Then for another period they had their base in the Isle of Wight and drew their supplies meanwhile from Hampshire and Sussex.

1001*   In this year there were constant hostilities in England because of the pirate host ... they overran the countryside and followed their usual tactics of slaying and burning ... the vast levies of the men of Devon and **Somerset** were mustered and they joined battle at Pinhoe ... No fleet by sea nor levies on land dared approach them, however far inland they went. It was in every way a hard time for they never ceased from their evil deeds.

1002*   In this year the king and his councillors decided to pay tribute to the fleet and to make peace ... this was accepted and they were paid twenty four thousand pounds. Then in the midst of all these events ... the king gave orders for all Danish [Viking] people who were in England to be slain on St Brice's Day [13 November] ... [fearing they would kill him by treachery and seize the kingdom].

1003   In this year Exeter was destroyed ... utterly laid waste ... [then] Swein led his host into Wilton and they sacked and burnt down the borough and then went to Salisbury ...

* * * * * * * *

Wulfsige died in West Dorset in Beaminster, one of his episcopal manors, on 8 January 1002, and the event is recorded by Goscelin (Love, 'The Life of St Wulfsige', this volume). As noted earlier, it was less than four seasons before, in 998, the year of the charter, the Vikings had come up the River Frome and penetrated deep into Dorset 'in whatever direction they pleased' and 'and always had the victory'. But Beaminster lies to the west across the watershed, well upstream on the Brit and, like Sherborne, all but impossible to access safely by boat. The Chronicle remains silent about the fortunes of Dorset in 1002, and so does Goscelin. But it was later that same year that twenty-four thousand pounds of tribute was raised to pay off the Viking fleet, and the king, in fear of his life, ordered the killing of all Danish (that is, Viking) people in England on St Brice's Day, 13 November. And neighbouring shires had seen – or were yet to see – major action as described above. Entries for the year before Wulfsige's death, 1001, refer to 'vast levies of men of Devon and Somerset' engaged in battle at Pinhoe (near Exeter), and for the year after, 1003, of 'great levies assembled from Wiltshire and Hampshire', and the destruction of both Exeter and Wilton.

    Bishop Wulfsige's body was carried safely back to Sherborne through a troubled countryside. With little doubt it was a world both 'dangerous and difficult'. We may only speculate as to the precise route taken. It took the bier and its bearers – described by Goscelin (Love, 'The Life of St Wulfsige', this volume), – through the episcopal hundreds of both Beaminster and Yetminster, climbing northwards up the steep route out of Beaminster, along the ridge and on down through Corscombe (possibly the *Wulfheardigstoke* of 998; Barker, 'Sherborne in AD 998', this volume), then continuing through Halstock

[*Halganstoke 998*, holy *stoc* or place] remembered for St Juthwara (also Goscelin, Love, 'The Life of St Wulfsige', this volume), turning east and meeting the River Yeo at the 'broad ford' – Bradford (Abbas) [*Bradanforda 998*] and so on up the Yeo valley to Sherborne. The procession will never have left Sherborne land, accompanied perhaps not only by hymn-singing mourners, but by armed members of the episcopal hundred levy. The latter-day representatives of such a route are winding and rural, nicely surfaced for motor vehicles, helpfully sign-posted from Beaminster – but not to Sherborne.

Note

1   'Shire' from Old English *scieran* – 'to cut'; being the division of the kingdom into administrative areas. Hampshire is first mentioned in the Chronicle in 757, and the other five shires of the old kingdom of Wessex, including Dorset, are mentioned, in succession, between 800 and 860 as units of organised resistance against the Vikings. All six may be a century or so older. 'The shiring of England was notably systematic ... a creation of an integrated system of administration [which] was far-reaching and long-lasting.' Each shire was, by the tenth century, divided into hundreds (wapentakes in the north) each assessed at a round number of hides for the payment of tax and for purposes of military service 'a system of formidable and integrated power' (Campbell 1993).

Bibliography

Campbell, J, 1993, *The History of the English Shires*. Hampshire County Council.
Chaney, W A, 1999 (first published 1970), *The Cult of Kingship in Anglo-Saxon England*. Manchester.
Domesday Book, Dorset, 1983, C and A Thorn (eds). Chichester.
Garmonsway, G N (trans), 1954, *The Anglo-Saxon Chronicle* (2nd Edition). London.
Swanton, M (trans and ed), 1996, *The Anglo-Saxon Chronicle*. London.

12. Sherborne:
Saxon Christianity *be Westanwuda*

Teresa Hall

The first mention of the diocese of 'Sherborne' occurs in the Anglo-Saxon Chronicle in the year AD 709 when we are told of the death of Aldhelm, its first bishop. He had been appointed four years earlier to a newly created diocese – *be Westanwuda* – to the west of Selwood (Thorpe 1861a, 68, 69; 1861b, 38). This paper will look at the conversion of the West Saxons and the establishment of Sherborne, the influence of trends within the English church at the time and the organisation of Christianity in Wessex in the late seventh and eighth centuries.[1]

The origins of Christianity in Wessex and the West Saxon bishopric
The origins of the West Saxon church and its relationship with Canterbury form an important backdrop to the foundation of Sherborne. In the second quarter of the seventh century, the kingdom of Wessex centred on the Upper Thames basin (Yorke 1995, 57). Bede tells us that Birinus, a Frankish bishop, arrived among the Gewisse in AD 634 and finding them completely heathen he remained with them, bent upon their conversion. Their king, Cynegils, whether for religious or political reasons, was obviously sufficiently impressed with the new religion to become a Christian. He was baptised under the sponsorship of Oswald, king of Northumbria who then married one of Cynegils' daughters. Dorchester on Thames (Fig 11) was given to Birinus and it became the first West Saxon see (HE iii.7).

The path to conversion was strewn with pitfalls, however. An initial set-back followed the death of Cynegils when his son, Cenwalh, a pagan, succeeded to the throne. Cenwalh was driven from Wessex by Penda, king of the Mercians when he rejected his wife (Penda's sister) in favour of another woman. This inadvertently led to his conversion when he took refuge with Anna, king of the East Angles, a devout Christian. Cenwalh was restored to his kingdom and (as Birinus had died) he accepted an offer from Agilbert, a Gaulish bishop who had been studying in Ireland, to evangelise the kingdom. All went well for about ten

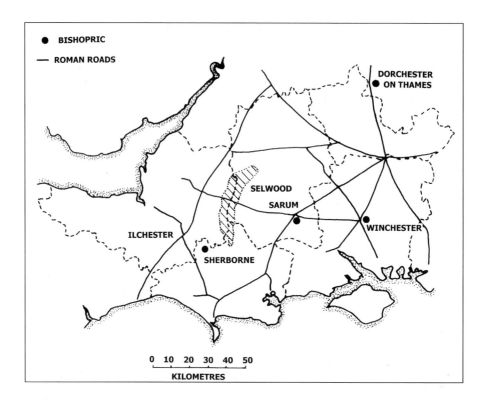

Figure 11. Map showing the dioceses of Sherborne (west of Selwood) and Winchester (east of Selwood).

years, but in *c* AD 660, the Mercians were pressing heavily on the northern borders of Wessex, and Dorchester on Thames fell into their hands. Cenwalh appears to have used the situation to rid himself of Agilbert – as he 'grew tired of the bishop's foreign speech' – and he installed a new bishop, Wine (who had been consecrated in Gaul but spoke English), at Winchester (HE iii.7). Bede tells us that Agilbert returned to Gaul to take up the bishopric of Paris, but before this happened, he went to Northumbria where he attended the Synod of Whitby in AD 664.

Wine did not remain long in Wessex after this event. He too, was driven away by Cenwalh, leaving Wessex again without a bishop. Wine seems to have been unorthodox in his approach. He must have accepted Cenwalh's offer of the bishopric of Winchester behind Agilbert's back, and in AD 665, he conducted the consecration of the Northumbrian Chad as bishop, uncanonically, with the help of two British bishops (HE iii.28). Enforcing the impression that he was of rather dubious profession, we hear that he purchased the bishopric of London from King Wulfhere of the Mercians (before AD 670) where he remained until he died. The situation in Wessex stabilised when Agilbert (following a plea by Cenwalh to return), sent his nephew, Leuthere, to be bishop as he could not forsake the bishopric of Paris (HE iii.7). From this time the bishopric became more firmly established and remained a single see based at Winchester until the death of Bishop Haedde.

So it was that when the West Saxons began their conquest of Dorset and Somerset, in the second half of the seventh century, they had already been converted to Christianity. Archaeologically, this is apparent in Dorset and Somerset where there are only a few small clusters of pagan burials – a very insignificant number compared with the widespread occurrence in neighbouring Wiltshire and Hampshire (Geake 1997, 203).

The choice of Sherborne as the site of the bishopric

With the arrival of Archbishop Theodore in AD 668 the structure of the English church was thoroughly overhauled. Many of the existing dioceses consisted of whole kingdoms and Theodore set about dividing up those that were over large whenever a suitable opportunity arose. The process was not without opposition, witness Wilfrid and Northumbria (Colgrave 1927, 48–51; HE v.19). The diocese of Wessex, however, was not divided during Theodore's lifetime, possibly because of his friendship with Haedde – Theodore's only surviving poem is dedicated to Haedde (Bischoff and Lapidge 1994, 186–9). It remained intact during Haedde's long episcopate (twenty-nine years) and was finally divided on his death in AD 705/6. A new see was created for Aldhelm, west of the great forest of Selwood (Fig 11), covering the expanding Saxon area of control – probably Dorset, Somerset and parts of Devon. Winchester, under Bishop Daniel, would continue to serve as bishopric for Berkshire, Hampshire and Wiltshire.[2]

What made Sherborne a suitable contender for the seat of the new diocese of Selwood? On the continent, bishops' sees were founded in important Roman administrative centres. This was obviously problematical in England where Roman towns had ceased to function, but the course of action taken was to plant the bishoprics in places that formerly had been Roman towns, such as Canterbury itself, and Dorchester on Thames and Winchester in Wessex. Sherborne does not fit this pattern. It has some Roman settlement remains, but was never a Roman town, so we must look elsewhere to explain why it was chosen for the bishop's seat. It is surprising that nearby Ilchester, a former Roman town and a royal estate, was not the preferred choice. An alternative explanation of Sherborne's attraction must be sought.

As Laurence Keen has pointed out, an important factor must have been the availability of a large area of land to support the bishop (1984, 208–9).[3] Indeed, David Farmer ('The monastic reform of the tenth century', this volume, and see below) suggests that Aldhelm may already have held the land. Fowler suggested that Sherborne had another attraction: it may already have possessed an established ecclesiastical status 'with traditions of its own'. He refers to a charter of Cenwalh, dated AD 671, which grants privileges to 'the pontifical Church of Sherborne', suggesting that whilst the text is clearly spurious, partly because it refers to a bishopric at this early date, it might preserve the tradition of a grant by Cenwalh to an earlier church (Fowler 1951, 30–1). Finberg moved the debate forward, citing a grant of land made to Sherborne, again by Cenwalh, which is recorded in a fourteenth-century list of benefactors of Sherborne (1964, 98).[4] The entry reads, '*Kenewalc rex dedit Lanprobi de . c . hydis* (Cenwalh, king, gave one hundred hides of *Lanprobi*)', implying that Cenwalh gave one hundred hides of land associated with a place called *Lanprobi* (O'Donovan 1988, 81). The word *Lanprobi* in the text probably represents a place-name, **Lanprobus*, which would derive from the Cornish elements lann, an enclosure, especially a cemetery, and Probus, a west country saint (Padel 1985, 142–4; Farmer 1978, 408). As early as 1913, Baring-Gould and Fisher (1913, 107) noted that the implication of the name, which they equated with Sherborne, was that Sherborne had been the site of a British monastery.[5]

The site of Lanprobi

The whereabouts of *Lanprobi* has been much debated (Barker 1980, 229–31; Hinton 1981, 222–3; Keen 1984, 209–12; O'Donovan 1988, 86–7; Hall 2000, 11, 52–3). Katherine Barker suggested that it lay under the town of Sherborne itself (1980, 229–31). Finberg drew attention to papal bulls of 1145 and 1163 which point to the site that is now the Old Castle in Sherborne (Fig 12) (1964, 98). The first reference links *Propeschirche* with an area called Stocland, which has been fixed, variously, as the Sherborne Out-hundred (Barker 1982, 109) or, as seems more likely, an area of meadow land to the east of the castle (Keen 1984, 211–12). The second papal bull refers to the church of St Mary Magdalene next to Sherborne Castle, with its chapels of St Michael and St Probus. *Propeschirche* and the chapel of St Probus (which must be the same church) are interpreted as the site of *Lanprobi*. The implication is that the new cathedral of Aldhelm did not centre itself at the earlier British site of *Lanprobi*, but about half a kilometre to the west, down the valley where a minor south-flowing stream enters the River Yeo.

An examination of the plan of Sherborne in the immediate vicinity of the abbey church, shows it to be rectilinear in form, a characteristic of many of the minster church settlements in Dorset (Hall 2000, 49–78). There is, therefore, evidence of a change of site and plan associated with Aldhelm's new cathedral church (whether from under the northern part of Sherborne, as suggested by Katherine Barker, or from what is now the Old Castle). The *lann* element of the *Lanprobi* name suggests a curvilinear form: Sherborne now presents a very rectilinear layout. This can be seen as a deliberate move by the West Saxons to emulate the classical Roman form thereby reinforcing the links with the Roman church which preferred to found its churches in Roman towns. It is another

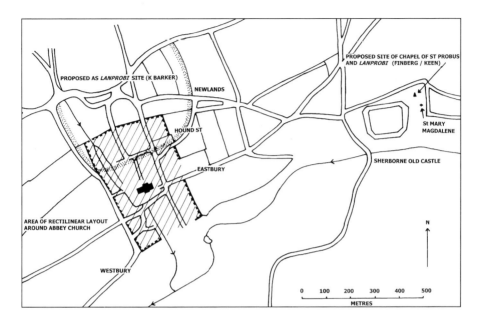

Figure 12. Map showing the possible sites of Lanprobi and the suggested rectilinear enclosure around the former cathedral. The area of Sherborne outside the rectilinear area (which roughly represents the area of the Abbot's Fee tithing) were separate tithings in the medieval period (Eastbury, Westbury, Hound Street). Newland was founded by Bishop Roger le Poore in 1227– 8 (Hall 2000, 53). (The plan was produced by regressive mapping)

facet of the thinking behind the reuse of Roman building material which enforced the idea of the antiquity of the church and the catholic Roman orthodox tradition. Bede refers to the building of stone churches as a Roman way of doing things (HE v.21).

The evidence points to a situation where the early eighth-century cathedral displaced an existing British community, *Lanprobi*, probably making use of its lands as part of the see's foundation grant. It is necessary to examine the wider religious climate of the time to account for such an event.

The Synod of Whitby and the absorption of the British Church by the English

The differences in practices between the indigenous churches of the British Isles and those that had direct links with Rome, were apparent from the time of Augustine's first attempts to contact the British (HE ii.24). The Christian churches already present in the British Isles had lost contact with the continent and were using antiquated practices including their method of fixing the date of

Easter. The southern Irish became aware of the problem and amended their
ways in AD 640, but the northern Irish, the Scots of Iona and its colonies, and
the Britons in the west of England and Wales adhered to their old customs.

When Agilbert was forced out of his see at Dorchester on Thames he took
refuge with King Oswiu of Northumbria. It may well have been the presence of
this Frankish bishop that set in motion the Synod of Whitby in AD 664, but the
agenda of King Oswiu seems to have been political rather than religious – in
order to consolidate his powerbase south of the Humber, Oswiu needed to
disassociate himself from the British church (Higham 1997, 254–8). Agilbert's
motives were religious, however, as the debate would help to consolidate the
position of the Roman church. Agilbert was deputed by King Oswiu to explain
the catholic observance of Easter (though he delegated the role to the more
fluent Wilfrid) whilst Colman, the bishop of Lindisfarne supported the customs
of Iona and the northern Irish (HE iii.25). Whether a real debate took place
resulting in King Oswiu making a decision on the spot, or if it was a set piece,
played out to a predetermined result as Higham suggests, the result was the
same (Higham 1997, 254–8). The synod was followed by a spate of withdrawals
by the more hard-line bishops and clergy who followed the Scots customs, and
the reallocation of their positions, churches and lands to Rome-friendly
replacements. Both Bede and Eddius Stephanus recount instances of this transfer
of lands (HE iii.28; HE v.19; Colgrave 1927, 36–7), the church at Ripon being
a famous example:

> He [Alhfrith] had first offered this site to some who followed the Irish ways,
> so that they might build a monastery there. But when they were given the
> choice, they preferred to abandon the place rather than accept the catholic
> Easter and the other canonical rites of the Roman and apostolic church; so he
> [Alhfrith] gave it to one [Wilfrid] whom he found to be trained in better rules
> and customs. (Colgrave and Mynors 1969, 521–3)

Bede was very concerned with the orthodoxy of the church and his *Historia
Ecclesiastica* (otherwise HE) is, essentially, a history of the triumph of the Roman
orthodox church over the diverse customs existing in the British Isles in the
seventh century. Approximately one in five of his chapters include some
reference to the struggle for orthodoxy. Bede was not the only churchman at
that time with this prime concern – both Theodore and Aldhelm were obviously
worried as well, as indeed was the papacy itself (Lapidge 1999, 26, 445). On one
of his trips to Rome, Wilfrid was summoned to a synod to combat the
Monothelite heresy where he had to affirm his beliefs and those of the English
church (HE v.19). Orthodoxy is something that would have been high on the
agenda of the West Saxon bishops.

British Christianity in Wessex

Is there any evidence for this 'religious cleansing' outside Northumbria? The
situation in Wessex is nowhere described clearly for us (there is precious little

information in Bede) and has to be pieced together from various clues. Here we are dealing with a different ethnic group from the Scots of Northumbria and Iona who had refused to be converted to Roman ways at the Synod of Whitby. The Britons of the south-west and Wales had a real hatred of the Saxons. Their stubbornness over the question of Easter probably arose as much from the political problem of not wanting to be seen to side with their enemy, as anything else (John 1970, 53). For them to have admitted they were wrong would be tantamount to accepting the ecclesiastical overlordship of the Saxons in the form of the archbishop of Canterbury. Whilst they still had their freedom this was unlikely.

Before the West Saxon expansion into Dorset, Somerset and Devon, contact with the British church may have been minimal, and Agilbert may not have had to deal with the problem.[6] During Wine's episcopacy, however, there was contact between the two churches, evinced by his use of two British bishops to help with the consecration of Chad. Wine's action was considered by Theodore to be unorthodox and Chad was deposed from his see in York, reconsecrated, and then appointed as bishop of the Mercians. There must be a possibility that the bishops who helped Wine were attached to British monasteries (as was the British custom) within the newly expanded area of Wessex. If *Lanprobi* had had a British bishop it would be another reason to have installed the new West Saxon bishop in Sherborne.

From the time of the next candidate, Leuthere, Agilbert's nephew, the bishopric would have taken a more orthodox line and there would be no co-operation with any British who were not prepared to conform to the Roman ways. Certainly in the time of Haedde's bishopric we find disdain for the British church. Aldhelm, as abbot of Malmesbury, writes to King Geraint and the bishops of Dumnonia (roughly Cornwall and that part of Devon which was not under Saxon control). Aldhelm's high-handed tone suggests that the Christianity that the West Saxons found present in the south-west was unacceptable and indeed, he links their practices with other heretical movements – the British clergy wore the wrong tonsure, after the fashion of the heretic Simon; they calculated Easter wrongly; and when suffered to meet with members of the English church, insisted that they fast for forty days before they would meet with them, imitating the heretics who called themselves *cathari* (Lapidge and Herren 1979, 155–60).[7]

Bede relates Aldhelm's letter in the following manner (HE v.18):

> ... Aldhelm, when he was still priest and abbot of the monastery known as Malmesbury, by order of a synod of his own people wrote a remarkable book against the British error of celebrating Easter at the wrong time, and of doing many other things to the detriment of the pure practices and the peace of the Church; by means of this book he led many of those Britons who were subject to the West Saxons to adopt the Catholic celebration of the Easter of the Lord. (Colgrave and Mynors 1969, 515)

The implication here is that there were a number of British Christians in Wessex in the period before Aldhelm became bishop of Sherborne. Amongst these can surely be counted the British church at *Lanprobi*.

From archaeological and documentary evidence we can begin to pinpoint some additional British church sites. Glastonbury in Somerset is a good example. The traditions of the house record a British foundation though there is nothing in the charters (that is not blatantly spurious) to support this (Abrams 1996, 5–6). The archaeological work by Rahtz on the Tor led him to the conclusion that 'the Tor was the pre-Saxon Christian nucleus of Glastonbury' (1991, 34; 1993, 60, 72). There is documentary evidence, however, of another British church in the vicinity. A grant of three hides of land at *Lantocal* or *Lantokai* (S 1249) to Glastonbury by Bishop Haedde (Sawyer 1968, 363) survives only as a fourteenth-century copy of a charter. The land, which has been identified as Leigh in Street, forms part of one of Glastonbury Abbey's core estates, and this has led Lesley Abrams to accept it as containing a genuine tradition (1996, 153–4). The place-name evidence here is similar to that of Sherborne – a *lann* dedicated to a British saint, in this case Saint Kea (Doble 1964, part 3, 101–2). This presents the possibility that the site at Street may have been the core of the original British monastery. Glastonbury Tor, and perhaps Marchey with its church of St Martin,[8] could then be seen as hermitages attached to *Lantokai* (along the lines of the early monastic site at Lérins which had a group of hermitages around the main monastery) (see Aston 2000, 58). The new Saxon monastery was founded on the flat ground below the Tor at Glastonbury in a large rectangular enclosure, and it may have been then that the old British monastery was put into the hands of the bishopric of Wessex to ensure that orthodox Christian practices were followed.

Further work by Rahtz presents another possible site of a British monastery; Cadbury-Congresbury, which is traditionally linked with a British bishop, St Congar (Rahtz *et al* 1992, 250).[9] The same fourteenth-century list that records *Lanprobi*, also records the granting of twenty hides at Congresbury to the church at Sherborne (the bishopric) by King Ine. The history of Congresbury is not straightforward, but it was later given by Alfred to Asser, perhaps in anticipation of the creation of the new see of Wells to whom it belonged at a later date (O'Donovan 1988, xlvi, 81). It has been suggested that the hillfort at Cadbury was the original site of Congar's monastery. This was replaced by a new church in a large rectangular enclosure at the foot of the hillfort – the present Congresbury. Recently discovered carved stonework from near Congresbury has been identified as part of the shrine of St Congar, who features in the Saxon list of the resting places of saints, and who is still venerated in the thirteenth and fourteenth centuries (Doble 1964, 3–29; Rollason 1978, 92; Oakes and Costen 2003). Again, this is an instance of a British monastic site ending up in the hands of the West Saxon bishopric.

Wareham in Dorset with its collection of inscribed stones must also fit into this group of possible British monasteries and it is one of the sites where Aldhelm is recorded as having founded a church (RCHM 1970, 310–12; Hinton 1992, 260).

A characteristic of this group of possible early British sites is the link between them and the early West Saxon bishops: it has been argued above that *Lanprobi* was dispossessed and granted to the West Saxon bishops; the site of *Lantokai* appears to have been in the hands of Haedde; Marchey, was in the hands of Forthere (Aldhelm's successor at Sherborne); Congresbury appears to have been given initially to Sherborne and then to the bishopric of Wells; and Aldhelm founded a church at Wareham. In addition, there is evidence of changes of site – *Lantokai* and the Tor to the present site of Glastonbury and Cadbury hillfort to Congresbury – and both the present site of Glastonbury and the church at Congresbury sit within large rectilinear enclosures. It would appear that the British Christian sites were put into the hands of the West Saxon bishopric, and new churches established along Roman lines.

Aldhelm as bishop

As we have seen, Aldhelm was a great supporter of the orthodox catholic church which was no doubt drummed into him at Canterbury – he may have spent as much as ten years studying under Theodore and Hadrian (Lapidge 1999, 25). Bede tells us that he presided energetically over his bishopric (HE v.18) which must have included much travelling through the region as Bede considered it necessary that a bishop should visit every hamlet and homestead within his care at least once a year – a tall order considering the size of the Selwood diocese. The *Carmen Rhythmicum*, one of Aldhelm's poems, begins, 'When I had set out for nasty Devon and was proceeding through Cornwall', suggesting that he was active in areas that probably still lay outside Wessex in his day (Lapidge and Rosier 1985, 177).

Aldhelm built several churches within the diocese, probably after he became bishop, two of which were in Malmesbury, but also minsters at Bruton, Bradford on Avon, Wareham and Frome (Lapidge and Herren 1979, 9, 183). William of Malmesbury tells us that he built a cathedral of marvellous construction (Lapidge and Rosier 1985, 8), and the analysis of Gibb and the Taylors of the Saxon remains at Sherborne Abbey suggests that the cathedral was modelled on a form of church more common on the continent, again emphasising the Roman links (Taylor and Taylor 1965, 540–3; Gibb 1975, 71–110; Taylor 1978, 991–2, 1004). This church must have stood in great contrast to the British church which may have been like Finan's church on Lindisfarne, built of hewn oak thatched with reeds (HE iii.25). Aldhelm was reportedly of royal blood, a kinsman of Ine, and he was involved in the drawing up of Ine's laws which reinforce Christian practices in the West Saxon kingdom. It may well have been during his episcopacy that the minster church system was established in Wessex (Hall 2000, 82–3).

The minster church model

Over the last thirty years or so, it has been recognised that from about the end of the seventh century a system of minster churches with distinctive locations was established on a systematic basis by royal personages and bishops to provide pastoral care within well-defined territories corresponding closely with royal estates and areas of judicial administration (Blair 1988, 1, 2; Blair and Sharpe 1992, 226–66). The word *mynster*, which is Old English for the Latin word *monasterium*, covers many different types of religious community, all of which took an active role in the pastoral care of the population in the surrounding countryside. These were not the strictly enclosed monasteries introduced in the tenth century by Dunstan and his fellow reformers (Foot 1992, 212–17).

The model of a minster church at the centre of a large royal or episcopal estate (something in the region of 15,000 acres), staffed by a group of priests or monks (with nuns present as well in some cases), and serving the pastoral needs of the estate, holds true for Dorset (Hall 2000). The term 'minster' is a familiar one in the county through its inclusion in place-names such as Wimborne Minster, Beaminster, Yetminster, Sturminster (two instances), Charminster and Iwerne Minster.[10] As far as we can tell, the minster system did not provide total coverage for Dorset in the first instance and secondary minsters were founded at a later date, filling in some of the gaps (Fig 13). A similar picture can be painted for Somerset, with minsters at the centre of royal estates at Bruton,

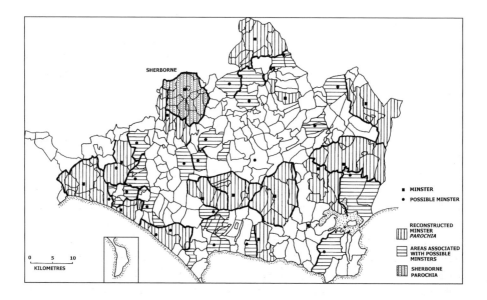

Figure 13. Map showing the reconstructed parochiae or early minster parishes of Dorset.

Milborne Port, Wells, Wedmore and Ilminster, amongst other places (Aston 1986, 54–8, 74–6; Costen 1992, 106–7). The geographical bases of these large multiple royal estates is reflected in their place-names (as has also been shown for Devon by Hoskins (1952, 300–10), which often comprise a river or topographical name that applied to the whole estate; Wimborne on the river Win (now Allen); Bruton on the Brue; Ilminster on the Isle; Tawton on the Taw.

As the large royal estates served by the minsters started to fragment, from about the ninth century onwards, proprietary church foundations took place on the new independent land units thus sowing the seeds of the parish system as we know it today (Blair 1988, 1–19). The minster churches exercised rights over these 'daughter' churches, however, in order to guard their income, including such practices as a monopoly on burial at the minster church. This hampered the passage of the newly founded churches to independence. Some of the more powerful minsters in Dorset, such as Gillingham, retained the majority of their chapelries until the Reformation (Hall 2000, 15). So it is possible to reconstruct what the Saxon church in the early eighth century must have been like: newly founded minster churches, in large rectangular enclosures, staffed by a variety of religious, at the centre of large royal estates for which they provided pastoral care.

Sherborne as a minster church

Whilst Sherborne was the centre of the newly created bishopric, its church would have functioned as a minster providing pastoral care for the episcopal estate donated to sustain the bishopric. Aldhelm's church would have been staffed by his *familia*, probably a group of canons or priests, and as far as we know would have continued thus until it was reformed by Bishop Wulfsige who replaced the canons with Benedictine monks in AD 998 (O'Donovan 1988, 45–6). A group of eight members of the Sherborne *familia* are recorded in a Sherborne charter of AD 864 (O'Donovan 1988, 21, 24).

It is possible to reconstruct Sherborne's *parochia* (Latin 'parish', the modern term for an area served by a minster church), by looking at the extent of the influence of Sherborne and the whereabouts of its dependent chapels (Hall 2000, 11, 13, 33). Up until the end of the eighteenth century Sherborne had about thirteen chapels dependent upon it, many of which had some element of the cure of souls, but none of which had achieved independence (Fig 14). A list of chapels paying Pentecost money to the vicar of Sherborne includes: Oborne, Caundle Marsh, Folke, Lillington, Holnest, Thornford, Beer Hackett, Nether Compton, Over Compton and Haydon (Hutchins 1870, 263). In Lincolnshire, Pentecostal payments were made by parishes to the cathedral church in return for holy oil or chrism (Owen 1971, 107). These are the only instances of this payment in Dorset, and they may represent a relict payment, surviving solely in the churches dependent on Sherborne. Dean Chandler, in the early fifteenth century, mentions additional chapels at Pinford, Long Burton, and within the

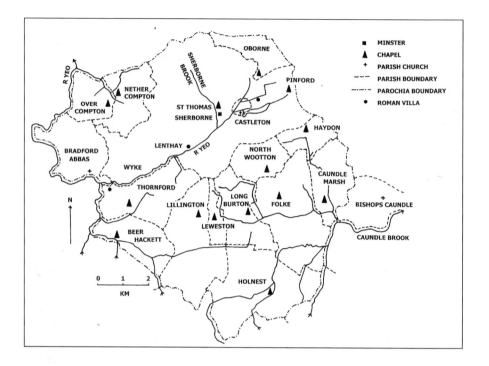

Figure 14. Map showing the reconstructed parochia or early minster parish of Sherborne.

town, at St Thomas in the Green (Timmins 1984, 22, 24). Most of the aforementioned chapels depended on Sherborne for burial; the inhabitants of Over Compton were not granted a licence for sepulture until AD 1431 and a pension of 12 pence per annum had to be subsequently paid to the vicar of Sherborne as compensation for lost revenue (Hutchins 1870, 170; Timmins 1984, 21). This is a classic, though late, example of a parochial chapel gaining in status. Undoubtedly, Sherborne's power to retain its daughter churches was reinforced by its status, initially as a cathedral church, and later as an important abbey, enabling it to exercise a great deal of control over its chapelries.

Conclusion

A picture has been painted of Sherborne, initially as a British monastery dedicated to Saint Probus, probably with its own British bishop, and then, after falling into West Saxon hands, as the centre of the newly created West Saxon bishopric of Selwood, covering Dorset, Somerset and Devon. Two main reasons may have influenced the choice of Sherborne as the site of the bishopric: one, the presence of an existing British ecclesiastical centre which needed to be reformed; and two, an area of ecclesiastical land that could be reassigned to the new bishopric. There are hints that other British holdings such as Congresbury and Street also formed part of the endowment of West Saxon bishops. This would have ensured that the new bishopric had sufficient lands and it would facilitate the reform of the British churches. The choice of what may have been a British bishopric would have made the imposition of the new West Saxon church much easier to accept in the eyes of the British of the area.

The link between the holdings of the West Saxon bishopric and British monastic sites would repay further examination as they appear to be closely connected in the newly formed diocese. This may well be the West Saxon equivalent of the transfer of lands that is recorded by Bede in Northumbria and which has recently been suggested in Mercia where there seems to be a substratum of British churches which lost their early authority but were allowed to continue as dependent churches (Bassett 1992, 13–40).

The West Saxon bishops, especially Haedde and Aldhelm, were deeply involved in the setting up of the new system of minster churches, put in place to provide pastoral care for the diocese. The cathedral church of Sherborne, whilst being the chief church of the diocese,[11] would also have fulfilled the functions of a minster with its canons providing a cure of souls for the *parochia* immediately surrounding it. This state of affairs appears to have continued up until the reforms of Wulfsige in the tenth century when the canons were replaced with monks who were not involved in the pastoral care of the Sherborne *parochia*.

This paper has also identified a change from British to orthodox Roman Christianity in late seventh- to early eighth-century Wessex. It presents a model in which the British church was disenfranchised under West Saxon control: its lands were confiscated and given to the West Saxon bishopric; British church sites were moved to new locations, often from hilltop to low-lying sites. The overall plan of the sites was restructured, with the curvilinear enclosures of the British church giving way to Roman-style rectilinear layouts. The internal plans of these new sites was highly structured and often based on grid layouts. These physical changes were the outward signs of new practices which would bring the church in Britain in to line with the orthodox continental Roman tradition. Reformed ecclesiastical practices for the British church included the date of the reckoning of Easter; the style of tonsure; and doubtless many other matters of which there is little record, including baptism and monastic practices. These momentous changes resulted in many of the currently observed physical features in the ecclesiastical landscape. These have been little appreciated by scholars in the past but their recent recognition provides a stimulating model for future research.

Notes
1 I wish to thank Katherine Barker for allowing me additional time to add new ideas that have been brewing since the conference, and Mick Aston for drawing some of the Somerset sites to my attention and for much useful discussion on the subject.
2 This arrangement is implied in the term 'west of Selwood', but for discussion on the subject see F Magoun (1939).
3 The history of the debate on the origins of Sherborne, up to 1984, is given in detail by Laurence Keen (1984, 208–12). I have summarised the main points here.
4 Finberg based this article on a paper that he had read to the Royal Historical Society in 1952 (1964, 95).
5 Mary O'Donovan does point out, however, that in the charter evidence, there in nothing definite to link the putative *Lanprobi* with Sherborne itself as a place, beyond it heading the list of places in the possession of Sherborne (1988, 83–8).
6 Malmesbury, for example, appears to link with the Irish rather than with the British.
7 One of Aldhelm's pupils, Bishop Pecthelm, became the first English bishop of Whithorn, which has been shown by Hill through excavation to have been remodelled at about this time. The plan form changed from circular to rectilinear (Hill 1997, 36, 44).
8 Marchey is also referred to in an early charter which only survives in a fourteenth-century copy (S 1253). It was reputedly granted to Glastonbury by Forthere, bishop of Sherborne, in AD 712 (Costen 1992, 107; Abrams 1996, 165–6).
9 Rahtz presents a British monastery as one possible interpretation of the site.
10 Lytchett Minster was not a minster but was owned by the minster at Sturminster Marshall (Mills 1980, 33).
11 The diocese of Selwood was further divided in 909 on Asser's death with new sees at Wells and Crediton.

Abbreviations
HE   *Historia Ecclesiastica* (see Colgrave and Mynors 1969)
RCHM   Royal Commission for Historical Monuments
S   Sawyer charter number (Sawyer 1968)

Bibliography
Abrams, L, 1996, *Anglo-Saxon Glastonbury: Church and Endowment*. Woodbridge. Boydell.
Aston, M A, 1986, Post-Roman Central Places in Somerset. In E Grant, *Central Places, Archaeology and History*. Sheffield. Sheffield University, 49–77.
Aston, M A, 2000, *Monasteries in the Landscape*. Stroud. Tempus.
Baring-Gould, S, and Fisher, J, 1913, *The Lives of the British Saints* (Volume 4). London.
Barker, K, 1980, The Early Christian Topography of Sherborne. *Antiquity*, 54, 229–31.
Barker, K, 1982, The Early History of Sherborne. In S Pearce (ed), *The Early Church in Western Britain and Ireland: Studies Presented to C A Ralegh Radford*. British Archaeological Reports British Series 102. Oxford, 76–116.
Bassett, S, 1992, Church and Diocese in the West Midlands: the transition from British to Anglo-Saxon control. In J Blair and R Sharpe (eds), *Pastoral Care Before the Parish*. Leicester. Leicester University Press, 13–40.
Bischoff, B, and Lapidge, M, 1994, *Biblical Commentaries from the Canterbury School of*

Theodore and Hadrian. Cambridge Studies in Anglo-Saxon England 10. Cambridge. Cambridge University Press.

Blair, J (ed), 1988, *Minsters and Parish Churches: The Local Church in Transition 950–1200*. Oxford University Committee for Archaeology Monograph 17. Oxford.

Blair, J, and Sharpe, R (eds), 1992, *Pastoral Care Before the Parish*. Leicester. Leicester University Press.

Colgrave, B (trans), 1927, *The Life of Bishop Wilfrid by Eddius Stephanus: Text, Translation, and Notes*. Cambridge. Cambridge University Press.

Colgrave, B, and Mynors, R A B (eds), 1969, Bede's *Ecclesiastical History of the English People*. Oxford. Clarendon.

Costen, M, 1992, *The Origins of Somerset*. Manchester. Manchester University Press.

Doble, G H, 1964, *The Saints of Cornwall* (Part 5). Oxford. Holywell Press.

Farmer, D H, 1978, *The Oxford Dictionary of Saints*. Oxford. Oxford University Press.

Finberg, H P R, 1964, *Lucerna*. London. Macmillan (especially 'Sherborne, Glastonbury and the Expansion of Wessex', 95–115).

Foot, S, 1992, Anglo-Saxon Minsters: a review of terminology. In J Blair and R Sharpe (eds), *Pastoral Care Before the Parish*. Leicester. Leicester University Press, 212–25.

Fowler, J, 1951, *Mediaeval Sherborne*. Dorchester. Longmans.

Geake, H, 1997, *The Use of Grave-Goods in Conversion-Period England, c.600–c.850*. British Archaeological Reports British Series 261. Oxford.

Gibb, J H P, 1975, The Anglo-Saxon Cathedral at Sherborne. *Archaeological Journal* 132, 71–110.

Hall, T A, 2000, *Minster Churches in the Dorset Landscape*. British Archaeological Reports British Series 304. Oxford.

Higham, N J, 1997, *The Convert Kings: Power and Religious Affiliation in Early Anglo-Saxon England*. Manchester. Manchester University Press.

Hill, P, 1997, *Whithorn and St Ninian: The Excavation of a Monastic Town, 1984–91*. Sutton. Stroud.

Hinton, D, 1981, The Topography of Sherborne – Early Christian? *Antiquity* 55, 222–3.

Hinton, D, 1992, The Inscribed Stones in Lady St Mary Church, Wareham. *Proceedings of the Dorset Natural History and Archaeological Society* 114, 260.

Hoskins, W G, 1952, The making of the agrarian landscape. In W G Hoskins and H P R Finberg, *Devonshire Studies*. London. Jonathan Cape, 289–333.

Hutchins, J, 1870, *History and Antiquities of Dorset* (3rd Edition, Volume 4). Westminster. Bowyer Nichols.

John, E, 1970, The Social and Political Problems of the Early English Church. In J Thirsk (ed), *Land, Church and People: Essays Presented to Professor H P R Finberg*. Reading. British Agricultural History Society, 39–63.

Keen, L J, 1984, The towns of Dorset. In J. Haslam (ed), *Anglo-Saxon Towns in Southern England*. Chichester. Phillimore, 203–47.

Lapidge, M, 1999, Aldhelm. In M Lapidge, J Blair, S Keynes and D Scragg (eds), *The Blackwell Encyclopaedia of Anglo-Saxon England*. Oxford. Blackwell, 25–7.

Lapidge, M, and Herren, M (trans), 1979, *Aldhelm: The Prose Works*. Ipswich. Boydell Brewer.

Lapidge, M, and Rosier, J (trans), 1985, *Aldhelm: The Poetic Works*. Cambridge. Brewer.

Magoun, F P, 1939, Aldhelm's Diocese of Sherborne Bewestan Wuda. *Harvard Theological Review* 32, 103–14.

Mills, A D, 1980, *The Place-Names of Dorset* (Part 2). Cambridge. English Place-Name Society.

Oakes, C M, and Costen, M, 2003, The Congresbury Carvings: an eleventh-century saint's shrine? *The Antiquaries Journal* 83, 281–309.

O'Donovan, M A, 1988, *Anglo-Saxon Charters III: Charters of Sherborne*. Oxford. Oxford University Press.

Owen, D, 1971, *Church and Society in Medieval Lincolnshire*. Lincoln.

Padel, O J, 1985, *Cornish Place-Name Elements*. English Place-Name Society, Volume 56–7. Nottingham. English Place-Name Society.

Rahtz, P, 1991, Pagan and Christian by the Severn Sea. In L Abrams and J P Carley, *The Archaeology and History of Glastonbury Abbey: Essays in Honour of the Ninetieth Birthday of C A Ralegh Radford*. Woodbridge. Boydell, 3–37.

Rahtz, P, *et al*, 1992, *Cadbury Congresbury 1968–73: A Late/Post-Roman Hilltop Settlement in Somerset*. British Archaeological Reports British Series 223 Oxford.

Rahtz, P, 1993, *English Heritage Book of Glastonbury*. London. Batsford.

Rollason, D W, 1978, Lists of Saints' Resting-Places in Anglo-Saxon England. *Anglo-Saxon England* 7, 61–93.

RCHM, 1952, *An Inventory of the Historical Monuments in the County of Dorset, Volume 1 (West)*. London. HMSO.

RCHM, 1970, *An Inventory of the Historical Monuments in the County of Dorset II (South-East)*. London. HMSO.

Sawyer, P H, 1968, *Anglo-Saxon Charters: An Annotated List and Bibliography*. London. Royal Historical Society.

Taylor, H M, and Taylor, J, 1965, *Anglo-Saxon Architecture* (Volume 2). Cambridge.

Taylor, H M, 1978, *Anglo-Saxon Architecture* (Volume 3). Cambridge.

Thorpe, B (ed and trans), 1861a, *The Anglo-Saxon Chronicle, according to the Several Original Authorities* (Volume 1, original texts). London. Longman.

Thorpe, B (ed and trans), 1861b, *The Anglo-Saxon Chronicle, according to the Several Original Authorities* (Volume 2, translation). London. Longman.

Timmins, T C B (ed), 1984, *The Register of John Chandler 1404–17*. Devizes. Wiltshire Record Society.

Yorke, B, 1995, *Wessex in the Early Middle Ages*. London. Leicester University Press.

13. Sherborne in AD 998:
the Benedictine abbey and its estate

Katherine Barker

Introduction

A Benedictine abbey was maintained by tithes and dues from its estates which financed – or provisioned – the everyday running of the house and its spiritual, pastoral, administrative, building – and defence – obligations. As can be seen from the charter dates (Table 1), the estates listed in 998 were not recent acquisitions granted to support the new foundation. From the early eighth century the Sherborne church had enjoyed landed resources sufficient to support both a non-monastic minster community of individual landholder/clerics and a bishop. The charter of 998 is a carefully worded legal document which communalised the estate in the name of the refounded abbey and its newly instituted monastic community thus overturning established family rights. Sherborne is one of a large number of abbeys refounded during the tenth century both here and across the channel, effecting what one writer has described as a 'tenurial revolution' which was to place the king – and his bishops – in positions of great power (John 1966, 168, 176; 1996, 126).

The Sherborne estates

In the charter of 998 the home estate is described in two parts as the hundred *agelli* in *Stocland* and the monastic *predium*, and then follows a list of eleven named estates, all but one in West Dorset, ten assessed in terms of number of *cassates,* the eleventh, Lyme, as a single *mansa*. Figures given can be compared with numbers of *hides* entered for the bishop of Salisbury's estate in 1086 and there is a striking correlation; only Halstock is missing. Both *cassate* and *hide* connote a unit of taxation. In eight cases out of the eleven, the identification of the estate is reasonably certain. There are several Holcombes in the area, but *Holancumb* is thought most likely to be Holcombe Rogus on the Devon/ Somerset border, an estate which, a few years later was clearly coveted property (Keynes, 'Wulfsige, monk of Glastonbury', this volume), and presumably to be

King Æthelred to Wulfsige, bishop ...	Domesday Book	Present Name	Anglo-Saxon Charter dating from AD 774–998
AD 998	AD 1086	AD 1998	
Hoc est in ipsa Scireburna centum agelli in loco	*Scireburne xliii* [43]	Sherborne, Dorset	S 895, AD 998
qui dicitur Stodland et predium monasterii sicut	*Scireburne ix* [9]		
Wlsinus episcopus fossis sepibusque girare curauit	*carucatae terrae xvi* [16]		
	et dim [+ one half]		
Deinde novem [9] *cassatos in ...Holancumb*	*Holceone ix* [9]	Holcombe Rogus, Devon	
Item in Halganstoke xv [15]	no entry	Halstock, Dorset	S 290; AD 842*
in Thornford vii [7]	*Torneford vii* [7]	Thornford, Dorset	S 516; AD 903 for 946/51*
in Bradanforda x [10]	*Bradeford x* [10]	Bradford Abbas, Dorset	S 422; AD 933*
in Wonburna v [5]	*Wocburne v* [5]	Oborne, Dorset	S 813; AD 970/75
in Westun viii [8]	*Westone viii* [8]	Stalbridge Weston, Dorset	S 423; AD 933*
in Stapulbreige xx [20]	*Staplebrige xx* [20]	Stalbridge, Dorset	
in Wulfbeardigstoke x [10]	?	?	
in Cumbtun viii [8]	*Contone vi + iii V* [6+]	?Over/Nether Compton (Dorset)	
in Osanstoke ii [2] *et*	?	?	
et mansam unam [1 mansa] *aet Lim*	*i caruca* [1]	Lyme [Abbas], Dorset	S 263, AD 774

Table 1. The abbey estates are shown in the order in which they were listed in AD 998 (first column), as compared with their respective entries in the Domesday Book of 1086 (second column), their present name if known, and finally, earlier Anglo-Saxon charter records which survive for some of them. A translation of the Latin listing of 998 is given below the Table. For a translation of the whole charter see Keynes ('King Æthelred's charter', this volume). The estates are plotted on a map (Fig 16).

Notes: lower case Roman numerals refer to *cassates* (998) or *hides* (1086) of land; in three instances they refer to ungelded/tax free units of land or *carucates*; *V* = *virgate* or a quarter *hide*; 3 are recorded for Compton. *S* = Sawyer 1968; *denotes the charter is accompanied by a written boundary survey of the estate*

Translation: AD 998. There is in Sherborne itself one hundred *agelli* [small fields/land units] in the place which is called *Stodland* and the monastic estate which bishop Wulfsige had enclosed by hedges/fences and ditches. Next nine *cassates* [of land] in the place which is known to the inhabitants as *Holancumb* [Holcombe Rogus in Devon]. Also in *Halganstoke* [Halstock] 15; in *Thornford* [Thornford] 7; in *Bradanford* [Bradford] 10; in *Wonburna* [Oborne] 5; in *Westun* [Stalbridge Weston] 8; in *Stapulbreige* [Stalbridge] 20; in *Wulfbeardigstoke* 10; in *Cumbtun* [Compton] 8; in *Osanstoke* 2 and one *mansa* of land beside the seashore which is called *at Lim* [Lyme; see Barker, 'The Sherborne estate at Lyme', this volume].

– or become – the site of a *rogus*, 'beacon'. The charter of 998 makes mention of 'beacon service', part of the bishop's military obligation (Keynes, 'King Æthelred's charter', §6, this volume).[1] By 1086 Holcombe was held by the sheriff of Devon for nine hides (S 1422 and S 1474; Domesday Devon, 2, 16:76). Bounds are recorded for Thornford, Bradford and [Stalbridge] Weston; those for the single *mansa* at Lyme are defined by the neighbouring Glastonbury estate of Uplyme (see Barker, 'The Sherborne estate at Lyme', Fig 24, this volume). There is no extant charter in the Sherborne archive for either Stalbridge or for Compton, nor for *Wulfheardigstoke* and *Osanstoke* the whereabouts of which are not known, although the name element 'stoke', OE *stoc*, 'a religious place, a secondary or dependent settlement' is, in the context, an appropriate one (Smith 1970, II, 153–5). *Osanstoke* ['Osa's place'] probably formed part of Stoke Abbot (Fowler 1951, 44); Ekwall (1936, 20) suggested *Wulfheardigstoke* was also part of the same place.

The making of the endowment

Whilst it is section 5 of the charter which lists the estates, section 4 is of considerable interest, providing the spiritual *rationale* – and the pretext – behind the making of the endowment.

Section 4 opens with a significant quotation from the Bible, from the first Book to the Corinthians. 'We are', we read, 'those "upon whom the end of the ages have come"'. Here is the ultimate justification for a 'restructuring' of the church estate in preparation for an event the precise time – and character – of which could not be known.[2] In everyday practical terms we find a carefully expressed strategy for managing what appears to have been a land shortage. Whilst the tenth century is taken to be a time of population growth (see note 3), there is a 'very great pestilence' recorded in the Anglo-Saxon Chronicle for 962, followed up in 986 by what is described as the first outbreak of 'the great pestilence among cattle' in England (Barker, 'Bishop Wulfsige's lifetime', this volume). The longer-term results of such calamities may at least partly be reflected in the wording of the charter of 998 which makes specific reference to the sin of *philargiria*, 'love of money' 'covetousness'. Two classes of people, including both those with a plough-team and those with only a spade, had nowhere to support themselves. A growth of 'customary' tenure by landholding *mundani*, 'wordly' that is, non-monastic, lay people, presumably claiming rights to sell, inherit or exchange, were rights henceforward claimed by the Benedictine foundation in an overarching statement designed to bring about harmony by agreed legal means. Thus it was to be that everyone would be able to cultivate a portion of land for himself.[3]

Use of the word *tellus* 'earth', 'ground' as the subject of *excolo* is something to consider. There is c*olo, colui, cultum,* Latin 'to cultivate' 'take care of', but here we have *ex-colo,* 'improvement', 'development'; literally, 'cultivating out'. This may well be a reference to assarting, that is to the cultivation of marginal land, to the expansion of land under the plough (see Duby 1968, 61–87). The bishop had deprived some of the clerical landed rich – the 'secular canons' – and, we take it, the politically influential, of some of their rights, whilst literally breaking new ground. 'Communalization of the endowment was commonly the first stage in the reform of the monastery concerned ... English reformers knew, revered and borrowed practices of such reformed houses as Fleury' – itself reformed from Cluny about 930 – (John 1966, 168). Anyone who attempted 'to annul this our donation' reads the charter of 998, 'will render account ... at the last judgement ... *Christo iudicante*' (Keynes, 'King Æthelred's charter', §7, this volume).

So what of the following section in the charter of 998 – the estates themselves? This section will be considered in three parts. The first discussed are *predium* and *stocland*, the Sherborne home estate (Fig 15). Second follow the eleven named estates which appear both in Table 1 and Figure 16. Of some interest here is the order in which these places are listed in 998 not hitherto explored. Thirdly, and of further interest is their location in relation to the three episcopal Hundreds of Sherborne, Yetminster and Beaminster which bring into focus the administrative geography of the troubled years of the late tenth century; the fiscal – and military – significance of the shire and its boundary.

The Sherborne home estate and hundred

In the charter of 998 the [country] estate (or *rus*)[4] '*in ipsa Scireburna* (in Sherborne itself)', is described in two parts, firstly the one hundred *agelli* in *Stocland* and secondly the monastic *predium*. This double element in estate structure is evidenced in a continental Carolingian – and Benedictine – context; that is, the 'demesne' or in-estate worked by a largely unfree population and a largely free out-estate tenanted in return for labour services (John 1966, 167–8; Blois 1989, 6). Here, for Sherborne, we can suggest that the in-estate is represented by the *predium monasterii*, and the out-estate by *Stocland*.

Sherborne enters the brighter light of late medieval history as the centre of a large administrative and judicial Hundred reckoned in two parts, the Sherborne in-hundred and the Sherborne out-hundred (Fowler 1951, 220); extensive areas which are noticeable by their apparent omission from the Domesday Survey.[5] The in-hundred Fowler associates with the ancient manor of Sherborne which forms a large arc of land around the town itself shaded eloquently in green on the Tudor map of *c* 1570 (Barker 1991, 33). This was the great parish of Sherborne, the dimensions of which were graphically described by Leland, as having a 'compass... nere four miles and the procession grownd [bound beating] about 13 miles' (Toulmin-Smith 1964, I, 152), proportions suggestive of a circle (see Fig 15). Wulfsige had the monastic estate, the *predium*, marked out by a hedge and ditch boundary which suggests open country – and by implication perhaps, the creation of a route (Faith 1997, 20). From the wording of the charter, it is clear that this is something he had already done by 998.[6] If the Sherborne parish does *not* represent the *predium monasterii* and the charter is referring to the monastic precinct, or to what later becomes Barton Farm, or to something else – this large home estate is not mentioned.

The other part of the home estate – listed first – is described in terms of the one hundred *agelli* in the place which is called *Stocland*. We find a reference to one hundred small land units of some kind occupying an area, a 'land', prefixed by a *stoc* name (see above). Gelling notes that a number of place-names ending with *-land* are at the limits of cultivable land on the edge of moors, which may refer to reclamation of coastal or river marsh, include Stockland in east Devon and Stockland at the mouth of the Parrett.[7] 'A reasonable case has been established for a meaning "land broken from marsh/moor/heath/wood"' (Gelling 1984, 247–8). It may be that we might add to these *Stocklands* this extensive tract of Sherborne land extending south down the limestone dip-slope and out into the heavy Oxford clays of the great common of Blackmore where reclamation and enclosure go back into medieval times. How early is not established, but the wording of the charter of 998 noted above may provide us

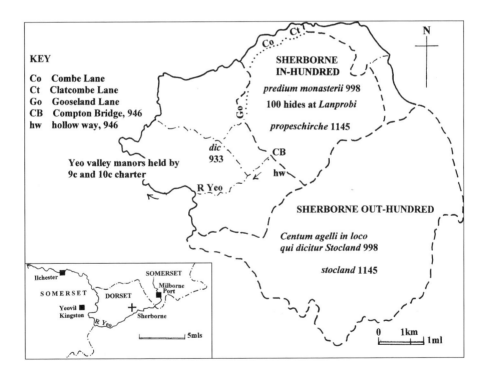

Figure 15. Map of the Benedictine manor of Sherborne in 998, showing the suggested location of the double estate comprising the centum agelli in Stocland *and the* predium monasterii *and (inset), the adjacent royal manors of the Yeo Valley. Dates shown are of tenth-century boundary surveys. For full discussion of the Sherborne Hundreds see Barker (1984).*

with an important clue. The slope is traversed by a number of north-south drove routes leading out into Blackmore; the associated settlements (not listed in 1086) present a discrete group of *-tun* names, Knighton, Leweston, Lillington, Allweston, Burton, and Wootton; four of the six prefaced by a personal/family name. An interesting exception here is Folke, a parish with an unusual place-name – indeed 'unparalleled' – and possibly of early tenurial significance, 'land held by the "folk" or common people' (Mills 1989, 330) and which presents a very distinctive field system by the early nineteenth century. A series of large ring-fence enclosures at Holnest out in the moor, betrays the site of at least one medieval vaccary; Holnest remained part of the bishop's personal estate as late as 1570, and included two areas of woodland and wood pasture (Barker 1991, 36–41).

A case can be made for *stocland* as representing the later Sherborne out-hundred. *Stocland* thus denoted a land category and not just an estate; rendered in the vernacular, not in Latin, and already so-called. The reference to the *centum agelli* there – in Latin – may be indicative of a newly imposed quasi-hundredal status,[8] a *territorium*, where assarting and improvement was henceforward to be controlled – licensed – by the abbey. As with the *predium*, if *Stocland* is in fact something else, somewhere else, then this extensive multiple estate which forms an integral part of the manor of Sherborne in 1086 is, quite simply, not mentioned in 998.

We find another reference to a *Stocland* in 1145 (Dugdale 1817, I, 338–9). A much lengthier recitation than that of 998 of the *'possessiones, terris, redditibus et libertatibus ... et aliis pertinentiis suis ...'* of the monastery, which lists the items in a coherent order placing *Stocland* in a context which has been confused with a meadow name Stocland/Stockland near Sherborne Castle, itself the site of a chapel, the dedication of which has made for further difficulty (Keen 1984, 212; see Hall, 'Sherborne', this volume). The *Confirmatio Terrarum Monasterium Scireburniensis* of 1145, lists firstly churches, then local manors, then certain places in the town before continuing with tithes and with manors and their dues further afield. Listed at the beginning among the churches, we find '*Ecclesiam sanctae Mariae Magdalenae juxta castellum cum duabus capellis·et appendiciis suis* (the church of St Mary Magdalene next to the [Sherborne] castle with two chapels and their appurtances)'. Moving on to the local manors, we find listed Weston, Thornford, Bradford, Wyke, *Hloscumbe*, the two Comptons, and then immediately following, '*Propeschirche et Stocland, cum silvis et pratis, et cum duobus molendinis* (*Propeschirche* and *Stocland* with timber/woodland and meadow/grassland and with two mills)'.

But this time *Stocland* is paired not with the *predium monasterii*, but with *Propeschirche* (Barker 1982, 82–4; 1984, 25–6). A fourteenth-century list of benefactors to the Sherborne Church starts with a 'foundation' grant by Cenwalh (*c* 670) of one hundred hides [of land] at *Lanprobi*, and the name 'Propus church' has every appearance of being an anglicised version of the same name.[9]

A few years later, the *bulla Alexandri tertii,* a papal bull of Alexander III of 1163, also lists Sherborne possessions, this time as '*capellis, terris, decimis, et adjacentiis suis, terras, hospites, et domos censuales ...*'. Then follows a list of places in much the same order as in 1145. Starting again with the churches we find, once more listed among them, '*Ecclesiam sanctae Mariae Magdalenae sitam juxta castrum Sherborne cum capellis sancti Michaeli et sancti Probi, et omnibus pertinentiis suis* (the church of St Mary Magdalene sited next to the castle of Sherborne with chapels of St Michael and St Probus and all their appurtenances)' (Dugdale 1817, I, 339). Then comes the town, and then the local manors, and then those further away. There is no mention of either *Propeschirche* or *Stocland.*

The order of listing of places is, as in 998, worthy of careful attention even if its significance is not fully understood. We note that whilst the 998 recital puts *Stocland* first – *Stocland et predium* – in a position which makes it the first listed of *all* the Sherborne estates, in 1145 it concludes the list of the local manors, with *Stocland* taking second place after *Propeschirche.* Then come monastic properties in the town. In 1163 neither appear.

It thus looks as if we have two distinct references to this pre-Saxon dedication in the mid-twelfth century; one related to the 'home estate', that is, the monastic *predium* and later great parish, described as *Propeschirche*, and the second, to the dedication of a chapel (a *capella*, not an *ecclesia*, church) of St Probus at Sherborne Castle – built between 1107 and 1135 (RCHM *Dorset West* 1952, I, 64). Michael is often associated with subordinate foundations especially those in high places, and with cemetery sites (Farmer 1997, 348; Everitt 1986, 252) and this was apparently a joint dedication with *Probus* the earliest known reference to an obscure saint retrospectively credited with beqeathing his name to the 'founding' estate granted to Sherborne by Cenwalh.

Twelfth century historiography is notoriously 'patchy' in its attributions (Campbell 1986, 209–28), and Probus does not get the treatment of Juthwara, another obscure Sherborne saint, who not only appears in the *Life* of Wulfsige (Love, 'The Life of St Wulfsige', chs XXI, XXII, XXIV, this volume) but was awarded an entry in the Sherborne Missal *c* 1400. Yet we may take it that the territorial significance of the name was both understood and acknowledged in 1145 and further, deemed of sufficient importance to merit a *capella* dedication by a second generation Norman bishop of Salisbury, recorded just a few years later. Probus was again invoked almost two centuries later in the name *Lanprobi* cited as the 'original' hundred-hide Sherborne estate.

St Magdalen's is marked on a map dated *c* 1570 immediately to the east of the castle – but not the chapels. Likely to have been commissioned by the then bishop of Salisbury as part of an attempt to reclaim lost land (Barker 1991, 29) a very small church is drawn. Fields adjacent are coloured as part of *Castletowne,* and named. *Stockland* is omitted, occupying an undifferentiated area outside *Castletowne* but well within the great parish of Sherborne; not ***et*** *predium monasterii* but ***in*** *predium monasterii.* If, earlier, it had been part of the Magdalene/Michael/

Probus *appurtenance*, the bishop's mapmaker did not see fit to record it. First recorded in 1377 as *pratum*, meadow, *Stocland* occupies low-lying marshy land. Leland describes Sherborne Castle as surrounded by *morisch grounde* to the west, north and east (Toulmin-Smith 1964, 154). It is found again as *Stockland*, a field name east of the castle in 1600 and again on the 1733 map of the manor of Sherborne occupying about forty acres. It would fit the Gelling criteria (see above) for land reclaimed from marsh; another *Stockland*, but this time, rather smaller.

The eleven outlying estates

After *Stocland* and *predium* there are eleven named estates which appear on the map in the order in which they are listed (Fig 16). Holcombe Rogus comes first, an outlying estate. Then they read from Halstock (*halgan stoc*, 'holy place', remembered for St Juthwara (see Love, 'The Life of St Wulfsige', ch XXI, this volume), round the Sherborne home estate east as far as Stalbridge, and then swing south-west reaching the coast '*aet Lim*', at Lyme. There is one estate, *Cumtun*, which, if it is indeed to be identified with Over/Nether Compton north-west of Sherborne, is out of sequence. With the now conventional map orientation to the north, the first estate in the list, Holcombe, enters the picture from the left. Given the spiritual significance of the right hand, we may perhaps take it that the tenth-century writer was – in his mind's eye at least – facing south, when composing the list of estates which then enter from the right, swing round behind him and on clockwise in a wide arc embracing the whole of the out-estate before deviating to Lyme on the coast.[10]

So what happens after Stalbridge? Where is *Wulfheardigstoke* the next estate in the sequence? There is a small estate at Stock Gaylard south-west of Stalbridge on the northern edge of Blackmore; 'Toli held this land in pledge before 1066 from the land of Sherborne' (Domesday Dorset, 34:14), but unless it was formerly much larger (it was a single hide in 1086) it is not *Wulfheardigstoke*, which at ten *cassates*, is an estate at least the size of Bradford [Abbas]; and ten can connote a territorial 'whole' – a unit of taxation. Chardstock (*Cerdestoche*, 1086) is a possible candidate. On the Somerset/Devon/Dorset boundary it was an outlying part of the Domesday Hundred of Beaminster (it is now in Devon). The primary settlement, Chard, was held by the bishop of Wells (Domesday Somerset, 3:6). In 1086 the Chard *stoc* was held by the bishop of Salisbury assessed at twelve hides, with twenty ploughteams. But this would mean that firstly the estate is rather too big, and secondly the list, reading from Stalbridge to Chardstock, would then have to double back for *Cumbtun, Osanstoke* – and Lyme.

Keynes ('Wulfsige, monk of Glastonbury', this volume) draws attention to the curious omission of Corscombe from the charter of 998, 'an estate known to have been out on lease since the 970s'. *Corscuba* is listed three times in 1086; two small one-hide estates, and one large ten-hide (less one virgate) estate held by

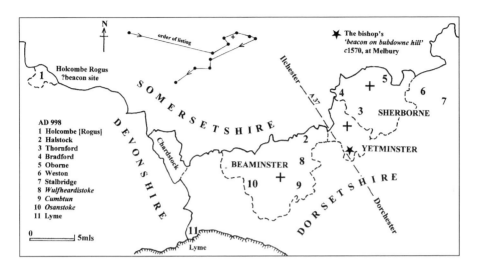

Figure 16. Map showing the suggested location of the Sherborne estates listed in the charter of 998 and (inset) their order of listing, in relation to the three episcopal hundreds of Sherborne, Yetminster and Beaminster, the bounds of which are those suggested by the Domesday Book. The estates are numbered in the order in which they are given; Holcombe [Rogus] is the first and Lyme, the last. The shire boundary is shown as an unbroken line. The bishop's hundreds are at least in part complemented by a series of royal manors on the Somerset side of the shire boundary.

the bishop. Corscombe should surely stand as a candidate for the ten *cassates* at *Wulfheardigstoke*. By 1086 it is no longer a *stoc* held by Wulfheard[11] and for some reason the name was not retained. A surviving *stoc* in this area is *Osanstoke* (Osa's *stoc*) which, assessed at two *cassates*, may be represented by the two untaxed *carucates* listed for the bishop at *Stoche* (Stoke Abbott) in 1086[12] (Domesday Dorset, 3:8, 3:9). Listed between *Wulfheardigstoke* and *Osanstoke* is an estate of eight *cassates* called *Cumbtun*, Compton, which poses the question as to whether this can really be Compton north of Sherborne. In 1086 the Sherborne *Contone* was held by the monks assessed at six hides and three virgates; Wulfsige's charter gives us eight *cassates*.

A route from Corscombe to Stoke Abbot takes us through Beaminster held by the bishop in 1086 assessed at sixteen hides and one virgate with twenty ploughteams. A large estate known to have embraced a number of places which are not recorded by name (Domesday Dorset, 3:10 and note) there may be a case here for exploring in more detail the area immediately east of Beaminster town, Coombe Down, the slopes of which are today occupied by Whitcombe and Coombe Down Farms. It may well be that all three estates do indeed occupy much the same area (as Ekwall suggested, see above) and are listed in terms of the route taken between them – thus from *Wulfheardigstoke* (Corscombe), on to *Cumbtun* (Coombe in Beaminster) and then *Osanstoke* (part of Stoke Abbot) (see Fig 16).

Of further interest is the order of estates given in 1086 which echoes the listing of 998.[13] Here Stalbridge is once again immediately followed by Corscombe and Stoke Abbot, thus giving us Bradford-Compton-Stalbridge-[Stalbridge]Weston-Corscombe-Stoke Abbot (Domesday Dorset, 3:4–9). The Compton [*Contone*] here listed after Bradford [Abbas] can convincingly be identified with Over/Nether Compton north-west of Sherborne, whilst *Wulfheardigstoke*, *Cumbtun* and *Osanstoke* of 998 look likely to have become, by 1086, respectively, Corscombe, a part of Beaminster and a part of Stoke Abbot.

Problems with identifying these three estates may suggest an area which, at least tenurially speaking, was in some 'flux' in 998, for reasons which are presumably related to those of change of status in the drawing up of the charter – we may also suspect matters relating to tax and/or the shire boundary. Keynes ('King Æthelred's charter', introduction, this volume) notes the list of estates 'is opaque ... [and] seems to reflect the settlement of an outbreak of disputes over land ... providing a context or pretext for the listing of landed property'. The status of these estates listed is presumably implied in the terms of the charter; whether they had been changed *by* the terms of the charter – as we might suspect – is impossible to know. It may be that all eleven named places represent former hereditary parcels or *prebends*, now made over to the abbey. Continuing difficulties may be evidenced in the loss of two 'personalised' Sherborne-held *stoc* named places (respectively those of *Wulfheard* and *Osa*) in the following century. Echoes here, perhaps of the kind of eventuality cited by John (1966, 173), that whatever misfortune befell these [landowning] people any 'land forfeit would [through the terms of the charter] come back to the church' – divested of their family names.[14]

The status of the eleventh estate at Lyme, is clearly not the same as the others if only by virtue of the fact the wording in the charter is different. For the first ten, it is 'in Thornford' (or whichever estate) and then the number of *cassates*. For Lyme we have one *mansa*, the geographical location of which is precisely described, and this is not *in Lim*, but *aet Lim. Mansa,* is from Latin *manere*, 'to reside', and we note that in 774, it is earlier described as a single *mansio* (for a discussion see Barker, 'The Sherborne estate at Lyme', this volume).

The three episcopal hundreds

The hundred formed the basis of Anglo-Saxon local government and jurisdiction. A subdivision of the *shire* (later county), it is likely to be of continental Carolingian origin. The shires played an essential part in the defence of the kingdom; shire levies of men and of tribute fill the pages of the Anglo-Saxon Chronicle for this period (Barker, 'Bishop Wulfsige's lifetime', this volume). Part of the tenth-century 'tenurial revolution' effected by King Edgar, was the transference of certain delegated powers from the local *ministri*, the *ealdorman* and *reeve*, to the local abbot or bishop, thus burdening the bishop with certain judicial and even military obligations – ensuring at the very least, that any risk to ecclesiastical endowments was avoided (John 1966, 175).

Bishop Wulfsige held three hundreds which were contiguous, each centred on an earlier minster, that is, Sherborne, Yetminster and Beaminster (see Fig 16). The three hundreds define much of the boundary of west Dorsetshire endowing them with something of a 'frontier' significance. The hundred boundaries shown on Figure 16 are those given for the Domesday hundreds. Already mentioned (above and note 1) is the distinct likelihood that the beacon on *bubdowne hill* recorded on a map of *c* 1570 represents the site of a tenth-century antecedent, and further, that the bishop of Sherborne may also have had a responsibility for the maintenance and manning of the beacon on the Devonshire/Somersetshire border implied for *Holancombe*.

A slightly later record belonging to Wulfsige's immediate successor Æthelric, throws light on the weighty fiscal and naval responsibilities of the bishop as major landholder in troubled times. The bishop complained that some of the lands which should have helped him meet the charge of a ship on the three hundred hides of his episcopal estate, or *ship-scot*, dues payable on thirty-three hides had been lost to him, dues which had clearly been paid to his predecessor(s). Following a levy of ships imposed in 1008 (probably not the first) it is clear the bishop was responsible for fitting-out and manning a warship; every 310 hides had to provide a *scegth* of approximately sixty-four oars; every eight hides were to provide a helmet and mailcoat. 'An association of hundreds in groups of three for the provision of ships ... is to be traced here and ... seems to indicate another unit of assessment, namely 300, the unit which appears [in Bishop Æthelric's complaint]' (*ASC* 1972, 138; Abels 1988, 93; Harmer 1989, 266–70).[15] The charter of 998 list finishes on the coast at Lyme, that place *iuxta ripam maris*, on the seashore (Barker, 'The Sherborne estate at Lyme', this volume). Somewhere in the Borough of Bridport of 1086, a little further along the coast, the bishop of Salisbury held *'dimidiam acram* (half an acre)'. Given the early thirteenth-century importance of the place for the manufacture of rope and rigging we may wonder as to the significance of this Domesday entry in terms of the early eleventh century for Sherborne (Barker 2003).

Wulfsige was clearly a major player in the management of what we would now call 'resources'. While there is evidence that bishops were ultimately responsible for weights and measures, for regulating trading and market dues, and that Benedictine foundations thus played a considerable role in the (re)creation of towns, Wulfsige was clearly not responsible – unlike some of his continental counterparts (Bois 1992, 86) – for coins and for coining which was also regularised by the English Crown during the later tenth century (Campbell 1986, 155–7). A mint was established at Milborne [Port] a royal manor only a few miles east of Sherborne, but in the neighbouring shire of Somerset (Fig 15). It was moved under Æthelred II to the security of the hillfort of South Cadbury (Aston 1984, 170–1, 185).

Notes

1   On a Tudor map of north-west Dorset *c* 1570 (BL Add ms 52522) probably
    commissioned by the then bishop of Salisbury to show his estates in the Sherborne
    and Yetminster Hundreds (Barker 1991, 33, 41–2), 'The beacon on bubdowne hill'
    is shown by means of a curious little device sited on what is now Melbury Hill.
    This is a conspicuous high point offering good views in all directions but
    particularly to the north across lowland Somerset towards the Parrett estuary, and
    west-north-west along the ridge that forms part of the shire boundary. Was the
    bubdowne hill beacon intervisible with that implied for Holcombe *Rogus*? Quite
    apart from its natural vantage point, the former occupies a strategic site alongside
    the Dorchester–Ilchester Roman road (much of which is still in use as the A37),
    close to the edge of the (Domesday) Hundred of Yetminster, near the present
    Melbury Bubb/Osmond parish boundary (see Fig 16). It is tempting to suggest
    that this represents the site of a much earlier beacon and had remained the
    responsibility of the bishop – which is why it appears on the map and in an area
    for which little other information is shown.

2   The end of the Sixth Age since Adam had been awaited at least since the time of
    Augustine of Hippo (Reuter, 'Introduction', Campion, 'Thousand is a perfect
    number ...' and Barker, *'Anni Domini Computati'*, all this volume).

3   Bois (1992, 45, 52, 95–8; 101–5) cites continental Frankish evidence for significant
    population growth by the tenth century – together with a number of technical
    developments, particularly that of the water mill. Daniel (1975) notes that despite
    'sustained attacks' by the Vikings the ninth and tenth centuries saw a 'silent
    agricultural revolution'. Bois (1992) also notes a newly recognised social division
    between those able to keep draught animals and those who only had spade and
    hoe. This distinction is clearly made in the charter of 998 between those who,
    because of a lack of land, could neither win a living *arando* [by ploughing] or
    fodiendo [by digging]. The steady increase in donations of land in favour of the
    church towards the end of the century were not, he notes, just simple acts of piety,
    but also a search for security and protection when local circumstances, political or
    economic, turned nasty. Campbell (1986, 161) also notes points of resemblance in
    styles of land management between English and Carolingian systems where the
    evidence suggests something more than common origins and common needs; a
    case in point is the establishment of the hundredal system; see note 8.

4   *Rus*, 'countryside' as distinct perhaps from *urbs*, 'town'. Bois (1992, 85–6) notes the
    separation of 'country' and 'town' in the growth of markets and periodic fairs
    encouraged – and controlled by – the church; in essence representing a new phase
    in town development.

5   Campbell (1986, 140) notes that the location of a bishop's *sedes episcopalis*, 'seat',
    was not necessarily at major centres with a Roman past because – as Bede seems
    to imply – kings had given away so much land it was not easy to find an estate
    sufficient to sustain a bishop. 'What made Lichfield suitable may be guessed from
    the Domesday Book which shows it as the centre of a vast multiple estate ...
    Sherborne [was] not improbably of the same type' *(ibid)*.

6   There are extant boundary surveys for two neighbouring Sherborne estates both
    of which pre-date 998; for Bradford [Abbas] AD 933, and Thornford AD 946. A
    ditch and double bank forms the axial north-south cross-valley boundary between
    Bradford and Sherborne Wyke. Described as an *ealden dic* [old dyke] it remains a

prominent feature in the landscape. A length of the boundary between Thornford and Sherborne is a *holen weg*, 'hollow way' which remains part of the parish boundary and which can still be walked (Grundy 1933, 25–253; 1938, 87; see Fig 15). It could well have been incorporated into the Wulfsige 'circuit'.

7　Stockland in Devon was held by Milton Abbey in Dorset. 'This manor was always part of the monks' lordship for their supplies and clothing' (Domesday Dorset, 12:14).

8　'No instance is known before the tenth century of the word "hundred" [or any English or Latin numerical equivalent] being used in England to denote a unit of government or of jurisdiction ... the case for the institution when it appears in the tenth century having been developed under Continental [Frankish] influence is supported by the adoption of a corresponding name' (Campbell 1986, 161). The reference to the '100 hides at Lanprobi', we take to be a latter-day – and by the fourteenth century, well understood term – denoting a single, discrete administrative unit.

9　There is another instance of **Lanprobus/Propeschirche* represented in Cornwall. The canons of *Sanctus Probus* held *Lanbrebois* [in Cornwall] in 1086; this is the church of *Sanctus Probus* 1123, *Seynt Probus* 1466; *Lamprobus Mill* 1759. 'Nothing is known of him; he is first found as patron saint of this parish in the form *Propus*, in the 10th century. It is unlikely that the saint of this parish is one of the various universal saints called Probus; but one of the same name was honoured at Sherborne in the Middle Ages' (Padel 1988, 146). 'Sherborne Abbey was formerly called Lanprobi or the church of Probus or else *Propeschirche*, but its calendar retains no memory of its former patron. If Probus ever existed and is not just a name meaning "honest" he was probably a Celtic or British saint of the West Country of whom all is forgotten except his dedications' (Farmer 1997, 418; see Hall, 'Sherborne', this volume).

10　It may be of significance that the Tudor map commissioned *c* 1570 by the then bishop of Salisbury to show the Hundreds of Sherborne and Yetminster (see note 1) is drawn with south at the top. Sherborne is towards the bottom of the map and the eye reads up the map, southwards.

11　Wulfheard may not have been an uncommon name but we note in the Anglo-Saxon Chronicle (see Barker, 'Bishop Wulfsige's lifetime', this volume) that in 837 [840] 'ealdorman Wulfheard fought at Southampton against thirty-three ships' companies, and made great slaughter there ... and the same year ealdorman Æthelhelm fought against a Danish host at Portland with the men of Dorset, but the Danes ... slew [him]'. This is the first reference to the Dorset levy. Wulfheard, we take it, led the men of Hampshire (Edwards 1988, 148–50).

12　The nature, status (and indeed, the origin) of these Domesday ungelded/untaxed *carucates* – including those of Beaminster and Netherbury (two each in 1086, not mentioned in 998) and, notably those of the home manor, Sherborne, remains a mystery; their distribution has already been noted (Barker 1982, 85–99). The monks held nine and a half ungelded carucates in Sherborne. It may be of interest that Goscelin's *Life* tells us 'the blessed Wulfsige had granted the brothers of the monastery the tithes and the half carucate of land which were the possession of the bishop' although the text here seems in some way to be corrupt (see Love, 'The Life of St Wulfsige', ch XVIII and note 70, this volume). The ungelded *caruca* recorded for Lyme later became a Salisbury cathedral prebend.

13 The only other time both Stalbridge and Compton estates are listed together is in a fourteenth-century compilation (BL Cotton Faustina Aii, fo 25), an attempt at an all-embracing 'trawl' of Sherborne estates (beginning with Cenwalh and *Lanprobi*) which includes those lost to Crediton and others to Wells when the see was divided in 909. Stalbridge and Compton occur one after the other as in 998, *Stapulbrige de xx hidis et Cuniton de viiii hidis* with the same hidages as entered in 1086, both seemingly granted to Sherborne by Æthelbert; Edwards (1988, 248) gives *Cuniton* as Nether/Over Compton.

14 Goscelin in his *Life* of Wulfsige (Love, 'The Life of St Wulfsige', ch XX, this volume) refers to an occasion when the king's judges tried to appropriate a parcel of land belonging to the bishop, and to the law-suit which culminated in the bringing in of Wulfsige's relics for a holy adjudication.

15 In 1086 we find the bishop of Salisbury (immediate successor to the bishop of Sherborne) holding *dimidium acrum*, 'half an acre' in the royal borough of Bridport (Domesday Dorset, 2:12). By the reign of King John, Bridport was already well-known for the provisioning of ships – for rope and linen manufacture – and entry in Domesday of the Bishop's holding here may not be without significance.

Abbreviations

ASC   *The Anglo-Saxon Chronicle*
RCHM   Royal Commission on Historical Monuments

Bibliography

Abels, R, 1988, *Lordship and Military Obligation in Anglo-Saxon England*. London. British Museum.

Aston, M A, 1984, The Towns of Somerset. In J Haslem (ed), *Anglo-Saxon Towns of Southern England*. Chichester. Phillimore, 167–202.

The Anglo-Saxon Chronicle, 1972, G N Garmonsway (trans). London. Dent.

Barker, K, 1982, The Early History of Sherborne. In S Pearce (ed), *The Early Church in Western Britain and Ireland, Papers Presented to CA Ralegh Radford*. British Archaeological Reports, British Series 102. Oxford, 71–116.

Barker, K, 1984, Sherborne in Dorset: an early ecclesiastical settlement and its estate. *Anglo-Saxon Studies in Archaeology and History* 3. Oxford University Committee for Archaeology, 1–33.

Barker, K, 1991, An Elizabethan Map of North-West Dorset: Sherborne, Yetminster and surrounding manors. In K Barker and R Kain (eds), *Maps and History in South-West England*. Exeter Studies in History, 31. University of Exeter, 28–53.

Barker, K, 2003, *The Bridport Charter of 1253, Making and Meaning*. Based on a lecture given to mark the 750th anniversary of the granting of the Borough Charter. Bridport History Society and Bridport Charter Fair, 50.

Bois, G, 1992, *The Transformation of the Year 1000. The Village of Lournand from Antiquity to Feudalism*, J Birrell (trans). Manchester.

Campbell, J, 1986, *Essays in Anglo-Saxon History*. London. Hambledon Press.

Daniel, N, 1975, *The Arabs in Mediaeval Europe*. Longman, Librarie de Liban.

Domesday Book, Devon, 1985 (2 parts), C and F Thorn (eds). Chichester. Phillimore.

Domesday Book, Dorset, 1983, C and F Thorn (eds). Chichester. Phillimore.

Domesday Book, Somerset, 1980, C and F Thorn (eds). Chichester. Phillimore.

Duby, G, 1968, *Rural Economy and Country Life in the Medieval West*. Edward Arnold; see especially Book II, Ch 1, 'The Extension of the Arable'.

Dugdale, W, 1817, *Monasticon Anglicanum* (Seven volumes). London.

Edwards, H, 1988, *The Charters of the Early West Saxon Kingdom*. British Archaeological Reports, British Series, 198. Oxford.

Ekwall, E, 1936, *Studies on English Place-names*. Stockholm.

Everitt, A, 1986, *Continuity and Colonization, the Evolution of Kentish Settlement*. Leicester. Studies in Local History. Leicester University Press.

Faith, R, 1997, *The English Peasantry and the Growth of Lordship*. Studies in the Early History of Britain. Leicester University Press.

Farmer, D, 1997, *The Oxford Dictionary of Saints* (4th Edition). Oxford.

Fowler, J, 1951, *Mediaeval Sherborne*. Dorchester. Longmans.

Gelling, M, 1984, *Place-names in the Landscape*. London. Dent.

Grundy, G B, 1933, Dorset Charters: Bradford Abbas. *Proceedings of the Dorset Natural History and Archaeological Society*, 55, 250–3.

Grundy, G B, 1938, Dorset Charters: Thornford. *Proceedings of the Dorset Natural History and Archaeological Society*, 60, 87–9.

Harmer, F E, 1989, *Anglo-Saxon Writs* (2nd Edition). Stamford. Paul Watkins.

John, E, 1966, *Orbis Britanniae*. Leicester.

John, E, 1996, *Reassessing Anglo-Saxon England*. Manchester.

Keen, L, 1984, The Towns of Dorset. In J Haslem (ed), *Anglo-Saxon Towns of Southern England*. Chichester. Phillimore, 203–48.

Mills, A D, 1989, *The Place-names of Dorset* (Part 3). English Place-name Society, LIX/LX.

Padel, O, 1988, *A Popular Dictionary of Cornish Place-names*. Penzance. Hodge.

RCHM. *Dorset, West,* 1952, *An Inventory of the Historical Monuments in Dorset* (Volume I). Royal Commission on Historical Monuments in England.

Sawyer, P H, 1968, *Anglo-Saxon Charters, an Annotated List and Bibliography*. London. Royal Historical Society.

Smith, A H, 1970, *English Place-name Elements* (Two volumes). Cambridge.

Toulmin-Smith, L (ed), 1964, *The Itinerary of John Leland in or about the years 1535–1543*. London. Centaur Press.

14. Benedictine books, writers and libraries: some surviving manuscripts from Sherborne and south-west England

Rachel Stockdale

Benedictines have long been associated with scholarship and learning, book production and fine printing, and from the Maurists onwards, the monks and nuns of the order, with their pupils, have been pioneers in palaeography and manuscript studies.[1] Injunctions to write, copy or illuminate manuscripts are not found in the Rule of St Benedict, but frequent references to reading presuppose that, even in his time, most monks were literate and books were available to them. Reading and spiritual exercises occupied about four hours a day in St Benedict's summer *horarium*, and these activities were equated with manual labour as a useful way of combating idleness, the enemy of the soul. Indeed, a General Chapter regulation of 1277 called specifically for monks to 'study, write, correct, illuminate and bind books according to their capacities, rather than labour in the fields'.

Sherborne Abbey has given its name to two of the most intriguing manuscripts to survive from an identified medieval monastery: the Sherborne Missal and the Sherborne Cartulary. Regrettably, however, there is insufficient evidence to assess the whole output of its *scriptorium* or to reconstruct the contents of the monastic library. Recent research has concluded that for Sherborne 'almost nothing is known of the provision of books. In the early fourteenth century the compilers of the *Registrum* reported some twenty-five common patristic titles and a little twelfth-century theology. The identifiable survivors include nothing that could be considered a library book' (Sharpe *et al* 1996, 590).

When the antiquary John Leland paid a visit *c* 1536–40, he noted ten titles, of which possibly three can be identified with manuscripts which survive today.[2] The fact that apparently early medieval volumes were still to be found at Sherborne at that time, suggests that the fire a century earlier had spared at least part of the library. Ker (1964, 179) listed eight extant manuscripts possibly from Sherborne, though he appended question marks to four of them to indicate doubts about their provenance, and he rejected two more outright. Five of these are discussed below. Sherborne did not have an easily recognised *ex-libris* like that of Rochester Cathedral Priory, which was written on to flyleaves of its books as a matter of course, so apart from Leland's list, identification rests on content of local interest or liturgical indications such as the saints and feasts mentioned in calendars, special prayers and order of services.

Sherborne is by no means unique in the relatively few surviving books which can now be attributed with any certainty to its monastery. However, to place in proper perspective the achievements of Benedictines as authors, scribes and illuminators in the south-west of England between the tenth-century revival of learning and the fifteenth century, it will be necessary to consider some examples associated with neighbouring houses, especially the nunnery of Shaftesbury.

The missal (Figures 7 and 17)

Missals were needed in all monasteries for the daily celebration of the mass. It must be assumed that the magnificent volume now known as the Sherborne Missal was a treasured object for display or use only on special days, and that less spectacular copies were in regular use.[3] Imposing in its physical dimensions, it consists of 347 leaves each measuring approximately 535 × 380 mm and weighs over 40 pounds in its present cover. The sheer quality and exuberance of the illumination must have impressed contemporaries and appealed to later collectors alike, and thus contributed to its survival. The text is that of a missal of Gregorian use comprising Temporal, Ordo, Canon, Sanctorale, Common of Saints and votive masses, preceded by a Benedictine calendar. Backhouse (1999, 7–12) places it in the context of two other missals also made about 1400, the Carmelite Missal (Add 29704-5 and Add 44892) and the Westminster Missal (Westminster Abbey 37).

Marginal illustrations of Benedictine monks and scenes from the history of Sherborne confirm the local provenance. On the left of the lower margin of page 397 St Wulfsige is shown welcoming the black monks to its church, whilst in the centre, the secular clergy are led away to fortified Old Sarum, and on the right the move onward to Salisbury, a church with towering spire, is in progress. The dedication of Sherborne Abbey church is represented on page 492 and its feast is noted in the Calendar (18 July), together with the feasts of Saints Benedict, Wulfsige and Juthwara (a saint from Halstock whose relics were at Sherborne). Grants made to Sherborne by benefactors are mentioned: some of these benefactors are depicted as busts in medallions, and the cartulary sometimes provides supporting evidence of their gifts. There are also many coats of arms in the border illustrations, not just those of Sherborne but of other houses with property in Dorset such as Abbotsbury, Milton, Cerne and Glastonbury.

Figure 17. The Sherborne Missal, c 1400; the Sunday after Epiphany, the Christ Child disputing with the doctors in the Temple. The illustration may draw its inspiration from a medieval schoolroom. (BL Add 74236, p 55. Reproduced by permission of the British Library)

Four local personalities connected with the missal appear in its pages. The abbot, who can be identified as Robert Bruyning or Brunyng, in office from 1385 to 1415, clearly played a prominent role as he is shown about a hundred times, in vestments or habit with a crozier. The bishop of Salisbury from 1395–1407, Richard Mitford or Medford, appears much less frequently, always in the company of the abbot. He is not named but is known from his personal arms. These influential men seem likely to have commissioned the book. The scribe was John Whas, as stated in four colophons, probably a Benedictine monk working alone on the manuscript. There is some evidence that the family name was a local one, but nothing further is known of him. By contrast, the most prominent of the (possibly five) artists was John Siferwas, who wears a white Dominican habit under his black cloak (see, for example, p 225) and who is also known from his self-portrait which forms the frontispiece of the Lovel Lectionary (Harley 7026). Members of his family can be traced in the south of England back to the early thirteenth century. Identification of these individuals raises the question of how and why members of different religious orders and ecclesiastical positions might be associated in the commissioning and production of a single manuscript. There was no Dominican house in Dorset before 1418, and it has therefore been suggested that the manuscript might have been produced at Glastonbury, as was probably the Lovel Lectionary. Even if the missal was not made entirely at Sherborne, there can be no doubt that it was created for the abbey, possibly ordered and financed by the abbot himself. It can be dated within a fairly narrow timespan, after 1399 and before 1407, determined by the form of arms of Henry, Prince of Wales, and the term of office of Bishop Mitford.

The only full-page miniature in the Sherborne Missal is the Crucifixion on page 380. However, it is the border images, up to thirty on some pages, together with the decorated and historiated initials which qualify it as a masterpiece of the International Gothic style. The realistic portrayals of native birds on pages 363–93, labelled with their vernacular, sometimes dialect, names are justly well known and have often been reproduced.[4] In contrast to these, which are clearly drawn from life, are exotic animals – a porcupine with a camel on page 268.[5]

The missal seems to have remained at Sherborne until the Reformation. It is unclear how it reached France where it remained for most of the eighteenth century and received its present binding, but in 1800 it came into the hands of the 2nd Duke of Northumberland whose family was to own it for very nearly two centuries.[6]

The psalter
The psalter was one of the most widely used devotional books of the Middle Ages. There are no surviving psalters from Sherborne, but two which are now in the British Library are associated with the neighbouring nunnery of Shaftesbury, for a time the largest and richest female Benedictine community in England.

Lansdowne 383 was written about 1130–40. G F Warner (1903, no 13) thought that the original owner must have been connected with Shaftesbury Abbey, though he did not claim that it was necessarily written there. Subsequent research has questioned whether a female community would have commanded sufficient skills to execute work of such a high standard, whilst stylistic comparisons have been made with manuscripts from Hereford or elsewhere in the south-west. However, the evidence of the liturgical calendar seems strongly to favour Shaftesbury, for it gives prominence to King Edward the Martyr, assassinated by his stepmother in March 978/9 at nearby Corfe, whose relics were preserved at Shaftesbury, and St Ælgifu, a nun buried there, is mentioned in the litany.

The Calendar is illustrated with the signs of the Zodiac and the occupations of the months. A cycle of six full-page miniatures precedes the psalter text, and two further miniatures occur later in the volume. Historiated initials mark the liturgical divisions of the psalms and are an early example of such usage in a western psalter. A woman in a brown garment with a green hood is depicted more than once, most notably adoring the Virgin and Child on folio 165. Clearly she was important in relation to the manuscript but it is not certain whether she was the abbess or a nun, or a secular benefactress who commissioned the work. The figures have the solid, statuesque appearance typical of English Romanesque art.

The second psalter, Cotton Nero C iv, was almost certainly not made at Shaftesbury, though it must have been there in the thirteenth century when the feast of the dedication of the abbey church was added to the calendar. Formerly known as the St Swithun Psalter from a presumed connection with the Winchester house, it is now more usually called the Psalter of Henry of Blois after one of the most influential Benedictines of his age, brother of King Stephen, papal legate, abbot of Glastonbury and bishop of Winchester from 1129–71. It is thought that he commissioned it from Hyde Abbey, formerly the New Minster, Winchester between *c* 1140 and 1160 and it may be his own gift or bequest to Shaftesbury. By the mid-twelfth century, devotional manuscripts for private use were becoming more common. Henry was in a position to command the finest craftsmanship and is known to have been something of a connoisseur, for on a visit to Rome he showed an interest in the classical statues considered unseemly in a monk. His psalter begins with a total of thirty-eight pages of miniatures, with inscriptions in Anglo-Norman French. The figures are angular, with lively facial expressions, and many wear contemporary dress. The drawings are tinted rather than full colour, but have suffered from removal of some pigments and deliberate splitting of the leaves, as well as sustaining damage in the Cotton fire.

The pontifical
A pontifical contains offices and prayers, services and ceremonies proper to a bishop or an abbot acting as bishop, such as orders of service for the

consecration of a church, ordinations to office, the blessing of a new abbot and crowning of a king. The pontifical to which Sherborne has given its name (also known as the Pontifical of St Dunstan) is now MS lat 943 in the Bibliothèque Nationale in Paris.[7] Written in the late tenth century (960–90), probably at Christ Church Canterbury, it was at Sherborne by the early eleventh century, on the evidence of local additions (a list of bishops of Sherborne folio 1v, a letter to Wulfsige on the front flyleaves and further letters at the back). It is thus the only pre-Conquest manuscript with Sherborne connections to have survived. There are coloured initials and musical notation in Anglo-Saxon *neums*.[8] As in the case of the missal, the Sherborne Pontifical would not have been the only book of its kind in use there. Another pontifical, Cotton Tiberius C i, of the eleventh century, was assigned to Sherborne by Ker on the grounds of content, though he indicated his uncertainty with a question mark. This text is now bound up with other material originating from the Benedictine house at Peterborough.

The cartulary

Devotion to the Work of God did not prevent the followers of St Benedict from attending to the worldly interests of their communities, and it is fortunate for modern scholarship that Benedictines were such conscientious record keepers. The British Library holds a number of cartularies, including the earliest survivor from any English religious house,[9] but the mid-twelfth-century Sherborne Cartulary, Add 46487, is quite unique. Between thick oak boards, which are certainly medieval but possibly not original, are bound two distinct books.[10] The cartulary proper, on folios 3–38v, consists of copies of pre- and post-Conquest documents in Latin and Anglo-Saxon relating to Sherborne Abbey, followed by those of its subordinate house of Horton, and papal charters recording the quarrel between the monks and Bishop Jocelin.

First among them, on folios 3–4, is a copy of the charter of 998 by which King Æthelred granted Bishop Wulfsige permission to convert Sherborne to a Benedictine monastery.[11] A grant on folios 10v–11 of five hides of land at Oborne by King Edgar purports to have been witnessed by St Dunstan himself. Documents such as these drew attention to the volume long before it reached the British Museum – all the charters appeared in print as listed in Wormald's article (1957, 111–17). Those of the Anglo-Saxon period are more recently transcribed and annotated in O'Donovan's edition (1988).

The second part of the volume, folios 39–86b, is a liturgical collection for the use of the abbot, consisting of passion narratives, gospels and collects, and prayers and blessings for liturgical ceremonies. This section is adorned with decorated initials and two evangelist miniatures in early Romanesque style (the other two are presumed to have been removed). St John, who occupies a full page on folio 52v, is shown in an unusual standing position, whilst St Mark (half-page on fo 43v) is seated. Both lack the conventional evangelist symbols.

Although it was common practice in the eleventh and twelfth centuries to copy important single charters on to the vacant flyleaves of service books for reference, the Sherborne Cartulary is the only example known of liturgical and secular material being accorded equal weight in a single volume. Sherborne's struggle to retain its privileges after the loss of the seat of the bishopric to Old Sarum is well documented. In February 1145/6, just before the compilation of this manuscript is believed to have begun, a bull of Pope Eugenius III had settled in Sherborne's favour a dispute with Jocelin, bishop of Salisbury over the right of electing the abbot, and had at the same time confirmed its territorial possessions. The monks would naturally be anxious to record their victory for posterity, and to ensure that the evidence would not be tampered with or called into question. They therefore copied out the precious charters and bound them up with a gospel book destined for permanent display on their altar, where both would remain inviolable.

Shaftesbury provides an example of a more conventional cartulary (Harley 61), neat but functional. It was compiled during the reign of Henry V between 1413 and 1422 and consists of 124 leaves, uniformly written with rubricated headings and initials by a single scribe (or by collaborators with very similar hands). On the flyleaf a later hand has entered the title *Registrum peruetustum Abbatie Shaftoniensis sive Shaftisbiriensis.* G R C Davis (1958, 100) thought it was 'Intended apparently as a register of rights and privileges etc. given and conceded rather than of title-deeds'. The arrangement is only partially chronological. Folios 1–22 contain the only surviving copies of thirty charters, diplomas and writs of the Anglo-Saxon period, six of which pre-date the foundation of the nunnery and are probably preserved as evidence of title to some of its landholdings. Not all are necessarily authentic. Following the common practice of the period some, including the foundation charter in the name of King Alfred (fos 21v–2), may have been written later to support the status quo rather than to record a contemporary transaction. The rest of the volume is made up of later documents including private charters and agreements, inquisitions and a list of tenants. Several stages of copying must have intervened between the source documents and this volume, in the course of which inaccuracies and misreadings have been introduced. The contents are listed and some of the charters published in full in Dugdale (1846, II), and there are extracts in Hutchins (1873, III). The Anglo-Saxon charters are printed with extensive notes in a recent edition by S E Kelly (1996).

Produced about the same time as Harley 61, Egerton 3135 is a register containing copies of a group of deeds relating to the endowment of a chantry by Robert Osegod, alias Fovent, and his wife, the parents of Cecilia Fovent who was abbess of Shaftesbury from 1398 to 1423. The property donated for this purpose was situated in Fovant, Wiltshire, and in Shaftesbury itself, and the deeds range in date from the thirteenth century until *c* 1406. A third Shaftesbury book, Egerton 3098, is a *Kalendare munimentorum* or inventory of muniments, compiled by order of Margery Twynyho, abbess from 1496 to 1505, to help locate material needed as evidence of rights and possessions. The confusion which existed in the abbey treasury, and the frustration of having to search through various chests and boxes for missing muniments, are amusingly described in a preface (fos 1–2) which is quoted in translation in an article by H I Bell (1933–4). The task of listing the documents under the manors to which they related, noting briefly the subject and the grantors, was entrusted to the sacristan Alexander Katour. He began work in 1500, though it is clear from the preface that the present manuscript, perhaps a copy of his original, was completed after the death of the abbess in 1505. Some of the items listed can be identified with entries in Egerton 3135 and Harley 61, but the three sources do not match as closely as might have been expected. Although the intention was to facilitate retrieval, only once did the compiler actually record where a document was to be found. Extracts are printed in Hutchins (1873, III).

The *compotus* or account book
Daily life in the Sherborne community is reflected in a *compotus* or account book (Cotton Faustina A ii), begun *c* 1395 and continued into the fifteenth century, recording details of financial and domestic administration. The arrangement is haphazard, suggesting that it was intended as a source of ready reference, rather than a formal compilation. There are lists of the pre-Conquest English and Saxon kings who were benefactors of the church of Sherborne, with the names and often the hidage of the lands they donated,[12] local bishops, and monastic officials at the time of Richard II. Military dues, spiritual and temporal taxes, extents of lands owned, and rents are noted. On folio 31 are set out the half-yearly wages for 1387–8 of outdoor and indoor servants of the abbey, including the swineherd, drover and cook, followed by a memorandum of those with the right to receive vegetables as payment in kind (Fig 18). A calendar and copies of the Benedictine Constitutions of Abingdon and Oxford are also found in the volume.

The chronicle
The keeping of the annals or writing the history of a monastic foundation was often passed down the generations from one anonymous writer to the next. But some historian monks are identifiable by name, Matthew Paris of St Albans being perhaps the most prominent. Whilst Sherborne lacks a named chronicler, its neighbour Glastonbury produced three: William of Malmesbury, Adam of Domerham and John of Glastonbury. John, who flourished *c* 1400, tells in his prologue how he approached the task, consciously 'following in the footsteps' of his predecessors but adding details which William had omitted, rearranging the whole in better order and pruning Adam's prolixity. One copy of his Chronicle is Cotton Tiberius A v, a curious volume now bound along the short sides of the leaves at the foot of the text. This version is incomplete, ending in

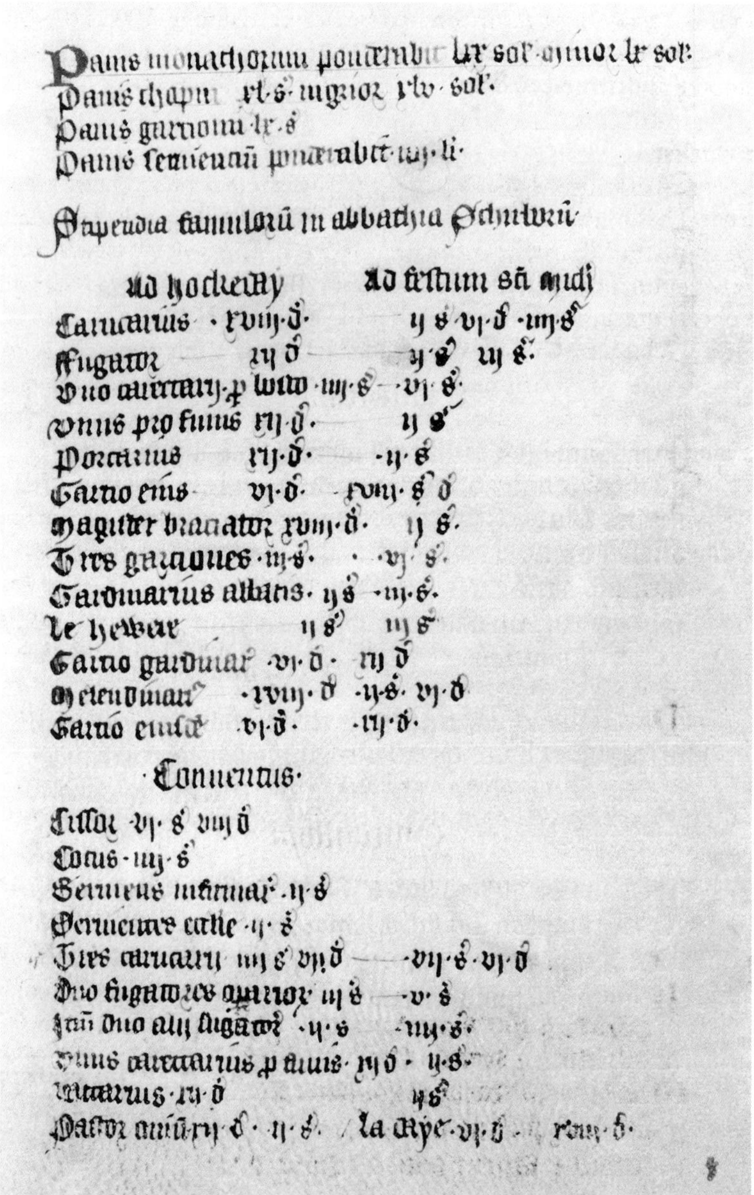

*Figure 18. A page from the Sherborne compotus or account book showing a list of abbey servants'
wages. Set out on the page are the half-yearly wages for 1387–8 of outdoor and indoor servants
of the abbey, including the swineherd, drover and cook, followed by a memorandum of those with
the right to receive vegetables as payment in kind. (BL Cotton Faustina A. II, fo 31. Reproduced
by permission of the British Library)*

1334 with the account of Prior John of Breynton. Ashmole 790 in the Bodleian Library contains not only the rest of John's work but a continuation from 1400–93 by another Glastonbury monk, perhaps Thomas Wason.

Other works

It is ironic that Adam of Barking, a monk of Sherborne who is believed to have lived around 1217, and a writer of prose and verse whose works are mentioned three times in Leland's list, has no surviving manuscripts which can be attributed with certainty to Sherborne.[13] Similarly Ælfric 'The Grammarian', biographer of St Æthelwold and abbot of the neighbouring Benedictine house of Cerne, where he is known to have compiled his *Homilies*, has no manuscripts with local connections to represent his prolific writings. The absence of manuscript evidence from Sherborne must therefore be regarded as a failure of survival, rather than any lack of interest in authorship as an intellectual and creative activity.

Manuscripts from other Benedictine houses in the south-west of England also suggest that a range of literature was available in monastic libraries for monks to read, even if their authors were not members of the order. Three examples must suffice. Firstly from Shaftesbury, comes a fifteenth-century compilation of religious works (Add 11748), comprising the Treatise on the Contemplative Life by the Augustinian Canon Walter Hilton (died 1396), a chapter from Bonaventura on the Life of Christ, and verses on the instruments of the Crucifixion, all in English. Folio 1 records that the volume was in the custody of the abbess and convent of Shaston [Shaftesbury].

From Cerne there is a thirteenth-century manuscript of John of Sacro Bosco (fl. 1230), his *Tractatus de Sphaera*, together with other astronomical works and tables (Egerton 843). The *Tractatus*, which was very popular in the Middle Ages and survives in a number of manuscripts as well as translations and printed editions, was a little work in four chapters dealing with the terrestrial globe, circles great and small, the rising and setting of the stars, and the orbits and movements of the planets. The manuscript is illustrated with explanatory diagrams in colour. It was once bound together with Trinity College Cambridge MS O.2.45, which contains evidence of the Cerne provenance. It was extracted in the early nineteenth century in circumstances in which J O Halliwell-Phillipps was thought to have been implicated, though no charge was ever proven.[14]

Finally from Abbotsbury comes a volume containing, among other miscellaneous items, an anonymous treatise in Norman French explaining the game of chess through problems and solutions (Cotton Cleo. B ix). Part of the text is in verse, and each example is illustrated with a diagram of a chess board showing the positions of the pieces.[15] The manuscript was written towards the end of the thirteenth century. At the end (fos 54v–60) is a calendar with entries for the Feast of the Dedication of the Church of St Peter at Abbotsbury on 12 October, and those of Saints Wulfsige, Juthwara and Edwold, a hermit of Cerne. Unfortunately, it is not known whether there was ever a budding chess champion among the Abbotsbury monks.

Sherborne and its immediate neighbours bear witness to the strong bond between Benedictines and their books, as patrons, producers, collectors, custodians and readers, but the relatively small numbers of volumes which can now be positively connected with these houses demonstrate also the accidents and uncertainties in the survival of medieval manuscripts.[16]

Notes

1 This paper was originally prepared as a slide lecture for the Sherborne Abbey Millennium to celebrate in pictures some highlights of Benedictine book-production in Sherborne and the south-west. It is not a comprehensive survey and does not contain any new research. The examples were selected purely from personal interest and from manuscripts known to me through my work at the British Library. Manuscripts are identified here by their customary references, and are part of the British Library collections unless otherwise stated. All are well served by existing scholarly publications covering their history, texts, decoration and iconography. The main printed sources consulted are listed in the Select Bibliography (generally in the most recent or easily-accessible editions), and are cited in abbreviated form in the text and notes.

2 See his *Collectanea* (IV, 150). The three survivors are: Adam of Barking 'Carmen de sex aetatum serie' and Claudius of Turin, Commentary on Matthew; both Cambridge, Corpus Christi College, MSS 277 and 88 respectively, and Wulfstan Cantor, Life of St Swithun, Bodleian Library MS Auct. F. 2.14. Ker thought the first two were not Sherborne books. See Sharpe *et al* (1996, 590).

3 Some portions of the Sherborne Missal were published in facsimile with an introduction by J A Herbert (1920). At the time of the Sherborne Millennium meeting in 1998, the manuscript was on loan to the British Library from its then owner the 12th duke of Northumberland. Later that year, it was acquired for the nation with the help of the National Heritage Memorial Fund and became British Library Add 74236, though it will doubtless continue to be known as the Sherborne Missal. To mark the acquisition, a thoroughgoing and richly illustrated study was published by the BL's former Curator of Illuminated Manuscripts, J M Backhouse (1999). This should be consulted for further bibliography relating to the manuscript. Another missal, possibly from Sherborne and of eleventh-century date, is in Cambridge (Corpus Christi College 422).

4 See for example Yapp (1981).

5 Medieval animal lore and allegories of Christian behaviour, with the associated images, were certainly known to monastic communities. The British Library holds a very fine Bestiary with the *ex-libris* of Rochester Cathedral Priory (Royal 12 F xiii).

6 Backhouse (1999, 55–61) makes a detailed examination of the available evidence relating to its custody and sale from 1703 onwards.

7 I have not examined this manuscript myself. The contents and physical description can be ascertained from Delisle (1868–81, I, 320 and III, 268–70) and Lauer (1939, 335–6). O'Donovan (1988, 46–8) prints the writ of Bishop Æthelric to Æthelmaer from fo 170v.

8 *Neum(e)*, is the 'generic name for each of the various signs in the old musical

notation (superseded by the current staff notation) showing the note(s) to which a syllable of vocal music was to be sung. As surviving plainsong notation, the *neums* give precise indication of pitch; but, originally from the seventh century, they were only approximate reminders of the shape of the melody' (Jacobs 1958, 256).

9 Cotton Tib. A xiii fos 1–118, early eleventh-century cartulary from the Benedictine monastery of Worcester.

10 The cover with its Limoges enamel of a half-length angel, now mounted upside down, was noted and drawn by Thomas Hearne in his *Itinerary of John Leland* (1744, ii). The cartulary was rebound in the medieval fashion, in the original order, and replaced in its covers at the British Museum in 1967. For a modern examination of the boards and a description of the make-up of the volume discovered when it was pulled see Borrie (1968). For an account of the order of leaves before rebinding, see Wormald (1957, 102–3). A concordance of the present and previous foliations, photographs of the disbound volume and the interleaved paper with notes by previous owners Thomas Lloyd and Sir Thomas Phillipps are kept separately as Add 46487*.

11 Printed with notes in O'Donovan (1988, 39–44). Another badly burnt twelfth-century copy of this charter is in Cotton Otho A. xviii. f 132.

12 This list gives significant information about the estates before the division of the diocese. It is printed as Appendix I in O'Donovan (1988, 81–2).

13 See the *Dictionary of National Biography* (1885, I, 76–7). Ker rejected Cambridge, Corpus Christi College MS 277.

14 See D A Winstanley, 1948, Halliwell Phillipps and Trinity College Library. In *The Library* (5th series), II, 250–82.

15 Excerpts, including diagrams, were published in Murray (1913, 579–88). The calendar was printed in full in Wormald (1939, 2–13).

16 Some of the British Library manuscripts mentioned here are generally on display in the public exhibition galleries. Intending visitors should consult the BL website at http://www.bl.uk and enquire in advance about specific items. Catalogue descriptions of some, but not yet all, can be accessed through the same site.

Select Bibliography

Backhouse, J M, 1999, *The Sherborne Missal*. London. The British Library [see bibliography for further reading].

Bell, H I, 1933–4, A Register of Deeds from Shaftesbury Abbey. In *British Museum Quarterly*, VIII, 19–20. [Egerton 3098].

Borrie, M A F, 1968, The Binding of the Sherborne Chartulary. *British Museum Quarterly* XXXII, 96–8.

Collins, A J, 1935–6, A Chartulary of Shaftesbury Abbey. *British Museum Quarterly* X, 66–8 [Egerton 3135].

Davis, G R C, 1958, *Medieval Cartularies of Great Britain. A Short Catalogue*. London. Longmans.

Delisle, L V, 1868–81, *Le Cabinet des Manuscrits de la Bibliothèque Nationale*. Paris. Imprimerie Nationale.

Dictionary of National Biography, 1885.

Dugdale, W, 1846, *Monasticon Anglicanum* (New Edition). London. James Bohn [I, 331–41 Sherborne; II, 471–88 Shaftesbury; 621–4 Cerne; III, 52–61 Abbotsbury].

Herbert, J A, 1920, *The Sherborne Missal*. Oxford. Roxburghe Club.

Hutchins, J, 1873, *The History and Antiquities of the County of Dorset* (3rd Edition). Westminster. John Bowyer Nichols.

Jacobs, A, 1958, *A New Dictionary of Music*. Harmondsworth. Penguin Reference Books.

Kauffmann, C M, 1975, *Romanesque Manuscripts 1066–1190* (= A Survey of Manuscripts Illuminated in the British Isles III). London. Harvey Miller [Lansdowne 383 is no 48 and Add 46487 is no 60].

Kelly, S E (ed), 1996, *Charters of Shaftesbury Abbey* (= Corpus of Anglo-Saxon Charters V). Oxford. Oxford University Press for The British Academy.

Ker, N R, 1964, *Medieval Libraries of Great Britain: a list of surviving books* (2nd Edition), and Watson, A G (ed), 1987, Supplement. London. Royal Historical Society.

Lauer, Ph (ed), 1939, *Catalogue Général des Manuscrits Latins* I. Paris. Bibliothèque Nationale.

Leland, J, 1964 (Reissue), *The Itinerary of John Leland* (first published 1744). London. Centaur Press.

Murray, H J R, 1913, *A History of Chess*. Oxford. Clarendon Press.

O'Donovan, M A (ed), 1988, *Charters of Sherborne* (= Corpus of Anglo-Saxon Charters III). Oxford. Oxford University Press for The British Academy.

Scott, K L, 1996, *Later Gothic Manuscripts 1390–1490* (= A Survey of Manuscripts Illuminated in the British Isles VI). London. Harvey Miller [The Sherborne Missal, here BL Loan 82, is no 9].

Sharpe, R, *et al* (eds), 1996, *English Benedictine Libraries. The Shorter Catalogues*. London. The British Library in association with The British Academy.

Warner, G F, 1903, *Illuminated Manuscripts in the British Museum* (Series I–IV). London. The British Museum.

Winstanley, D A, 1948, Halliwell Phillipps and Trinity College Library. In *The Library* (5th series, Volume 2).

Wormald, F, 1939, *English Benedictine Kalendars after A.D. 1100* (= HBS lxxvii) London. Henry Bradshaw Society.

Wormald, F, 1957, The Sherborne 'Chartulary'. In D J Gordon (ed), *Fritz Saxl 1890–1948. A Volume of Memorial Essays*. London. Nelson & Sons, 101–19.

Yapp, B, 1981, *Birds in Medieval Manuscripts*. London. British Library.

Additional Sources

Fowler, J, 1951, *Mediaeval Sherborne*. Dorchester. Longmans.

Gibb, J H P, 1981, *The Book of Sherborne*. Buckingham. Barracuda Books.

Leland, J, 1970, *Antiquarii De Rebus Britannicis Collectanea* (Reprint). Farnborough. Gregg International.

Miller, A, 1999, *The Monasteries of Dorset*. Bournemouth. Albemarle Books.

Page, W (ed), 1908, *Victoria County History: Dorset*. London. Archibald Constable [See especially article by M M C Calthorp, 2, 62–70].

Turner, D H, *et al*, 1980, *The Benedictines in Britain*. London. The British Library.

15. Picturing the beginning of the Age of Saints: the iconography of last things

Katherine Barker

The great legacy of the tenth century was its view of the future which was one to frame the basis of thinking for many generations to come (Leonardi 1999, 211). A sense of direction brought in its wake a renewed sense for the need to prepare for the beginning of the end of history which would see the final battle with the Devil and the ultimate victory of Christ for all men. Suffering and evil would be things of the past. 'We are those upon whom the ends of the ages have come' declares the writer of the Sherborne charter of 998, quoting from the first Letter to the Corinthians: and 'when the trumpet of the archangel is sounding ... equity and justice shall be made known to all with Christ as judge' (Keynes, 'King Æthelred's charter', §7, this volume). The words ring out, *clangente*, from the page. And so it was that the tenth century witnessed a growth of artistic activity which included some powerful evocations of the Apocalypse.

Royal patrons

Charlemagne (crowned 800) was patron of what we might well call 'monastic literature and fine arts'; the production of books, of illuminated manuscripts including musical notation, and, of course, richly appointed church and monastery buildings in which such things were both made and kept. Standards and conventions adopted and promoted under the aegis of Charlemagne persisted for many generations across much of Christian Europe.

It was a rich, colourful – and busy – world for *ars sacra*, 'the sacred arts' which used some of the most expensive materials and pigments available; purple silks, silver and gold inlays, lapis lazuli and precious stones. Most of this has been lost. A few years ago Dodwell (1982) explored Anglo-Saxon literary references to artistic and precious objects and rediscovered 'a long-lost breathtaking world of finely ornamented book covers, reliquaries, chalices, crosses, candlesticks ... fine linens and silk embroidered vestments and hangings ... speaking eloquently of the marriage of art and ceremony ... between monastic life ... and high liturgical culture' (Mayr-Harting 1999, 218).

Emperors Otto I, II and III (whose combined reigns embrace the greater part of the tenth century, from 936 to 1002) inherited a rich tradition in the iconography – the 'symbolic' style – of the Apocalypse as it appeared in Carolingian books and which was emulated both in Franconia and Anglo-Saxon England. The high-point of Ottonian book illustration came with a series of books made at Reichenau or Regensburg for Otto III (996–1002) and his successor Henry II, and which 'are among the summits of Western Civilisation' (Mayr-Harting 1999, 227).

Otto III had a sense of destiny which seems to have been closely bound up with the imminence of the year 1000, a sense heightened by the intellectual climate in which he had grown up (see Barker, '*Anni Domini Computati*', this volume). Adso, later abbot of Montier-en-Der had an apocalyptic view of kingship. He saw rulers as divine agents. Writing in West Francia, he dedicated his thesis to Otto I's sister, wife of Louis IV, Otto III's great aunt. Otto I was married to an Anglo-Saxon princess and, modelling himself on Charlemagne, was crowned in Rome in 962. Otto II adopted the Roman imperial title in 982 (during a disastrous campaign in Italy against the Moors) and was by then already ruling an area rather larger than modern Germany. His queen, Theophana, was a Byzantine princess, and mother of Otto III who succeeded to the throne at the age of five. Adso's teaching, together with that of both Abbo of Fleury and of Gerbert of Aurillac, who become Pope Sylvester II, clearly had an impact on the young Otto III. The latter was to see things in terms of *renovatio*, the Christian renewal of the whole of the Roman Empire. Indeed, in the year 1000, Otto III had the idea of transferring his throne to the Eternal City, on the Aventine. A gesture which was symbolic and to be without sequel (Duby 2000, 21). But Otto approved prestige publication to complement his reforming ambition; and his reign marks the high-point of Ottonian book illumination (Mayr-Harting 1999, 227).

Seeing Revelation
So what of the Apocalypse? The scriptural source is Revelation (in Greek 'Apocalypse') the last book in the Bible, then as now (see Woods, 'The Revelation of St John', this volume). Written by St John the Divine, it remains a difficult work to understand. An almost cinematic narrative of highly imaginative images drawn from Jewish biblical tradition – and, we must take it – from surrounding Graeco-Roman culture, it is rich in colour, in allegory and allusion, and while being intensely visual, it is, as Boxall notes, an extremely noisy book, permeated by music and loud 'noises off'. As it tells us, it is a work intended to be read aloud – indeed, to be *performed*. There are echoes here perhaps of a lost *genre* of fantastical other-worldly drama understood – surely recognised – by audiences of early second-century Asia Minor for whom it was originally written

(Boxall 2002, 2–9). It was also non-Roman if not actually anti-Roman. As Woods notes ('The Revelation of St John', this volume), apocalyptic writing has a special appeal for the persecuted and downtrodden.

> And I heard the voice of many angels round the throne ... and the number of them was ten thousand times ten thousand ... and I beheld ... a great earthquake; and the sun became as black as sackcloth of hair and the moon became as blood ... and the heaven departed as a scroll when it is rolled together; and every mountain and island were moved out of their places ... and I saw a great red dragon having seven heads and ten horns and his tail drew the third part of the stars of heaven and did cast them to earth ... and there was war in heaven ... and I saw as it were a sea of glass mingled with fire ... and them that had gotten victory over the dragon ... having the harps of God and they sang the song of Moses ... and I saw an angel come down from heaven having the key of the bottomless pit and a great chain in his hand. And he laid hold on the dragon ... which is the Devil ... and bound him a thousand years ... And I saw a great white throne ... and I saw the dead stand before God; and the books were opened; and the dead were judged ... And I saw a new heaven and a new earth ... saw the holy city, new Jerusalem, coming down from God out of heaven ... (Revelation 5:11; 12:3, 4, 7; 15:2, 3; 20:1, 3; 11, 12; 21:2)

There are twenty-two carefully structured chapters of surreal narrative, heavy with mystical (and political) *double-entendre*. But nothing contemporary remains as to how this might have been rendered in two-dimensional graphics. If we intended to illustrate this today so as to reach as wide an audience as possible we could only use what are recognisable images. We would look through our stock of dragon and angel types, perhaps use footage of an erupting volcano for the bottomless pit and a Disney-style walled medieval city for the new Jerusalem. And then, perhaps, we might commission some 'other-worldly' music to accompany a computer simulation, but certainly written using the standard tonic scale.

There were already a number of commentaries on Revelation circulating in the early medieval world on how it might best be understood. That written by Beatus of Liébana (died 798) enjoyed wide currency from the ninth to the thirteenth centuries: 'his Apocalypse commentary was immensely influential in the West during the Middle Ages' (Boxall 2002, 125). Writing in what is now Spain, his work might, perhaps, have attracted less attention had it not been illustrated. Two years after Beatus' death Charlemagne was crowned, and with the new emphasis on books and their illustration, Beatus' work found favour and contributed to what became, in the fullness of time, a distinctly Ottonian style.

It was the illustrations that proved as arresting as the text itself. Beatus took special care to make learning available in easily memorable form – specific images found in Revelation were rendered in a graphics 'code' by which individual images, and the relationship between them, could be understood and explored as a counterpart to the written commentary. Under divine guidance, Beatus tells us, he sought to enhance the *allegoria* of the sacred images, whereby something represented in two dimensions might be understood in another and spiritual dimension. Early Medieval Christian graphics, like their counterparts, words and numbers, had a strong allegorical content. They too, were a language.

Reading carefully 'between the lines' Beatus tells us why today we find the pictures very strange – if not, in some cases, almost alien. He took special care to make learning 'accessible'. Pictorial representations of happenings in Revelation were to be timeless. 'He never separates the present time from the Last in which Antichrist [the Devil] will be revealed, because what will then be visible is now invisibly carried on in the Church' (Nolan 1977, 61–2). In other words, he finds a liturgical justification in using the style of his own time; images of people and objects and things drawn in a way which would appeal to a contemporary audience.[1] They do not immediately appeal to us without interpretation – indeed, without *translation*. Beatus' forms are set within what was then a familiar cosmos, that is, 'an absolute Up and Down ... the medieval model is vertiginous ... while unimaginably large, [the universe] was finite, and thus had ... a perfectly spherical shape ... artists were not interested in strict illusionism ... there was no scale ... the relative sizes of objects ... was determined by their relative importance and not their distance from one another in the real world' (Lewis 1964, 98–101). Beatus' pictures will thus have had a powerful immediacy for his audience, for only the present moment has no time. The pictures will represent something going on invisibly just beyond the range of human sight and hearing. No one – then as now – can presume to know what the Antichrist might actually look like, nor how the seating arrangements might work for the Day of Judgement. And when these events occur, they too will be in the present.

The *mandorla* – a 'celestial time capsule'

The apocalyptic images selected here are all book illustrations dating from the tenth century and featuring a symmetrical, elliptically shaped, 'capsule-like' aureole or *mandorla* – from the Italian word for 'almond'. The illustrations are by different schools of illumination and each has an individual character. But they all clearly belong to the same family of artistic conventions; they share an iconography which, at least in part, has its inspiration in the Byzantine world of the east Mediterranean.

The *mandorla* frames the Christ figure which may either be standing or sitting within it, and holding items appropriate to the occasion. In the mind's eye the *mandorla* can move up or down and is often seen through – or set in – an arched window or opening of some kind. The occupant of the *mandorla* may also move; that is, stepping up or down or – during the Ascension – having been smoothly transported skywards, perhaps in the process of leaving it altogether. In the examples shown here, an arch above the *mandorla* implies it is in descent, and a horizontal line, in ascent, or perhaps motionless and invisibly held, and so rendered visible for the viewer. Around or beneath the *mandorla* are images which narrate what is going on. This is a pictorial record of those persons attending – including angels – their significance and their role, and whether they were talking or singing. All the originals are in full colour, but the significance of colour cannot, alas, be explored here.

The four images illustrated here (Figs 19–20 and 22–23) may be compared with a fifth portraying King Edgar offering up a charter of 966 by which he refounded New Minster, Winchester (see Farmer, 'The monastic reform of the tenth century', Fig 4, this volume). It is very similar in style to that of about fifty years later which shows Cnut presenting an altar cross to the New Minster. The 'Edgar *mandorla*' may be compared with that drawn for Cnut which is shown here as a simplified line-drawing (Fig 21e).

Figure 19, The Second Coming of Christ, is a miniature from the Benedictional written for St Æthelwold, bishop of Winchester, between 975 and 980. The *mandorla* is tilted to the right and Christ, looking down, is moving to step out of it, carrying a staff and a Book of Judgement. The two sides of the 'hull' of the *mandorla* are different, giving a certain substance to it, almost a sense of perspective. It is seen through an archway, emerging from swirling clouds of glory, and above are angels and archangels – probably singing. Talbot Rice (1952, 186) notes this work is 'strikingly Byzantine in character' and suggested the prototype came via the *scriptorium* at Metz.

Three further representations of an Ascension *mandorla* are included here as line drawings for comparison (Fig 21a–c). A fourth (Fig 21d), shows both the *mandorla* and the hand of God in a representation of Pentecost.

By the same artist in the same work is a depiction of the **Ascension** with which the Second Coming may be compared (Fig 21a). This time Christ is looking up out of the *mandorla*, again to the right; the staff is now in his left hand, he offers his right hand to God who is represented by a much larger right hand, palm forward, emerging from a circle against the top edge of the frame. The division between Heaven and Earth is represented by a wavy 'cloud' line.

Another version of the **Ascension** is found in the Sacramentary of Robert of Jumièges (Fig 21b) (Rouen, BM, MS Y6, fo 81v; see Talbot Rice 1952, pl 139). The top half of the *mandorla* is already in heaven above the wavy 'cloud' line. Two angels watch him go, that on the left is gesturing to the disciples below, and that on the right is looking up and raising his right hand – transcendence completed. Christ's two feet and the margin of his robe 'protrude' from the margin at the top of the page. They are rather too large for the *mandorla*, which is shown without detail. What we see is Christ moving smoothly upward and out of our sight, just at the point of leaving the 'capsule' on his safe arrival in Heaven.

A third version of the **Ascension** is found in the twelfth-century Winchester Psalter (Fig 21c) (BL MS Cotton Nero C.IV, fo 27; see Haney 1986). The artist

Figure 19 (left). The Second Coming of Christ, a miniature from the Benedictional written for St Æthelwold, Bishop of Winchester, between 975 and 980. (BL Add. MS 49598 fo 9v. Reproduced by permission of the British Library)

Figure 20 (right). Christ enthroned within a double mandorla with choirs of martyrs, confessors and virgins assembled behind Him, illustration from the Æthelstan Psalter. (BL Cotton MS Galba A. XVIII, fo 21v. Christ enthroned from the Æthelstan Psalter. Reproduced by permission of the British Library)

shows the top of the *mandorla* already entering Heaven, the 'frontier' is once again, a wavy line, and again we watch it moving upwards out of human sight off the top of the page. Two angels face downward, their wings embracing the 'hull' of the *mandorla* and this time assist in its upward course. A very elongated pair of legs suggests we are seeing Christ from the ground; in rapid ascent to his destination.

Pentecost illustrated in the Sacramentary of Robert of Jumièges (Fig 21d) uses some familiar imaginary in a slightly different way. The full circle located at the top of the archway, contains the 'Hand of God' in like-style to that of the Ascension (Fig 21a) except this time the disc containing the hand is shown in full and is aligned on a vertical axis that runs straight down the page. The disciples seated on a lower arch are receiving the 'tongues of fire' which pour forth from the beak of a large bird flying head-first down-page in a *mandorla*. This time we take the *mandorla* to signify the divine status of the message.

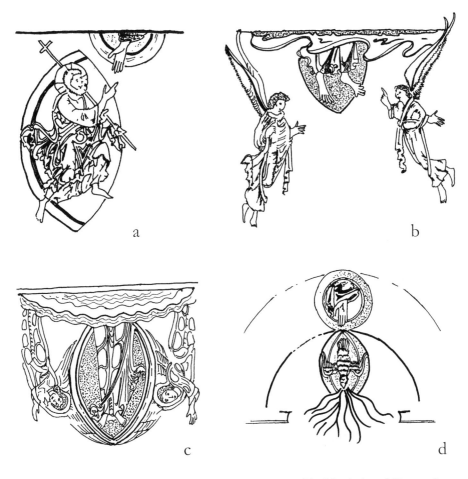

Figure 21. The Mandorla and Transcendence, outline drawings of the mandorla sketched in outline, taken from tenth-century manuscript examples: a, depiction of the Ascension from The Benedictional of St Æthelwold (BL Add MS 49598 fo 56v); b, the Ascension illustrated in the Sacramentary of Robert of Jumièges (Rouen, BM, MS Y6, fo 81v); c, the Ascension illustrated in the twelfth-century Winchester Psalter (BL MS Cotton Nero C.IV, fo 27); d, Pentecost illustrated in the Sacramentary of Robert of Jumièges; and e, the mandorla drawn above King Cnut and Queen Ælfgifu presenting a cross to the New Minster, Winchester (The New Minster Liber Vitae, 1016-20; Dedication, BL MS Stowe 944).

Figure 20, depicts **Christ enthroned** with choirs of martyrs, confessors and virgins assembled behind him. The illustration was probably added by a tenth-century English artist to a ninth-century psalter, probably from the Liège area, and given by King Æthelstan to the Old Minster at Winchester. It is very similar in style to the Christ-figure who presides at the Last Judgement where the assembled human company is then divided into two; the 'good' (to the right) and the 'bad' (to the left); the former led to heaven, the latter thrust into hell. The Æthelstan Psalter features a 'double' *mandorla*, a central chamber 'encased' in an outer shell. This has a certain rigidity about it, the whole is seemingly 'trapped' by the borders of the page and thus rendered motionless. There could, however, be an unexpected dimension here. The figures grouped in six compartments face inwards and clearly continue behind the central *mandorla*. Christ, the Alpha and Omega (the two Greek letters read from his right to his left), is surely moving forward towards us in the promise of things to come, as the voices of this great chorus swells in praise.

Figure 22 (left). Detail of Christ seated in Majesty from a drawing made by an Anglo-Saxon artist working at the Abbey of Fleury in the late tenth century. (MS 175, fo 149. Detail of Christ in Majesty. Reproduced with permission of the Orléans Bibliothèque Municipale)

Figure 23 (right). The Aachen Gospels, the emperor Otto III seated in majesty, about 996. (Photo copyright Ann Munchow, Aachen. Aachen, Dom Schatzkammer, The Liuthar evangeliary, Aachen Gospels. Reproduced with permission)

Figure 22 is a detail of **Christ seated in Majesty** from a drawing made by an Anglo-Saxon artist working at the abbey of Fleury in the late tenth century. Bishop Æthelwold of Winchester who commissioned the Benedictional (see above) had close contacts with Fleury. Christ is seated, a decorated halo touching the apex of the *mandorla*, and his feet resting on its base, his toes just over the edge. He is giving a blessing with his right hand and holding a book of Judgement in his left. The standing figures, not immediately identifiable, are positioned in front of the *mandorla* which is 'suspended' between them. Both are standing on the same level, one, holding a staff is presenting a book, the other, a scroll; and both are wearing halos. If Christ steps out of the *mandorla* and stands up, he will dwarf both. A very small (ie low status) kneeling, hooded and suppliant figure is seeking intercession from the figure on the left. Note the position of the hands of all four figures; they are all speaking.

The Christ figure may be compared with that redrawn in Figure 21e, that presides over the presentation by Cnut and Emma of an altar cross to New Minster, Winchester (see above and Fig 4).

The *mandorla* and Otto III
Figure 23 is a page from the Aachen Gospels showing **Otto III seated in majesty** in a style normally reserved for the Christ figure. Otto III was crowned emperor on Ascension Day 996, and the iconography of this composition immediately recalls scenes both of Majesty and of Ascension. We have a seated figure in a *mandorla* holding a symbol of Christian imperial authority, and the Hand of God emerging from a circle immediately above it. In western fashion Christ is usually shown standing as he ascends into Heaven (see above), but here the figure is shown seated very much in the style of tenth-century Byzantine ivories (Mayr-Harting 1999, 228). And it is Otto, not Christ, who is enthroned in the *mandorla*. Seated 'in majesty' Otto will not, of course, complete the Ascension, but he has clearly penetrated the celestial realm. God is reaching down and actually touching the emperor's crowned head, not palm forward, but in a manner so as to hold the crown. The Four Apostles are there in spirit, Matthew (a man), Mark (an eagle) Luke (a calf) and John (a lion). This is a Foursome which may in itself be a symbolic representation of the Four Empires of history established by St Jerome (died 420) who saw Rome as the final Empire, a scheme not favoured by Augustine (Campion 1994, 326–7). Is this Otto presiding over the beginning of a potential Fifth? A refounded Roman Empire? In Rome? A figure crouches (in subjection?) beneath the imperial throne as Otto simultaneously moves upward. On earth, below the banner held by the Gospel writers, we find six standing figures. The end of the Sixth Age since Adam had long been imminent; Otto makes up the Seventh human figure of significance. The six standing figures comprise two crowned heads bowing in deference, and along the bottom of the page, two members of the military and two of the church; the former to his right, the latter to his left.

Otto's sense of apocalyptic destiny has already been noted (see above). And here it is, it seems, most eloquently – most graphically – expressed on an illuminated page of the Aachen Gospels dating from the turn of the tenth century. It was in 998, two years after his coronation, that Otto III set out his programme on a seal based on that of Charlemagne. And in 1001 we find Otto declaring himself '*servus apostolorum et secundum voluntatem Dei salvatoris Romanorum imperator augustus* (Otto, servant of the Apostles and according to the will of God our saviour august emperor of the Romans)' (Canning 1996, 76). Otto is an exact – if younger – contemporary of Wulfsige. And both men were to die the following year, 1002.

Note

1   This continued to be the practice in 'apocalyptic' representation throughout the Middle Ages and into more recent times. *The Wisdom of God displayed in the works of the Creation from the Beginning to the Consummation of all Things*, by Bishop Burnet, published in 1816, the year after the Battle of Waterloo, is illustrated in arresting early nineteenth-century style. This large and handsome leather-bound volume of 716 pages was recently recovered by the writer from a skip. Found in a local recycling bin was a less substantial work published just after the First World War, *A short explanation of some portions of Daniel and Revelation shewing the wonderful fulfillment of these and other Bible prophecies*. The author, unnamed, sees The Great War as 'evidently foreshadowing' the beginning of the End. The illustrations include some delightful Edwardian-style lady angels. What today makes bizarre reading is the significance assigned to one of the Pope's titles, *Vicarius Filii Dei* (Representative of the Son of God). Rendered in Roman numerals VICARIVS FILII DEI, the author notes that we have, with the [deliberate] omission of A, R, S, F and E, the sum of $5 + 1 + 100 + 1 + 5 + 1 + 50 + 1 + 1 + 500 + 1$ which makes 666. 'Let him that hath understanding count the number of the [second] beast [which emerged from the earth] for it is the number of a man; and his number is Six Hundred threescore and six' (Rev 13:18). The incomplete nature of Six has already been noted (Barker, '*Anni Domini Computati*', this volume), and three Sixes only serves to emphasise its imperfection. Knight (1999, 100), notes that Greek and Hebrew letters had a designated numerical value or *gematria*. 'The question of who this figure [of 666] identifies is much discussed in the commentaries'; it occurs in some versions as 616. 'The most common solution is that it stands for [the Roman emperor] Nero.' Boxall (2002, 124–5) notes that other candidates for 666 include Pope Innocent IV, Napoleon and Saddam Hussein. Beatus of Liébana reasoned that in Roman numerals 666 is DCLXVI and was therefore an anagram of DICLUX, one of the titles of the Antichrist. Did he, one wonders, ever work this into any of his illustrations? Suffice to say, the text of Revelation can be endlessly reinterpreted to serve the purposes of the present, as other writers have noted.

Bibliography

Boxall, I, 2002, *Revelation: Vision and Insight*. SPCK.
Campion, N, 1994, *The Great Year, Astrology, Millenarianism and History in the Western Tradition*. Penguin Arkana.

Canning, J, 1996, *A History of Medieval Political Thought*. London and New York. Routledge.

Dodwell, C R, 1982, *Anglo-Saxon Art, A New Perspective*. Manchester Studies in the History of Art, 3. Manchester University Press.

Duby, G, 2000, *Art and Society in the Middle Ages*, Jean Birrell (trans). Cambridge. Polity Press.

Haney, K E H, 1986, *The Winchester Psalter, an Iconographic Study*. Leicester University Press.

Knight, J, 1999, *Revelation*, J Jarick (ed). Readings: A New Biblical Commentary. Sheffield Academic Press.

Leonardi, C, 1999, Artists and Patrons. In T Reuter (ed), *The New Cambridge Medieval History* (Volume 3, *c* 900–1024). Cambridge University Press, 186–211.

Lewis, C S, 1964, *The Discarded Image, an Introduction to Medieval and Renaissance Literature*. Cambridge University Press.

Mayr-Harting, H, 1999, Artists and Patrons. In T Reuter (ed), *The New Cambridge Medieval History* (Volume 3, *c* 900–1024). Cambridge University Press, 212–32.

Nolan, B, 1977, *The Gothic Visionary Perspective*. Princeton University Press.

Talbot Rice, D, 1952, *English Art 871–1100*. Oxford. Clarendon Press.

16. The dissolution of the abbey and after at Sherborne

Joseph Bettey

The dissolution of the ancient and wealthy Benedictine abbey at Sherborne, the eviction of the monks and the rapid dispersal of lands, provides a classic example of the way in which such sweeping and far-reaching changes were accomplished without any murmur of protest or any local voice raised in support of the long-established situation. Here was a well-endowed abbey, set in a town which it dominated through its property holdings and because of the size and magnificence of its church and monastic buildings. Its widespread estates in Dorset provided a large income, but the charity which it dispensed did little to endear it to the townsfolk. The abbey had a much greater impact as a landholder and collector of rents and dues than it did as the focus of spiritual life. The contrast between the splendour of the abbey church and the much smaller parish church of All Hallows at its west end, illustrated the gulf between the opulence of the monks and the comparative poverty of spiritual provision for the town (Fowler 1951, 263–9).

Classic also is the close involvement of local gentry families in the administration of the abbey estates and the election of abbots. Among these families were the Strangways of Melbury, Fitzjames of Lillington, Leweston of Leweston, and most notably of all, the Horseys of Clifton Maybank. Sir John Horsey, who died in 1531, was typical of the rising Tudor gentry families who were to profit so much from the destruction of the monasteries. He had taken a prominent part in local government, had served the King at Court and had been careful to ingratiate himself with Cardinal Wolsey. At the time of his death his estates stretched from Horsey near Bridgwater via Charlton Mackerell to Melcome Horsey in central Dorset. His residence was at Clifton Maybank on the Somerset-Dorset border, only a short distance from Sherborne. Here he was well placed to maintain a close interest and involvement in the affairs of the abbey and in the administration of its estates (Webb 1977, 28–32; 1978, 22–30). Nevertheless at the time of Sir John Horsey's death in 1531 there can have been few who would have believed that within a decade the abbey would be suppressed, the monks departed, and the abbey buildings and most of the lands in the possession of the Horseys. Sir John was succeeded by his son, also John, who continued the family prominence in local government as well as being active at Court. His status was confirmed in 1535 when he was one of those knighted at the coronation of Anne Boleyn. He was steward to the lands of the monasteries of Athelney and Montacute, and chief steward of Sherborne Abbey lands; he was thus thoroughly familiar with their nature, extent and value, and well placed to gain eventual possession of them.

The process of the dissolution
The details of the suppression of the abbey at Sherborne and the transfer of most of its lands to Sir John Horsey are well known, and can be briefly summarised. As early as 1533 local gentlemen, London lawyers and court officials were seeking to ensure that their nominee was appointed as abbot of Sherborne in succession to the current abbot, John Meere. Sir John Horsey evidently supported John Barnstaple or Bastaple, one of the monks as his candidate, and was prepared to offer a bribe to Thomas Cromwell to achieve his purposes. When Meere resigned in 1535, Barnstaple was duly elected abbot, and Horsey wrote to Cromwell agreeing to pay him 500 marks (£333 6s 8d) 'according to my promise'.[1] John Barnstaple also wrote to Cromwell, thanking him for the preferment and promising to carry out Cromwell's instructions, including the payment of £40 per annum to his predecessor, John Meere.[2] The scene was thus set for the events which were to follow, with a compliant abbot ready to submit when required.

Sir John Horsey was one of the Dorset commissioners for compiling the *Valor Ecclesiasticus* in 1535. This revealed for the first time the true extent of the monastic estates in Dorset, including those of Sherborne. Sherborne had a net annual income of £682 14s 7d to support an abbot and fifteen monks, and its wealth was derived from widespread estates in Dorset, properties in Sherborne, Lyme Regis and Taunton, a flock of 885 sheep and tolls from markets and fairs in Sherborne.[3]

During 1535 Cromwell had also ordered an enquiry into the state of all the monastic houses and into the conduct of the monks and nuns. Unfortunately we have no account of the results of this visitation for Sherborne, unlike Abbotsbury and Cerne, there were no disgruntled monks to write directly to Cromwell with extravagant claims concerning the behaviour and sexual exploits of the abbot and senior monks. We can only suppose that at Sherborne there were no overt scandals, and that religious life and the ancient round of festivals and regular services continued to be observed in the time-honoured fashion. Had there been anything seriously amiss, Cromwell's commissioners would assuredly have reported it since they were well aware that their primary purpose was to find evidence of evil-doing which could be used to justify the overthrow of the monasteries (Bettey 1989, 43–56).

The surrender of the abbey

With its large annual income, Sherborne was well outside the provisions of the
Act of 1536 which suppressed all monasteries with less than £200 per annum.[4]
No sooner than this Act was passed, and all the lands and possessions of the
smaller monasteries had been seized by the Crown. Pressure was then exerted
on the larger monasteries, urging them to make a 'voluntary' surrender of their
houses in return for pensions for the abbot and monks. Most west country
monasteries, including Sherborne, withstood this pressure and continued.

Eventually they could resist no longer. For Sherborne the end came on 18
March 1539. The king's commissioner, John Tregonwell, who was later to be
richly rewarded with the site and estates of Milton Abbey, made a tour through
the west country, from Wiltshire to Cornwall and back through Dorset, receiving
the surrender of monastic houses throughout the region. On 18 March 1539 he
reached Sherborne, and the day was to witness the most dramatic change ever to
occur in the long history of the town. When the day began the ancient abbey was
functioning as it had done for five centuries and more; by the end Abbot John
Barnstaple and sixteen monks had departed, having been granted pensions,
while all their property including the abbey and its magnificent church had been
handed over to the Crown. John Barnstaple received the handsome pension of
£100 per annum; in March 1540 he was instituted as rector of Stalbridge, the
richest of the former abbey's livings, and remained there, living in considerable
style, until his death in 1560. Abbot Barnstaple owed his presentation to
Stalbridge to the influence of Sir John Horsey, and Horsey was duly remembered
in the abbot's will. The other monks were awarded pensions ranging from £12
to the prior, John Dunster, to £6 per annum for junior monks. Many were from
local families, and several of them were later to obtain benefices in the district.
John Dunster, the former prior, became curate of North Wootton and vicar of
Oborne where his name is inscribed over the north window of the surviving
chancel. Thomas Caple or Capel became chaplain of the almshouse and
remained there until his death in 1563. The infirmarer, William Vowell, remained
with Abbot Barnstaple and became curate of Stalbridge. Thomas Ellyot became
curate of Bishop's Caundle, and later was appointed rector of Lillington;
Augustine Grene became curate of Chetnole. Others moved away from
Sherborne, such as Robert Pytman who was appointed vicar of Woolavington
near Bridgwater. He was married during the reign of Edward VI, and deprived
under Mary in 1554. Bartholomew Sterre became rector of Thorn Coffin near
Taunton; he got married in 1552 and was deprived in 1554 when he was said to
be forty.[5]

Dispersal of the estates

As with most monastic property, the Sherborne estates were disposed of very
rapidly by the Crown. The bulk was obtained by Sir John Horsey, but other
gentlemen were able to enjoy a minor share of the spoils. George Duke of

Camberwell, Surrey and John Sterre of Sherborne acquired the New Inn and numerous other houses and tenements in Sherborne for £557 8s 1d.[6] Thomas Godwin, John Hassard and others obtained the Sherborne Abbey properties in Taunton and Lyme Regis.[7] Sir John Horsey's acquisitions were much greater. First he had purchased the site and demesnes of the abbey together with several of the estates including Bradford and Wyke, as well as former monastic lands at Cannington in Somerset, Longleat in Wiltshire, and Creech in Purbeck. Later he also purchased the former Sherborne properties of Thornford, Over Compton, Nether Compton, Stowell and Pinford.[8] By 1543 Sir John Horsey had spent £2,793 6s 6¼ d on the purchase of monastic lands, not all of which he retained in his own hands.[9] The result of these and other purchases of former monastic land was greatly to enhance Sir John Horsey's estate and make him one of the wealthiest of the Dorset gentry. All this was not obtained without a struggle, for courtiers, lawyers, speculators, royal commissioners and local gentry all competed to acquire as much as possible of this 'golden shower of the dissolved abbey lands [which] rained well-near into every gaper's mouth'.[10] Like many other purchasers of monastic land, Sir John Horsey was anxious to recoup his heavy expenditure as soon as possible. The quickest way to provide a return on the outlay was by selling the lead which covered the monastic buildings. A great deal of lead was immediately stripped from Sherborne buildings, and without a covering many of them, including the cloisters, rapidly deteriorated and collapsed. Some survived to be granted to the Governors of the school which was established in 1550; while in a remarkable transaction the great abbey church was sold to the parishioners of Sherborne. The complex history of the former abbey buildings has been carefully traced by Joseph Fowler and need not be repeated here.[11]

The Horsey family
Sir John Horsey's successors did not long enjoy the fruits of his success in building up a great estate. Sir John Horsey II died in 1564 and was buried beside his father beneath an elegant tomb in the former abbey church at Sherborne. Sir John appears to have suffered from the strain of reckless extravagance which in subsequent generations was to bring ruin upon the family. He was addicted to gambling, or as he himself put it 'havinge small experiens and consideration unto his estate and vocation and lesse unto his helthe and commoditie was oftentymes enticed and overmuche used and disposed to dyce play, which in small tyme seemed almost to his undoinge'. In 1558 he entered into a bond of £300 with his brother-in-law, Thomas Phelips or Phillips of Montacute that he would forsake the playing at dice. Apparently he did not keep his bargain. Like many other contemporary gentlemen, he was also remarkably litigious, and the numerous extended lawsuits over lands in which he was involved must have been a heavy drain on his resources.[12] The estates passed to his son, also Sir John Horsey, who died without issue in 1588. He appears to have been

distrusted by his father who in his will, made in 1546, eighteen years before his death, required heavy penalties to be imposed on his son if he failed to respect his father's wishes. Sir John Horsey III was responsible for alienating part of the estate he had inherited, and by the time of his death in 1588 he had disposed of some lands and had leased others including the valuable manors of Wyke and Pinford to George Sydenham of Brympton D'Evercy.[13] The remaining lands were inherited by a second cousin, Ralph Horsey, who was in financial difficulties and continued to dispose of parts of the estate, having lost much of his fortune by investing in an unsuccessful project to smelt iron using coal. After his death in 1612, the ruin of the family was completed by his son George Horsey, who spent huge sums of money on an ill-conceived plan to drain the Fleet, the area of tidal water along the Dorset coast between Chesil Beach and the mainland. George Horsey was finally imprisoned for debt in Dorchester gaol where he died in 1639. Much of the family mansion at Clifton Maybank was demolished, and part of it was later incorporated into the Elizabethan house at Montacute. By curious irony, one of his sons, John Horsey, died while fighting for Parliament during the second siege of Sherborne Castle in 1645.[14]

The effects of the Dissolution in Sherborne

The suppression of the monastery which had for so long dominated Sherborne could not fail to have a profound effect upon the economic and religious life of the town. The abbey had provided employment, charity and a market for supplies of all sorts. But Sherborne was fortunate in that its size, its geographical position on the major route from London to the west, the continuing importance of its markets and the variety of trades provided a cushion against the economic collapse which monastic suppression produced elsewhere. The contrast with Cerne Abbas is notable, for Cerne, being much smaller, was devastated by the closure of its abbey, and did not recover for decades (Bettey 1988, 43–53). At Sherborne the markets and annual fairs continued to draw people from the villages and farms of the fertile Blackmore Vale, and their importance was recognised in further market grants of 1564–88.[15] In *c* 1540 John Leland visited Sherborne and wrote 'The town of Sherborne ... stondith partly by making of Clothe, but most by al maner of craftes'. Apart from the port of Poole, Leland considered Sherborne to be 'the best toun at this present tyme yn Dorsetshire' (Toulmin-Smith 1907, I, 152). Sherborne certainly possessed a remarkable number of different trades and, for example, casual references in the churchwardens' accounts for the 1530s and 1540s reveal the existence of clothmakers, weavers, tanners, candlemakers, glaziers, mercers, carpenters, plumbers, beer-brewers, smiths, shepherds, bakers, inn-keepers, cordwainers, drapers, parchment-makers and cutlers. Likewise, the surviving wills and probate inventories provide similar evidence of the range of crafts and trades in the town.[16] It was this diversity which enabled it to survive the closure of the monastery.

Religious life

The dissolution of the abbey inevitably affected the religious life of the town profoundly. The parish church of All Hallows was attached to the west end of the abbey church, and the vicar, John Chetmill, had been appointed in 1536. A local man, he was to remain as vicar through all the religious changes until his death in 1566 (Fowler 1951, 297–8). The departure of the abbot and monks marked a great change in John Chetmill's status, and he recorded their departure in the parish register under 18 March 1539 with the simple statement '*Expulsio Monachorum de Sherborne*'. An equally remarkable change in his fortunes was soon to occur, for in 1540 the parishioners of Sherborne purchased the former abbey church and churchyard from Sir John Horsey. The initial payment was 100 marks (£66 13s 4d), but further payments for the bells and the lead on the church roof meant that the total cost to the parishioners was about £320. This far-sighted and enterprising action by the parishioners was also recorded by John Chetmill in the parish register (Fowler 1951, 317–18).

We have no evidence of how this purchase was arranged, who were the leading figures in securing it, or how the money was raised and parish agreement reached. The churchwardens' accounts which are so informative concerning parochial affairs during the 1520s and 1530s are missing for the crucial years 1538–42.[17] We can only imagine the thoughts of John Chetmill and his parishioners at Easter 1540 when they used the great abbey church for the first time. Certainly they lost no time in demolishing their old church of All Hallows; the churchwardens' accounts are full of references to the sale of stone, lead, timber and glass from the old church and to the demolition of various parts of the structure including the tower.

The impact of the change was no doubt softened by the fact that the ancient services and rituals continued as before, since another decade was to pass before sweeping changes were imposed on the parish churches and the time-honoured Latin mass was abolished. At Sherborne, the churchwardens' accounts for the 1540s record the traditional processions at Easter, Rogationtide, Whitsun and Corpus Christi, the liturgical dramas of Holy Week, the boy bishop ceremony, the provision of costumes for the church players, and the continuing large income from the annual church ales.[18] With the accession of Edward VI in 1547, however, changes came thick and fast. The chantries were abolished, images were smashed, the stone altars were removed, the wall paintings obliterated with whitewash, and in 1549, 3s 6d was paid for the first English prayer book. In 1552 came the second book of common prayer and the confiscation of many of the church's treasures by the King's Commissioners. The inventories kept by the churchwardens reveal the extent of the losses. There is amazing contrast between the large number of precious items which are listed in the pre-Reformation inventories and the chalice, two surplices, two table cloths and a desk cloth which are all that remained in 1552–3.[19]

During the short reign of Queen Mary 1553–8, Catholicism was restored, and many of the items which had so recently been destroyed or confiscated had to be replaced at great expense. In 1553–4, for example, the Sherborne churchwardens spent nearly £12 on song-books, vestments and a processional cross. Similar heavy expenditure is recorded during the next few years. The accession of Elizabeth in 1558 and the Elizabethan Settlement of 1559 brought another wave of destruction. In all these changes, the Sherborne churchwardens faithfully obeyed every twist and turn of government policy, apparently without complaint. At least, none appears in their annual accounts. Throughout this period John Chetmill remained as vicar, and apparently accepted the successive changes. There is no reason to suppose that this was mere time serving or cynical clinging to office, since he appears to have been a conscientious parish priest; certainly his name appears as a witness on many of the wills made in Sherborne, which would indicate that he was a regular visitor to the sick and dying. One small piece of evidence suggests that he may not have welcomed the return of Protestant worship under Elizabeth. In May 1559 a parishioner called John Cock wrote a long and intemperate letter to William Cecil. He pleaded for further Protestant reforms in the Church, and, among other complaints, refers to the continuing popish practices of the vicar of Sherborne. The letter is written in a minute hand, entirely in Latin apart from occasional phrases in Greek, and it is evidently the work of a fanatical Protestant. Accordingly it should be treated with caution, but it provides the only indication we have of Chetmill's own views.[20]

Break up of the diocese

Sherborne was also greatly affected by another consequence of all the Reformation changes. This was the break up of the ancient diocese of Salisbury and the transfer of Dorset to the newly established diocese of Bristol in 1542. The change meant that Sherborne Castle, together with the lands of Sherborne manor, all of which belonged to the bishops of Salisbury, was no longer in Salisbury diocese, and the castle ceased to provide for a diocesan residence for the bishops, although they continued to enjoy the income from their widespread lands in the manor and hundred of Sherborne.

The bishop of Salisbury from 1539 to 1557 was John Capon, who contrived to retain his bishopric through all the successive changes of religion. Following the accession of Edward VI in 1547 the bishop faced great pressure to lease the profitable Sherborne lands to Edward Seymour, duke of Somerset and uncle to the king. In 1548, in the face of 'grete and unlawful threatinge of the said Duke of Somerset', the bishop unwillingly granted him a lease of the lands for ninety-nine years. The duke of Somerset was executed in 1552, but in 1550 had sub-leased the castle, manor and hundred of Sherborne to Sir John Paulet, Lord St John. Following the accession of Queen Mary in 1553, the lease had been acquired by Sir John Horsey who had also obtained the deeds, court rolls and other documents relating to the manor. In 1555 Bishop Capon began a long suit against Horsey in the Court of Chancery, alleging waste of resources of the manor and destruction of the castle. Horsey was accused of cutting down the timber and spoiling the woods on most of the estate, and of turning the castle into a ruin. Specifically the bishop alleged that Horsey had

> defaced the castell of the same manor of Sherborne and hath taken away and severed from the same all the lead that was layed for the covering of the towers and cloysters of the said castell, and hath taken awaie and pulled down dyvers and sundry houses and buyldings standinge and beinge within the precyncte of the same castell, and has also taken the glassed oute of the windows and pulled downe all the iron barres and casements that were in the same windows.

The value of the lead, stone, timber and glass sold by Horsey from the castle was said to be more than £1,500. The remaining timber in the castle was alleged to be rotten through lack of covering, while the lack of a stronghold meant that the surrounding countryside was left unprotected in case of foreign invasion.

Following this long and expensive suit, Horsey was treated leniently by the Court of Chancery. He was obliged to surrender the property and hand over all the records, but the bishop was ordered to pay him 200 marks (£133 6s 8d) in compensation for the lease, while Horsey and his son were to have 'the office of bailiwick of the manor of Sherborne' and custody of Sherborne Park for fifty years at £8 per annum. Lord St John was to have three bucks and four does from the park each year.[21] The castle appears to have been abandoned and gradually fell into ruin. Certainly by 1569 it was being used as a convenient quarry for stone to repair the parish church (Fowler 1951, 338).

During the episcopacy of Bishop Edmund Gheast (1571–7), the queen herself began to attempt to gain control of this profitable estate. In this connection an interesting incident took place in Sherborne in 1576, providing a glimpse of Sherborne society and of characters reminiscent of Shakespeare's Dogberry and Verges in *As You Like It*. The queen's attempt to obtain Sherborne lands had evidently been entrusted to officials of the Exchequer Court, and on 25 June 1576, the Lord Treasurer and the barons of the Exchequer wrote to the town constable of Sherborne, William Phelps, instructing him to seize the deeds, court rolls, evidences and other writings relating to the manor of Sherborne. The documents were said to be in possession of Walter Baker, steward of the manor.

Clearly William Phelps was overwhelmed by this official command from such an august source, and his subsequent actions were described in an enquiry which was later held into the whole episode. Apparently unable to read the letter himself, Phelps took it first to Nicholas Engleberd, a prominent Sherborne resident and former churchwarden, who read it aloud. Still uncertain, Phelps and Engleberd together took the letter to Hugh Meyer, the collector of the bishop's rents in Sherborne, who also read it aloud. By this time a small crowd of interested spectators had assembled, and the whole party set off for Walter Baker's house. Baker, however, adamantly refused to release any of the records to them, whereupon the crowd urged Phelps to force an entry and break open the closet and chest in which the records were stored. Nicholas Engleberd also pressed Phelps to act, warning him that he might 'kiss the Fleet', in other words might find himself in the Fleet prison if he did not obey the Exchequer orders. Phelps, fearing that he would be personally liable for the considerable damage he would cause by breaking into Baker's house claimed that, as the law officer, he was unwilling to cause a breach of the peace. He therefore contented himself with having the letter read yet again, and ordering the crowd to disperse.

Two days later, on 27 June 1576, a further enquiry by the Exchequer produced evidence of the vicissitudes of the various records relating to the manor of Sherborne, including those of Burton, Holnest, Wootton, Bishop's Caundle, Yetminster, Newland and Castleton. Henry Sterre, gentleman, who lived in Bradford Abbas and whose father, John Sterre, had been steward of Sherborne manor and of the Sherborne almshouse, admitted that he had inherited from his father three bags full of parchment rolls, each bag containing more than two bushells, as well as a large quantity of loose records. Uncertain what to do with them, he had delivered some to Walter Baker, while others he had given to John Fitzjames of Lillington, 'for the good will he bore unto him'.[22]

A year later, in 1577, John Piers became bishop of Salisbury and, succumbing to royal pressure, granted a ninety-nine-year lease of Sherborne manor to the queen. She granted it to Thomas White. In 1592 this lease was transferred to Sir Walter Raleigh.[23]

St Mary's churchyard

The final piece of evidence concerning the long period of controversy and confusion in Sherborne following all the upheavals of the Reformation comes from a dispute over rights to St Mary's [the Abbey] churchyard which was tried before the Exchequer Court in 1603. Sir Ralph Horsey, the fourth generation of the Horsey family to hold the former abbey lands of Sherborne, was already in financial difficulties, and had sold the parsonage of Sherborne to John Stocker, a merchant of Poole. The dispute arose between Stocker and the vicar of Sherborne, Francis Scarlett. It involved tithes and perquisites due to the vicar, and evidence was taken from numerous elderly inhabitants of Sherborne whose memories stretched back to the reign of Queen Mary and the accession of Queen Elizabeth, and to the time of John Chetmill, the long-serving vicar of Sherborne who had died in 1566. One man, John Dyer aged eighty-eight and living in the almshouse could even remember the last days of the abbey and the rule of abbots Ramsam, Meere and Barnstaple. In support of the claim that the vicar was entitled to the trees in the churchyard and to the grass growing there, one witness, Austin Kinge, beer-brewer aged fifty-eight, recalled that he had been a servant to Mr Chetmill and at the beginning of Queen Elizabeth's reign he had accompanied the vicar to Blandford to see the burning of the image, and that on their return Mr Chetmill 'did put his horse to the churchyard of Sherborne where he fed and depastured without contradiction'. John Downton of Beer Hackett, clerk aged fifty, also deposed that the vicars of Sherborne had always had rights to the trees and grass of the churchyard, and to the profits of the fair which was held there. He also mentioned the site of All Hallows which now formed part of the churchyard, that in Queen Mary's time the parishioners went in procession about the bounds of the churchyard every Sunday and that the Corpus Christi play was performed there.

All the witnesses agreed that the income of the vicar of Sherborne was meagre. Before the Dissolution the abbot of Sherborne as rector of the parish had been entitled to the major part of the tithes and offerings paid by the parishioners, and this right had passed to the Horsey family who became lay rectors. The Horseys were said to receive more than £300 per annum from the parish, whereas the vicar was paid only £20 per annum which was derived from the small tithes of eggs, apples, garden produce and hemp. No glebe land was attached to the vicarage, but only a small garden. Moreover, the abbots had always provided the vicars with food and clothing, but that perquisite had ceased at the Dissolution.

Clearly the repercussions of the Dissolution were still being felt in Sherborne, even after a lapse of more than sixty years.[24]

Notes

1   *Letters and Papers, Henry VIII*, VIII, 693.
2   *Letters and Papers, Henry VIII*, VIII, 852.
3   *Valor Ecclesiasticus*, Record Commission 1810–34, I, 281–4.
4   *Statutes of the Realm*, III, 733, 27 Henry VIII, c28.
5   *Letters and Papers, Henry VIII*, XIV(i), 566; *Miscellanea Genealogica et Heraldica*, 2nd Ser., II, 48; W Dugdale, 1817, *Monasticon Anglicanum*, I, 331–41; Fowler 1951, 317. Somerset Record Office, D/D/Vc66. I am grateful to Dr Robert Dunning for the last reference.
6   *Letters and Papers, Henry VIII*, XIX(ii), 527(6).
7   *Letters and Papers, Henry VIII*, XIX(ii), 340(51); 690(67).
8   Public Record Office, E318/14/622; E318/14/623; SC6/Henry VIII 654–62. *Letters and Papers, Henry VIII*, XV, 436(54); 611(47); 733(29); 1032(568). P Webb, 1977, 100; 1978, 26–7; W Dugdale, 1817, 335–40.
9   *Letters and Papers*, Henry VIII, XVIII(i), 981(78).
10 The phrase comes from Richard Carew's *Survey of Cornwall*, 1602. For details of Sir John Horsey's struggles and acrimonious disputes over the acquisition of monastic lands see PRO C78/24/4; C78/30/17; C3/83/14; REQ2/39/13; REQ2/44/85; REQ2/131/56. *Letters and Papers, Henry VIII*, Add 1372.
11 J Fowler, 1951, 325–36.
12 PRO C78/19/12; C78/38/1; C78/38/11.
13 PRO C78/19/12; P Webb, 1977, 100; 1978, 29.
14 PRO C78/30/17; E178/5626; E178/6202; SP16/342/247; J Hutchins, 1866–70, *History of Dorset* (3rd Edition), IV, 427–9. J H Bettey, 1987, *Rural Life in Wessex*, 25.

15 Dorset Record Office, D/SHA/CH9.
16 Wiltshire Record Office Diocesan Records – Sherborne Wills and Inventories.
17 The churchwardens' accounts are printed in successive volumes of *Somerset and Dorset Notes and Queries* XXIII–XXV, 1939–50.
18 *SDNQ* XIV and XIV 1943–47.
19 *Dorset Natural History and Archaeological Society Proceedings,* 25, 196–274; 26, 101–59.
20 PRO SP12/4/26, 21 May 1559.
21 PRO C78/14/18; C24/38/11.
22 PRO E133/1/336; E133/1/337. Four generations of the Sterre family served as stewards on the Sherborne lands of the bishops of Salisbury and subsequently to Sir Walter Raleigh, PRO E134/7 James I M24.
23 Calendar of State Papers, Domestic 1591–4, 212, 27 January 1592.
24 PRO E134/1 James I Mich. 22; E134/1 James I Hil. 33.

Bibliography

Bettey, J H, 1987, *Rural Life in Wessex.*
Bettey, J H, 1988, The Dissolution and after at Cerne Abbas. In K Barker (ed), *The Cerne Abbey Millennium Lectures.* Cerne Abbas Millennium Committee.
Bettey, J H, 1989, *The Suppression of the Monasteries of the West Country.* Gloucester. Alan Sutton.
Dugdale, W, 1817, *Monasticon Anglicanum* (Volume 1).
Fowler, J, 1951, *Mediaeval Sherborne.* Dorchester, Longmans. (Details the long history of the conflict between the abbey and townsfolk during the later Middle Ages.)
Hutchins, J, 1866–70, *History of Dorset* (3rd Edition, Volume 4).
Toulmin-Smith, L, 1907, *Leland's Itinerary in England and Wales* (Four volumes).
Webb, P (ed), 1977, John and Jasper Horsey: Two Tudor Opportunists. *Dorset Natural History and Archaeological Society* 99, 28–32.
Webb, P (ed), 1978, John and Jasper Horsey: Two Tudor Opportunists. *Dorset Natural History and Archaeological Society* 100, 22–30.

17. The Sherborne estate at Lyme

Katherine Barker

> *Ego Æthelredus ... episcopo Wlsino ... et ... Scirburnensis ecclesiae ... mansam unam iuxta ripam maris qui dicitur aet Lim.*
>
> I, [King] Æthelred ... to Bishop Wulsinus [Wulfsige] ... and ... to the Sherborne Church ... one *mansa* [of land] beside the shore of the sea which is called (at) Lyme (Charter of 998)

Lyme is the last estate listed in the charter of AD 998 (see Keynes, 'King Æthelred's charter', §5, this volume) and the only one to receive this kind of descriptive treatment. The subject concerns a single unit of land at *Lim* – Lyme – called a *mansa*. The ten other named estates are listed in terms of number of *cassates* involved (see Barker, 'Sherborne in AD 998', this volume). This is not the first time we hear of a Sherborne church estate at Lyme, and the charter of 998 is clearly confirming the possession of land held there before the introduction of the Benedictine Order. We look firstly at the wording of the charter of 998 and then at the possible significance of *mansa*.

Two Lyme charters, AD 774 and 998

In a charter of AD 774, just over two centuries earlier, in the name of King Cynewulf of Wessex (S 262),[1] we find a grant of land at Lyme made to the church of Sherborne for a salt-pan. The description of the estate is longer as might be expected in a first-time legal agreement. The grant concerns '*unius mansionis terram ... juxta occidentalem ripam fluminis illius quod vulgo Lim vocatum est. Haut procul a loco ubi meatus sui cursum in mare mergit ...*', that is, 'one *mansio* of land ... beside/on the west bank of the stream which is commonly called the *Lim* [Lyme]. Not far from the place where the opening of its watercourse flows/plunges into the sea' (Birch 1885–94, no 224; Barker 1982, 88–90).

We have a single unit of land, this time called a *mansio*, and a more detailed description as to its precise location. The estate is on the sea coast as we already

know, but we also learn that it lies on the west bank of the Lyme stream. Both
these charters are authentic (O'Donovan 1972, 1988) but neither is accompanied
by a boundary survey. There is, however, such a survey for the neighbouring
estate of Uplyme first published by H S A Fox in 1970. In AD 938 King
Athelstan granted to his namesake, in favour of Glastonbury Abbey, a six-hide
estate at *Lim* which was resurveyed by the abbey in 1516 (S 442). It can be seen
that the boundary of the Glastonbury Abbey estate skirts round an area of land
on the west bank of the stream, climbs a steeply facing slope west from the
Salteford then turns south and reaches the sea at *Sigilmere* (Fig 24). Thus neatly
defined is an area of land lying between the stream and the coast which fits with
the wording of both Sherborne documents, and places yet another of Wulfsige's
estates on a shire boundary. So it is we may plausibly identify the *mansio* of
Cynewulf with the *mansa* of Wulfsige – a single well-defined unit of land which
provides something of a 'key' to an understanding of the shape of the later
manorial history of Lyme.[2]

The question has to be posed as to why the location of this estate should be
described again in 998 when, presumably, the clearly worded terms of the charter
of 774 were still 'in force'. No other named Sherborne estate with an earlier
charter receives such treatment.

In 774 we find the Sherborne estate – the *mansio* – located '*iuxta occidentalem
ripam fluminis* (beside/on the west bank of the stream)'. Given that we know
with a reasonable degree of certainty where this is, the only query might lie with
the precise meaning of *haut procul* which describes its location with reference to
the coast. And it is the coast which receives mention in 998. Here we find a
much shorter description of the whereabouts of this estate which this time is
located '*iuxta ripam maris* (beside/on the shore of the sea)'. Thus in 774 we have
iuxta ripam fluminis which, in 998, reads *iuxta ripam maris*. It is the same estate but
the emphasis is different. The charter of 998 has its focus on the coast.

Lyme today is well-known for the Cobb, a breakwater first recorded in 1294
(Fowles 1982, 10), and which may represent an early (but perhaps not the first)
attempt at coastal defence. This is a difficult length of coast for the mariner and
renowned for landslips. The Cobb is located on the west bank coast within the
former Sherborne estate, together with Broad Street (formerly West Street), the
main street of the present town which presents some of the characteristics of a
thirteenth-century planned market street of a type found on other episcopal
manors (Beresford 1967). The coastline of 774 is lost and changes between 774
and 998 are surely irrecoverable. The location of the salt-pan is not known,[3]
neither the location of the early *Lim* settlement(s) which are likely to have lain
back from the coast, safely protected from both the elements and unwelcome
visitors.[4] We may envisage temporary, seasonal settlement – salt and fish – on
the beach during the summer months.

The precise meaning and significance of the word *ripa* in 774 and two
centuries later in 998 is difficult to determine – it was soon to connote a landing

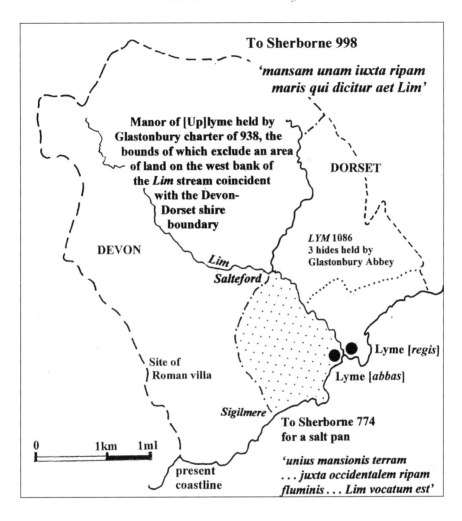

To Sherborne 998

'mansam unam iuxta ripam maris qui dicitur aet Lim'

Manor of [Up]lyme held by Glastonbury charter of 938, the bounds of which exclude an area of land on the west bank of the *Lim* stream coincident with the Devon-Dorset shire boundary

DORSET

DEVON

Lim

Salteford

LYM 1086
3 hides held by Glastonbury Abbey

Lyme [*regis*]

Lyme [*abbas*]

Site of Roman villa

Sigilmere

To Sherborne 774 for a salt pan

'unius mansionis terram ... juxta occidentalem ripam fluminis ... Lim vocatum est'

0   1km   1ml

present coastline

Figure 24. Map of the Sherborne estate at Lyme and the mansa aet Lim *in 998 which is shown stippled. This is a territorial arrangement evidenced by the eighth century and again in Domesday (Barker 1982, fig 7.6).*

stage or wharf (Latham 1965, 409) – but a difference there clearly was, or the matter would surely not merit a remention. The reference to the *ripa maris*, certainly turns our attention seawards and thus to matters of defence – protection of the salt-pan(s) from the sea and the population from the Vikings, thus imposing, we may take it, additional obligations on Wulfsige. The bishop was responsible for the building and manning of a warship and *Lim* is Sherborne's only manorial access to the coast. If the grant of land to Huna by King Eadwig in 957 (S 644) represents the later royal coastal estate of Lyme Regis on the east bank of the stream, then the whole *Lim* coast was, by 998, supervised by a combination of Crown and Church agencies both on the Dorset border; the Dorset/Devonshire boundary itself by Sherborne and Glastonbury – indeed Glastonbury managing the whole of the *Lim* hinterland. The 'frontier' location of the bishop's three West Dorset hundreds has already been noted (see Barker, 'Sherborne in AD 998', Fig 16, this volume). We may reasonably suspect there to have been an early-warning coastal beacon site at *Lim*; the 1539 coastal map shows a beacon on a headland between Charmouth and Lyme long since lost to the sea. Beacon service/construction, *rogi constructione*, receives specific mention in the charter of 998 (see Keynes, 'King Æthelred's charter', §6, this volume).

The *mansa* at Lyme

The significance of the term *mansa* used in the charter deserves exploration. Both *mansio* and *mansa* derived from the Latin *manere*, 'to reside'. In the Domesday Book of 1086, we find a bishop's *domus*, residence or house, recorded there. There are four Lyme-named manors listed in 1086 distinguished only by their respective landowners. The single hide held by the king's sergeant represents the later Lyme Regis, and the two other estates, both held by Glastonbury Abbey for respectively six and three hides, represent the six hides of the Uplyme charter (in Devon, already mentioned) and the other – on the east bank of the stream (in Dorset) became the medieval manor of Colway. The Sherborne estate appears in the guise of an ungelded (untaxed) single *caruca* of land held by the bishop of Salisbury (Domesday Devon, 4:1; Domesday Dorset, 2:5, 8:6, 57:14; Fig 24).

> Lym. Land for one caruca; it never paid geld, fishermen hold it; they pay 15s to the monks for fish. Meadow 4 acres. The Bishop has 1 house [domus] there which pays 6d.

The Domesday reference to a bishop's house at Lyme adds some weight to the possibility that the term *mansio* (774) and *mansa* (998) both connote an estate with a residence – a 'mansion'. It is the only Sherborne estate to record such an item in 1086. Bois (1992, 37) notes that (across the Channel), a reference to a *manse* [in a charter] 'emphasises the particular importance of a house [a term] frequently used in close proximity to a Gallo-Roman villa'. There is the site of a large Romano-British villa in Uplyme.[5] We may only speculate as to whether this played some role in the management of a one-time undivided estate based on the catchment area of the Lyme stream. Also of interest here is the ungelded status of the bishop's Lyme estate in 1086, which by 1405 was accounted a prebend of Salisbury cathedral (Wanklyn 1944, 64–7). The distribution of the other ungelded *carucae* on the bishop's Sherborne estate has already been noted (Barker 1982, 90–4; 1984, 23–8). Their significance has yet to be explained.

The earlier history of the *Lim* estate remains a matter for speculation, but the apportionment of the production – and lucrative proceeds – of salt and fish between early Anglo-Saxon Crown and Church gave rise not only to manorial boundaries, rights and obligations, but to the division between two shires effected by later Anglo-Saxon rulers faced with a serious military threat. The shearing of Lyme in half between Dorset and Devon at least a thousand years ago is an arrangement still firmly in place today.

Notes

1 Charter numbers in the text are referenced by S (Sawyer) and the number.
2 The Sherborne estate was later known as *Netherlym* (as distinct from Uplyme), also as the manor of *Lyme Abbots* or *Sherborne Holme* (Roberts 1996, 200). The site of the medieval Sherborne prebendal farm occupied a focal area of the west bank *mansa*, recorded as twenty-seven acres of arable and three of meadow, lying between Pound Road (formerly Prebendary Lane), Sidmouth Hill, Clappentail Lane and Silver Street (Wanklyn 1944, 66). East of the stream was the royal manor of Lyme Regis; a borough charter was granted in 1284. This is likely to be the single hide at *Lim* held by the king's sergeant in 1086. After the Dissolution the whole of the coastal settlement either side of the Lyme – or *Buddel* – became Lyme Regis. In 1145 and again in 1163 (Dugdale 1817, I, 337, 338) there is mention of a Sherborne Church in *Lim* the site of which is uncertain. Two church towers are shown for Lyme on the coastal landmark map of 1539 (Fowles 1991, frontispiece), one of which may have belonged to the Sherborne manor. The present parish church of St Michael is sited on the east bank.
3 John Fowles in a note to the author dated 20 September 1984 cites a letter he had received from a marine biologist noting that it was Linnaeus who, in the eighteenth century, had given Lyme as one of the classic sites of the Briny Shrimp which needs a very salty habitat indeed. The biologist wrote to ask the whereabouts of the salterns. Fowles was only able to suggest that a last remnant of a salt-pan may perhaps be found at low tide in the 'hewn rock' on the east side of Broad Ledge where a tradition persists there were once houses. He also notes (*pers comm*) there are streets recorded for medieval Lyme which have no known location.
4 Part of the tourist attraction of Lyme today – which it has enjoyed for several centuries – is the existence of what are essentially a unique pair of small medieval towns which now find themselves virtually on the beach. The town of 2005 still presents a very different character east and west of the stream.
5 An even larger Roman villa is found at Halstock another Sherborne manor – fifteen *cassates* in 998, but not mentioned in 1086. *Halganstoke* or 'holy place' it is associated with St Juthwara, who was revered at Sherborne and is mentioned in Wulfsige's *Life* (see Love, 'The Life of St Wulfsige', ch XXI, this volume).

Bibliography

Barker, K, 1982, The Early History of Sherborne. In S Pearce (ed), *The Early Church in Western Britain and Ireland*. BAR British Series, 102. Oxford, 77–116; esp 88–9, and 111–12.

Barker, K, 1984, Sherborne in Dorset: an Early Settlement and its Estate. *Anglo-Saxon Studies in Archaeology and History* 3. Oxford University Committee for Archaeology, 1–33.

Beresford, M, 1967, *New Towns of the Middle Ages, Town Plantation in England, Wales and Gascony*. London.

Birch, W de Gray, 1885–99, *Cartularium Saxonicum* (Three volumes and index).

Bois, G, 1992, *The Transformation of the Year One Thousand: the village of Lournand from antiquity to feudalism*, J Birrell (trans). Manchester University Press.

Domesday Book, Dorset, 1983, C and F Thorn (eds). Chichester. Phillimore.

Domesday Book, Devon, 1985, 2 parts. C and F Thorn (eds). Chichester. Phillimore.

Dugdale, W, 1817, *Monasticon Anglicanum* (Seven volumes). London.

Fox, H S A, 1970, The Boundary of Uplyme. *Transactions of the Devonshire Association* 102, 33–47.

Fowles, J, 1982 (Reprinted 1991), *A Short History of Lyme Regis*. Dorset. Dovecote Press.

Latham, R E, 1965, *Revised Medieval Latin Word List from British and Irish Sources*. London. The British Academy, Oxford University Press.

O'Donovan, M A, 1972, Studies in the History of the Diocese of Sherborne. Unpublished PhD dissertation. University of Cambridge.

O'Donovan, M A, 1988, *Charters of Sherborne*. Oxford.

Penn, K, 1980, *Historic Towns in Dorset*. Dorset Natural History and Archaeological Society Monograph Series no 1, 69–74.

Roberts, G, 1834 (Reprinted 1996), *History and Antiquities of Lyme Regis and Charmouth*. London. Lymelight Press and the Philpott Museum, Lyme Regis.

Sawyer, P H, 1968, *Anglo-Saxon Charters, an Annotated List and Bibliography*. London. Royal Historical Society.

Wanklyn, C, 1927, *Lyme Regis, a Retrospect*. London.

Wanklyn, C, 1944, *Lyme Leaflets*. London. Privately printed.

18. Sherborne Abbey *c* 1530 and Sherborne School 1500–2000: two drawings with numbered keys

J H P Gibb

Editors' note

Jim Gibb is highly regarded for his skilful reconstructional drawings of Sherborne Abbey and its monastic range. It seemed particularly appropriate to include in this volume a suggested reconstruction of the buildings as they were on the eve of the Dissolution (see also Bettey, 'The Dissolution of the abbey', this volume). Equally appropriate, it seems to us, is also to include a drawing, in the same style, of the view as it appears today. We suspect this will already be of interest by 2050; by the year 2550 (should it survive) it will be without equal. Whilst thinking so much about the past, it is easy to forget that we ourselves are part of history. The opportunity to commission a second drawing, an accurate record of the everyday appearance of the abbey and school buildings as they are now at the turn of the new millennium, is not one to be missed. The keys provide an index of their changing use.

Figure 25. Reconstruction drawing of Sherborne Abbey, c 1530, with a numbered key. (Drawing by J H P Gibb)

Sherborne Abbey circa 1530

Figure 25: reconstruction of Sherborne Abbey, c 1530

Key

1   **East Gatehouse**, fifteenth century, now Sherborne Museum and part of Bow House.
2   **Monastic Almonry**, late fifteenth century, where the poor were fed; now an extension to Sherborne Museum.
3   **The Lady Chapel**, *c* 1250, Early English three-bay chapel. Only the west bay survives.
4   **North-east Chapel**, fifteenth century, probably the monks' mortuary chapel; now the clergy vestry.
5   **Monks' Graveyard**.
6   **Bishop Roger's Chapel**, *c* 1250, probably the abbey's sacristy.
7   **Chapter House**, late twelfth–thirteenth century, daily meeting chamber for monastic business.
8   **Dormitory**, on the first floor, late twelfth century. Chapter house and various rooms on the ground floor.
9   **(?)Necessarium**. Monks' latrine attached to the dormitory and flushed by a main drain.
10   **Cloisters** built by Abbot Frith, 1248–73. Demolished 1550s.
11   **Conduit** or **Lavatorium**, *c* 1520, fountain house and monks' wash place.
12   **(?)Refectory** or dining hall. Demolished 1550s.
13   **Monks' Kitchen**, fifteenth century, with large chimney, survives as school offices.
14   **Abbot's House**, fifteenth century, note elaborate entrance, stair turret, and abbot's parlour above. Now school offices.
15   **Abbot's Hall**, fifteenth century on twelfth-century undercroft, greatly expanded as school chapel.
16   **North-west Wing** attached to the abbot's hall, fifteenth century. (?)Guest chambers. Demolished 1853.
17   **Great Hall**, thirteenth century with fifteenth-century roof and windows, hall and ante-room above, stores and inner parlour below. Now school libraries.
18   **Abbot's Chapel**, (?)fourteenth century about south-west corner of cloisters. Only a piscina and entrance survive.
19   **All Hallows Church**, *c* 1400, Chapel of Ease for the parish; became the parish church after the fire of 1437. Demolished 1540s.
20   **Old Vicarage**, fifteenth century, a medieval 'hall house' demolished *c* 1850. Housed the priests of All Hallows. Site of house of Saxon bishops.
21   **Abbey Mill and Leat**, became a silk mill in nineteenth century. Demolished *c* 1850.
22   **Combe Stream**, supplied the abbey fish ponds and the great drain.
23   **The Great Drain**, controlled by sluice gates, and flushed latrines.
24   **The Newell Water**, twelfth century, piped down valley from the Newell spring, it supplied drinking water to kitchen and conduit.
25   **Prior's House**, (?)fifteenth century, survived as a private house until demolished in 1749.
26   **Infirmary**, (?)thirteenth century, for sick and infirm monks, with its own chapel, kitchen and latrines. Demolished (?)*c* 1550.Figure 26: Sherborne School, 1550–2000

Figure 26. Sherborne Abbey and school, 1500–2000, with a numbered key. (Drawing by J H P Gibb)

Figure 26: Sherborne School, 1550–2000

Key

1   **Bow House**, fifteenth and ?seventeenth century. Acquired in 1921 for the Masters' Common Room with staff accommodation above. Earlier part of the east gatehouse of the monastery, it became the Sun Inn – with a reputation for rowdiness – and served as a billet for as many as sixty or seventy First World War troops.

2   **Sherborne Museum**, Abbey Gate House (fifteenth and nineteenth century). Originally the gatehouse and almonry of the monastery. It was the abbey verger's house (before becoming the museum in 1958). Several hapless participants of the Battle of Sedgemoor, 1685, were hanged under the fifteenth-century gateway which still stands.

3   **The Old School Room** 1606, the site acquired in 1605 on a thousand-year lease. This in fact was the second schoolroom on this site built to house the Edward VI Grammar School founded in 1550. Now School House dining hall. Over the door lintel are the arms of Edward VI; inside on the east wall is a coloured statue of Edward in Portland stone set up in 1614. It remained the main teaching room of the school for over two centuries. Within these walls the assizes were held, and both Charles I and Cromwell's troopers installed themselves during the Parliamentary occupation of the town during the Civil War.

4   **Bell Building** (1835). The site was first occupied by a brew house put up in 1642 with cellars beneath and dormitory accommodation above. Demolished in 1835 it was replaced by the present structure, a schoolroom on the ground floor and sleeping accommodation above, 'surmounted by a handsome Gothic cupola for the bell'. It now serves as kitchen, larder and storerooms.

5   **Former Headmaster's House**, 1560–1860. The end of the abbey building was demolished and a purpose-built Tudor house built to accommodate the headmaster, later also served as a staff common room. Reverted back to the lady chapel of the abbey in 1921; only one Tudor bay remains including the 'headmaster's eye' – a small oval window which looked down into the schoolroom. Mounted on the south wall are the royal coat of arms, together with those of the principal founding benefactors of the school.

6   **The Slype** (passage), thirteenth century, the former south bay of the monks' dormitory. Acquired by the school in 1550. In 1598 it was the 'plumb house' (for brewing); by 1732 it served as the school laundry.

7   **Site of the Monks' Cloisters**, twelfth century, rebuilt during the fourteenth century. Some of the arches can still be seen in the remaining east-facing wall. It was from here the conduit (*lavatorium* or fountain house) built by Abbot Meere (1505–35) was removed in 1553 and reconstructed in the (meat) market place, or *Shambles* at the bottom of Cheap [market] Street. The pipe that carried the Newell Water to the conduit was lengthened and clean water was thus brought into the heart of the town. It remained the principal clean water supply until the 1850s. Initially held in trust for the town by Sherborne Almshouse, it was held by the Governors of the school from 1629 until 1933 when it was given to the town who adopted it as their insignia. The derelict cloister area was

known as the 'Ball Court' an area popular as a fives playground.

8   **School House**, occupied by the housemaster. Built 1860, designed by W Slater, served as the headmaster's house 1860–1950. The first occupant was Hugo Daniel Harper, under whom, following the Endowed Schools Act and the coming of the railway, the school acquired much of its present character.

9   **School House Dormitories**, built 1860. The foundation stone was laid by the earl of Shaftesbury, the great philanthropist. Designed by W. Slater, the doors and windows reflect that of the medieval buildings opposite.

10   **Medlycott History Classrooms**, built 1955 by Oswald Brakspear, OS. Named in memory of a distinguished Chairman of Governors.

11   **Sixth Form Green**, site of the prior's house. With the enormous expansion of the school in the nineteenth century, the layout of the place was changed opening up what was to become the 'new court' – now Sherborne School Courts – enclosed by the acquisition of the library chapel and studies, and the building of the big schoolroom. The first school gate (25) was built in 1853. An old right of way across the area and through the abbey was thus finally extinguished.

12   **Headmaster's Offices**, fifteenth century, built by Abbot Ramsam. Formerly the abbot's lodging and monks' kitchen. The finely carved doorway with its empty niches still remains; so also the massive kitchen chimney. Seemingly a private residence for a time it was, by the end of the eighteenth century incorporated into the nearby silk mill. Acquired by the school in 1851. The upper landing became part of the school chapel in 1851. Scheduled as an Ancient Monument in 1937.

13   **School Chapel**, central part originally the abbot's hall used as part of a silk mill after the Dissolution. Became part of the school by gift of Lord Digby in 1851. Extended in 1853, 1865 and 1922. The north aisle was added in 1878 by R H Carpenter; there is a twelfth-century undercroft now used as part of the school library.

14   **School libraries and muniment room**, tenth, thirteenth and fifteenth centuries. Formerly the abbot's guest hall above, cellarer's stores and outer parlour below. There are remains of the corner of the north-west transept of the Saxon cathedral in the wall of the muniment room. The roof of what is now the upper library suggests the room was once divided by a screen or minstrel's gallery; the lower floor was probably used for malting and/or a wine store. From about 1740 the main body of the library formed part of a great silk mill one of many for which the district became well known. In 1851 by gift of Lord Digby it became part of the school; used initially as a place of assembly. Hugo Daniel Harper, headmaster at the time, wanted to restore the cloisters.

15   **Fifth Form Green**, originally a garden known as 'Little Court'. The south wall was the north wall of All Hallows church, and by implication, stands over the north wall of St Aldhelm's cathedral church.

16   **Classrooms** that enclose the western side of the above were built in 1869–70 by R H Carpenter; 'classrooms for Science and Art' later 'English Classrooms' were four in number; the original desks on rising tiers remained until the 1970s. One 'doubled up' as a Governors' Board Room.

17   **Chapel War Memorial Stairs** and Roll of Honour, designed in 1920 by Sir Reginald Blomfield and consecrated in 1922 by the bishop of Madras. The names of the Fallen of both World Wars are recorded on the walls. There are 221 names listed for the First World War, the equivalent of the whole strength of the school in 1914. In 1926 the Harper Memorial window was moved to the east end with the installation of a new chapel organ.

18   **Stage** and **Stairs** of the big schoolroom, were added in 1956 as a Second World War memorial.

19   **The Big Schoolroom** and west cloisters behind. Designed to serve as a place of assembly for the now much-enlarged school, the new hall was opened in 1879. Partly intended for teaching, it was soon in use for music. The interior has been changed several times. Damaged by Sherborne's only air raid in 1940, in 1956 a handsome new north gallery was built on the site of the old raised dais, and a much enlarged stage with rooms beneath constructed at the south end thus serving – most successfully – to reorientate the audience.

20   **Devitt Workshops**, 1921. Designed by Sir Reginald Blomfield, put up 'regardless of expense'. The foundations are deep, made necessary by the very swampy nature of the ground formerly that of the abbey mill leat. The open ground to the west is the Devitt Court in which survives parts of the abbey mill buildings which sprawl across the present site. Out of the picture to the west is the site of the swimming bath opened in 1873 and filled initially by both the waters of the Combe Stream and the Newell Water – until the first proved too dirty. The earth dug out was used to fill the medieval fishpond a little further up the valley now the site of the sports centre of 1976 – and a new swimming pool. The 1873 bath was drained in the mid-1980s and a new science block facing Acreman Street opened on the site in 2000.

21   **Carrington Buildings**, designed in 1910 by Sir Reginald Blomfield, named after a parent and generous benefactor. In distinctive Queen Anne style 'dedicated to Art Science and Arms', the building houses the original science block once also the site of the school's museum so badly damaged during the air raid of 1940 it was never reassembled.

22   **North-west Classrooms**, built in 1833 by R H Carpenter.

23   **Classics Classrooms** designed by Sir Reginald Blomfield and completed in 1913.

24   **Mathematics Classrooms** also designed by Blomfield and opened in 1923, thus finally enclosing the school courts. Among the earliest schoolboy occupants was Alan Turing (1912–53), Enigma code-breaker and 'father of the digital computer'.

25   **Tower Gateway** of 1923, again by Blomfield, replaced an earlier school gate first constructed in 1853 which was dismantled and re-erected as an entrance way to the games fields. Over the gateway are mounted the school coat of arms; shields and initials of governor, headmaster and architect.

26   **School Lodge** built in 1853 to complement the first school gateway.

Bibliography with additional notes

Barker, K, 1990, *Sherborne Camera*. Wimborne. Dovecote Press.
Plate 2 shows a view looking north-west from the abbey tower across the school as it was in 1879, and plate 15 is an axiometric plan of the eastern end of the abbey and range drawn in the early 1920s showing the part-demolition of the Tudor headmaster's house as part of the proposed rebuilding and expansion of the lady chapel.

Fowler, J, 1951, *Mediaeval Sherborne*. Dorchester. Longmans.
A remarkable work containing much valuable material from original written sources.

Gibb, J H P, 1975, The Anglo-Saxon Cathedral at Sherborne. *The Archaeological Journal* 132, 71–110.
An account of excavations at Sherborne Abbey 1968–73 by Sherborne School Archaeological Society. Reprints are obtainable from the Friends of Sherborne Abbey bookstall, price £1.00.

Gibb, J H P, 1981, *The Book of Sherborne*. Buckingham. Barracuda Books.
See especially pages 48–68 on the growth and development of the abbey and precinct, and pages 92–106 on the school. See also pages 24–5 for a reconstruction drawing of the Saxon cathedral, and a reproduction of part of the charter of King Æthelred, AD 998.

Gibb, J H P, 1985, The Fire of 1437 and the Rebuilding of Sherborne Abbey. *Journal of the British Archaeological Association* 138, 101–24.

Gibb, J H P, 1986, The Battle of the Fonts and the Fire of Sherborne Abbey. privately printed.
Includes extracts from the Sherborne Annals written between 1437 and 1456, in the monastery at Sherborne, BL Harley 3906. Copy in Sherborne Museum, and obtainable from the Friends of Sherborne Abbey bookstall, price £1.00.

Gibb J H P, 1988, Sherborne Abbey – Addendum to the Fire of 1437. *Journal of the British Archaeological Association* 141, 161–9.

Gourlay, A B, 1971, *A History of Sherborne School* (2nd Edition). Sawtells of Sherborne.
For a full account of the history of the older school and monastic buildings, see pages 260–315.

Keen, L, and Ellis, P (eds), forthcoming, Sherborne Abbey Excavations 1972–1976. English Heritage.

Monckton, L, 1999, Late Gothic Architecture in South West England, Wells, Bristol and Sherborne. Unpublished PhD thesis, University of Warwick (Two volumes).

Monckton, L, 2000, The Late Medieval Rebuilding of Sherborne Abbey: a re-assessment. *Journal of the Society of Architectural Historians*.

19. Sherborne today: aspects of the Benedictine legacy

Katherine Barker

A comparison of the two views of Sherborne Abbey and its precincts drawn by Jim Gibb (see Gibb, 'Sherborne Abbey', Figs 25 and 26, this volume,) graphically illustrates the scale of the ecclesiastical legacy to the town; a legacy shaped by the adoption of the Benedictine Rule a thousand years ago (Bettey, 'The dissolution of the abbey', this volume). Over five and a half centuries, perhaps as many as twenty generations, Benedictine living – and building requirements – imposed and maintained an Order not only over the religious community, but a much wider community round about. Without such it seems unlikely the town would have inherited an Edward VI Grammar School, and – in the fullness of time – the large independent school of today. Stockdale ('Benedictine books, writers and libraries', this volume) notes the Benedictine involvement in writing, in the production of books, and in education.

The size of the medieval Sherborne library is not known. John Leland noted the existence of ten (surviving) titles in 1536–40; Stockdale (*ibid*) discusses five of them. One of them, the Sherborne Missal of *c* 1400 includes, for the Second Sunday in Epiphany, a scene of the Christ Child found by his parents disputing with the doctors in the Temple (see Stockdale, 'Benedictine books, writers and libraries', Fig 17, this volume). The room in which the 'lesson' is taking place is worthy of closer inspection, as is the furniture. There is a reference to a schoolmaster, a *magister scholarium*, in 1437, and indications that the monastery, certainly during the last century of its existence, delegated the task of teaching the choristers to 'an outside man'. One of the mid-fifteenth-century choir misericords shows a schoolmaster, wearing a round cap, beating a recalcitrant pupil watched by laughing boys (Gourlay 1971, 6–7). The Edward VI charter of 1550 set Sherborne back on a course which has made it well known for education.

Through the Benedictines, Sherborne not only became part of a well-established wider world of European learning, but was known to – and acknowledged by – the leaders of Christendom, papal and episcopal, royal and military. The twelfth-century fortified residence of Bishop Roger of Caen at Castleton (Sherborne Old Castle) survived a century after the Dissolution to be of strategic use during the Civil War. The successor residence nearby, formerly the bishop's hunting lodge (Sherborne New Castle), was granted out by the Crown to royal favourites, most notably Walter Raleigh. In 1617 the estate was acquired by Sir John Digby, first earl of Bristol, in whose family it remains. What is now Sherborne Castle Estates Ltd surrounds the town, just as the Benedictine estate once did.

Medieval bishops were not only builders of large monuments, they were also urban developers. The town plan of Sherborne includes two small thirteenth-century planned medieval 'new towns' or suburbs – the one at *Newland* established by Bishop Le Poor's charter of 1227–8, and the other at *Castleton* adjacent to the castle. First mentioned in 1537, it is not known which bishop was responsible for its creation (Fowler 1951, 155); much of it was destroyed by the coming of the railway in 1860. Both were styled 'boroughs' and whilst rents were paid to the bishop, the inhabitants enjoyed a degree of self-government. Each had a court leet, a market and a fair. But whilst the life of the community was surely much enriched by the abbey foundation in its midst, it perhaps missed out in other ways. The town of Sherborne as a whole was never accorded the rights enjoyed by a borough; there were no burgesses, no burgage rights, and certainly no member of parliament. Thus it was the reforms of the Corporation Act of 1835 passed it by.

A town hall was opened in 1681 on the south side of the abbey graveyard, the money was raised by the warden of the King Edward VI Grammar School. Here the county Justices met, having previously met in the Edward VI schoolroom. But the only popular assembly which all inhabitants were entitled to attend was the Parish Vestry. Principal landowner in the town was the Digby family to whom market dues were paid. The town hall was demolished in 1884, and in the fullness of time the then Lord Digby built Sherborne a meeting hall, succeeded by another in 1972. But the town itself has inherited no civic centre, there is no 'town hall'. By the middle of the nineteenth century the other landowner of note was Sherborne Almhouse, founded in 1437, and still administered by the Master and Brethren. The relative poverty of the centuries after the Dissolution meant the survival of a number of old houses and there was in fact to be no major redevelopment until the early twentieth century in the building of local authority housing on the northern and western edges of the town.

The most far-reaching change – which set the scene for today – was brought about by the Public Health Act of 1848 which created a central Board and Inspectorate to deal with the problems of water supply and sewerage. We 'are bound to state' notes the Report, 'that [we have nowhere found] to exist better material for an efficient local Board' (Gibb 1981, 126). Conditions in the town were bad. A large number of medieval cottages were condemned as unfit for human habitation (creating a number of what are now secluded walled gardens) and St Mary's (the abbey) graveyard was closed and a new cemetery opened on the western edge of the town. But there was to be no town government as such until the setting up of the Urban District Council in 1894 and which was – a generation later – to use the conduit, the monks' *lavatorium*, as its insignia. Sherborne's coat of arms was granted in 1986 following the creation of Sherborne Town Council in 1974.

Sherborne history in its insignia

Figure 27a depicts the Sherborne Abbey seal. Dated to the eleventh century it is the only representation known of the late Anglo-Saxon church, clearly quite different from the building known today. It shows a church with a west tower with a circular belfry opening, a high lantern turret and possibly an apsidal chancel. An old right-of-way through the eastern end of the present building suggests the Normans not only rebuilt, but extended the Anglo-Saxon church – building on, as it were, to the right-hand end of the structure represented here.

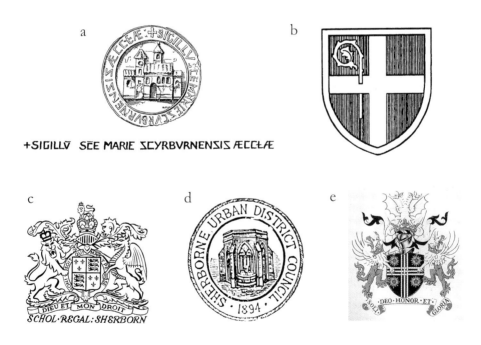

Figure 27. Sherborne history in its insignia: a, the Sherborne Abbey seal redrawn by J H P Gibb; b, the arms of Sherborne Abbey; c, the royal arms of Edward VI; d, insignia adopted by Sherborne Urban District Council in 1933; and e, Sherborne's coat of arms granted by the College of Arms in 1986.

The earliest recorded use of the arms of Sherborne Abbey (Fig 27b) is to be found in the Sherborne Missal, *c* 1400, together with those of the abbeys of Glastonbury, Abbotsbury, Milton and Cerne. The crozier or pastoral staff, is a symbol which can be used for either bishop or abbot. 'Gules, a cross argent, in the dexter half a crozier in pale or debruised by the arm of the cross', the arms were adopted by the town of Sherborne after the Dissolution; there was no alternative insignia available until 1933.

The royal arms of Edward VI (Fig 27c) were mounted over the doorway of the schoolroom (see Gibb, 'Sherborne Abbey', Fig 26: 3, this volume,) in 1608; 'tinctured' at great expense by a certain Roger Moore, ordered to be 'washed over with Oyle' in 1670, and subsequently restored to their former glory, in which state they remain. Another set were mounted on the headmaster's house (Fig 26: 5) destroyed during the Civil War and replaced in 1660. The royal arms over the present tower gateway (Fig 26: 25) were 'incised' in 1889 and mounted over the new gate in 1923.

Abbot Meere's (1505–35) Conduit House, the monks' *lavatorium*, was the Insignia adopted by Sherborne Urban District Council (Fig 27d) in 1933, the year Sherborne School Governors gave it to the town. Constructed in the cloister north of the abbey, it was moved at the Dissolution – together with the water supply – to the market place at the bottom of Cheap Street where it still stands. It remained an important source of drinking water, both human and animal, until the 1850s.

Sherborne's coat of arms (Fig 27e) was granted by the College of Arms in 1986. The silver cross represents the abbey interlaced to represent the town's former weaving industry; the rose badges, Edward VI, founder of the grammar school; the double-headed wyvern Sherborne's Saxon origins; the Crowns are of those Kings Æthelbald and Æthelbert buried in the abbey, and the griffin supporters are legendary guardians of treasure – the town's tradition as a centre of education. The motto comes from the Sherborne Missal: SOLI DEO HONOR ET GLORIA [Through God the Foundation, Honour and Glory].

Bibliography
Fowler, J, 1951, *Mediaeval Sherborne*. Dorchester. Longmans.
Gibb, J H P, 1981, *The Book of Sherborne*. Buckingham. Barracuda Books.
Gourlay, A B, 1971, *A History of Sherborne School*. Sawtells of Sherborne.

20. Constants and contrasts: monastic tradition and renewal

Dom Aidan Bellenger

Monastic history means little out of context and it is spirituality which makes sense of the desire to seek God as a consecrated vocation for life which is the essence of monasticism. This lifetime's quest is not a common way even for committed Christians but it has formed part of the Church's experience, especially in the Orthodox and Catholic traditions, from the earliest of times. Dorset has a special place in that tradition. 'Dorset' as the Victoria County History puts it, 'enjoyed a unique pre-eminence for the number and importance of its religious houses founded during the Saxon period' (VCH 1908, 47). These formed the foundation of a wide monastic network which flowered in the Middle Ages. In medieval Dorset ten monasteries followed the Rule of St Benedict. These were the monasteries for men at Abbotsbury, Cerne, Milton and Sherborne, the monastery for women at Shaftesbury, two male Benedictine priories at Cranborne and Horton, a Cluniac priory at Holme, a Cistercian abbey for men at Bindon and a Cistercian abbey for women at Tarrant Keynes. All were founded by the end of the twelfth century with the exception of Tarrant which was established in the mid thirteenth. In addition there were a number of alien priories, dependent on foreign monasteries, most of them Benedictine, including Frampton, Loders, Povington, Spettisbury and Wareham. These were lesser establishments, in some cases no more than farms (*ibid,* 1908, 48–122).

After the Dissolution a handful of Dorset men joined the revived English Benedictine Congregation (Dolan 1901, 264–7) and from the years 1795 to 1807 a small community of English Benedictine nuns exiled by the French Revolution from Paris were settled at Marnhull (Eaton 1929, 63–75). In modern Dorset there is no living Benedictine presence although until 1989 there was a community of Cistercian nuns, also originally refugees of the French Revolution, at Holy Cross Abbey, Stapehill (Holy Cross Abbey, 1937) founded in 1802 which until 1817 had a brother house of monks at Lulworth, the abbey of St Susanna, the first English-based monastery to be given abbatial status since the

Reformation (Bellenger 1986, 83–90). This was an appropriate distinction since Dorset and Sherborne were to provide in the person of Stephen Harding (d. 1134) the effective architect of the Cistercian reform. The monks of Lulworth returned to France in 1817 and were the founding fathers of many now flourishing communities including Mount Melleray in Ireland and Mount St Bernard in Leicestershire (Lekai, 1977).

According to the *Benedictine Year Book* for 1998 the Benedictine Confederation, which does not included Cistercians, numbers some 8,694 Benedictine monks world-wide and about 10,208 nuns. Of these 480 monks and 470 nuns are resident in England. All these are Roman Catholic. There are, in addition, 38 Anglican monks and 120 Anglican nuns following the Benedictine way. I call it the Benedictine <u>way</u> rather than the Benedictine <u>order</u> because the Benedictines have never been a centralised religious institute like the Dominicans, Franciscans of Jesuits.

Monastic rules compiled by founders of monasteries were numerous in the years from the era of the traditional first monk, St Antony of Egypt (251–356), to the time of St Benedict (c. 480–550). These rules were accompanied by books of sayings, constitutions and biographies of holy monks. A tradition emerged which placed increasing emphasis on the community aspects of monastic life. The most influential pre-Benedictine writers were probably John Cassian (*c* 360–422) and Basil the Great (330–379). Cassian saw monastic life as apostolic in origin, a re-capturing of the life of the first Christians. While seeing the importance and to some extent the superiority of the eremetical life, he also legislated for monks living together, under a spiritual father, following the lead given by Pachomius (d. 346), the founder of Christian community monasticism. Basil the Great, Bishop of Caesarea, went further than Cassian in his emphasis on community life stressing the centrality of shared liturgical prayer and manual labour rather than the individual feats of sometimes outlandish asceticism which characterised the earliest monks. This living monastic tradition informed the life and spirituality of St Benedict (Fry, 1980).

In the medieval world there was great respect for founders of religious houses and the saints which they sometimes nourished, but there was little respect for what we would now call copyright. If something made sense you incorporated it complete in your own writing. It was a compliment to the original author to do so. Much academic controversy has been aroused by the integrity of the text of St Benedict's *Rule* and its relationship, in particular, to another monastic rule, *The Rule of the Master*. This controversy, as well as revealing the use of traditional texts in monastic rules, also throws light on the nature of St Benedict's *Rule* itself. St Benedict's 'School of the Lord's Service' provides not a proscriptive book of laws but an open-ended, spiritually-based attempt to provide the essentials of a monastic life. Each monastic family has its own particular way of living out the *Rule*.

The *Rule* reflects Benedict's own personal search for God and the monastic life which was not always easy. He learnt, at his first monastery at Subiaco, how to govern the hard way. His monks objected so strongly to his reforming oversight that he was forced to start again at Monte Cassino. After his death Cassino was to be destroyed several times but manuscripts of his *Rule* survived, circulated beyond Italy and eventually became, during the Carolingian renaissance of the ninth century, the standard monastic text for the West. The text was rarely used in its purest form and when many of the Dorset monasteries following the *Regularis Concordia* of the English tenth century monastic revival, adopted the *Rule*, it was the *Rule* established by time and experience, based on the good practice of good monasteries and set within the experience of other rules. Good practice was what distinguished a good monastery but most Benedictine monasteries have common features which are apparent across the centuries. Each independent Benedictine house is a distinct family ruled by an abbot (form *abbas*, father) and has its own monastic nursery, the novitiate, where fledgling monks are trained. The novitiate is essentially an apprenticeship in the spiritual life, a craft, which demands, in the continuing search for God, an ongoing formation. A monk's life is one of continuing learning. The principal work of every Benedictine monastery is the performance of the Divine Office, God's work (*Opus Dei*), the public worship of the Church and the community, reflecting the liturgical year, the rhythm of the day and night, and the seasons. This *Opus Dei* is complemented by a structured community life, periods of silence and *lectio divina*, meditative reading, and manual work.

Local conditions influence the details of the life and St Benedict made provision for abbatial initiative in adapting, for example, the Divine Office (Chapter 18) and the food and drink (Chapter 40). Although autonomy is the ideal, monasteries have been grouped together over the centuries to help development and from the early thirteenth century, following the Fourth Lateran Council's advocacy of provincial chapters, national congregations were formed. Sherborne, a Cathedral priory, and then from 1075, an autonomous abbey, was a part of that English congregation as is my own monastery at Downside. The English Benedictine Congregation is the only survivor of those original congregations and continuity is displayed in the appointment of members of the Congregation to titles of the old monasteries. Thus in 1998, Dom Matthew Stark, formerly Abbot of Portsmouth, Rhode Island, in the United States, is now titular abbot of Sherborne. The title is one of honour, not of jurisdiction.

The English Benedictine Congregation was revived in the early years of the seventeenth century with a number of English monastic communities on the continent feeding a network of chaplaincies and Mass centres on the English mission. The first monastic house for men was established at Douai, in Flanders, and dedicated to St Gregory the Great. This is the ancestor of modern Downside. The English Benedictines were a missionary body centrally organised under a President General until 1899 when a new constitution, approved by the Holy See, which has always protected the independence of monasteries from local interference, promoted the communities to the rank of abbey. The first three abbeys of Ampleforth, Douai and Downside are the senior houses in a Congregation which now has ten abbeys of men, seven of them in England. In 1998 their manpower, according to *The Benedictine Year Book* was as follows: Ampleforth (100), Belmont (45), Buckfast (38), Douai (30), Downside (36), Ealing (25), and Worth (27). All of them are numerically greater than Sherborne, which rarely attained a community of twenty, and it is very difficult, rather in the way it is so difficult to translate currency over the centuries, to make contrast and to draw out similarities between medieval and modern monasticism. I have already underlined the tradition. It is perhaps in the three Benedictine vows that the heart of Benedictine spirituality makes itself most clear and on which the 'feel' and character of the continuing Benedictine charism across the centuries is most obviously displayed.

After his profession, a Benedictine monk makes three vows, not as generally thought, those of poverty, chastity and obedience, but rather those of stability, *conversio* or *conversatio morum*, and obedience. Stability is a promised attachment to a particular community for life and this generally implies a particular place. Such commitment is reflected in the great churches built by St Benedict's disciples, places built to last which gave Benedictine foundations so strong a sense of *genius loci*. Stability also implies a calm rootedness in God. *Pax*, peace, is often seen as a Benedictine gift and this should flow from the life of the community. *Conversio* or *conversatio morum* is about changing one's self in conformity with the monastic life, crudely translated as 'a conversion of manners.' At one level this vow is about becoming a monk in the traditional way – as the 998 Charter for Sherborne puts it taking on a life of 'chastity, humility and subjection' (VCH 1908, 63). At another level 'conversion' is in creative tension with stability – always changing, always purifying, always examining motives. Change is always difficult to take even if it is change for the better. It has been said that a good family gives its children 'roots and wings' and that is perhaps what *stability* and *conversatio* provide for a monk.

The third vow, obedience, may have, for the modern world a rather harsh negative sound about it akin to the 'subjection' of the 998 Charter. But it has a more sensitive meaning based on the root of the word 'obedience' which means *listen* and is also the opening word of the *Rule* of St Benedict. Learning to listen to the word of God, to the commands of the abbot, to the wisdom of the brethren all form part of the monastic *ascesis* and this vowed listening is as crucial now to any Benedictine as it was a millennium ago. Listening to God in the stable enclosure of the monastery is the normal vocation of the monk but the consequences of that listening can lead to a new way of looking at things. Monasticism is not about inertia but about the interplay between tradition and renewal which, in the lives of individual monks, can often lead to crisis and sometimes to enlightenment. The impact of such conflict comes out clearly in the lives of two monks, among the most famous of their respective houses:

Stephen Harding at Sherborne, David Knowles at Downside.

This year is very much Stephen Harding's as it is Sherborne's because it was in 1098 that the abbey of Cîteaux, the mother of so many monasteries, was founded. Stephen was a native of the south-west of England, born in the last quarter of the eleventh century, who entered the monastery of Sherborne as a monk or possibly only as a pupil. He did not stay long and he seems to have left to become a full-time student, but having re-discovered his faith and a personal life of prayer which included the daily recitation of the whole psalter, he entered Cîteaux as one of its seven founding fathers. In 1109 he became the third abbot of the monastery and was instrumental in compiling the *Carta Caritatis* which became, after the *Rule* itself, perhaps the most influential document in the history of Benedictine monasticism. Its title reflected its gentle tone, a charter of love, its details provided a simple but formidable constitution, especially its scheme of visitation from one house to its daughter foundations and an annual general chapter of abbots of Cîteaux, which gave the Cistercians an organisational edge over their Black Monk, Benedictine contemporaries in the twelfth century. The White Monks, as the Cistercians were called from the colour of their habits, injected a new vitality into the monastic order. Stephen Harding secured an important part in the history of the European Church (Farmer 1992, 442–3).

The greatest twentieth century chronicler of English Medieval Monasticism was Dom David Knowles (1896–1974) a monk of Downside (and a former pupil of Downside School) who went on to become Regius Professor of Modern History at Cambridge (Brooke, 1991). Clothed as a novice in 1914, solemnly professed as a monk in 1918 and ordained priest in 1922, the research for his magnum opus, *The Monastic Order in England*, eventually published in 1940, was undertaken in the monastic library at Downside between 1929 and 1939 at a time when he was experiencing a spiritual crisis, perhaps not unlike Stephen Harding's, which was moving him to a life of renunciation and asceticism which he felt he could not find at Downside. He wanted to make a new foundation whose rule of life was even stricter than the Cistercian (Morey 1979, 144–53). The foundation was never achieved although among the possible places explored as a possible home for it was Milton Abbas in Dorset. Sherborne, it was assumed, was unavailable. In 1939 Knowles left Downside for ever and went on to pursue 'his monasticism of the soul' at Peterhouse, Cambridge, and elsewhere. He could only be satisfied with the perfection gained from cultivating his own garden.

Disputes and difficulties, scandal and conflicts of jurisdiction; these are what emerge from many of the surviving records of medieval monasteries which tell us less of the normal rhythm of life and prayer of the communities. Monastic history can too often be less than an edifying spectacle. But this is perhaps to miss the point. Monasticism is about the sinner seeking sanctity and not always attaining it. It is about perseverance as well as success. Perfection is not easily

Figure 28. An architect's line drawing of the interior of Downside Abbey.

achieved and when we judge monastic observance perhaps we should aim less high than that from the perspective of the revolutionary reformer. Abbot Cuthbert Butler, of Downside, suggested that the life of the humdrum and seemingly uninspiring community, like medieval Sherborne perhaps, had its message to give:

> I think monastic history written from the standpoint of reforms will be a picture of our own perspective. At all times there has been some monastery, some congregation, some reformer, in the limelight, salt of the earth: my knowledge of monastic history leads me to that belief that at all times there has been a background of old-fashioned houses in which a very respectable religious life, with good, if not showy, observance and real spiritual religion, was being lived in a quiet way outside the reform-circle of the hour. (Brooke *ibid*, 45)

Human frailty is a common theme throughout monastic history and:

> St Benedict nowhere suggests that he is legislating … for any uncommon type of temperament. His monks are ordinary men, and he will lead them in a way accessible to ordinary men. St Benedict intended the perceptive portions of the Rule to be … the minimum standard of evangelical life, which could be demanded of all, but which proficients could transcend while yet fulfilling. (Brooke *ibid*, 43)

Hence there is always the danger of monastic tepidity.

> St Benedict's humanity and gentleness … have often been degraded into something merely human and commonplace by leaving out of the reckoning the complete self-sacrifice without which they cannot be attained … St Benedict never confuses charity with mere good nature, filial respect and obedience with him an affection, peace and order with comfort and ease, measure and discretion with faintheartedness and mediocrity. (Brooke, *ibid*)

Sometimes, moreover, monasteries can be too closely mixed in the secular society and this can lead, as in 1436 at Sherborne, to physical violence and destruction. A monastery and its monks are always searching and in a profound sense it is only with death that final fulfillment of the monk's vocation is found. Each Benedictine monastery has its own story, even if they are variations on a theme. Yet, the *Rule* provides a pivotal document and the gold standard. As David Knowles conclude at the end of his study of monastic history:

> At the end of this long review of monastic history, with its splendours and miseries, and with its rhythm of recurring rise and fall, a monk can but ask himself what message for himself and for his brethren the long story may carry. It is the old and simple one; only in fidelity to the Rule can a monk or monastery find security. A Rule, given by the founded with the acknowledged fullness of spiritual wisdom, approved by the Church and tested by the experience of saints, is a safe path, and it is for the religious the only safe path. It comes to him not as a rigid, mechanical code of works, but as a sure guide to one who seeks God, and who seeks that he may indeed find. If he truly

seeks and truly loves, the way will not be hard, but if he would love and find the unseen God he must pass beyond all things seen and walk in faith and hope, leaving all human ways and means trusting the father to whom all things are possible. When once a religious house or a religious order ceases to show then the rigours of the narrow way that leads to the imitation of Christ in His Love, it sinks to the level of a purely human institution, and whatever its works may be, they are the works of time and not of eternity. The true monk, in whatever century he is found, looks not only to the changing ways around him or to his own mean condition, but to the unchanging everlasting God, and his trust is in the ever-lasting arms that hold him. Christ's words are true: 'He who doth not renounce all that he possesseth cannot be my disciple.' His promise is also true: 'He that followeth me walketh not in darkness but shall have the light of life.' (Brooke *ibid*, 44)

Bibliography

Bellenger, D A, 1986, *The French Exiled Clergy*. Bath.

Brooke, C, (ed), 1991, *David Knowles Remembered*. Cambridge.

Dolan, G, 1901, 'Chapters in the History of the English Benedictine Missions,' *Downside Review* 20, 264–7.

Eaton, R, 1929, *The Benedictines of Colwich*. London, 63–75.

Farmer, D H, 1992, *Oxford Dictionary of Saints,* third edn. Oxford.

Fry, T, (ed), *R B 1980*, Collegeville, 3–151, includes a discussion of *The Rule of the Master,* and provides a useful survey of the monastic tradition in English in the introduction.

Morey, A, 1979, *David Knowles,* includes the Knowles Rule for a contemplative monastery. London.

La Trappe in England, 1937, by a religious of Holy Cross Abbey, Dorset. London.

Lekai, L J, 1977, *The Cistercians,* Kent State; especially Chapters XIII and XIV.

VCH, 1908, Calthrop M in Page W (ed) *Victoria County History of Dorset, Institute of Historical Research/Oxford University Press,* vol II. London.

21. St Benedict:
guide and prophet in today's world

Esther de Waal

What we were celebrating in Sherborne in April 1998 was ultimately due to a short guide no more than nine thousand words, written in the sixth century for a household of men in rural Italy who were trying to live a life of prayer and of study, while also having to earn their living – an ideal that could hardly be more basic and simple[1] (Fry 1981; Parry 1990; de Waal 1995).

Yet the text that St Benedict wrote as a practical handbook for their way of life has shaped and influenced men and women, individuals and communities, for more than fifteen hundred years so that throughout the world today there are Benedictine communities – and they continue to grow. Last year I was in Zimbabwe when Ampleforth made a new foundation there; and Anglican Benedictines have recently made a new foundation in South Africa. What is there, we must be tempted to ask, in a text which has given it such flexibility and resilience, that it can not only still be creative today but promise even more for the future? For increasingly (this is very much a sign of the times), individuals across all denominations, are turning to St Benedict and to his way of life as he sets it out in his Rule. There they find a guide, who brings them support and reassurance, and they also find a man who challenges them. The Rule of St Benedict brings a message of both comfort and discomfort.

Fr Lawrence Freeman, OSB, has called the Rule the most decisive document for Christian living after the Bible. It is, he says, written for ordinary people, not for the great or the mystical. It is never pious or platitudinous. It has a character of ordinariness and universality, it speaks with moderation and compassion – just like the Gospel itself. But this simplicity and shortness should not be allowed to mislead us, for each word is distilled from scripture and from experience. This is basic Christianity taken seriously and made practical – and it thus becomes practical and accessible. It also becomes inescapable. Here we are given the very radical demands of the Gospel applied to daily life not in any abstract moralising way, with ethical demands presented in didactic terms, but through examples taken from ordinary life, in real life situations, or through portraits on which we can model ourselves. In other words presented in terms that become difficult to evade. For although St Benedict is the clear-sighted legislator, addressing problems likely to arise in a community situation, he also speaks to the individual. His writing is direct and personal, with many touches of penetrating insight for, in the words of Patrick Barry, until recently abbot of Ampleforth the largest Benedictine community in this country, St Benedict never quite forgets the individual standing before him into whose eyes he is looking as he offers guidance to anyone seeking God in the world of the sixth century, which was one of conflict, decay and baffling confusion (Barry 1997).

The Rule touches us because it is addressed to the heart. We are told early on that we are to listen 'with the ear of the heart'. This is the sort of writing that engages us: vivid, concrete images, short effective quotations from the scriptures (and above all the psalms) words that touch the senses, ask us to take time, so that we have to ponder and to reflect. They bear little relation to the 'vision statements' that seem to beguile the churches today, or to the jargon, buzz words, and functional and information-filled language that daily besieges us all.

The voice of St Benedict, in other words, addresses something that is common, universal, fundamental to all our humanity. He begins right at the start in the Prologue (that wonderful lyrical opening which is like the prelude to all that is to come later), by addressing us as the prodigal, an image that has appealed to artists throughout the centuries, one that speaks to each of us: we identify with the person who has strayed, who is eating empty husks, who come to themselves, who decide to move forward in a process of transformation, in order to return home – a word that has so many levels but above all speaks of being at home in one's own self. This is a journey which we all have to make, and it is never an easy one. St Benedict never patronises, he does not minimise demands: instead he speaks of commitment, or perseverance and endurance, of hanging on and not giving up. He uses military imagery, of combat and battle. But he also promises that although the way is narrow at the start it will open us as we progress along it, 'our hears overflowing with the inexpressible delights of love'.[2]

This awareness of the need to be tough is balanced by the tone of compassion. The abbot who is the exemplar of Christ to his monks is both tender and tough, and he is the example of how we are to behave not only towards others but also towards our own selves. Acceptance is the basis of St Benedict's understanding of human behaviour, accepting each one as unique. In practice in the community it means that each member is treated as special. St Benedict is always saying that a person is special because they are old, or because they are young, or sick or weak. So there is an absence of labels, or judging, or putting people into categories and heaping expectations upon them. St Benedict alerts us to just how easy it is to label people and thus to imprison them.

St Benedict does not dictate. He is making a statement in effect that he believes in the unique and personal responsibility of each individual to make their way to God in their own time and on their own terms. This is, however, far from any easy-going liberalism – it is instead a belief in the potential of each one. Early on in the Prologue he asks us whether we want life, to be fully alive: his offer is that of a life-giving way, and it is up to us to respond or not. His concern is with the disposition of the heart, not with any outward obedience.

'How to be human, how to be more fully human' is how an American Benedictine prior summed up what he believed the Benedictine way could bring to anyone who discovered it and followed it, 'a love of true life and a longing for days of real fulfillment'. Balance has always been one of the most familiar aspects of the Benedictine approach, the balance of body, mind and spirit, of work, study and prayer. St Benedict laid out a daily *horarium* which recognised the human being as a tripartite person in which each element is God given, so that physical, intellectual and spiritual are all brought into relationship in such a way that each person may experience a pattern to bring them fullness of living.

The monastic buildings themselves reflect this, for they provide us with images which illuminate the monastic life. The cloisters are the link-line relating the buildings serving the daily needs of the community: the dormitory and the refectory (the Rule is clear on the need for enough sleep and sufficient food); the *scriptorium*, for the reading and writing of books, and the chapter house, in which a chapter of the Rule was read daily before matters of business and administration were discussed; but above all, the church itself, which anchors the cloisters just as it anchors the whole life. 'At the sound of the bell drop everything.' The priority in this life is the *Opus Dei*, the work of God, the daily offices which punctuate the day with prayer and praise.

The totality of the way of St Benedict is one of its more refreshing and energising gifts. Many of us were brought up to think that to be spiritual meant saying prayers and going to church. There was little idea that the handling of matter and of material things could be a way to God. Now St Benedict tells us that we are to handle the tools of daily life, the implements of the kitchen, garden or pantry, as though they were the sacred vessels of the altar. For he wants us to honour matter; everything is to be handled with care, just as each person is to be handled with care – the two go together.

When a community is tied to the land by the vow of stability, and cannot go wandering off since they know that the monastic site is a heritage to be handed on from generation to generation, there is a real sense of commitment to place. That means serving the land well, recognising its potential, and so Benedictines have always been open to advances in technology and human skill right from the beginning when it was said of them that they conquered the Europe of the Dark Ages by book and plough. This was always responsible husbandry which looked to the common and shared good of the whole, the enhancement of the land itself, and its sharing with the people around. Environmental care and ecological concern have always been part of the implication of living by the

Rule. It is tragic that this aspect of Christian understanding was for so long neglected and lost and that in fact it has been through a largely secular movement that it has again been brought back to the fore. Here are extracts of two statements from Benedictines about stewardship and the responsible care for God's creation. The first is from the American Benedictine sisters:

> Creation is the Lord's and we are its keepers; we hold it on trust. We must always remember that the earth is not so much inherited from our parents as borrowed from our children. We owe a debt to the next generation ...

The second comes from a daughter house of Ampleforth in St Louis:

> As Benedictines we see creation as a gift of God to be lovingly nurtured so that it fulfills its purpose in serving human frailty ... We do not grasp. We try not to waste. We believe that in having sufficient but not the superfluous. We have the cautious optimism to believe that with the humble effort to understand and co-operate with the Creator's abundant gifts we can bring about on this planet a truly human life for all.

In the three Benedictine vows we also find something which addresses fundamental aspects of our humanity, which can become practical, life-enhancing tools for anyone who is trying to live out their Christian discipleship in today's world. They are not the more widely known evangelical vows of the later medieval religious orders, poverty, chastity and obedience, which are difficult, if not impossible to apply generally. The trio of stability, *conversatio morum* and obedience, which might at first sound startling and rather strange, do in fact reveal St Benedict's quite extraordinary grasp of the human psyche and of human relationships.

Stability means essentially to stand, to stand still, firm, firmly rooted in the inner centre of one's own being, not trying to escape or to run away. In effect this vow is leading us into maturity by making us face reality, and helping us to confront whatever it is in our depths that must be confronted. The early desert fathers had a simple little phrase: 'stay in your cell and your cell will teach you everything'. The words of the vow *conversatio morum* really have to be rewritten in words more suitable for the twentieth-first century: a commitment to continual conversion, to moving forward, change, to the new. It is the counterpoint to standing still, and St Benedict always loves to present us with paradox. Again he is here touching something universal and fundamental: the image of the journey, the quest, the search, life as a process of continual and never-ending transformation which will not allow us to become static, to play safe, to live and half live.

When we come to obedience we find a word that can very easily have so many negative connotations, but it is in fact quite simply nothing more than the willingness to listen, *ob audiens*, the Latin meaning to listen intently to the voice of God. Commitment to obedience is thus essentially the process of listening, hearing and responding daily to the word of God, so that we live, as it were, with a dialogue between ourselves and God, in total awareness, mindfulness of his presence instead of what we so often do, and, which is so easy and so attractive, having an interior monologue with ourselves. Obedience seen in this way is no longer threatening, for it is above all a free, open and willing response of saying Yes to the voice of God, the voice of the loving father who cares for each one as the prodigal whom he wishes to bring home.

The vows are not three separate things but parts of a whole, and it is vital to see how they hold together as a process, an inter-connected and inter-related process in which each is necessary and cannot be understood apart from the others. We are to stand firm, as we are to journey, in an ever-moving stability and the point of reference is not our own selves, our will, our selfish interests but word of God which, if we listen to it, will prevent us from becoming a law unto ourselves.

The vows can work at differing levels: they show an excellent grasp of the individual human psyche and its needs; they apply in relationships, not only in the monastic community but in a family, parish, school or workplace. They also apply to the institution of the church itself where they can become quite prophetic, as I discovered when I was in South Africa in the years immediately following the ending of apartheid, exploring the insights of the Rule as a means of building a future for the church and society there. They present a series of questions: Are you a people who are standing firm, or a people trying to escape what is difficult and demanding? Are you a people who are clinging to the past, to idols, or are you a people prepared to move forward? Are you a listening people, or a people in denial? These are questions that might also be asked here in this country by an institutional church as it prepares itself to meet the challenge of the future.

By now it will be apparent that St Benedict is a master of paradox, of the holding together of different things. In an age which is looking for certainty, which enjoys flying banners and shouting slogans, he gives us a different message: learn to live with contradictions, in a way that will make them life-giving and creative. The keynote of his approach is growth, dialogue, the opening up of a conversation, whether with others or with one's self. Historically St Benedict showed great insight in bringing the two streams of monasticism into the Benedictine life and letting them stimulate each other: the eremetical and the coenobetic, the hermit-style of the life of the solitary as it had been experienced in the desert, and the shared, community life of the love of brothers as St Pachomius knew it.

The significance of this is enormous. In the words of a present day American Cistercian monk, Thomas Keating: 'His breadth of view provides a milieu in which both of these kinds of monks, with their respective attractions can live together, help one another, and, by being different, enrich each other.'[3] Be open to different, even divergent aspects of the truth, live open to both, let two poles flow in and work dynamically. Thomas Keating then goes on to show that in doing this St Benedict is not simply juxtaposing them but he is also trying to harmonise them by the limits which he imposed on each, so that neither takes off in its own direction to the practical destruction of the other. Here is the interaction which produces growth. In a world and a church which seem to be so increasingly polarised St Benedict is again speaking with urgency and relevance. The flexibility and the durability of the Benedictine way of life is perhaps the most obvious vindication of the practical wisdom of the Rule.

In *Conjectures of a Guilty Bystander* Thomas Merton (1966), twentieth-century American Trappist whose writings have made the monastic life accessible to so many people today, tells us that 'there is nothing whatever of the ghetto spirit in St Benedict. That is the wonderful thing about the Rule and about the Saint: the freshness, the liberty of spirit, the sanity, the broadness, the healthiness of the Benedictine life.' He himself of course as a Trappist was living by the Rule: he is writing out of his own personal experience. And Professor Owen Chadwick, one of the most distinguished of contemporary ecclesiastical historians, writing as an academic, makes a similar point when he says that it is as 'fresh and living, clear, simple and wise today as when it was first written'. The Rule of St Benedict has the character of any great text: it transcends its age. Successive generations come to it, asking different questions – as I have also done at different points in my own life – and finding that as we make fresh demands upon it so it opens up new depths and new riches.

Notes

1   There are many different texts, translations and commentaries on the Rule. Amongst the most definitive and recent is *RB 1980*, edited by Timothy Fry OSB, the Liturgical Press, Collegeville, Minnesota, USA published in 1981, which sets out the Latin and English with notes. There is also a translation by Abbot David Parry OSB, reissued by Gracewing in 1990. *A Life-Giving Way, A Commentary on the Rule of St Benedict*, by Esther de Waal, published by Geoffrey Chapman in 1995, gives a chapter by chapter commentary intended for lay people. The simplest introduction to the Rule is my own *Seeking God, the Way of St Benedict*, originally published in 1948, new edition Canterbury Press, 1999.
2   This is the penultimate sentence of the Prologue to the Rule.
3   *Cistercian Studies*, 1976, xi, 2, 263. I explored this theme in *Living with Contradiction*, originally written in 1989 and re-issued by the Canterbury Press, Norwich, 1997.

Bibliography

Barry, P, 1997, *St Benedict's Rule A New Translation for Today*, Ampleforth Abbey; see the Preface.
Fry, T (ed), 1981, *RB 1980*. Collegeville, Minnesota USA. Liturgical Press.
Keating, T, 1976, *Cistercian Studies* 11, 2, 263.
Merton T, 1966, *Conjectures of a Guilty Bystander*. New York. Doubleday.
Parry, D, 1990, *The Rule of St Benedict*. Geoffrey Chapman, Gracewing.
de Waal, E, 1995, *A Commentary on the Rule of St Benedict*. Geoffrey Chapman.
de Waal, E, 1989 (Reissued 1997), *Living with Contradiction*. Canterbury Press.

de Waal, E, 1998, *The Way of Simplicity, The Cistercian Tradition.* Darton, Longman & Todd.
de Waal, E, 1999, *Seeking God, the Way of St Benedict.* Canterbury Press.

List of Further Reading

Ker, W P, 1957, *A Catalogue of Manuscripts Containing Anglo-Saxon*. Oxford.
Knowles, Dom D, 1949, *The Monastic Order in England*. Cambridge.
Sawyer, P, 1997, *The Oxford Illustrated History of the Vikings*. Oxford.

Index

Illustrations are denoted by page numbers in *italics*. The letter n following a page number indicates that the reference will be found in a note.

F

Finan, St 141
Fitzjames family 188
    John 196
Flete, John 56
Fleury (France), abbey 24, 27, 46, 47,
    152, 185; *see also* Abbo of Fleury
Focillon, Henri 6, 38
Folke (Dorset)
    chapel 143
    place-name 154
Forthere, bishop of Sherborne 141,
    146n
Fovant (Wilts), chantry property 170
Fovent family
    Cecilia 170
    Robert and wife 170
Fowler, Joseph 191
Frampton (Dorset), priory 217
Francis of Assisi, St 3
Freeman, Fr Lawrence 225
Fried, Johannes 7
Frith, John, abbot of Sherborne 207
Frome (Som), minster 27, 141

G

Geraint, king of Dumnonia 26, 139
Gerberga (wife of Louis IV) 45–6,
    178
Gerbert *see* Sylvester II
Gewisse 133
Gheast, Edmund, bishop of Salisbury
    195
Gillingham (Dorset)
    charter drawn up 61
    minster 143
Glastonbury (Som)
    abbey
        abbots/monks 24, 26, 60, 72
        arms 165, 216
        estates 140, 151, 200, 202

manuscripts 57, 70, 167, 171–
    3
monastic reform 24, 26, 27, 58
    Wulfsige at 56, 57
British monastery 140, 141
Tor 140, 141
Gniezo (Poland), Otto III visits 44
Goda, thegn 130
Godwin, Thomas 191
Godwine (abbot) 13
Godwine (bishop) 22
Gorze (France), abbey 24
Goscelin
    biographical details 76, 96, 98
    Life of St Wulfsige 55, 98–9, *100*,
        101–22
Gotha (Germany), manuscript 99, 102
Gregory the Great, St 22, 35, 43, 219
Gregory V (Bruno) 38
Grene, Augustine 190
Grosjean, P 99
Guthrum 55, 129

H

Hadrian of Canterbury 141
Hæddi, bishop of Winchester 54, 135,
    139, 140, 141, 145
Halliwell-Phillipps, J O 173
Halstock (Dorset)
    Juthwara, cult of 75, 97, 101, 115,
        132, 165
    Sherborne estate 12, 149, 150, 156
    villa 203n
    Wulfsige's body carried through
        131–2
Hampstead (Middx), Westminster
    estate 57
Hamworthy (Dorset), harbour 129
Harding, Stephen
    see Stephen Harding, St
Harper, Hugo Daniel 210
Hartland (Devon), Nectan of 99